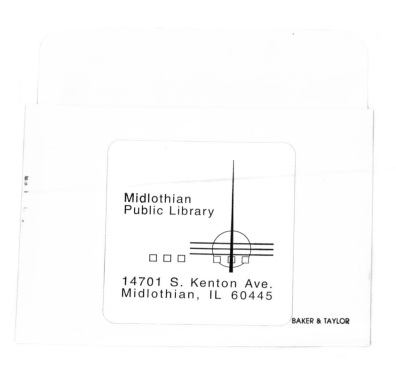

UP FROM INVISIBILITY

BETWEEN MEN ~ BETWEEN WOMEN

LESBIAN AND GAY STUDIES

LILLIAN FADERMAN AND LARRY GROSS, EDITORS

Up
from
Invisibility

LESBIANS, GAY MEN, AND THE MEDIA IN AMERICA

Larry Gross

COLUMBIA UNIVERSITY PRESS

NEW YORK

COLUMBIA UNIVERSITY PRESS
Publishers Since 1893
New York   Chichester, West Sussex
Copyright © 2001 Larry Gross

Library of Congress Cataloging-in-Publication Data

Gross, Larry P.
Up from invisibility : lesbians, gay men,
and the media in America / Larry Gross.
p. cm.—(Between men—between women)
Includes bibliographical references and index.
ISBN 0-231-11952-6 (cloth : alk. paper)
ISBN 0-231-11953-4 (pbk. : alk. paper)
1. Mass media and gays—United States
I. Title. II. Series.

P94.5.G38 G76   2001
305.9'0664'0973—dc21   2001042140

Columbia University Press books
are printed on permanent and
durable acid-free paper.

Printed in the
United States of America

c 10 9 8 7 6 5 4 3 2 1
p 10 9 8 7 6 5 4 3 2 1

This book is dedicated to Rita Addessa,
whose untiring efforts will ensure a
better world for the children of a future age

CONTENTS

No one looking at the young woman who walked into a lesbian bar in Los Angeles in the summer of 1947 would have suspected they were witnessing a milestone in American social history. A 26-year-old secretary who called herself Lisa Ben (an anagram of *lesbian*) was distributing copies of a new publication she had created called *Vice Versa*—"because in those days our kind of life was considered a vice." The magazine consisted of only fifteen type-written pages, but it signaled the first stirrings of the modern gay rights movement in the United States.

Fifty years later, in the summer of 1997, a 17-year-old high school senior in Wisconsin responded to Ellen DeGeneres's coming out on the cover of *Time*, the *Oprah Winfrey Show*, and nearly every other media forum by writing a column for *Oasis*, an "online magazine for lesbian, gay, bisexual, transgender, and questioning youth," in which she proclaimed her intention of living her life honestly, "because I have nothing to hide."

Between these two moments in modern American history lies a chasm bridged by transformations in culture, politics, and media that no one in 1947 could have foreseen.

This is a book about the emergence of lesbian and gay Americans from the shadows of invisibility and their entrance onto the playing fields of politics and culture. It is also a book about the role of media in bringing together a self-conscious community that was able to organize a movement and demand change; and about the role of media in portraying gay people to the majority and to gay people themselves, in ways that perpetuated harmful stereotypes and, eventually, also in ways that began to reverse some of that harm. While the stories told in this book constitute a chronology, because I am following several threads the narrative circles back occasionally to pick up another strand in the interwoven stories of media and movements, politics and performers. The primary focus of this narrative is on journalism, both minority and mainstream, and the two widest channels of American popular culture, movies and television. However, as we approach the present, the focus will broaden to encompass a wider range of media and genres, including pop music, sports, comics, pornography, and the Internet.

❖❖❖

A half century ago homosexuality was still the love that dared not speak its name: it was a crime throughout the United States (whereas today it is criminalized in eighteen states). In the fervor of the Cold War that gripped the country, homosexuals were targeted along with Communists. Newspapers and magazines referred to homosexuals only in the context of police arrests or political purges, as in a 1953 headline: "State Department Fires 531 Perverts, Security Risks." Hollywood operated under the Motion Picture Production Code, which prohibited the presentation of explicitly lesbian or gay characters and ensured that any implied homosexual characters would be villains or victims. Television was the new kid on the block, just barely beginning its colonization of the nation's living rooms. The emergence of a gay movement in the 1950s coincided with the societal transformations wrought by television and the increasing centrality of communications technologies in American society.

The lesbian and gay liberation movement that seemed to appear spontaneously across the country shortly after the 1969 Stonewall riots in New York City was in fact the result of a process begun in a post-World War II urban gay world that was largely invisible to heterosexual society, and whose growing self-consciousness in the decades prior to Stonewall can be traced in large part to the lesbian and gay press of which Lisa Ben was a pioneer.

Throughout the 1950s and into the 1960s, the homophile movement (as it was then called) expanded and deepened the self-awareness of lesbian and gay people as a distinct, self-conscious, and embattled minority. The movement was born behind a veil of pseudonyms and secrecy at the height of the Cold War, and its members, defined as criminal, mentally ill, and immoral, attempted to effect social change by persuading experts to speak in their behalf. With the advent of television, several brave activists appeared on the new medium, using pseudonyms but this did not protect them from being recognized and promptly fired.

By the early 1960s, movement leaders emerged who were inspired by the civil rights movement to proclaim that "Gay Is Good!" They began taking their struggle to the streets, demonstrating in front of government buildings, demanding an end to laws that criminalized gay people and promoted discrimination and harassment.

The Stonewall riots in June 1969 harvested a crop planted by a decade of political and social turmoil. The new movement was founded on the importance of coming out as a *public* as well as an individual act. The open avowal of one's sexual identity, whether at work, at school, at home, or before television cameras, symbolized shedding the self-hatred that gay men and women had internalized. To come out of the closet quintessentially expressed the fusion of the personal and the political that the radicalism of the late 1960s exalted.

Among the early targets of the newly militant gay liberation movement were the images presented in the media: Hollywood films and television programs, as well as the stories reported—or ignored—by the news media. From the earliest post-Stonewall days, mainstream news media and Hollywood's dream—or nightmare—factories were never far from the center of movement attention. While activists chalked up steady but modest victories—modifying a dramatic plot to dilute a stereotypic portrayal, persuading an editor to avoid the term "pervert" or adopt the term "gay"—it was still left to the struggling lesbian and gay press to keep a growing community informed about the matters of greatest concern to its fate. The importance of the gay press was evident as the backlash against the early gains of gay liberation took shape in the mid-1970s.

The advent of the AIDS epidemic in the early 1980s proved the crucial role of the gay press, as mainstream media largely ignored the epidemic or viewed it primarily as a threat to the "general population" if it spread beyond deviant "risk groups." Still, AIDS accelerated the process that was already under way and definitively ended the invisibility of gay people in American mass media.

As we begin a new century, broadcast and cable television dominate American culture and politics, while glancing nervously behind them at the oncoming Internet. Since the demise of the Production Code in the early 1960s, Hollywood has pushed the envelope in every direction, it seems, except toward greater artistic quality, and lesbian and gay people have gradually moved onto the media stage in growing numbers and greater verisimilitude. A media-dominated culture with an insatiable appetite for personality gossip has blurred the lines between private lives and public access, at least in the case of celebrities, and we all know more than we might wish about the sex lives of the rich and famous, including some who are queer.

Today, few can remain unaware of the existence of lesbian and gay people, and young people grow up reading words and seeing images that previous generations never encountered. In the final years of the twentieth century, lesbian, gay, bisexual, and transgendered people entered the ranks of our culture's permanent cast of characters, even though rarely in leading roles and almost never permitted to express physical affection. A queer presence has even been detected, or exposed, within the cuddly purse-carrying Teletubby, Tinky Winky. Gay and lesbian Americans have been identified as a certifiable market niche, one well-heeled enough to warrant targeted ads (especially ones that wink at us over the heads of straight people). We can confidently expect to show up as the subject of news stories, even some that do not presume that our existence is controversial or that simple equality is a special right.

Gay people did not, however, ascend from the pariah status of criminal, sinner, and pervert to the respectable categories of voting bloc and market niche without playing the familiar American game of assimilation. The rules of this game require the muting of a group's distinctive coloring in order that they might blend into the fabric of the mainstream. To the extent that gay people wish to be taken into the American fold—and many certainly do, although many others just as certainly do not—they face the same choice. And in the past decade the organized sector of lesbian and gay America has embraced assimilation as the realization of their ultimate goal. At the start of the new century, the country's largest lesbian and gay organizations—the Human Rights Campaign (HRC), the National Gay and Lesbian Task Force (NGLTF), and the Gay and Lesbian Alliance Against Defamation (GLAAD)—were each led by a professional woman, each partnered, with children, and presenting the face of middle-class normality and respectability.

Yet at the same time, the increasingly visible presence of queer people—women, men, and trans—has contributed mightily to the subversion of traditional sexual morality and the expansion of the range of personal possibilities. The media have served both as carriers and reflections of transformations that the forces of cultural reaction have been powerless to reverse. A few hours of cable-TV surfing, from *The Young and Restless* to Jerry Springer to MTV to *Will & Grace* to *Nightline*, will demonstrate that the cultural mainstream has overflowed the narrow channels in which it once was confined. The newest ratings magnets, "reality" programs of various sorts, from MTV's *The Real World* to CBS's *Survivor*, take the presence of openly gay people for granted, and this increasingly reflects the real world we live in.

American popular culture remains an active battlefield for the foreseeable future. Conservatives attempt to push us back to a largely mythical past of "traditional family values." The mainstream media, in their search for demographically lucrative audiences, inch cautiously toward a more accurate reflection of contemporary realities. In this seesawing progress lesbian and gay people find themselves simultaneously sought out by opportunistic marketers and scapegoated by equally opportunistic preachers. And we increasingly insist on speaking for ourselves, both behind the scenes and on the media stages. Gay advocates and our adversaries agree on one thing: the media are more than mere entertainment. The mass media are shifting the terms of our public conversation toward a greater acknowledgment of diversity. If we are lucky, this process will prove irreversible.

❖❖❖

This book is the culmination and distillation of many years of research and teaching, media-watching, reading, and listening, and it draws upon the work of many other scholars and activists. Anyone telling the story of lesbian and gay people and the media is indebted to the pioneering efforts of Vito Russo and Richard Dyer. I also owe much to Ed Alwood and Rodger Streitmatter for their comprehensive accounts of mainstream and minority journalism. The histories I am telling testify to the courage and dedication of those who created a gay and lesbian media presence during the chill of the Cold War years. I am especially grateful to Barbara Gittings, Frank Kameny, Jim Kepner (one of the great joys of this project was reading his work in the collection, *Rough News—Daring Views*), and the tireless Jack Nichols. Many, many others have added to my store of knowledge and shaped my understanding of the multiple, intertwined narratives I have traced in this book. Most of these people have enriched my life with friendship and conversation, others only through their writing and their activism. I would like to thank Leroy Aarons, Rita Addessa, Randy Alfred, Kevin Barnhurst, Howard Becker, David Bianco, Michael Bronski, Patrick Califia, Steven Capsuto, James Carey, Jim Chesboro, George Custen, Julie D'Acci, John DeCecco, John D'Emilio, Bill Dobbs, Alex Doty, Martin Duberman, David Ehrenstein, John Erni, Fred Fejes, Oscar Gandy, Josh Gamson, George Gerbner, Richard Goldstein, Herman Gray, Laura Grindstaff, Jessea Greenman, Darrell Hamamoto, Jason Heffner, Amber Hollibaugh, Elihu Katz, John Stuart Katz, Jonathan Ned Katz, Al Kielwasser, James Kinsella, John Loughery, Carolyn Marvin, Kathryn Montgomery, Michael Morgan, Marguerite Moritz, Peter Nardi, Charles Nero, Esther Newton, Gayle Rubin, Jay Ruby, Michael Schudson, Sarah Schulman, Michelangelo Signorile, Ken Sherrill, Kate Stimpson, Joe Turow, Carole Vance, Suzanna Walters, Tom Waugh, Andrea Weiss, Michelle Wolf, the late James Woods, and many other scholars, journalists, and activists. I am enormously indebted to freelance journalist Rex Wockner and to the incomparable duo known as Fenceberry for keeping me informed and aware of articles and developments in the media and the world.

The original impetus for the book was a request from Martin Duberman for a volume on the media for the series of lesbian and gay-themed books for young people he was editing for Chelsea House. That project died with the series, but it provided the kernel of the present book. Work on the book was generously supported by a Fellowship from the John Simon Guggenheim Memorial Foundation in 1998–99, and from the Annenberg School for Communication at the University of Pennsylvania, and Dean Kathleen Hall Jamieson.

Research assistance from many students over the years has made my work possible, and my thanks especially to John Campbell, Gus Dantas, David Gleason, David Gudelunas, and Steven Hocker. John Campbell and Alison Hector performed indexical wonders. As usual I am grateful to the peerless computer skills of Rich Cardona, Kyle Cassidy, Lizz Cooper, and Jon Stromer-Galley; Deb Porter and Ellen Reynolds helped me amass far too many videotapes.

I have been fortunate in working for a decade with Ann Miller, executive editor of Columbia University Press, on the series in which this book appears, and she was supportive and helpful to me as she has been to all our authors. Two anonymous reviewers (one of whom I would like to commission to write my obituary) provided both encouragement and sage advice. Roy Thomas provided copyediting with a delicacy that improved the final text.

As the project neared completion I was able to count once more on the advice and counsel of Richard Dyer, Lisa Henderson, and Barbie Zelizer, who each read the manuscript and helped me avoid many pitfalls.

As always, my greatest supporter and strictest critic has been Scott Tucker. After twenty-five years of shared life and love, he continues to administer a judicious mix of applause and admonition. My luck in finding him remains a cornerstone of my faith in the possibility of a just universe.

UP FROM INVISIBILITY

1

The Mediated Society

America at the start of the 21st century has often been described as a society dominated by the mass media, and so we are. How often have we heard someone say that if something doesn't happen in the media it "didn't happen"? And, of course, how much do we really know about the world beyond our immediate surroundings that doesn't come to us via the media? But what is it that makes important the images we see on television and on the movie screen, the stories that we read in newspapers, magazines, and books, the songs we listen and dance to? Why do they play such important roles in our lives? How did the media, and television in particular, acquire such power in a society of over 250 million people? Given the many ways in which we receive information about our society and our world—from parents and peers, teachers and preachers—how is it that the mass media have become so uniquely powerful?

The answer lies in the changes in technology and society in the past century. The world has become a single giant organism, whether we like it or not, and its nervous system is telecommunications. Modern industrial society has become ever more integrated and homogeneous—teenagers around the world at this moment are watching American-made music videos on Japanese-made television sets—and very few communities or individuals remain islands isolated from the media mainstream. Our knowledge of the world beyond our immediate surroundings is made up largely of what this electronic nervous system transmits to us. The mass media have become our common ground with countless other groups that make up the national and international community. The mass media thus bring together audiences that would previously have lived in separate worlds. Never before have all social classes, groups, and ages shared so much of the same cultural fare, while having so little to do with its creation.

There is more that makes the modern mass media different from the culture of past centuries. Today's mass media are not only centralized and remote from their audiences, they are also overwhelmingly commercial enterprises, in the business of buying and selling products—and their primary product is audiences. The selling to advertisers of our presumed attention is the transaction at the heart of the mass media economy in the United States and, increasingly, throughout the world.

The media have learned that they can attract our attention most effectively when they tempt us with enjoyable, amusing, engrossing images, songs, and stories. As a society we have become addicted to one of the most powerful drugs known to our species: entertainment. We consume entertainment in astounding amounts and varieties. Some numbers:

- In 1996 the music recording industry sold just over a billion albums, and the 10 to 34 age group accounted for about 65 percent of these purchases.
- After a post-TV falloff, radio listening was back to 3.25 hours by 1981. In 1997 there were more than 12,000 radio stations in the United States (most, however, owned by a small number of major media corporations).
- In the late 1990s about 420 movies appeared on the screens of more than 25,000 theaters, and Americans bought about 1.3 billion movie tickets per year (nearly half of these bought by 12–29-year-olds, who represent about 30 percent of the population).
- Daily television viewing per household has risen steadily from four and one half hours in 1950, when only few had TVs, to more than seven hours since the early 1980s, when nearly everyone had at least one. By 1986, 57 percent of U.S. households had two or more TVs; in 1999, 64 percent of American teenagers had TV sets in their rooms.
- When we watch television we are watching more than programs: the average television viewer sees more than 38,000 commercials every year.

All human societies have created, shared, and consumed with pleasure the symbolic products we can collectively call "culture" or "the arts." The very processes through which all human societies create and maintain themselves—that distinguish us from our animal ancestors—are those of storytelling in words, pictures, music, and dance. For most of human history the stories, songs, and images people knew were crafted by members of their own communities, with whom they shared the basic conditions of life. In stark contrast to preindustrial societies, in which the culture communities consumed was almost entirely dependent on what they could produce, we now are faced with endless competing choices, twenty-four hours a day, produced by industrial corporations with which we have no social contact whatever.

Remember: this dizzying array of media options is not there because anyone actually asked for all these images, songs, or stories. Rather, it exists because someone, somewhere, has a commercial interest in selling us a product—or more typically, in attracting our attention so that it can be "sold" to advertisers who wish to sell us something. While major corporations compete to spend hundreds of thousands of dollars to place a thirty-second ad during the Super Bowl halftime, there are usually small businesses eager to spend much lower sums to place their ads during late-night programs or on less popular cable channels. Whether larger or smaller audiences, in prime time or less desirable demographics, the media are selling audience attention all the time, on all channels.[1]

The businesses that manufacture and distribute media fare are increasingly interconnected, and this helps them coordinate their efforts in packaging and selling their products. While they seem on the surface to be separate and independent enterprises, we might wonder what happens when three of the five top-selling magazines in the country (*People*, *Time*, *Sports Illustrated*) are owned by the same company, Time Warner, which also owns major record producing and book publishing companies, as well as CNN and HBO (and that ended the century by merging with the Internet service AOL). Should we be surprised when the stars of Warner Brothers movies, or singers who record for Warner Records, are featured on the cover of *People* or *Time*, or profiled on CNN? No more than we should wonder why morning or late-night talk shows on the networks seem endlessly interested in guests who happen to have "specials" on those same networks that same week.

The corporations that create media fare also control how particular

---

[1] So-called noncommercial public broadcasting has long since yielded to dignified, upscale commercials in the guise of sponsorship notices. Cable systems offer commercial-free "premium" channels, such as HBO, but viewers pay monthly fees for these; CSPAN, the cable industry's public service channel, is probably the only real commercial-free venue on American television. (For further information on material cited in these notes, see Sources at the end of this book.)

social groups and issues are represented. Indeed, representation in the media is in itself a kind of power, and thus media invisibility helps maintain the powerlessness of groups at the bottom of the social heap. Not all interests or viewpoints are treated equally, and judgments are routinely made— by producers and writers, editors and reporters—about what to include or exclude. Sometimes these decisions are enforced by official rules: for example, the Federal Communications Commission once listed "seven dirty words" that could not be spoken on the air;[2] likewise, the Motion Picture Production Code in force from the 1930s through the early 1960s required that crime must never pay and that homosexuality was the love that dare not speak its name.

Whatever the motives of preindustrial storytellers, in our commercial media those who determine the content of our news and entertainment programming live and die by the bottom line. In such circumstances, their decisions are inevitably weighted toward the safe and predictable, toward formulas that have worked in the past, and their goal is to attract the largest possible audience of individuals whose spending power appeals to potential advertisers (which presently means younger audiences for the most part). Under these conditions, it is far safer to repeat previous successes—in the form of sequels, spin-offs, and imitations—than to introduce innovations that push the envelope too far or too quickly.

When previously ignored groups or perspectives do gain visibility, the manner of their representation will reflect the biases and interests of those powerful people who define the public agenda. And these are mostly white, mostly middle-aged, mostly male, mostly middle and upper-middle class, and overwhelmingly heterosexual (at least in public).[3] As of the late 1990s, the television networks and major film studios, with almost no exceptions, are all

[2] The FCC's ruling was upheld by the U.S. Supreme Court in *FCC v. Pacifica* (1974), and therefore you shouldn't be hearing any of these on broadcast radio or TV: *fuck, shit, piss, cunt, cocksucker, motherfucker,* or *tits.* Cable is another matter, as it is not bound by FCC rules, and the ability to offer dirty words, along with bare breasts, is among its distinctive features.

[3] While there certainly are gay men among the industry elite, very few are willing to be known as such. David Geffen, who came out after repeated outings in the gay press (all the while denying that he had ever been in the closet), is the most powerful and visible openly gay Hollywood mogul, and his close friend Barry Diller may be the most powerful closeted gay executive. Despite frequent media exposures—in 1995 *Spy* magazine identified him as the "smartest Don" in what they termed Hollywood's Gay Mafia—Diller persists in promoting such charades as his public "relationship" with designer Diane Von Furstenberg, who told the *New York Times* in 1993, that "Barry and I were together five years. . . . He's a little bit like my husband except that we are not married." When the couple suddenly decided to marry, in February 2001, the *New York Times*'s headline—"For Diller and Von Furstenberg, a Merger"—suggested business rather than romantic considerations.

run by men who fit this profile. While a woman has occasionally broken into the white boys' club of the studio complex, she rarely lasts long at the top.[4] In a closed world of writers, directors, producers, and so on, who read, watch, and listen to the same media, we can only expect that shared assumptions would be reinforced. The images of women and minorities that do appear on the country's big and little screens will be those that make sense to those who have decision-making power—the images that fit their own worldview or that have succeeded in the past.

Hollywood's calculus of casting risks and benefits is shifting, however, partially in response to societal changes and partially in tandem with advertisers' perceptions of the changing values of the "prime demographic" young audiences they crave. These shifts have eased the restrictions of lesbian and gays who work in the entertainment industries, while having little impact on people of color. The lineup of new TV series for fall 1999 included no African American leads among them. When the NAACP protested what it termed a "virtual whitewash," TV producer Marshall Herskovitz commented, "The overwhelming majority of TV executives and producers are white, so their concerns generally follow their own lives."[5] At the same time, the fall 1999 lineup forecast seventeen gay characters, about the same as the number of African American, Asian, and Latino characters combined. The *Los Angeles Times* noted that there are gays on television because there are gays in television. "Unlike Latinos, blacks and Asian Americans, gay people are fully integrated into the Hollywood power structure. They hold jobs from the upper ranks to the lower reaches of the industry, in much the way Jews have traditionally occupied a disproportionate number of positions in the entertainment business." Yet, as the *Times* continued, "This is not to say that executives are freely out of the closet and that writers work without constraints, creating fully realized gay characters without fear of reprisal from the network or advertisers. Executives still routinely live semi-closeted lives, and Joe

---

[4] In 1996 Jamie Tarses (daughter of veteran TV producer Jay Tarses) was appointed president of ABC-TV's entertainment division. Her tenure in the job was accompanied by frequent rumors and media stories predicting her imminent downfall, and she resigned in August 1999 after a reorganization downgraded her position.

[5] The NAACP's count referred to programming by the ABC, CBS, NBC, and FOX networks. The smaller UPN and WB networks have specialized in minority-centered programs, continuing a pattern of segmentation in which white and African American audiences watch effectively segregated programs. The 1999–2000 Nielson ratings for African American audiences turn up four UPN programs (*The Parkers, Moesha, Grown Ups, Malcolm and Eddie*) and three WB programs (*The Steve Harvey Show, The Jamie Foxx Show, For Your Love*) in the top ten. The only overlap between the white and black top ten was, as usual, *Monday Night Football*, and, a new arrival, *Who Wants to Be a Millionaire*.

Voci, who produces series with Mandalay Television, notes that although there are gay characters on TV, gay-themed shows—with the exception of *Will & Grace*—are still nonexistent."

TELEVISION AS THE MAINSTREAM

Print has been with us for 500 years, photography for 150, electricity and telephony for more than a century, movies and automobiles for about 100 years, radio for almost 80 years, and television for half a century. As we all know, the pace of technological innovation has greatly accelerated, and its cumulative impact is transforming the world. What do we know about the impact of television's first half century? As I have already argued, television now dominates the cultural environment, telling most of the stories to most of the people all of the time.

Unlike print, television does not require literacy. Unlike the movies, television (in the United States) is "free" (supported by a privately imposed tax on all goods) and it is always running. Unlike radio, television can show as well as tell. Unlike the theater, concerts, movies, and even churches, television does not require mobility. It comes into the home and reaches individuals directly. With its virtually unlimited access from cradle to grave, television both precedes reading and, increasingly, preempts it.

Marshall McLuhan's familiar claim that we live in a "global village" was both insightful and deceptive: he accurately pointed to the homogenization and sharing of common messages that television has brought about, but he falsely equated the sharing of received messages with the mutual interaction and regulation that is characteristic of authentic community.

Television has become the key source of information about the world, creating and maintaining a common set of values and perspectives among its viewers. In fact, given that the average American adult spends several hours each day with television, and children spend even more time immersed in its fictional reality, the media have become central agents of enculturation. Expanding this observation, the Cultural Indicators research project conducted by George Gerbner and myself, along with Michael Morgan and Nancy Signorielli, in the 1970s and 1980s, used the concept of cultivation to describe the resulting influence of television on viewers' conceptions of social reality. On issue after issue those who watch more television are more likely—whatever their background—to project television's versions of reality on to their conceptions about the world, its people, and how they function.

We ultimately isolated a pattern that we termed "mainstreaming." The mainstream can be thought of as a commonality of viewpoints and values that television tends to cultivate in its viewers. While light viewers in any particular demographic group may exhibit relatively divergent positions on a given topic, heavy viewers are more likely to agree with the viewpoint proffered by television. In other words, differences explained by the viewers' divergent backgrounds and life situations—differences that are readily apparent in the answers given by light viewers—tend to diminish or even disappear when heavy viewers in the same groups are compared. Heavy television use is thus associated with a convergence of outlooks, a mainstreaming of opinion.

Because commercial television seeks large and heterogeneous audiences, its messages are designed to disturb as few as possible. They tend to balance opposing perspectives and steer a course along the supposedly nonideological middle ground. We found that heavy viewers are significantly and substantially more likely to label themselves as "moderate" rather than either "liberal" or "conservative." Thus, on the surface, mainstreaming appears to be a centering of political and other attitudes. However, a look at the actual positions taken in response to questions about a number of political issues shows that the mainstream does not always mean middle of the road. When we analyzed responses by samples of American adults to questions on social issues that have traditionally divided liberals and conservatives, we found such a division mainly among those who watch little television. Overall, self-styled moderates are closer to conservatives than they are to liberals. Among heavier viewers of television, liberals and conservatives are closer to each other (often statistically indistinguishable) than among lighter viewers. In most cases, this is due to the virtual collapse of the typical liberal opinion among heavy-viewing liberals.

We have identified the mainstream as the embodiment of a dominant ideology, cultivated through the repetition of stable patterns and absorbed by otherwise diverse segments of the population. Yet it nevertheless has to contend with the possibility of oppositional perspectives and interpretations. What options and opportunities are available to those groups whose concerns, values, and even very existence are belittled, subverted, and denied by the mainstream? Can the power of the mass media's centralizing tendencies be resisted, can one avoid being swept into the mainstream?[6] The answers to such questions depend in large part on the group; while many segments and perspectives are similarly ignored or distorted by the mass media, not all have the same options for resistance, or the development of alternative channels.

---

[6] The research tradition identified with the British school of cultural studies has emphasized the possibilities of resistance to media power, but generally this resistance is more passive than active, more individual than organized, more stylistic than political.

In general the opportunities for organized opposition are greatest when a visible group can create and disseminate alternative messages. Numerous settlements have sprung up, as it were, along the right bank of the mainstream. Most organized and visible among these are the Christian fundamentalist cable television programs. These programs provide their (generally older and less educated) viewers with an array of programs, from news to talk shows to soap operas to church services and sermons, all reflecting perspectives and values that they quite correctly feel are not represented in mainstream, prime-time television or in the movies.

The religious sponsoring and producing organizations are not merely engaged in meeting their audiences' previously unmet needs for a symbolic environment in which they feel at home. They are also attempting to translate the (usually exaggerated) numbers of their audiences and their (constantly solicited) financial contributions into a power base from which they can exert pressure to alter the channel of the mainstream and bring it even closer to where they now reside, up on the right bank.

At the moment, and for the foreseeable future in the United States, at least, there is no comparable settlement on the left bank of the mainstream. Right-wing minority perspectives are ultimately supportive of the dominant ideology, however much the media's need for massive audiences might sacrifice or offend their interests. Minority positions and interests that present radical challenges to the established order will not only be ignored, they will be discredited.

Those who benefit from the status quo present their position as the moderate center, balanced between equal and opposing "extremes"—thus the U.S. news media's cult of "objectivity," achieved through a "balance" that reflects an invisible, taken-for-granted ideology. The fatal flaw in the credo of centrism is that how one defines the "responsible" extremes determines where the center will be. In the United States the mass media grant legitimacy to positions a lot further to the right than to the left, which puts the "objectively balanced" mainstream clearly to the right of center. Jesse Helms can be elected and reelected to the Senate, while his opposite number on the left, whoever that might be, couldn't conceivably claim or receive that degree of visibility, power, and legitimacy. Yet in the final analysis, the "legitimate" left and right both serve to buttress the ramparts of the status quo, and to keep the truly oppositional from being taken seriously.

In its early days, television in the United States brought entire communities "together" to absorb common messages, but the assembly was symbolic rather than physical. Americans watched television from their separate living rooms and were able to discuss their common media fare the next morning around the water coolers and in the school yards of the nation. When more than two-thirds of the nation watched network programs each night, when even larger proportions watched Lucy, and when astronomically large audiences watched Kennedy's funeral, the moon landing, the royal wedding, O.J.'s trial, and Princess Diana's funeral, television was able to bring national and even worldwide communities together, however briefly.

However, developments in recent years in the United States and around the world are changing these patterns. If the first era of television was one of heterogeneous audiences united in watching common programs on few channels, we are now well into the era of multichannel programming aimed at ever narrower demographic audience slices. Television is beginning to fragment its audiences and its messages, becoming more like print than early broadcasting, and thus we are likely to see changes in its effects. But the experience of the past half century should caution us against premature forecasts of an age of media differentiation that will fragment audiences into narrow coteries, each consuming a distinct and tailored diet. For, certainly, our experience so far has been one of illusory differences that don't, in fact, make much difference.

While we all know there are distinctions between television advertising and programming (or between ads and articles in newspapers and magazines), we should not overstate these differences, especially in the case of television. News, drama, quiz shows, sports programs, and commercials share many underlying similarities. Even the most widely accepted distinctions—such as those among news programs, drama, and commercials—are easily blurred. In Sarah Kozloff's nice phrase, "American television is as saturated in narrative as a sponge in a swimming pool. . . . Forms that are not ostensibly fictional entertainments, but rather have other goals—description, education, persuasion, exhortation, and so on—covertly tend to use narrative as a means to their ends."

Decisions about which events are newsworthy and about how to present them are guided by considerations of dramatic form and content drawn from fiction. For a story to be "newsworthy" it must contain a break in the usual order of things (a disaster, a murder, a scandal, etc.), followed by plot development and resolution. In 1963 Reuven Frank, executive producer of *NBC News* (and later president of NBC's news division), advised journalists that, "Every news story should, without sacrifice of probity or responsibility, display the attributes of fiction, of drama. It should have structure and conflict, problem and denouement, rising action and falling action, a beginning, a middle, and an end."

The amount of attention devoted to a news story is not necessarily a measure of importance on any "objective" scale, as opposed to its ability to attract and maintain audiences—how else to explain the news media's fixation on O. J. Simpson's trial, or the incessant repetition of that image of Monica and Bill embracing? Likewise, the polished minidramas of most commercials reveal a mastery of fictional style. Consider the compressed 30- or 60-second narrative structure of a typical commercial: a problem (dirty laundry, stomach ache, romantic difficulties) leads to plot development (use of the product: detergent, antacid, mouthwash) and the expected happy ending (clean socks, relief, romance).

The arrival of "infomercials" and home-shopping programs on the one hand, and so-called reality-based television, blending staged and documentary footage (such as *America's Most Wanted* and *Cops*), on the other, has made it even more difficult to distinguish between "informing," entertaining, and selling. Superficially different forms of programming support each other by using similar narrative structures and visual styles and dramatizing identical values of consumerism and the "good life." Commercials and programs generally look and sound alike, teaching complementary lessons. Programs that fail to reinforce these mainstream values often find themselves unable to attract sponsors and wind up in the vast graveyard of canceled programs.

Programs and commercials also have in common the formal conventions of realism. That is, despite a limited degree of reflexivity—in which a program deliberately calls attention to its own artificiality (say, when the cameras pull back at the end of a sketch on *Saturday Night Live* to reveal the set surrounded by the larger sound stage)—mainstream films and television programs are presented as transparent windows on reality that show us how people and places look, and how institutions operate—in short, supposedly the "way it is." But even "backstage" dramas about the media, such as *Murphy Brown* and *Frasier*, are highly unrealistic and conform thoroughly to the contours of other network fare. Nonetheless, for many viewers such programs may constitute their only source of information about the inner workings of a newsroom or radio station.

These depictions of the way things work are personified through characterizations and dramatized through plots that take us into situations and places we might otherwise never see. They show us the hidden workings of personal motivation, organizational performance, and subcultural life. Normal viewers, to be sure, are aware of the fictiveness of media drama; no one calls the police when a character on TV is shot. But how often and to what extent do viewers actually overcome the media's seductive realism? In truth, even the most sophisticated among us can find many components of our "knowledge" that derive wholly or in part from fictional representations. How many of us have been in an operating room—awake—or in a court-room during a murder trial? How many have been in a jail or a corporate boardroom? Yet we all possess images of and information about such places that is patched together from our experience with dramatic and news media. Through the media we have witnessed open-heart surgery, murder trials, jail riots, and high-level corporate deliberations. Are these images accurate? Most of us will never know, because our experiences are likely to be limited to what the media choose to show and tell us.

Thus, the media are likely to be most powerful in cultivating images of events and groups about which we have little firsthand opportunity for learning. By definition, most minority groups and "deviants" of various sorts will fall into the category of being relatively distant from the lives and daily experiences of those who are not members of a given minority group or "deviant" category. Lacking other sources of information, most people accept even the most inaccurate or derogatory information about a particular group or event.

Most mediated images reflect the experiences and interests of the major-ity groups in our society, particularly those who constitute the large audi-ences producers wish to sell to advertisers. A group of researchers examined fifty-six sitcoms and drama shows aired on ABC, CBS, NBC, and FOX between October 28 and November 3, 1991, and concluded that "characters on prime-time dramas and situation comedies are mostly male, white, single, heterosexual, in their 30's or 40's, and work in professional, managerial, or semi-professional, middle to high income jobs."

Figure 1 (suggested by sociologist Elihu Katz) shows the patterns of media images of majority and minority groups: the solid line represents the vast preponderance of programming that depicts majority images as pro-

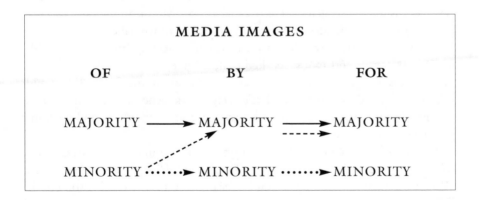

MEDIA IMAGES

OF   BY   FOR

MAJORITY ———▶ MAJORITY ———▶ MAJORITY

MINORITY ┄┄┄▶ MINORITY ┄┄┄▶ MINORITY

duced *by* and *for* the majority group; the broken line represents a much smaller proportion of programming that focuses on minorities, but this too is produced by, and largely for, members of the majority group. The dotted line represents the smallest portion of media content—programming produced by and for minorities.

SEXUAL MINORITIES AND THE MEDIA

The term *minority* has been applied to ethnically and racially defined people as well as to women (in terms of their relative powerlessness despite their numerical superiority), and it is now commonly applied to lesbian women and gay men. All of these categories are defined by their deviation from a norm that is white, male, Christian, and heterosexual, and these deviations are reflected in the mirrors that the media hold up before our eyes. In brief, minorities share a common media fate of relative invisibility and demeaning stereotypes. But there are differences as well as similarities in the ways various minorities are treated by the mass media. And because there are important differences in the conditions they face in our society, the effects of their media images are different for members of the various minority groups.

Unlike women, who might be viewed as minority spectators of images produced by and for male audiences, more "conventional" minorities have difficulty even finding their images reflected on the big and small screens of our mainstream media. The heterosexual male might be the center of everyone's (certainly of his) dramatic universe, but he will also be provided with appropriate female companionship (the spoils of the victor, one might say). Conversely, there is no demand for—and much resistance to—the frequent appearance of figures marked by their difference from the white, middle-class, Christian (if secular), heterosexual norm. Minority audiences facing their living room "window on the world" have had to make do with sparse fare. African American scholar Patricia Turner, reflecting back on her childhood in the 1950s and 1960s, recalled that, "While my mother loathed making long distance calls, even when there was a death in the family, she would call long distance to share news that a 'Negro' was scheduled to appear on a television program. . . . Our images were few and far between, and we hungered for more of them."

In a similar vein, Chinese American actor B. D. Wong, commenting on his role (as a Korean American) on the TV sitcom *All American Girl*, notes: "When we were growing up, when an Asian person came on TV, somebody would say: 'Come quick! Come into the living room. There's an Asian person on TV.' And everybody would run and go, with this bizarre fascination: 'Oh wow, look at that. That's amazing.'"

I would venture to suggest, however, that B. D. Wong would not have been called into the living room to witness one of the even more rare appearances of a lesbian or gay character on television. Despite the fact that Wong would have had particular reason to be interested in such appearances, it is highly unlikely that his family would have been aware of this interest, or that they would have indulged it had they suspected. Lesbian and gay people do not share the sort of fond recollections recounted by Turner or Wong.[7]

Sexual minorities differ in important ways from the "traditional" racial and ethnic minorities; in many ways we are more like "fringe" political or religious groups. Like other social groups defined by forbidden thoughts or deeds, we are rarely born into minority communities in which parents or siblings share our minority status. Rather, lesbians and gay men are a self-identified minority and generally only recognize or announce our status at adolescence, or later. Also, by their very existence, sexual and political minorities constitute a presumed threat to the "natural" (sexual and/or political) order of things, and thus we are always seen as controversial by the mass media. Being defined as controversial invariably limits the ways lesbians and gay men—or political and religious "deviants"—are depicted in the media on the rare occasions when they do appear. It also shapes the effects of such depictions on the images held by society at large and by members of these minority groups.

Close to the heart of our cultural and political system is the pattern of roles associated with sexual identity: our conceptions of masculinity and femininity, of the "normal" and "natural" attributes and responsibilities of men and women. And as with other pillars of our moral order, these definitions of what is normal and natural support the existing social structure. The maintenance of the "normal" gender-role system requires that children learn—and adults be discouraged from toppling—a set of expectations that channel their beliefs about what is possible and proper for men and for women.

The gender system is supported, in turn, by the mass media's treatment

---

[7] Take, for example, the experience of an 18-year-old gay male Cuban American college student: "My mother made us listen to this thing on the radio, and she made a big deal about it to the whole family. It was an interview with these homosexuals. . . . [My mother said] 'Look, how disgusting!' Things like that have made me never want her or anyone in my family to find out about it."

of sexual minorities. Lesbians and gay men are usually ignored altogether; but when they do appear, it is in roles that support the "natural" order and they are thus narrowly drawn. The stereotypic images are always present, if only implicitly, as when gay characters are depicted in a carefully "antis-tereotypic" manner that draws our attention to the absence of the "expected" attributes. Richard Dyer has pointed out that, "What is wrong about these stereotypes is not that they are inaccurate." They are, after all, often more than a little accurate, at least for some gay people, some of the time. Dyer continued, "What we should be attacking in stereotypes is the attempt of heterosexual society to define us for ourselves, in terms that inevitably fall short of the 'ideal' of heterosexual society (that is, taken to be the norm of being human), and to pass this definition off as necessary and natural." Sexual minorities are not, of course, unique in this regard— one could say the same for most media images of minorities. But our general invisibility makes us especially vulnerable to the power of media images.

Of all social groups, we are among the least permitted to speak for ourselves in public life, including in the mass media. Prior to Ellen Morgan's much publicized coming out (along with her real-life counterpart, Ellen DeGeneres) in 1997, and the following year's Will Truman of NBC's *Will & Grace*, no major network television program had a lesbian or gay lead character. Gay roles are no longer scorned as the kiss of death for movie stars— after all, both William Hurt and Tom Hanks won Oscars for playing gay men—but there is still not a single openly lesbian or gay major Hollywood star. This is not exactly a matter of personal choice. The entire industry operates on the principle that the American public is suffused by prejudices that must be catered to. In earlier decades the same logic required Jewish actors to submerge and hide their ethnicity. "In Hollywood, stars assumed neutral names like Fairbanks, or Howard, or Shaw; actresses underwent plastic surgery; some made a point of going to Christian churches or donating money to Christian charities."

Openly lesbian and gay reporters are absent from the news programs inhabited by the likes of Tom Brokaw, Carole Simpson, or Connie Chung. While we are certainly present in the story conferences and newsrooms in which such programs are assembled, it is generally on condition that we keep our identities hidden, from the audience if not always from our colleagues.

We are also the group whose enemies are generally least inhibited by the consensus of "good taste" that protects other minorities from the more public displays of bigotry. It is unthinkable in the 1990s that any racial or ethnic minority would be subjected to the sort of rhetorical attack that is routinely aimed at lesbian and gay people by public figures, who do not encounter widespread condemnation for their bigotry. When Roberta Achtenberg, a member of San Francisco's Board of Supervisors and a prominent legal activist, was nominated by President Clinton in 1993 as Under Secretary of Housing and Urban Development, Sen. Jesse Helms (R-NC) went on the attack: "She's a damn lesbian . . . working her whole career to advance the homosexual agenda. Call it gay-bashing if you want to. I call it standing up for traditional family values." One would have to go back decades to find such unabashed bigotry directed against a member of a racial or ethnic minority on the floor of the U.S. Senate.[8]

Our vulnerability to media stereotyping and political attack derives in large part from our isolation and pervasive invisibility. The process of identity formation for lesbian and gay people requires the strength and determination to swim against the cultural stream one is immersed in at birth. A baby is born and immediately classified in two critical dimensions. One is presumed to be known before birth—when a baby is born no one asks, "What race is it?"—because we believe in a rigid set of racial identities (and, in our white supremacist society, if you're not "all white" you're "not white"). The other identifying attribute is the subject of that familiar first question: boy or girl? The newborn infant is held up, inspected, and wrapped in an appropriately colored blanket. As we know, the blue-blanket babies and the pink-blanket babies are treated differently from that moment on, by doctors and nurses and parents and everyone else. Something else is taken for granted at the same time that also affects how that baby is treated: it is defined as heterosexual. It is made clear throughout childhood that this baby is expected to grow up, marry, have children, and live in nuclear familial bliss, sanctified by religion and licensed by the state. Over and over, through a multitude of messages in a myriad of

---

[8] In 1996 the Dole presidential campaign first accepted and then rejected a contribution from the Log Cabin Gay Republican organization. During the early stages of the 2000 presidential campaign, George W. Bush, who presented himself as a "compassionate conservative" urging his party to reach out to racial minorities, told NBC's Tim Russert that he would not meet with the Log Cabin group because it would create a "huge political nightmare. . . . I am someone who is a uniter, not a divider. I don't believe in group thought, pitting one group of people against another" (11/21/99). In April 2000, having sewn up the nomination, Bush met with a group of gay Republicans, later telling reporters, "I am a better person" for having met with this group. While he did not agree on some issues, he added, "I'm mindful that we're all God's children."

media, that child encounters the taken-for-granted assumption that his or her future is heterosexual.

How do those of us who are not white, male, middle class, Christian, and heterosexual come to a sense of identity and self-worth in a society that values attributes we do not and mostly cannot possess? Well, for one thing, we can observe the people around us as well as those we encounter through the lens of the media. Women are surrounded by other women, African Americans by other African Americans, and so forth, and can observe the variety of choices and fates facing those who are like them. Mass media may offer only a narrow range of roles and images for women and minorities, but their biases and omissions are also balanced by the audiences' own experiences.

In contrast, lesbians and gay men are a self-identifying minority. We are presumed to be straight, and are treated as such, until we begin to recognize that we are not what we have been told, that we are different. But how are we to understand and deal with that difference? We generally have little to go on beyond very limited direct experience with those individuals who are sufficiently close to the accepted stereotypes to be labeled publicly as queers, faggots, dykes, and so on. Increasingly, openly lesbian and gay people are present throughout society, but even so, nearly half of the people surveyed in polls say they know no gay people, and large majorities say there are none in their family. And we have the mass media. In the absence of adequate information in their immediate environment, most people—gay or straight—have little choice but to accept the media stereotypes they imagine must be typical of all lesbians and gay men.

The rules of the mass media game have had a double impact on gay people: not only have they mostly shown them as weak and silly, or evil and corrupt, but they continue for the most part to exclude and deny the existence of normal, unexceptional as well as exceptional lesbians and gay men. Hardly ever shown in the media are just plain gay folks, used in roles that do not center on their difference as an anomaly that must be explained, a disappointment that might be tolerated, or a threat to the moral order that must be countered through ridicule or physical violence. The stereotypic depiction of lesbians and gay men as abnormal, and the suppression of positive or even "unexceptional" portrayals serves to maintain and police the boundaries of the moral order. It encourages the majority to stay on their gender-defined reservation, and tries to keep the minority quietly hidden out of sight. For the visible presence of healthy, unapologetic lesbians and gay men does pose a serious threat: it undermines the unquestioned normalcy of the status quo, and it opens up the possibility of making choices that people might never have otherwise considered could be made.[9]

SUBVERSION AND RESISTANCE

We are all colonized to some degree by the majority culture. Those of us who belong to one minority group or another will inevitably have absorbed many mainstream values, even when they serve only to demean us. Similarly, although it might seem contrary to their interests, millions of nonwhites across the globe happily consume U.S. media products, with their distinctly "white-angled" view of the world. Recognizing these patterns is a first step toward demanding more even-handed media representation of all cultural groups. Yet this does not, in itself, guarantee a solution.

In the case of sexual minorities, there have been responses to the media's hostile treatment of sexual minorities that represent degrees of subversion and resistance. Sexual minorities are particularly vulnerable to the internalization of mainstream values, given that the process of self-identification generally occurs in isolation and relatively late in life. As gay liberationist writers Hodges and Hutter put it: "We learn to loathe homosexuality before it becomes necessary to acknowledge our own. . . . Never having been offered positive attitudes to homosexuality, we inevitably adopt negative ones, and it is from these that all our values flow." Without realizing it, even lesbians and gay men may be profoundly heterosexist in their thinking and outward behavior.

Individuals who internalize or fail to challenge mainstream beliefs often do not realize, however, that by defending antigay and antilesbian values, they are essentially doing the work of their oppressors. Political theorists use the term *hegemony* to describe this sort of collusion between master and slave, in which the oppressed are somehow persuaded that their oppression is just, inevitable, or natural. Once a hegemonic system is in place, those at the top of the hierarchy need only defend the ideologies and structures that convince those below that they belong there. Once homosexuals believe that they are in fact perverted, trivial, or unworthy of public recognition—and therefore lack the grounds to protest their mistreatment—their oppressors' work has

---

[9] In a refreshingly candid defense of antigay discrimination, psychologist E. L. Patullo acknowledged the importance of maintaining the status quo since, "In a wholly nondiscriminatory world, the advantages of heterosexuality would not be obvious."

been done for them. The Zionist polemicist Ahad Ha-'Am drew on a biblical analogy, in an essay on Moses, to describe this phenomenon: "Pharoah is gone, but his work remains; the master has ceased to be master, but the slaves have not ceased to be slaves." And as Raymond Williams pointed out, hegemony "is never either total or exclusive. At any time, alternative or directly oppositional politics and culture exist as significant elements in the society." One such oppositional strategy is the appropriation and subversion of mainstream media.

For gay males, the classic strategy of subversion is camp—an ironic stance toward the straight world rooted in a gay sensibility. As British gay writer Jack Babuscio defined it, camp reflects "a consciousness that is different from the mainstream; a heightened awareness of certain human complications of feeling that spring from the fact of social oppression; in short, a perception of the world which is coloured, shaped, directed and defined by the fact of one's gayness." This characterization would, of course, fit the comic or aesthetic styles of other oppressed groups (e.g., the fatalism of Jewish humor, the sense of loss in African American folk songs that gave rise to the blues), but the gay sensibility differs in that we encounter and develop it at a later stage in life; it is nobody's native tongue.

Moreover, while sharing much with other minority perspectives, camp is suffused with a theatrical view on the world that is rooted in the particular realities of lesbian and gay life. Forced to "pass for straight" in order to avoid social stigma or physical danger, one develops, Babuscio noted, "a heightened awareness and appreciation for disguise, impersonation, the projection of personality, and the distinctions to be made between instinctive and theatrical behaviour." In short, the gay sensibility incorporates a self-conscious role-playing and theatricality—and the knowledge that social and gender roles are ultimately no more than performances, arbitrary guises into which skilled players can step at will. Passing for straight involves play-acting, pretending to be something one is not, either by projecting untruths or withholding truths about ourselves that would lead others to the (correct) conclusion about our sexuality.

Rooted in this sensibility, camp serves several purposes. It supplies an opportunity to express distance from and disdain for mainstream culture. Exchanged in private settings, camp helps forge in-group solidarity, repairing some of the damage inflicted by the majority and preparing us for further onslaughts. Used as a secret code in public settings, it can also be a way to identify and communicate with other "club members" under the unknowing eyes of the straight world—itself an act of subversive solidarity. Politically, it can also be a form of public defiance, a flamboyant expression of sexual variation that dares to show its face. Finally, camp is the quintessential gay strat-egy for undermining the hegemony of mainstream media images. The sting can be taken out of oppressive characterizations and the hot-air balloons of conventional morality can be burst with the weapon of irony. Most impor-tantly, by encouraging viewers or readers to evaluate mainstream culture as outsiders, as spectators living beyond its perimeter, a camp sensibility creates a sense of detachment from the dominant ideology. In the words of Richard Dyer:

> The sense of being different . . . made me feel myself as "outside" the mainstream in fundamental ways—and this does give you a kind of knowledge of the mainstream you cannot have if you are immersed in it. I do not necessarily mean a truer perspective, so much as an aware-ness of the mainstream as a mainstream, and not just the way every-thing and everybody inevitably are; in other words, it denaturalizes normality. This knowledge is the foundation of camp.

Ultimately, the most effective form of resistance to the hegemony of the mainstream is to speak for oneself, to create narratives and images that counter the accepted, oppressive, or inaccurate ones. While many groups and interests are ignored or distorted in the media, not all have the same options for resistance. The opportunities for opposition are greatest when there is a visible and organized group that can provide solidarity and insti-tutional support for the production and distribution of alternative mes-sages.

In post-World War II America, lesbian women and gay men began, with difficulty, to create alternative channels of communication that would foster solidarity and cultivate the emergence of a self-conscious community. Typi-cally, the first alternative channels to appear are those with low entry barriers, minimal technological needs, and relatively low operating costs. Thus, news-papers and magazines have long been the principal media created and con-sumed by minority groups.[10] In recent decades, video technology has made it possible for anyone with a camera and editing deck (or at least access to them) to produce fictional and nonfiction programs. But the problem of dis-tribution remains a major hurdle (although video technology makes possible syndicated cable programs). Films, while far more expensive to make, can

[10] An important medium and genre of the 1950s and 1960s, particularly for lesbians, was paperback "pulp" fiction. Novels, such as Ann Bannon's Beebo Brinker series, featured lesbian heroines and plots, and did not invariably end in tragedy. Flourishing like weeds at the margin of literature, these novels represented a source of imagery and emotional support.

often recoup their investment by identifying and appealing to a relatively specific niche. Finally, the Internet now utilizes a relatively cheap technology to provide Web-based news and magazine sites, chat rooms, bulletin boards, and mail networks. By contrast, it is network television—with its numerous regulatory hurdles, high production costs, and demand for broad audiences—that remains the most insular and undemocratic of the media, largely unavailable to most minority groups.

Coming Out and Coming Together

To understand lesbian and gay liberation is to realize the central role that the minority press has played in the formation of identity-based politics, whether the case in point is the African American, feminist, or lesbian and gay movement. The lesbian and gay movement that seemed to appear "spontaneously" across the country shortly after the 1969 Stonewall riots in New York City was in fact the result of a process begun early in a post-World War II urban gay world that was largely invisible to heterosexual society, and whose growing self-consciousness in the decades prior to Stonewall can be traced in large part to the pioneering lesbian/gay press.

The first stirrings of the modern gay rights movement in the United States came about during a period of political and sexual repression. The United States in the late 1940s was obsessed with a desire to return to a state of prosperity and "normalcy" after nearly two decades of disruption: economic depression in the 1930s followed by the Second World War. The country was gripped by the anti-Communist fervor of the Cold War, which prompted the witch-hunts led by such politicians as Sen. Joseph McCarthy (R-WI). From the late 1940s through the 1950s, actual or suspected homosexuals were targets of persecution just as real or suspected Communists were; in fact, the categories were often collapsed into the commie-queer bogeyman. As historian John D'Emilio points out, it took little effort to incorporate lesbian women and gay men into the demonology of the period: "According to extreme anti-Communist ideologues, left-wing teachers poisoned the minds of their students; lesbians and homosexuals corrupted their bodies. Communists bore no identifying physical characteristics. . . . Homosexuals too could escape detection. Coming from all walks of life, they insinuated themselves everywhere in society, including the highest reaches of government."

Because most people confronted with accusations of homosexuality during these witch-hunts quietly resigned, it is impossible to determine the number of careers and lives that were destroyed. In 1949, during the early stages of McCarthyism, ninety-six "perverts" were fired by the State Department; by 1953 the Los Angeles Hearst newspaper could run the headline: "State Department Fires 531 Perverts, Security Risks." A Senate committee reported 4,954 cases between 1947 and 1950.

In 1948 America was shocked by the publication of Alfred Kinsey's *Sexual Behavior in the Human Male*, followed in 1953 by a companion volume on females. As gay critic Michael Bronski put it, the Kinsey Report (as it was popularly known) told homosexuals what they already knew: they *were* everywhere; at the same time, it also reinforced many heterosexuals' most basic fear—that the invisible, undetectable enemy *was* everywhere.[1]

In this environment, when gay people began to organize in order to fight back against their oppression, it is no surprise that the organizations they created emphasized secrecy and discretion. The earliest important organization, the Mattachine Society, took its name from mysterious medieval figures in masks, and its form was modeled on the Communist Party, in which secrecy, hierarchical structures, and centralized leadership predominated. Within a few years of its founding in Los Angeles in the winter of 1950, as the Mattachine Society began to attract attention and increased membership, the original leftist leadership was purged and the centralized structure relaxed. After 1953 the Mattachine Society was much more assimilationist than radical.

Throughout the 1950s and into the 1960s the homophile movement, as it was then generally called, slowly expanded and deepened the self-awareness of lesbian and gay people as a distinct, self-conscious, and embattled minority. Central to this awareness was the process known as "coming out"—the individual realization that one was homosexual, and the acknowledgment of this sexual identity to other gay people. As more lesbians and gay men came

[1] The Kinsey Report gave birth to one of the most resilient pseudostatistics in the history of social science: the familiar estimate that 10 percent of the population is homosexual. In fact, Kinsey and his colleagues give a number of different figures in the 1948 volume, ranging from a low of 4 percent (males who are exclusively homosexual) to a high of 37 percent (the percent of males reporting at least one same-sex orgasm), with a final estimate that "only fifty percent of the [white male] population is exclusively heterosexual throughout its adult life." The equivalent figures for women were lower in all categories. However, in the absence of a true probability sample survey—impossible to conduct with an invisible population that has reason to fear exposure—there is no way to obtain an accurate estimate of the lesbian and gay population.

out, they began to break the silence of decades, demanding an end to laws that criminalized gay people and promoted discrimination and harassment.

In 1951 the American homosexual movement received a significant boost with the publication of the first full-scale account and polemic for equality, Donald Webster Cory's *The Homosexual in America: A Subjective Approach*. Writing as a gay man (but under a pseudonym that referred to André Gide's homosexual apologia, *Corydon*), Cory presented a forceful argument that homosexuals constitute a minority within American society: "Our minority status is similar, in a variety of respects, to that of national, religious and other ethnic groups: in the denial of civil liberties; in the legal, extra-legal and quasi-legal discrimination; in the assignment of an inferior social position; in the exclusion from the mainstream of life and culture."

Cory's powerfully written, openly subjective description and analysis of the conditions of gay male life in midcentury America served as a stimulus to the emerging homosexual self-consciousness, and Cory was viewed as an inspirational leader of the nascent homophile movement.[2] In a 1963 follow-up book, *The Homosexual and His Society: A View from Within*, written with John LeRoy, Cory restated his thesis "that the invert is a member of a minority group, differing from ethnic and other minorities essentially in that his status as a minority group is unrecognized," and celebrated the "feeling of group recognition [that] has grown among these people," leading to the launching "of a struggle for the rights guaranteed to all citizens of a free democratic society." Describing the beginnings of that movement in "small secret underground groups," Cory and LeRoy note that, "With diminishing secrecy, several distinct groups and societies have found their way on the American scene, fighting a legal, social and political battle in order to help win public acceptance for the invert and his way of life."[3]

---

[2] Among the many "end of the millennium" lists in the year 2000 was the Web-magazine *Gay Today*'s list of the "Top 100 Gay Books of the 20th Century," which cited Cory's book as "The Gay Book of the Century," followed by the two Kinsey volumes. By contrast, the right-wing Intercollegiate Studies Institute at the same time listed Kinsey's book as the third worst book of the century, after Margaret Mead's *Coming of Age in Samoa* and Beatrice and Sidney Webb's *Soviet Communism: A New Civilization?*

[3] By the mid-1960s, however, something was happening to Donald Webster Cory, and his days as a leader of the homosexual liberation movement were numbered. In his 1963 book with John LeRoy, Cory had argued against the prevailing psychoanalytic view that homosexuality was a curable sickness and that "those who remain homosexual are trapped by their own perversity, since it is a matter of choice, after all. Nothing could be farther from the truth." Yet despite this apparent resistance to the claims of psychiatry, by 1965, under the influence of psychotherapist Albert Ellis, Cory was promoting the key positions he had opposed in his earlier writings. Cory's conversion to a psychiatric perspective and his abandonment of the minority analysis he had pioneered led to a struggle within the homophile movement and the rejection of Cory's position

GIVING VOICE TO THE VOICELESS

When the 26-year-old lesbian who called herself Lisa Ben created *Vice Versa* ("a magazine for gay gals") in 1947, she was reflecting the increasing sense of group recognition cited by Cory: "Whether the unsympathetic majority approves or not, it looks as though the third sex is here to stay." She wondered "whether the war by automatically causing segregation of men from female company for long periods of time has influenced fellows to become more aware of their own kind," and recognized the possibilities created by changing social and economic conditions: "Today, a woman may live independently from man if she so chooses and carve out her own career. Never before have circumstances and conditions been so suitable for those of lesbian tendencies."[4]

Lisa Ben worked as a secretary for RKO Studios and was able to use her office typewriter to produce her magazine. "I put in five copies with carbon paper, and typed it through twice and ended up with ten copies of *Vice Versa*. That's all I could manage. There were no duplicating machines in those days, and, of course, I couldn't go to a printer." *Vice Versa* only lasted for nine issues before Lisa Ben's work conditions changed and she could no longer type the magazine at the office, but in the words of Jim Kepner, founder of the International Gay and Lesbian Archives in Los Angeles, it "established the basic format for the general gay magazine—with editorials, with short stories, with poetry, with book and film reviews, and with a letters column." It certainly lived up to the subtitle on its front page: "America's Gayest Magazine."

---

by the New York Mattachine Society. At this point there occurred the strange and possibly unique example of a *reverse coming out*: the pseudonymous Donald Webster Cory suddenly disappeared from sight, and the space previously occupied by his body was taken by an apparently heterosexual sociologist named Edward Sagarin, now writing about the homophile movement under his real name, as an "objective" social scientist. In a 1973 essay surveying a spate of recent books on homosexuality, many of them works of the early gay liberation movement, Sagarin defined gay identity as "false consciousness" and criticized the minority model he had promulgated in his earlier (and now unacknowledged) existence as Donald Webster Cory. Sagarin ended his essay on a truly bizarre note by defending the continued hiding of "secret deviants" and warning that those who "call on gay people to accept and assert themselves, blatantly to proclaim themselves, . . . may be proceeding on the road to their own undoing."

[4] Lisa Ben's suppositions about the importance of wartime experiences for the formation of gay consciousness are supported by historian Allan Bérubé's research on *Coming Out Under Fire*. While her optimistic predictions for lesbians in an economy of opportunity for single women might have been dampened by the regressive spirit of the 1950s, her analysis presaged the work of gay historians like John D'Emilio, and well described conditions that emerged in the 1970s.

In the words of John D'Emilio, "the pioneering effort to publish magazines about homosexuality brought the gay movement its only significant victory during the 1950s." The magazines he referred to were all, like *Vice Versa*, published in California: *ONE* was founded in Los Angeles in 1953, *Mattachine Review* and the *Ladder* were launched in San Francisco in 1955 and 1956. But unlike *Vice Versa* they reached far beyond the editors' immediate circle—they were distributed nationally and built a combined circulation of about 7,000. They each lasted more than a dozen years, surviving attacks from government agencies and officials determined to shut them down. According to journalism historian Rodger Streitmatter,

> People in both large cities and small towns throughout the country were not only reading the articles but were becoming engaged in the debates. Readers of the magazines did not passively accept information from the editors, but they actively participated in forging the ideology of lesbian and gay liberation. Just as the founding of the first African-American newspaper has been credited with marking the beginning of a national movement to secure black civil rights in the early 19th century, by creating a communications medium that allowed women and men all over the country to converse with each other, *ONE*, *Mattachine Review*, and the *Ladder* began to build a national lesbian and gay community.

ONE was founded by a few gay men in Los Angeles who were frustrated by the feeling that they were just talking to themselves and the knowledge that the media wouldn't print anything about their cause. As Don Slater, one of the founders, later put it, "A social movement has to have a voice beyond its own members. Talking to each other in small groups does not create a social movement." They named the magazine (and the organization that produced it) from a quotation by Thomas Carlyle: "A common bond of brotherhood makes all men one."[5] America's first openly sold magazine by and for homosexuals, *ONE* took a more militant stand than did the Mattachine Society, which by then was adopting a strategy of achieving acceptance by conforming to heterosexual standards. The head of the Mattachine Society, which had relocated to San Francisco, was a former newspaperman, Hal

[5] Jim Kepner later elaborated on the origins of the name, citing "the ubiquitous World War II joke about an army sergeant teaching a group of rookies to count off, coming to one who didn't speak up, and barking, 'Hey! You! ain't you one?' 'Yes,' lisped the recruit, 'Are you one, too?'" Kepner continued, "'He's *one*' was common gay jargon."

Call, and in 1955 he founded the *Mattachine Review* as a tool to promote the organization's philosophy that public attitudes toward homosexuals would improve as soon as "sex variants began behaving in accordance with societal norms."

Neither Mattachine nor *ONE* attracted substantial contributions from women, and it took a group of lesbians to fill this vacuum. In 1955 four lesbian couples living in San Francisco began an organization they called the Daughters of Bilitis (the name came from French poet Pierre Louys's *The Songs of Bilitis*), and a year later DOB leaders Phyllis Martin and Del Lyon began to publish the *Ladder*. The first issue stated: "We enter a field already ably served by *ONE* and *Mattachine Review*. We offer, however, that so-called 'feminine viewpoint' which they have had so much difficulty obtaining. It is to be hoped that our venture will encourage the women to take an ever-increasing part in the steadily-growing fight for understanding of the homophile minority."

The three magazines carried news of developments around the country affecting lesbians and gay men, and *ONE*'s editor Jim Kepner accumulated a network of contributors scattered throughout the United States who sent him clippings that he then distributed to the magazines. They also monitored and reported on the efforts of the fledging homophile movement, as it was then called.

ONE, Inc., introduced an array of programs in addition to *ONE* magazine, all intended to support their mission of homosexual liberation: offering a book service, publishing a guide to homophile organizations and, in 1956, instituting lectures and classes on "An Introduction to Homophile Studies," "The Homophile in History," "The Homosexual in American Literature," "Introduction to the Sociology of Homosexuality," and "The Orthodox Freudian Texts on Homosexuality," among others. By 1959, Jim Kepner reported in *One Confidential*, the institute's newsletter, the basic course ran for thirty-six weeks and had attracted over two hundred people. The "Homosexual in History" course also ran for thirty-six weeks and "we've been amazed at the volume of material brought to light—not easily. . . . We were swamped in every age and country, despite the efforts of many historians to bury this material."

The courses, like the magazine, included arguments countering the claim that homosexuality is unnatural, or that homosexuals are necessarily mentally ill. *ONE* offered extensive accounts and detailed refutations of the arguments made by prominent psychiatrists of the period, exposing the contradictions and faulty logic in the writings of such noted authorities as Albert Ellis:

Having specifically defined exclusive homosexuals *and* exclusive het-erosexuals as similarly neurotic, Dr. Ellis inexplicably judges the former to be more urgently in need of therapy, and to compound the contra-diction, his concept of full cure seems to be to encourage a person to lose all interest in, or openness to, homosexual activity, even though, by his definition, this merely substitutes one exclusivist neurosis for another. His definition of neurosis is identical with his definition of cure.

ONE reported and commented on debates that were going on within var-ious religious denominations and informed its readers about developments in other countries, particularly the progress toward legal reform in Great Britain, where the *Wolfenden Report* of 1957 urged the abolition of laws against homosexual acts by consenting adults in private. *Mattachine Review*, which mirrored the Mattachine Society's belief that progress would be achieved through educating and encouraging progressive experts, was the first to publicize the groundbreaking research of psychologist Dr. Evelyn Hooker, who demonstrated that there were happily adjusted homosexuals and that there was no inherent association between psychopathology and homosexuality.[6] The *Ladder* led the way in arguing that lesbian and gay peo-ple had to think of themselves as a political force, not merely as an oppressed minority. Their role became influential when a candidate for mayor of San Francisco in the 1959 election accused Mayor George Christopher of trans-forming the city into "the national headquarters for sex deviants," and sin-gled out the Daughters of Bilitis in a warning to parents to guard their daughters. The editors of the *Ladder* responded with a special issue that helped bring the gay perspective into what became a major public debate. The mainstream media condemned the antigay tactic and Mayor Christopher was reelected by a wide margin. This was a turning point in the emergence of a politically active and visible lesbian and gay community in San Francisco.

The magazines operated with minuscule budgets and volunteer labor—Dorr Legg was hired by *ONE* in April 1953 as the first paid employee of the gay movement, for "$25 a week, when available. . . . It generally wasn't avail-able." Very few ads were ever placed by businesses; even businesses sup-ported by gay customers were afraid to advertise in these magazines. Despite these odds the circulation of the magazines rose throughout the 1950s, with

---

[6] As Hooker later said, "At that time, the 1950s, every clinical psychologist worth his soul would tell you that if he gave those projective tests he could tell you whether a person was gay or not. I showed that they couldn't do it."

ONE reaching 5,000 subscribers each month, and *Mattachine Review* around 1,000. The *Ladder* had the lowest circulation—a pattern to be repeated later with other lesbian publications—but its readership was much larger than its official circulation of around 700. One Washington, D.C., subscriber invited friends over every month for a "*Ladder* party" at which she would read the magazine out loud to as many as thirty or forty other lesbians. Similar gatherings were held around the country. Jim Kepner later noted, "Our reach was wider than our limited membership and circulation figures would indicate, as we challenged homophobic psychiatrists, legal, and religious 'authorities' and gave voice to those who had previously been voiceless. Gay gossip spread our ideas to many who never saw our magazine."

Gay people weren't the only ones who were paying attention to these small magazines: the FBI quickly began to investigate the publications, calling them subversive, disgusting, and shocking. In August 1953, Los Angeles postal officials tried to stop *ONE* from mailing issues on the grounds of obscenity, but the Post Office in Washington overruled them. Shortly thereafter a Republican senator from Wisconsin, Alexander Wiley, wrote to the Postmaster General, protesting "the use of the United States mails to transmit a so-called 'magazine' devoted to the advancement of sexual perversion." Now the Post Office began a serious campaign, confiscating the October 1954 issue of *ONE*, and the magazine had to take the matter to court. In the meantime, FBI agents maintained a constant harassment of the editors of all three magazines; the editors, in turn, infuriated the FBI by claiming that "everyone knew J. Edgar Hoover was queer." As Hal Call put it recently, "I told the FBI agents the same things forty years ago that historians are just saying today." Despite mounting legal costs, *ONE* pursued its appeal of the Post Office rulings through the federal courts. In January 1958 the U.S. Supreme Court overruled the decision of the lower courts in a landmark decision establishing that the subject of homosexuality was not, per se, obscene.

In the wake of the Supreme Court's decision the editors of *ONE* felt liberated to "advocate homosexuality." At a time when homosexual acts were illegal throughout the United States, the magazine's editors asserted the "right, even in the face of much opinion and some law to the contrary, to say that homosexuality is a good thing for homosexuals. We also have a constitutional right to add, for the sake of discussion, that we might think homosexuality a good thing for everybody. We wouldn't expect that opinion to be popular, but we have the right to express it." Reflecting on the role of the gay press in the 1950s, Jim Kepner noted: "Most gays then felt that our only concern was to get the police off our backs. My writings were central to advocating the need for Gay self-respect and education, and for building Gay community consciousness and institutions." And, he added, "We did the job while professional journalists stayed in the closet for thirty years."

PROVOKING CONCERN

In the spring of 1959 the *Village Voice* printed an article by Seymour Krim called "The Revolt of the Homosexual," which purported to be a dialogue between a homosexual and a skeptical heterosexual. The homosexual asserts a demand for "simple human rights" and easily refutes the standard arguments presented by the "heterosexual." Krim's imagined dialogue takes on a more militant tone, as he continues:

> Those who come after us will laugh at pressures now put on men to keep up a front of courage, indifference to delicacy, male superiority. If I prefer gentleness to harshness, I'm not being a woman. I'm being human, something you might be ashamed of with your strait-jacket notion of masculinity. Like it or not, we will force our way into open society and you'll have to acknowledge us.

Written a full decade before Stonewall, Krim's warning reflected the growing willingness of gay people to risk visibility and demand the right to speak for themselves.

In July 1962 a public radio station in New York City, WBAI-FM, broadcast a program, "The Homosexual in America," in which a panel of heterosexual psychiatrists spent ninety minutes talking about homosexuals and mental illness. This familiar pattern of talking about gay people rather than allowing them to speak for themselves was one time too many for a young gay activist named Randy Wicker. Wicker marched into the station the next day and demanded equal time. The station program manager agreed to the demand and scheduled a second program, this time featuring Wicker and seven other gay men. The announcement drew ridicule from some in the press: a radio-TV critic said the station was "scraping the sickly barrel-bottom" by giving these men the opportunity "to tell their perverted side of the admittedly sad but certainly sinful story." However, the program was greeted more favorably by others, such as Jack Gould in the *New York Times*, who believed it encouraged a "wider understanding of the homosexual's attitudes and problems."

The following autumn Randy Wicker received a call from a reporter at the *New York Times*. The reporter, Robert Doty, had been given an unusual assignment by the new metropolitan editor, Abe Rosenthal: to investigate the increasingly visible gay male community. The managing editor at the *Times*, Harrison Salisbury, later recalled a lot of discussion within the paper about the assignment, as "homosexuality . . . wasn't thought of as something you brought forward and you talked about. . . . They wondered if this was the sort of thing the *Times* should do." But if Salisbury and his colleagues were worried that Doty's story might glamorize the subject of homosexuality, their concerns were unfounded. True, Doty was taken on a tour of the gay world by Randy Wicker and introduced to "normal" gay men. He was given the pioneering studies by California psychologist Evelyn Hooker that found that gay men were as well-adjusted psychologically as were straight men. Yet when it came to writing his story, Doty reverted to the familiar journalistic practices of "objectivity" and "balance." What this meant was that Doty's direct contact with healthy homosexuals was overruled by the opinions of "official sources."

Thus, when the nation's leading newspaper first put gay people on its front page in December 1963, they were motivated to break their silence by the realization that gay people were beginning to live their lives more openly. That this was not a development welcomed by the *New York Times* itself could be seen in the headline and lead paragraph of this first-ever front-page article focusing on gay people:

GROWTH OF OVERT HOMOSEXUALITY IN CITY PROVOKES WIDE CONCERN

The problem of homosexuality in New York became the focus yesterday of increased attention by the State Liquor Authority and the Police Department. The liquor authority announced the revocation of the liquor licenses of two more homosexual haunts that had been repeatedly raided by the police. . . . The City's most sensitive open secret— the presence of what is probably the greatest homosexual population in the world and its increasing openness—has become the subject of growing concern of psychiatrists, religious leaders and the police.

Doty's article was typical for the period in that he accepted without question the views of those defined as "legitimate" authorities—political, legal, medical, and religious—and the only comments that came from gay people were buried at the end of the story. Reporters and readers are aware of the significance of sequencing in news stories: the most important facts and opinions come in the first paragraphs—the lead—and the rest of the article proceeds in descending order of importance. The message was both familiar and clear:

gay people were the least important sources of information and opinion about their own lives.

As hostile as it was, the *Times* article signaled an end to the pervasive silence about lesbians and gay men in the press. As the 1960s progressed, more and more articles focusing on gay people began appearing in newspapers and magazines, many of them echoing the *Times*'s concerns over the growing visibility of gay people. Even more alarming to the press was the insistence of many gay people that they were neither morally degenerate nor mentally ill. In March 1964 the *New York Times* ran its second front-page story about homosexuals. Spurred by a report from the New York Academy of Medicine, the article was headlined, "Homosexuals Proud of Deviancy, Medical Academy Study Finds."

The most influential national magazines of the period, *Life*, *Time*, and *Newsweek*, also noticed the presence of the emerging lesbian and gay community and its growing demand for an end to the stigmas imposed by law, medicine, and religion. In June 1964, *Life* magazine published an extensive article on "Homosexuality in America," although like most stories of the period it focused exclusively on gay men and ignored lesbians. The introduction to the story, printed over a two-page photograph of shadowy figures standing in a San Francisco leather bar, captures the stance of the media as they confronted the specter of homosexuality:

HOMOSEXUALITY IN AMERICA: A SECRET WORLD GROWS OPEN AND BOLDER. SOCIETY IS FORCED TO LOOK AT IT—AND TRY TO UNDERSTAND IT.

These brawny young men in their leather caps, shirts, jackets and pants are practicing homosexuals, men who turn to other men for affection and sexual satisfaction. They are part of what they call the "gay world," which is actually a sad and often sordid world. On these pages, LIFE reports on homosexuality in America, on its locale and habits, and sums up what science knows and seeks to know about it.

Homosexuality shears across the spectrum of American life—the professions, the arts, business and labor. It always has. But today, especially in big cities, homosexuals are discarding their furtive ways and openly admitting, even flaunting, their deviation. Homosexuals have their own drinking places, their special assignation streets, even their own organizations. And for every obvious homosexual, there are probably nine nearly impossible to detect. This social disorder, which society tries to suppress, has forced itself into the public eye because it does present a problem—and parents especially are concerned. The myth and misconception with which homosexuality has so long been clothed must be cleared away, not to condone it but to cope with it.

This article clearly reflects the familiar concern with "understanding" homosexuals in order to contain the social problem they represent—in an echo of McCarthyism the article asked, "Do the homosexuals, like the Communists, intend to bury us?" Still, it was relatively progressive, and *Life* later called on New York state to follow the lead of Illinois which, in 1961, became the first state to make homosexual behavior between consenting adults legal.[7] But these signs of progress were short-lived, and these national magazines soon reverted to the hostile patterns of earlier years.

In a January 1966 essay, "The Homosexual in America," *Time* paid brief acknowledgment to the growing belief among psychiatrists that homosexuals were not mentally ill, but then devoted most of the essay to undermining that perspective. It concluded:

It is a pathetic little second-rate substitute for reality, a pitiable flight from life. As such it deserves fairness, compassion, understanding and, when possible, treatment. But it deserves no encouragement, no glamorization, no rationalization, no fake status as minority martyrdom, no sophistry about simple differences in taste—and above all, no pretense that it is anything but a pernicious sickness.[8]

THE VOICE GETS LOUDER

The 1960s ushered in an era of social activism across the United States as the civil rights movement, followed by the antiwar movement and the women's movement, engaged thousands of citizens in grassroots political campaigns.

[7] *Life*'s extensive story, with its numerous photographs, had the presumably unintended consequence of informing gay readers around the country about developments in far-off places. A Texas man then in his forties recalled, "The first time I ever heard of *ONE* or Mattachine was in *Life*. It never would have dawned on me that anything like that was out there." Another account came from a man who had been a Virginia teenager: "I read it when nobody was around. . . . I hung on every word of it. I thought, *I* want to go to a big city. *I* want to find out what this is all about."

[8] The *Ladder* responded to "*Time*'s pernicious prejudice" in an article recounting a lecture by sexologist Isadore Rubin, who presented a detailed critique of *Time*, concluding that, "if they are not ignorant, the editors of this essay are intellectually dishonest, motivated by prejudice, and guilty of deliberate omission and distortion."

The lesbian and gay movement took on increased fervor as activists began appearing in the Northeast as well as the West Coast. In Washington, D.C., a government employee named Frank Kameny fought back after he was fired because of his sexuality and became one of the key figures in building the gay movement. Kameny founded the Mattachine Society of Washington, which pursued a far more active and militant strategy than its West Coast counterpart, and coined the slogan "Gay Is Good" in a deliberate echo of the familiar "Black Is Beautiful."[9]

One of the first vehicles for Kameny's arguments was the *Ladder*, which was taken over in 1963 by a new editor, Philadelphia activist Barbara Gittings. One of Gittings's first acts was to add the words "A Lesbian Review" to the front cover of the *Ladder*. As she explained, "The subtitle said, very eloquently, I thought, that the word 'lesbian' was no longer unspeakable." Even more daring, Gittings replaced the line drawings previously used on the cover with photographs of actual lesbians, many photographed by her lover and colleague Kay (Tobin) Lahusen.

Another new magazine was begun on the East Coast in 1964, this time in Philadelphia. *Drum*, published by the Janus Society, a homosexual rights organization founded in 1960, took its name from a famous statement by Thoreau: "If a man does not keep pace with his companions, perhaps it is because he hears the beat of a different drummer." Editor Clark Polak said that he "began *Drum* magazine as a consistently articulate, well-edited, amusing and informative publication. I envisioned a sort of sophisticated, but down-to-earth, magazine for people who dug gay life and *Drum*'s view of the world." Polak was on to something, as *Drum*'s circulation quickly climbed to 10,000, by far the largest for a gay publication. Like the *Ladder* under Gittings, *Drum* took a much more militant stance than had earlier publications. Polak criticized "hyper-conformist" gay people as sellouts for saying they had no problems as long as they didn't flaunt their homosexuality: "Individuals who pass for straight in the way that light-skinned Negroes pass for white are paying an extremely high price for their homosexuality."

In 1966 Frank Kameny and another leader of the Washington Mattachine, Jack Nichols, founded their own magazine, the *Homosexual Citizen*. Although Kameny and Nichols wrote much of the contents, the magazine was edited by a lesbian, Lilli Vincenz. In the first issue Vincenz wrote an editorial explaining the juxtaposition of "homosexual" and "citizen" in the

[9] Another of Kameny's successful linguistic innovations was the use of "sexual orientation" or "preference" as neutral terms to replace the various medical labels that implied pathology in describing homosexuality.

magazine's name: "These words must seem irreconcilable to the prejudiced. All we can say is that these people will be surprised—for patriotism and responsible participation in our American democracy are certainly not monopolized by white Anglo-Saxon Protestant heterosexuals."

In 1965 these activists—Randy Wicker in New York, Kameny, Nichols, and Vincenz in Washington, and Gittings, Lahusen, and Polak in Philadelphia— were among the small number who opened a new front in the struggle for gay liberation. Following in the footsteps of civil rights and antiwar groups who were taking their protests to the streets, these activists began marching with picket signs—in front of the White House, the Civil Service Headquarters, and the State Department in Washington, the United Nations in New York, and Independence Hall in Philadelphia. While their small numbers were dwarfed by the much larger protests against the war in Vietnam that often occurred on the same day, these early marches signaled a new visibility for the movement.

Word of the marches was spread not through the mainstream media, which largely ignored them, but in the pages and on the covers of the lesbian and gay magazines, especially the *Ladder*. When the mainstream media began to pay attention to the growing visibility of lesbian and gay people in the 1960s, their coverage tended toward alarmist expressions, as in the *New York Times*'s front-page headline, "Growth of Overt Homosexuality in City Provokes Wide Concern." The gay publications responded by printing their own reviews of the stories appearing in the *New York Times*, *Time*, and *Life*, blasting them for their prejudice and superficiality. After *Life* published its "Homosexuality in America" feature, Polak responded with an article in *Drum* on "Heterosexuality in America, signed by 'P. Arody'": "Heterosexuality shears across the spectrum of American life— the professions, the arts, business and labor. It always has. But today, especially in big cities, heterosexuals are openly admitting, even flaunting their deviation."

The gay press made major strides in reaching larger audiences in the mid-1960s with developments on both coasts. New York journalist Al Goldstein pushed the envelope of sixties' social tolerance by launching the sex-tabloid *Screw* in 1968. With contents ranging from reviews of pornographic films to nude photographs of men and women to uncensored classified ads, the magazine was an instant success that quickly reached a circulation of 150,000. One of the novel features of *Screw* was a column by gay activist Jack Nichols and his lover, Lige Clarke, for which they used the name of the Washington magazine, "Homosexual Citizen." The column, appearing in the biweekly tabloid, brought news of the gay liberation movement to many thousands—both gay and straight—who would never see the smaller movement magazines.

In one of their columns Nichols and Clarke heralded an important milestone of the movement: in November 1967 a young activist named Craig Rodwell opened the Oscar Wilde Memorial Bookstore in New York City, the first gay bookstore in the country. Donald Webster Cory's *Homosexual in America* had concluded with a 19-page annotated list of novels and dramas, from Sherwood Anderson to Arnold Zweig, "in which homosexuality is the basic theme, or in which it plays an important minor role." But even those familiar with Cory's list would have been frustrated in their attempts to track down many of these works. For them, as for others less aware of the existence of serious writing on homosexuality, walking into a bookstore emblazoned as the "Bookshop of the Homophile Movement" was a revelation and a sort of homecoming. The Oscar Wilde Memorial Bookshop, like its successors around the country, served as a catalyst for emerging lesbian and gay communities, and as an invaluable resource for thousands of queers searching for images and inspiration, affirmation and arousal.

Around the same time, a Los Angeles activist who used the name Dick Michaels took over a movement newsletter, renamed it the *Los Angeles Advocate*, and turned it into the country's first commercial gay paper. Focusing mostly on news, covering stories "the straight press wouldn't print, and what gay people needed to know about what was happening in the world," the paper was an immediate success. By the end of its second year the *Advocate* had reached a circulation of 23,000 and was distributed in cities across the country. It was becoming the first national gay news magazine—a role it continues to play today, with a circulation exceeding 80,000.

As activists turned the heat up during the turbulent years of the late 1960s, the *Advocate* encouraged their newly militant tactics, routinely using the slogan "Gay Power" and thus helping to solidify the identity of the gay movement. In August 1968 the patrons of the Patch, a Los Angeles gay bar, stood their ground and mocked police who raided the bar. The *Advocate* hailed this as a historic event that signaled "a new era of determined resistance." And so it did, as the New York City police learned on a June night the following summer. The Stonewall riots may have been the spark that ignited a movement across the country, but the kindling for the bonfire had been prepared over the previous two decades by small and scattered groups of activists who nurtured a movement through the words and pictures of their magazines.

The decade of the 1970s was a period of explosive growth for the lesbian and gay community around the United States, as thousands came out and joined the movement, and as commercial, political, religious, cultural, and social institutions sprang up everywhere. These institutions cultivated the growing sense of community identity and spread the word to a new genera- tion of young people who came out into a world that had been turned upside down.

Newspapers and magazines were founded by lesbian and gay organiza- tions and individuals all over the United States and beyond. Activists Karla Jay and Allen Young published a collection in 1972 called *Out of the Closets: Voices of Gay Liberation* that listed fifteen periodicals published across the United States and Canada in addition to the *Advocate* and the *Ladder*. Within a few years that number had more than doubled. Particularly notable was the phenomenal increase in lesbian feminist activism, fueled by the dual forces of the women's and the lesbian/gay movements. The early 1970s saw the founding of such journals as *Ain't I a Woman?*, *Amazon Quarterly*, *Aza- lea*, *Dyke*, the *Furies*, *Lavender Woman*, *Lesbian Connection*, *Lesbian Tide*, *Sinister Wisdom*, *Sisters*, and *Tribad*. Although most of these publications did not survive the 1970s, they played a major role in the emergence of lesbian- feminist consciousness and culture, and introduced readers to such powerful writers as Rita Mae Brown, Audre Lorde, and Adrienne Rich. At the same time, more significant lesbian and gay political journals were being founded, notably *Gay Community News* in Boston and the *Body Politic* (1971–1988) in Toronto.

Although published in Canada, the *Body Politic* (*TBP*) played a central role in the emergence of the U.S. gay movement during this period. The bor- der was not an insurmountable barrier. Many of the writers who contributed to *TBP* were American; Allan Bérubé, John D'Emilio, Amber Hollibaugh, Vito Russo, James Steakley, and Scott Tucker are among the leading writers of the U.S. movement who found a welcome there. *TBP* was easily the most sophisticated and ambitious in its intellectual and political scope, and its his- tory of struggle with government censorship and repression gave it an impor- tant place in the history of the gay press.

Gay Community News was started in 1973 as the local paper of the move- ment in Boston but within a few years was playing a larger role as the only national lesbian/gay news weekly, as well as the most significant venue for political analysis and a good deal of cultural writing. Many of the most important political debates of the period were conducted in the "letters" pages of *GCN*. It is no coincidence that many influential lesbian and gay writ- ers and activists began their movement careers at *GCN* (among them Michael Bronski, Richard Burns, Phillip Brian Harper, Sue Hyde, Neil Miller, Cindy Patton, and Urvashi Vaid).

The lesbian and gay press played a central role in the emergence of a newly self-confident and visible community that was demanding its share of the American dream. The political successes of the gay liberation movement, and the defeats, were reported in the pages of the lesbian and gay press while the mainstream press continued to ignore or denigrate their efforts. But the true value of the gay press did not become fully apparent until the early 1980s, when the AIDS epidemic brought down the curtain on the "golden age" of the lesbian and gay community in the decade following Stonewall.

COMING OUT IN THE NATION'S LIVING ROOMS

By the early 1950s the power of newspapers and magazines was being challenged by a new medium that was to become the most powerful source of images and information in the history of the world. In the beginnings of the television era, it did not take long before the host of a sensationalistic program in Los Angeles, *Confidential File*, decided to broadcast a program on homosexuality. The program, which aired in April 1954, included an interview with a young gay man who used the pseudonym Curtis White—but only after the host had interviewed a psychiatrist and a police department vice officer, who were presented as the representatives of official authority. "Curtis White," who said that he did not consider himself to be abnormal, was asked if his family knew that he was homosexual. In what may have been the first instance of what is by now a familiar response, White said, "Well, they didn't up until tonight . . . I think it's almost certain that they will . . . I think I may very possibly lose my job too." Asked why he had agreed to appear on the program, given these concerns, White said he hoped to be "a little useful to someone besides myself." Unfortunately, despite Curtis White's effective presentation, which was well-received by the Los Angeles press, his boss also watched the program and saw through the fake name and the blurring of his face. Curtis White, whose real name was Dale Olson, was promptly fired.

Despite the risks, lesbians and gay men continued to take whatever opportunities presented themselves to appear on television talk shows and tell their story. In 1958 the first gay man to appear on a television program in New York was a Mattachine Society member, Tony Segura, who wore a hood to disguise his identity. A typical feature of the radio and television talk shows that included lesbian or gay people was the apparently obligatory "balance" provided by an antigay psychiatrist or some other hostile challenger (often, the host himself played the role of attacker).

Radio and television producers of the period—and, unfortunately, many today as well—were unable, or unwilling, to allow lesbian or gay people to speak for themselves without the protection of a medical or religious expert to neutralize the threat to normalcy. The consequence of this balancing act, as the producers no doubt intended, was frequently a circus atmosphere of gladiatorial combat. When gay activists Frank Kameny and Jack Nichols made the first appearance by openly gay people on a Washington, D.C., television program in 1967, the host lost his cool and began yelling, "Get out of my studio, you vicious perverts! . . . You make me want to vomit!"

Although local radio and television stations found homosexuality suitably titillating for talk show audiences, it wasn't until 1967 that any of the television networks were willing to approach the topic. CBS producer Fred Friendly had commissioned a documentary "in which homosexuals have a chance to talk about their life and about what it's like to live in a world where a person is laughed at as homosexual." But when producer William Peters came back with such a program—built around a conversation with eight gay men in San Francisco—the CBS brass refused to air the program. The word in the office was that they found the program distasteful and risky. But the show had already been announced, and therefore another *CBS Reports* producer, Harry Morgan, was assigned to the task. This time, however, Morgan did it by the book, television style, and the program, narrated by Mike Wallace, was aired in March 1967. The program explicitly excluded lesbians from its discussion of "The Homosexual." The only gay men identified by name are white, middle class, and visibly respectable (Jack Nichols, who appeared under the pseudonym Warren Adkins, was fired the next day from his job at a Washington hotel). Others are shown strategically placed behind potted palms, or otherwise hidden from view, as their tormented psyches are bared.

As befits an objective reporter facing an aberration in the natural order, Mike Wallace seemed anxious to know what causes homosexuality (thus, presumably, helping society to prevent it). For authoritative answers Wallace turned to psychiatrists Irving Bieber and Charles Socarides, two leading proponents of the view—now officially discredited—that gays are mentally ill. Their statements were made with a confidence as assured as it was baseless, for they consistently failed to acknowledge the most elementary handicap facing any responsible scientist who wishes to study gay people: the impossibility of obtaining a nonbiased sample from an invisible population. In addition to the psychiatrists, Wallace spoke to members of the clergy—a Catholic priest and a Protestant minister—who admitted that homosexuals, while certainly sinners, are to be pitied and, if possible, saved. Viewers were also treated to the sight of a 19-year-old serviceman being arrested in a park for "soliciting" an undercover policeman and told that his commanding officer and parents would be informed of his arrest. After nearly an hour-long program in which gay men were defined and framed almost entirely from the outside, Wallace concluded: "The dilemma of the homosexual: Told by the medical profession he is sick, by the law that he's a criminal. Shunned by employers. Rejected by heterosexual society. Incapable of a fulfilling relationship with a woman or, for that matter, with a man. At the center of his life, he remains anonymous . . . a displaced person . . . an outsider."

And that's the way it was, Tuesday, March 7, 1967. But it didn't stay that way for long.

3

Stonewall and Beyond

The 1960s are known as a decade of street politics. From the attacks by Alabama police dogs on civil rights marchers to the urban riots in Watts, Newark, and Detroit; from the antiwar marches in front of the White House and the Pentagon to the riots at the Democratic National Convention in Chicago; from the Free Speech Movement at Berkeley to the shooting of students on the campuses of Kent State and Jackson State universities—one social conflict after another was taken outside. To gain the attention of the public, it seemed, one needed to do it in the streets, while the whole world was watching. But, of course, sometimes the media weren't interested.

Among the many landmarks of that turbulent decade few have achieved the fame and symbolic resonance of events that began as a fairly routine example of police harassment on a hot June night in 1969. Police raids on gay bars were neither new nor unusual, though they had become less frequent by the late 1960s. When the police raided the Stonewall bar in Greenwich Village on June 28, they did not expect to set off a riot—and they certainly did not expect to ignite the explosion of a militant gay rights movement. But when many of the bar's patrons fought back, soon joined by allies on the streets, the incident sparked several nights of rioting—and the Stonewall riots initiated a flurry of organizing that soon turned into a firestorm of activism across the country.[1]

---

[1] As has been noted, Stonewall wasn't the first bar whose patrons fought the police—that honor probably goes to the Patch in Los Angeles. Many theories have been put forward to explain why the Stonewall raid erupted in violence—among them that Judy Garland's funeral took place earlier that day. It might also be asked why this particular riot sparked the firestorm

The night of the Stonewall riots the media were unaware of the historic significance of the events in the Village. Even though the editor on night duty at the *New York Times* realized that "these guys are fighting the cops for the first time" and dispatched a reporter to the scene, he also knew that the topic of homosexuality was not popular with the top brass. The *Times*'s brief account of the historic event was buried on page 33 and told from the police's perspective. As the riots continued the *Times* ran a second story the next day, also on page 33, that again focused on the official point of view: "Police Again Rout 'Village' Youths."

Other New York media were less subtle than the *Times*, even if no more sympathetic to the Stonewall rioters. The *New York Daily News* waited until July 6 to cover the story, but its reporter was at least aware that something significant had occurred. This did not prevent him from treating the riots as an occasion for heavy-handed humor. The story was headlined "Homo Nest Raided, Queen Bees Are Stinging Mad," and it continued in that vein:

> She sat there with her legs crossed, the lashes of her mascara-coated eyes beating like the wings of a humming-bird. She was angry. She was so upset she hadn't bothered to shave. A day-old stubble was beginning to push through the pancake makeup. She was a he. A queen of Christopher Street. Last weekend the queens had turned commandos and stood bra strap to bra strap against the invasion of helmeted Tactical Patrol Force. The elite police squad had shut down one of the their gay clubs. . . . Queen power reared its bleached blonde head in revolt. New York City experienced its first homosexual riot.

The *Village Voice*, Greenwich Village's local countercultural paper, was no more delicate in the choice of language to describe the momentous events happening in its own backyard. *Voice* reporter Lucian Truscott, who came upon the riot as he walked through the Village that night, wrote an account that referred to "the sudden specter of 'Gay Power' [that] erected its brazen head and spat out a fairy tale the like of which the area has never seen," when "the forces of faggotry" rallied in protest against the raid. Truscott's article did capture some of the significance of the riots, however, in the words of gay poet Allen Ginsberg with which he ended his article: "You know, the guys

---

it did. The symbolic importance that Stonewall has assumed may also be the result in part of the fortuitous name of the bar chosen by the police that hot June night. Had the riots taken place at the Sewer, or The Snake Pit (to name two other contemporaneous Village bars), these names would hardly have had the militant resonance of Stonewall.

out there were so beautiful—they've lost that wounded look that fags all had 10 years ago."

The *Village Voice* was soon to learn that the "forces of faggotry" were willing to fight the media as well as the police. In the wake of the Stonewall riots a group of gay activists quickly organized a rally that led to the formation of the Gay Liberation Front (GLF) and the birth of a new, radical, gay liberation movement modeled on such sixties groups as Students for a Democratic Society (SDS) and the Black Panther Party. Writing in their column in the underground newspaper *Screw*, Jack Nichols and Lige Clarke wrote, "The revolution in Sheridan Square must step beyond its present boundaries. The homosexual revolution is only a part of a larger revolution sweeping through all segments of society."[2]

The GLF quickly grew and began to organize on several fronts. One of its first projects was to organize dances for young people as an alternative to the Mafia-controlled bars. But when they tried to advertise their dances in the *Village Voice*, they were told that the word "gay" was obscene and could not be used in the ad. To make matters worse the *Voice*, willing to use words like "faggots," "dykes," and "queers" in its news articles on the Stonewall riots, also ran ads for apartments that specified "no gays."[3]

GLF members showed up outside the *Voice*, not far from the Stonewall bar, on September 12, 1969, carrying picket signs denouncing their policies. After several hours some of the demonstrators were invited to meet with the publisher. The meeting was heated but the GLF was victorious. The *Voice* agreed to allow "gay" and "homosexual" to appear in ads without alterations. While not a total victory—the publisher reserved the right of his reporters to use derogatory language—this was a milestone of lesbian and gay media activism: it was a sign of the new militancy of a gay movement that was taking its demands directly to the media, making them targets of protest along with politicians, psychiatrists, and preachers.

[2] The name Gay Liberation Front was an obvious reference to the Vietnamese National Liberation Front, reflecting the activists' engagement in the antiwar movement. Karla Jay and Allen Young's 1972 collection, *Out of the Closets: The Voices of Gay Liberation*, included a listing of lesbian and gay organizations in thirty-six states, the District of Columbia, and ten other countries. California alone was represented by seventy-four organizations, sixteen of them called Gay Liberation Front.

[3] Such refusals were common at the time. A few years later an innocuous ad for the Canadian gay liberation journal the *Body Politic* was turned down by the *Toronto Star*, on the grounds that it would contribute to the recruitment of homosexuals. However, such outbreaks of bigotry continue to occur. In August 1999 the *San Diego Union-Tribune* rejected an ad for the film *Better Than Chocolate* containing the following quote: "One of the best lesbian movies ever! Sexy! Funny! A total refreshing delight!" The paper's advertising director explained: "I didn't like the word Lesbian. We have guidelines and do not want words of a sexual nature."

On the first anniversary of Stonewall, the first Gay Pride march was held in New York City—it is now an annual event in cities across the country and even beyond—and the *New York Times* took notice. The "quote of the day" was a statement by one of the organizers that summarized the core belief of gay liberation: "We're probably the most harassed, persecuted minority group in history, but we'll never have the freedom and civil rights we deserve as human beings unless we stop hiding in closets and in the shelter of anonymity."

"TURNING THEIR CONDITION INTO POLITICS"

Among the early efforts of the newly militant gay liberation movement of the 1970s was a focus on the images presented in the media: Hollywood films and television programs, as well as the stories reported—or ignored—by the news media. But one of their first targets was more upscale than either newspapers or television.

In September 1970, *Harper's* magazine, a long-established periodical with a reputation for intellectual and cultural analysis, published a cover essay by Joseph Epstein: "Homo/hetero: The Struggle for Sexual Identity." Epstein's essay was later described by conservative writer Midge Decter as "an elegant and thoughtful" account of "the tangle of his feelings and attitudes towards homosexuality and towards the then new question of homosexual rights." Gay readers saw the essay rather differently: it was an unabashed proclamation of homophobia masquerading as analysis. Epstein assured his readers that he had not "accepted" homosexuality; in fact, he continued, "If I had the power to do so, I would wish homosexuality off the face of the earth." The essay ended with an even more chilling declaration: "There is much that my four sons can do in their lives that might cause me anguish, that might outrage me, that might make me ashamed of them and of myself as their father. But nothing they could ever do would make me sadder than if any of them were to become homosexual." The Gay Activists Alliance sent a delegation to the offices of *Harper's* where they conducted a very gentle sit-in, greeting staff members by saying, "Good morning, I'm a homosexual. We're here to protest the Epstein article. Would you like some coffee and donuts?"[4] They occupied

---

[4] The Gay Activists Alliance (GAA) was organized in December 1969 by a faction that split off from the Gay Liberation Front (GLF) in a disagreement over organizational structure (they thought GLF didn't have enough) and programmatic focus (they thought GLF was diffusing the importance of achieving social and political rights for homosexuals by linking with nonhomosexual left-wing causes). Within a relatively short period, the more organized and reformist GAA supplanted the GLF as the primary gay liberation organization on the East Coast.

the offices for the day, trying to explain to the editors why the Epstein essay was so offensive and dangerous. Midge Decter, then *Harper's* executive editor, insisted that the article was "serious and honest and misread," to which GAA leader Arthur Evans replied, "You knew that his article would contribute to the suffering of homosexuals. You knew that. And if you didn't know that you're inexcusably naïve. You're a bigot and you are to be held responsible for that moral and political act." Years later, in a monumentally homophobic article in *Commentary*, Decter complained about the lack of style exhibited by the demonstrators; she expected more "dash and high taste" from the amusing fairies she preferred to these humorless activists who were "turning their condition into politics."

Another reaction to Epstein's article was set off when Merle Miller, a respected television writer, was lunching with two *New York Times* editors shortly after the *Harper's* article appeared.[5] After the editors expressed approval of the Epstein piece Miller exploded, "Damn it, I'm a homosexual!" The result was that the editors challenged Miller to write his own piece, which he did, and it was published in the *New York Times Magazine* in January 1971 under the title, "What It Means to Be a Homosexual." Miller's article talked about growing up as a "sissy" in Iowa and taking on the protective coloring of a tough journalist, joining in the laughter at "queer jokes." The article, which was probably the first time someone prominent had come out so publicly, generated a flood of mail—nearly five thousand letters, the vast majority from gay people expressing their gratitude to Miller for speaking out. Miller expanded the article into a book, *On Being Different*, in which he wrote, "It took me almost fifty years to come out of the closet, to stop pretending to be something I was not, most of the time fooling nobody."

The impact of the *Harper's* sit-in was also felt by the producers of the Dick Cavett show broadcast by ABC to a national audience. GAA activists had been demanding an opportunity to respond to antigay remarks comedian Mort Sahl made in the spring of 1970, but they had been rebuffed by the Cavett staff. When GAA members prepared to infiltrate and disrupt the show the evening of the *Harper's* sit-in, Cavett (who had seen coverage of the *Harper's* demonstration on the news) agreed to invite two GAA representatives on for a future show. In November 1970, GAA leaders Arthur Evans and Marty Robinson appeared on the *Dick Cavett Show* to express GAA's

---

[5] Epstein's article set off another, slightly more delayed reaction. Australian political scientist Dennis Altman, who was in New York at the time and participated in the *Harper's* zap, was moved to write what became *Homosexual: Oppression and Liberation*, one of the first major works of gay liberation analysis.

demands for cultural and political change. Asked what they were seeking, Robinson said, "Heterosexuals live in this society without any scorn—they live openly, their affection is idealized in movies, theater. Homosexuals want the same thing: to be open in this society, to live a life without fear of reprisal from anybody for being homosexual—to live a life of respect." Speaking of GAA's strategy, Evans added, "We feel that we have to come out politically, as a community which is aware that it is oppressed and which is a political power bloc feared by the government. Until the government is afraid of us—afraid of our power—we will never have our rights."

As political scientist Toby Marotta noted, the *Harper's* sit-in and the Cavett show marked a new stage: the approach of challenging culture-shaping institutions with demonstrations that combined consciousness-raising tactics with politicizing and pressuring tactics. In the long run, however, the decisive battles would not be waged over magazines like *Harper's*, where even articles as offensive as Epstein's reached an audience of thousands at most. But television programs were viewed by *millions* every week. Lesbian and gay activists began to pay close attention to the central role that television entertainment was playing in shaping the American cultural and social agenda. The success of the 1972 TV movie *That Certain Summer* drew the attention of activists because of the potential it demonstrated for television to reach national audiences. It was important to persuade the television networks to present more frequent and more truthful lesbian and gay images in prime time.

Operating first under the banner of the GAA and subsequently of the National Gay Task Force, founded in New York in 1973 (now the National Gay and Lesbian Task Force, in Washington), activists began to put pressure on the television networks, whose headquarters are also in Manhattan. One of the first tactics used by the GAA was the "zap," in which a small group of activists would infiltrate an event and provoke a scene by loudly protesting antigay oppression. The first zap was staged at the season opening of the Metropolitan Opera in New York in 1970, when Mayor John Lindsay was confronted by members of GAA who had infiltrated the event dressed in tuxedos, in order to dramatize their anger over the mayor's refusal to end police harassment of gays. As the mayor and his wife entered, the packed lobby was rocked by cries of "End Police Harassment!" and "Gay Power!"

Zaps were intended to garner publicity by staging actions where reporters and cameras were likely to be. One zap carried this tactic to its extreme in December 1973 when activist Mark Segal infiltrated the CBS News studio and, carrying a sign proclaiming GAYS PROTEST CBS BIGOTRY, suddenly leapt in front of the camera as news anchor Walter Cronkite read the evening news.[6] The interruption was quickly ended and few viewers were likely to have understood what happened, but the story of the zap was itself news, and Cronkite apparently was goaded into thinking more seriously about the issue. On the *CBS Evening News* broadcast of May 6, 1974, Cronkite included a major segment on gay rights, beginning by saying, "Part of the new morality of the '60s and '70s is a new attitude towards homosexuality. The homosexual men and women have organized to fight for acceptance and respectability. They've succeeded in winning equal rights under the law in many communities."

The zap was intended to reach gay people as much as those who were its targets. GAA leader Arthur Evans summarized the philosophy of the zap, which he termed political theater for educating the gay masses:

> Gays who have as yet no sense of gay pride see a zap on television or read about it in the press. First they are vaguely disturbed at the demonstrators for "rocking the boat"; eventually, when they see how the straight establishment responds, they feel anger. This anger gradually focuses on the heterosexual oppressors, and the gays develop a sense of class-consciousness. And the no-longer-closeted gays realize that assimilation into the heterosexual mainstream is no answer: gays must unite among themselves, organize their common resources for collective action, and resist.

Or, as one activist put it, "one good zap is worth ten years of analysis."[7]

EXPRESSING OUTRAGE

Besides the occasional zap, however, media activists had few truly helpful resources to call upon. They lacked the support of governmental authorities such as the Federal Communications Commission or congressional committees that would stand up for the rights of racial minorities in their dealings

---

[6] Segal had previously zapped tapings of *The Tonight Show with Johnny Carson* and *The Mike Douglas Show*, but the tapes were edited before broadcast; he had also caused NBC's *Today Show* to go blank for a few seconds when he ran across the studio shouting, " Gay people are sick and tired of NBC's bigotry towards us."

[7] The GAA's tactics, including the zap, were later revived by AIDS-era activists, especially ACT UP and Queer Nation, and in January 1991, during the Persian Gulf war, four ACT UP members repeated Segal's stunt, surprising Dan Rather and *CBS Evening News*'s audience by jumping in front of the cameras, shouting, "Fight AIDS, not Arabs!"

with the media. They knew that they could not count on mainstream institutions such as churches and civic groups to defend their interests. For these groups, as for the media, homosexuality was a controversial topic that they generally preferred to avoid. But the activists did have one effective secret weapon—their own social invisibility: many lesbian and gay people who worked inside the media industries, but could not work openly for the gay cause, could nevertheless provide valuable information. These "agents in place" as they were sometimes called, often smuggled advance copies of television scripts to activists who then confronted network executives (they also assisted activists infiltrate television studios for zaps).

A leaked script for an episode of ABC's popular "doctor show" *Marcus Welby, M.D.*, in which Dr. Welby counsels a married gay man to suppress his homosexuality, served as the impetus for the Gay Activist Alliance's efforts. Working with an office plan provided by another insider, GAA members led by *Variety* reporter-turned-activist Ron Gold infiltrated ABC headquarters in New York on February 16, 1973, and challenged surprised executives. The sit-in led to arrests rather than negotiations, and the program aired two days later with only minimal changes, but the network executives did learn something from the episode. They began to invite gay activists to comment on scripts dealing with homosexuality—an understandable tactic, once they realized the activists would get their hands on the scripts in any case. But if the network learned something from this experience, the lesson apparently did not reach the producers of *Marcus Welby, M.D.*

The following year they came up with a script for an episode called "The Outrage" which revolved around a male teacher who molests a teen-age boy. Ron Gold had recently joined the newly formed National Gay Task Force (NGTF) and was positioning it to be the primary gay organization in consulting and negotiating with national media. Gold and his fellow activists responded with their own outrage when the network proposed only minor modifications in a script that was fundamentally unacceptable. The entire premise of the program held up precisely the sort of stereotype that NGTF was trying to eradicate: the familiar but false linkage of gay men with child molestation. The network refused to make the major changes that would have been required to satisfy the activists, and talks broke down. Led by Boston media activist Loretta Lotman, who moved to New York to spearhead the campaign, NGTF, along with GAA president Morty Manford and longtime L.A. activist Morris Kight, began to organize a nationwide protest against the outrageous *Welby* episode. The activists aroused lesbian and gay groups around the country to pressure their local ABC affiliates (and provided instructions on what to say to station general managers and on how to jam the station's phone lines), while simultaneously addressing companies planning to buy ad time on the program.[8] Capitalizing on its recent victory in persuading the American Psychiatric Association to remove homosexuality from their list of mental illnesses, NGTF now obtained a statement from the APA condemning the *Welby* program for promoting a false image. The National Organization for Women and the National Educational Association were also enlisted to condemn the program.

The protest efforts failed to stop the episode, but it was softened in some ways and the term "homosexual" was replaced by "pedophile" as a description of the sex offender. Several major sponsors withdrew their ads, and at least five affiliates refused to air the program. While some of these stations would likely have been equally unwilling to air an episode with positive gay images, others were clearly responding to the NGTF's campaign. The general managers of the ABC affiliates in Boston and Philadelphia both rejected the show because they were persuaded by the protesters that it would reinforce the false notion that gays are child molesters.

The campaign demonstrated to the networks that the gay movement was able to mobilize on a national basis.[9] There were also lessons here for the movement. The topic of homosexuality was controversial even when handled in a fashion that was acceptable to lesbian and gay activists. If the activists were to succeed, they had to encourage positive images and not simply fight against negative stereotypes. After all, they were confronting an industry— the term actually used to describe Hollywood's production operations—and one in which "artistic" considerations were routinely bent to the real or perceived demands of the marketplace. In other words, activists aiming to influence the shape of the product had to become an inescapable part of the producers' landscape.

Further, because most production was located in Los Angeles the New York activists too often found themselves in the position of reacting to programs after they were already completed and even after they had been broadcast. A new front in the media struggle was opened when a Los Angeles–based psychologist and former screen writer, Newton Deiter, created the Gay Media Task Force in L.A. as a one-person West Coast complement to

---

[8] A GAA member who worked in ABC's computer room would call Lotman whenever an advertiser cancelled, and she would immediately inform media reporters.

[9] How far NGTF still had to go was shown by the response from a media executive to the organization's request that "The Outrage" be removed from syndication: "If as you indicate, there are 20 million homosexuals in America, then there must be at least 180 million heterosexuals. To our knowledge not one heterosexual has ever pressured us or attempted to dictate program content."

STONEWALL AND BEYOND 49

the NGTF. By the late 1970s the networks were regularly consulting with Deiter on scripts involving gay characters. Having a presence on both coasts permitted activists to circumvent the networks' strategy of responding to protests by telling New York activists that a decision was being made by the producers in L.A. and telling L.A. groups that the same decision was a corporate matter, handled in New York.

Whatever lessons ABC learned from the "Outrage" campaign had to be repeated for NBC after that network ran an episode of *Police Woman* called "Flowers of Evil." In this program, unfortunately typical of many queer appearances on the cop and doctor shows of the early 1970s, three lesbians murder patients in their old-age home until they are stopped by policewoman Angie Dickinson, who informs them, "I know what a love like yours can do to someone." This outrage provoked a zap at network headquarters by a group of lesbians; one even brought her children, who wandered into the executive washroom.

In February 1975 Loretta Lotman, who had succeeded Ron Gold as NGTF's media director, became the first openly gay person invited to speak at the National Association of TV Program Executives. She confronted the top programming executives in the industry: "When you show only the stereotype of gays, you're telling lies. No other minority is as abused, exploited, misrepresented, or demeaned as gay people are." Lotman's appearance was crowned by her success in eliciting a public commitment from the three network presidents to adopt nondiscrimination statements in their employment policies.

Communications researcher Kathryn Montgomery observed the efforts of the organized gay movement in the 1970s to improve the ways network programmers handled gay characters and themes. Between 1973 and 1978 there were seven major protests, and all three television networks were targets of campaigns against negative and damaging images of homosexuals. In all these instances the activists demanded changes in program content, deletions of material, or even the canceling of particular episodes. While these demands were not fully met, and no episodes were canceled in their entirety, in most cases the activists did succeed in modifying the more negative aspects of a lesbian or gay character's portrayal, and in three of the cases the objectionable episode was not rerun. However, protests from antigay organizations have sometimes resulted in episodes with *positive* gay images not being included in rerun schedules—thus the networks can accurately be described as more anxious to avoid controversy than to overcome prejudice.

Montgomery concluded that "the decisions affecting the portrayal of gay life were influenced by the constraints which commercial television as a mass medium imposes upon the creation of its content. . . . These requirements served as a filter through which the issue of homosexuality was processed, resulting in a televised picture of gay life designed to be acceptable to the gay community and still palatable to a mass audience."

Acceptability to the gay community meant that a portrayal did not attack or deny their basic humanity; but these portrayals would never reflect their values or perspectives. But of course television producers are not looking to please gay and lesbian people; they are merely trying to avoid arguing with them afterwards. In Vito Russo's words, "Mainstream films about homosexuals are not for homosexuals. They address themselves exclusively to the majority."

TALKING BACK TO THE MEDIA

Media activism was not limited to entertainment programming or to the national media. Grassroots efforts focused on media sprang up around the country in the early days of lesbian and gay liberation. In Philadelphia, community protests against an article in the *Philadelphia Inquirer*'s Sunday magazine spurred the creation of a Gay Media Project that functioned for several years in the mid-seventies. In Boston, Loretta Lotman and others organized a local media advocacy group, Gay Media Action, that negotiated with local news executives but had disappeared by the late 1970s. The Lesbian and Gay Media Advocates (LAGMA) was formed after the October 1979 March on Washington for Lesbian and Gay Rights, an event attended by over 100,000 people but which went largely unreported in the media.

The *New York Times* carried a brief account (on page 14), but the television networks barely mentioned the march, and *Time* and *Newsweek* ignored the largest lesbian and gay demonstration ever held to that point. Boston activists returning from the March were outraged at the minimal coverage and demanded meetings with newspaper editors and TV station managers. LAGMA set up a system of local media monitoring and meetings with reporters and editors, accompanied by style guidelines and story suggestions (one immediate result was the agreement by the *Boston Globe* to allow "gay" to be used as a noun), and in 1982 published a short book, *Talk Back! The Gay Person's Guide to Media Action.*

On April 26, 1980, *CBS Reports*, which had presented the first network documentary on gay men in 1967, returned to the topic with "Gay Power, Gay Politics," a program about San Francisco. The presentation proved to be biased and manipulative. Gay men *were* interviewed, but the framing and editing turned their words and meanings to the producers' purposes. Reporter George Crile put words in people's mouths and asked blatantly leading questions. People appeared to speak for themselves, but in fact were being used in the service of Crile's "angle": that gay men have become a powerful force in San Francisco and are using that power to destroy traditional values in their demand for "absolute sexual freedom."

It seems likely that at some point in making the documentary the producers found the dramatic theme they would use as the news frame for their story, and everything was then shaped to fit that frame. The program opened and closed with footage of the 1979 March on Washington in which longtime CBS correspondent Harry Reasoner played bookend anchor. Reasoner introduced the program by telling viewers that the homosexuals gathered in Washington "publicly proclaimed themselves to be the newest legitimate minority. . . . In this program we'll see how the gays of San Francisco are using the political process to further their own special interest, just like every other minority group before them. . . . What we'll see is the birth of a political movement and the troubling questions it raises for the eighties, not only for San Francisco but for other cities throughout the country." In fact, what CBS was presenting was the dread specter of the Lavender Menace.

Despite the opening promise, CBS did not show "how the gays of San Francisco are using the political process" because it focused on only one political issue—the 1979 mayoral election—and presented it in a distorted and misleading fashion. Crile, as narrator on the scene, began with the false implication that gay political engagement was a recent phenomenon, claiming with obvious absurdity that, until the candlelight march on the night of Harvey Milk's assassination, in 1978, "few people had realized the size and strength of the gay community," as if Milk's election the year before hadn't conveyed that message.[10] Starting to build his case that gay political power was used almost exclusively for the procurement of "absolute sexual freedom," Crile states that, "By the end of 1978, the homosexual community here had not only achieved full civil rights and economic power, but it was moving provocatively into the political arena." Crile avoided the question of how "full civil rights" were earned without being engaged in the political

[10] Crile's errors must be attributed to incompetence or simple dishonesty. Minimal research would have uncovered articles such as "Gay Power in San Francisco," in *Newsweek* in June 1977, before Harvey Milk was elected to the Board of Supervisors: "Of a total population of 680,000, an estimated 120,000 are homosexuals, and officials reckon that 28 percent of the city's voters are homosexual. As a result, homosexuals in San Francisco lead a more open life—and have more political clout—than in any other American city."

arena, because, presumably, he wanted to inject the loaded term "provocatively" to describe gay political engagement.

In order to make the story credible it was necessary to ignore or deny many facts, beginning by limiting the program's view of the gay community to men. Lesbians remained invisible, although several women prominent in the city's political life had been interviewed by the producers. The spectrum of San Francisco's large lesbian and gay community was narrowed to two categories of (mostly white) men: the smoothly dangerous elite backstage power brokers, and the menacing, leather-clad, sex-obsessed street gays who frightened children with unrestrained animal lust.

Throughout the program, facts were misrepresented or distorted to tell the story of a dangerous political grab by sexually outrageous gay men and the capitulation of mainstream politicians. The culmination of this tale featured the supposed surrender of Mayor Diane Feinstein to the demands of the gay politicos, in which, "She'd offered them a gay police commissioner and political appointments in proportion to their numbers in the city. In short, she had given them all they had asked for." This summary was amplified in the "FYI CBS NEWS" press release issued by the network shortly before the program aired on April 26, 1980: "Not only did Feinstein publicly apologize [for hostile remarks made in a magazine interview], she promised to appoint a gay police chief and give homosexuals other political appointments in proportion to their numbers." There are at least two problems with this summary. First, what viewers unfamiliar with San Francisco would conclude—and what the CBS press release states—is that Feinstein agreed to appoint a gay police chief. However, the head of the San Francisco police is not called the "police commissioner," as is common in many cities, but the Chief of Police. What Feinstein actually promised was to appoint an openly gay member to the San Francisco Police Commission, an advisory body that is supposed to represent segments of the community. Appointing a gay member to this commission was far from the capitulation Crile claimed and, after the election, Feinstein did appoint a lesbian activist to this body. Second, granting political appointments to a group in proportion to their numbers seems fairly democratic.

The program concludes with a speech by Cleve Jones—a gay activist and former Milk aide who had been interviewed (and used) by Crile throughout the program—given at a candlelight memorial service a year after the assassinations of Mayor George Moscone and Harvey Milk. Crile introduces the speech: "There had been growing concern here about the homosexual community, but until the election the city's establishment hadn't taken this new political movement seriously, hadn't tried to challenge or control it. And now, the gays were warning the city that gay power had come of age and that this was only the beginning." What followed was the concluding portion of Jones's speech, carefully edited to narrow its political focus and eliminate the real context and scope of the issues raised by San Francisco's lesbian and gay community (only the italicized portions below were included in the broadcast):

> Yes, we know that Harvey Milk was not our first martyr. Harvey had a lover named Jack, and one day in '78, Harvey came home to find Jack's body hanging from the ceiling, a suicide. I wonder, how many of you here tonight have lost a friend or a loved one to suicide? Raise your hands. How many? How many of you know a woman who has experienced the terror of rape? Raise your candles. How many of you have been attacked? How many of you have been beaten? Raise your candles?
>
> *How many of you have heard from behind, "Hey, faggot! Hey, dyke!"? That is why we are here tonight. That is why we marched on Washington. That is why we will keep on marching.*
>
> That is why we will not rest until Harvey's dream is fulfilled: when lesbians and gay men of every age, race, and background come out to join in the struggle with all those who seek lives of dignity and freedom and joy.
>
> *It will be a long struggle,* a very long struggle, *and we will have leaders and slogans and martyrs aplenty. But let no one misunderstand.*
>
> Our movement is powered by the determination of a people too long denied, too long abused, a people seeking the freedom to live, to work, and to love. Let no one misunderstand, *we are deadly serious. We are growing in power with every day that passes and we will not be stopped!*

The program then returned to Harry Reasoner, standing in front of the Washington Monument to drive the point home once more:

> Gay political organizations are acting all across the country. The right of homosexuals to organize like any other minority seeking to further its own interests is no longer in question. The question is, what will those interests be? Will they include a demand for absolute sexual freedom, as they did in San Francisco? And if so, will this challenge to traditional values provoke far more hostility and controversy when it is put to the test elsewhere? It is no longer a matter of whether homosexuals will achieve political power, but what they will attempt to do with it.

The program was probably the most vicious piece of propaganda ever made by a television network and it was greeted with outrage around the country, but especially in San Francisco. The mayor and City Council objected to the distortions of the program, and the local CBS affiliate followed it with a program in which the producers were confronted by local activists. But, of course, local San Francisco audiences were the least likely to be fooled by the program's lies and omissions. The real danger of the program was in its effect on people unable to compare it with their firsthand knowledge of San Francisco, and it was widely cited and used in antigay political campaigns around the country. A Moral Majority billboard in San Jose, California, south of San Francisco, used an image from the program along with the slogan: "Don't Let It Spread!" as part of a successful campaign leading to the defeat of a gay rights ordinance.

One gay activist fought back vigorously. Journalist Randy Alfred carefully documented the program's many errors and distortions in a lengthy complaint to the National News Council, a media self-policing body (since abolished). Alfred's complaint covered forty-four separate charges that, he said, "contribute to the cumulative effect of patterned distortion." After hearing the case, the council found that CBS had been unfair in numerous respects, a rare rebuke to a national network. The council concluded that, "By concentrating on certain flamboyant examples of homosexual behavior, the program tended to reinforce stereotypes. The program also exaggerated political concessions to gays and made those appear as threats to public morals and decency." CBS reluctantly made a minimal public acknowledgment on the air.[11]

One side effect of "Gay Power, Gay Politics" was to stimulate another local media activist group. The Philadelphia Lesbian and Gay Task Force (PLGTF) took up the role formerly played by the Gay Media Project and demanded a meeting with the general manager of the local CBS affiliate, one of the six stations around the country owned and operated by the network. Although the general manager, like his network bosses, would not admit

---

[11] George Crile survived criticism by the lesbian and gay community, only to become embroiled in a much wider public controversy when he used what appear to be the same unethical methods to "get" Gen. William Westmoreland in the CBS Reports program, "The Uncounted Enemy: A Vietnam Deception," in November 1982. As described by critics Stephen Klaidman and Thomas Beauchamp, "The bias . . . was manifested mainly in Crile's skillful selection and marshalling of information to make his case as convincingly as possible, even though a fair and distanced reading of all the available evidence would not necessarily have yielded the same conclusion. . . . [Crile] chose a method of inquiry that, together with his personal convictions, was predestined to yield biased or otherwise distorted results." Once again, CBS stood by their man.

there had been anything wrong with the program, the meeting initiated discussions and negotiations that were soon extended to the other Philadelphia television stations and then to radio and newspapers. One immediate result of the meetings was the agreement of local TV station managers to run (and, occasionally, to produce) public service announcements (PSAs) for PLGTF that focused on issues of discrimination and violence. In the two decades since the CBS documentary started them off, PLGTF leaders met repeatedly with local media executives in order to raise their awareness of the concerns of the lesbian, gay, bisexual, and transgendered communities.

4

At the Movies

If we are to understand the role of the media in the lives of gay people, we must turn to the darkened caves and silver screens of the cinema. Like other minorities, gay people were mostly invisible on the screen, and thus the process of studying the relationship of gays and the media began with the archaeology of mainstream images. This enterprise was initiated by film critic Parker Tyler, whose 1972 *Screening the Sexes* was an early post-Stonewall view of movies with an openly gay eye. The serious study of homosexuality in the movies was largely stimulated by the work of Vito Russo, who combined an involvement in gay politics with a fascination for movies. Gathering material while working in the film library of the Museum of Modern Art, Russo developed an extensive survey of homosexual images (both explicit and implicit) in Hollywood film and took to the road with an illustrated lecture called "The Celluloid Closet"; this was also the title of the book version published in 1981 (a second edition in 1987 included an extensive updating, as well as analyses of television programs).[1]

Much early work of gay activist-scholars—and the term is appropriate, as no one unengaged by the gay movement was pursuing these matters publicly—focused on the delineation and analysis of the stereotypic portrayals of gay people in the media. In 1977, when the British Film Institute published *Gays and Film*, a thin volume edited by Richard Dyer, it had few companions on library shelves. Two of the three articles included ("Lesbians and Film: Some Thoughts," by Caroline Sheldon, and "Stereotyping"

---

[1] After Russo's death in 1990 of AIDS-related causes, filmmakers Rob Epstein and Jeff Friedman made a documentary film version, *The Celluloid Closet* (1995), based on Russo's work.

by Dyer) focused on stereotypes. As Dyer put it, stereotyping was "relatively little explored in any systematic way and full of contradictions and confusions. Yet it remains an important area, for it is from representations of social groups that people get their 'knowledge' about those groups—and that goes for members of those groups themselves." In the two decades since, the number of books and articles on gay people in/and the media has expanded to fill several feet of shelf space, but the issue of stereotyping remains a constant and conflicted concern.

One of the first films made at the Edison Studio in New Jersey in 1895 was a five-minute experimental film directed by William Dickson, that showed two men dancing together to the music of a waltz played on an Edison gramophone. It was called *The Gay Brothers*. While we don't know what Dickson intended this light-hearted scene—or its title—to suggest, we do know that this brief curtain-raiser did not prove typical of the thousands of movies that have followed.

When the movies did approach homosexuality it was almost always within a narrow range of roles. When members of a minority begin to appear on movie and television screens, the roles they are permitted to play are generally limited to two categories: victim or villain. In the case of African Americans these two types can be seen, on the one hand, in D. W. Griffith's *Birth of a Nation* (1915), in which black men are vicious rapists whose attacks on white women are foiled by the white male heroes of the KKK, and on the other, in the caricatured lazy and foolish servants portrayed by Stepin Fetchit and Butterfly McQueen. By representing a threat to be defeated or by serving as a fun-house mirror that highlights the hero's normal image, both villains and victims upheld the importance of staying on the straight and narrow path.

Characters representing racial and ethnic minorities—African Americans, Asian Americans, and through the 1950s even "white ethnics" such as Italian, Polish, and Jewish Americans—may have represented a threat to the values but not the identity of "mainstream" Americans (although the frequency with which stories of "passing" by light-skinned African Americans appeared in movies suggests that threats to white identity were a concern in this case). Lesbian and gay characters posed a more serious problem for mainstream values and identities. Unlike racial minorities, sexual minorities are not easily identifiable by skin color, facial features, or accents, and they are not segregated in ethnic neighborhoods. As with the "Red Menace" of the 1940s and 1950s, in which Americans were warned that Communists were, metaphorically, hiding under their beds, in the case of lesbians and gays, Americans were afraid of who might literally be *in* their beds.

American movies have been preoccupied with lesbian and gay people, but for decades this took the form of hidden and coded representations. In the case of women the disguise was often just that: cross-dressing that allowed the audience to enjoy the discomfort of the characters because they were "in on the joke." Women dressed as men were allowed to evoke ambiguous responses from their male costars, as long as the roles were "straightened out" by the final clinch. But while the mystery lasted it sent mixed messages to audiences, and we can assume that lesbians and gay men sitting in darkened theaters in 1936 paid particular attention when Cary Grant told Katharine Hepburn, whose character in *Sylvia Scarlett* was disguised as a young man, "There's something that gives me a queer feeling every time I look at you."

In 1932, when Hollywood was preparing to film the biography of Queen Christina of Sweden, starring Greta Garbo, a New York journalist noted the evidence that Christina's one persistent love was for a Swedish countess and wondered, "Will Garbo play such a Christina?" Of course, Garbo did no such thing, but the role she played in *Queen Christina* (1933) gave lesbian audiences a lot to contemplate. Christina prefers to wear men's clothing (which Garbo herself was known to do), scorns the male suitors she is urged to accept, and then reveals real affection by greeting Countess Ebba with a passionate kiss; and when the Chancellor groans, "But your majesty, you cannot die an old maid!" she replies, "I have no intention to, Chancellor, I shall die a bachelor!" Although Christina does ultimately fall in love with a man (who falls in love with her while she is disguised as a boy!), the film may speak most truly when Christina muses, "It is possible to feel nostalgia for a place one has never seen."

As film scholar Andrea Weiss has noted, "Rumor and gossip constitute the unrecorded history of the gay subculture." In the 1930s sexually ambiguous stars like Marlene Dietrich and Greta Garbo—both since revealed to have been bisexual—created an image of the androgynous woman that was taken to heart by lesbians who followed their screen roles and gossiped about their private lives. Gay men had few such opportunities, however, as there was no male equivalent to these female stars. For men any appearance of androgyny, far from being alluring and mysterious, was a threat that had to be countered through ridicule. The early history of the movies, and especially the period after the introduction of the Motion Picture Production Code in the 1930s, was full of what Vito Russo described as "frivolous asexual sissies" who provided comic relief playing sidekicks, servants, and scapegoats. What was almost completely forbidden was any character who was explicitly lesbian or gay.

There is a Hollywood legend that producer Sam Goldwyn was told that

Radclyffe Hall's *The Well of Loneliness* wouldn't work as a movie because it was the story of a lesbian, to which Goldwyn was supposed to have replied, "So what? We'll make her an American." That exchange may never have occurred, but in 1936 Goldwyn produced a film version of Lillian Hellman's Broadway play, *The Children's Hour*, in which lesbianism *was* erased completely. In the film *These Three*, Hellman's play about two women schoolteachers whose lives are destroyed when a vicious child falsely accuses them of being lovers was transformed by Goldwyn and director William Wyler into a more suitably American tale in which the liar accuses one teacher of an affair with the other teacher's fiancé.

Throughout the period of the Code lesbian and gay characters were often implied in movies, but always as threatening or pathetic or ridiculous figures. Female characters with sinister lesbian overtones appeared in prison and mental hospital plots (*Caged*, *The Snake Pit*), and as predatory and unscrupulous (*Young Man with a Horn*, *All About Eve*). Male roles with gay overtones depicted sad young men (*Tea and Sympathy*, *Rebel Without a Cause*) and vicious degenerates (*Suddenly Last Summer*).

By the end of the 1950s the Motion Picture Production Code was weakening, and one of those working to undermine its authority was director Otto Preminger. In 1953 Preminger made one of the first challenges to the authority of the Code by producing *The Moon Is Blue*, a comedy that not only failed to condemn adultery (although none occurred in the movie) but actually used the forbidden word "virgin"! In 1961 Preminger filmed the best-selling novel *Advise and Consent*, a story of political intrigue in Washington, D.C., in which a senator commits suicide when an early homosexual episode is brought to light. The Motion Picture Association of America was forced to accept that times had changed and issued a policy on October 3, 1961, stating that, "In keeping with the culture, the mores and the values of our time, homosexuality and other sexual aberrations may now be treated with care, discretion and restraint." Discretion and restraint meant, as the MPAA cautioned, that "sexual aberration could be suggested but not actually spelled out." It also still meant that lesbian and gay people would be depicted, in Vito Russo's words, as "pathological, predatory and dangerous; villains and fools, but never heroes."

Director William Wyler took advantage of the new rules to make a second film version of Lillian Hellman's *The Children's Hour* (1962), and this time he retained the original version of the lie told by a little girl. Wyler was quoted as saying that, "The lie has to have such a devastating effect that to be credible it must be appalling." Apparently he also meant it had to be unspeakable: although it is clear that the child is alleging that the teachers are carrying on a lesbian relationship, the word *lesbian* is never uttered. What is more, no one in the film suggests in any way that were it true it would not be a tragedy. The climax of the film occurs when one of the teachers realizes that she is, in fact, attracted to the other woman. "I'm guilty!" she cries. "I've ruined your life, and I've ruined my own. I feel so damn sick and dirty I just can't stand it anymore." The consequence of this realization of her lesbianism is that she promptly commits suicide, only one of many lesbian and gay characters of the period who take their lives when faced with the "awful truth" about their sexuality.

"SHOW ME A HAPPY HOMOSEXUAL
AND I'LL SHOW YOU A GAY CORPSE"

The 1960s ushered in a period of cultural change and growing openness to aspects of sexuality previously denied and repressed in American society. As has been noted, the ferment of the 1960s fertilized the ground in which the seeds of gay liberation sprouted. But in Hollywood the climate remained chilly for lesbian and gay characters. The relaxed Code did permit writers and directors to include homosexuals in their films, but only as long as they were unhappy.

The 1961 British film *Victim* told a story that was influenced by the landmark *Wolfenden Report* of 1957, a parliamentary document that argued for the legalization of homosexual conduct between consenting adults (this recommendation was adopted by the British government in 1967). The *Wolfenden Report* had used as an argument the fact that their criminal status made gay men unusually susceptible to blackmail, and *Victim* tells the story of a blackmail victim who fights back.[2] When the producers wanted to show the film in the United States, they were denied approval by the Code office because of the "candid and clinical discussion of homosexuality and its overtly expressed plea for social acceptance of the homosexual." The British producers distributed the film without a seal, but Hollywood studios were

---

[2] Although the death penalty for buggery was abolished in England in 1862, the Criminal Law Amendment Act of 1885 included the infamous Labouchere Amendment, which made "acts of gross indecency" between men punishable with up to two years at hard labor (the sentence meted out ten years later to Oscar Wilde), and in effect brought within the scope of the law all forms of male homosexual activity. The Labouchere Amendment was often referred to as the "Blackmailer's Charter." British law ignored lesbians in 1885, and when an unsuccessful attempt was made in 1921 to extend the Labouchere Amendment to women, it was opposed on the grounds that, "You are going to tell the whole world that there is such an offence, to bring it to the notice of women who have never heard of it, never thought of it, never dreamt of it."

more cautious. They avoided the risk of being denied a seal by steering clear of depictions of sympathetic or happy homosexuals.[3] Lesbian and gay villains showed up with relentless frequency, only to be defeated by the heterosexual heroes. James Bond, perhaps the quintessential symbol of straight male virility in this period, was responsible for disposing of several lesbian and gay male killers, among them Lotte Lenya's evil Rosa Klebb in *From Russia with Love* (1963), and a gay couple in *Diamonds Are Forever* (1971), who are shown hand-in-hand before Bond burns them to a crisp. But homosexuals didn't have to be killers in order to end up badly, and they could administer their own punishments.

The storyline pioneered by *The Children's Hour* was repeated with variations by other writers and directors, except that the exposure of a character's homosexuality did not depend on the perceptiveness of a vicious child. In *The Sergeant* (1968), Rod Steiger plays a sexually repressed homosexual who doesn't understand why he is obsessed with a handsome young soldier. When his secret eventually explodes in his face—Steiger kisses the enlisted man and is rebuffed—he runs off into the woods and shoots himself. These two films share the core plot components of fictional depictions of queers in that period (and which haven't entirely disappeared): The story is set in a homosocial environment (a girl's school, an army base). The homosexual character is love with a straight person, and neither the gays nor the straights realize what's going on; the gay characters are in the closet, even to themselves. Self-realization leads to rejection by the heterosexual loved one, and despair and disaster for the queer character.[4] In *Reflections in a Golden Eye* (1967), Marlon Brando is another sexually repressed military man, this time a colonel who follows a young private around, spying on him at night. When he realizes that the private is attracted to his wife, not to him, the colonel shoots the young man.

---

[3] The Code was superseded in 1968 by the Motion Picture Association of America's "alphabet soup" ratings system, still in effect today. The MPAA's film ratings are determined by a secret twelve-person jury who are paid to watch and rate every film released in America. In 1999 the jury comprised seven women and five men, varying by age, race, and level of education, but all were parents and, presumably, heterosexual. Instead of adhering to hard and fast guidelines, they are encouraged to react subjectively to what they see on screen. In practice, while homosexuality is no longer prohibited, as it was under the Code, any sign of queerness will trigger a more restrictive rating. Even more influential than the MPAA's ratings themselves, however, may be the policies of the largest video rental chains, such as Blockbuster, whose refusal to stock NC-17 as well as X-rated videos can doom a film's commercial future.

[4] Needless to say, these characters don't have sex. Nor, in the minds of some viewers, would this be possible. Film critic Pauline Kael, reviewing *The Children's Hour* in 1962, opined that the audience felt sympathy for the two women because they "didn't really *do* anything, after all;" adding: "I always thought that was why lesbians needed sympathy—because there isn't much they *can* do."

As the decade of the sixties moved toward the explosion of the Stonewall riots, two movies presented unusually explicit portraits of lesbian and gay life. However depressing the lives they portrayed, these films did expand the angle of vision to encompass lesbian or gay relationships. *The Killing of Sister George* (1968) and *The Boys in the Band* (1970) were presented by the producers and accepted by the critics as unflinching glimpses of gay life: "tacky, tawdry, repellent and true," in the words of *Life* critic Richard Schickel. Sister George is the name of a character in a British television soap opera, and she is "killed off" in the program because the real-life actress who plays her is too blatantly lesbian for the producers. George's aggressively butch personality—and her heavy drinking—lead to her complete ruin. She loses both her job and her lover through the efforts of a smoothly seductive BBC executive who personifies the sinister lesbian. The message of the film was not merely hostile to lesbians, it was a demonstration of the dangers of being open about it. As director Robert Aldrich put it, "She doesn't fit into the machine."

Although the film was condemned by lesbian and gay critics as yet another story of a doomed homosexual, Sister George has also been seen in a more positive light as an unapologetic feisty lesbian who is undone as much by her own honesty as by her abrasiveness.[5] The real message of the film was that being out of the closet was dangerous to your health. This message was repeated eightfold in *The Boys in the Band*.

Based on a successful Off-Broadway play by gay writer Mart Crowley, *Boys in the Band* was translated to the screen with very few changes and with the original New York cast. The decision to use the stage actors in the movie version was not, strictly speaking, a tribute to their theatrical skills. Few film actors were willing to be seen in gay roles—a situation that remained little changed over the next thirty years. This is not to say that stage actors were unconcerned about the images they portrayed. When the play opened in New York in 1968, Cliff Gorman (the actor playing Emory, "the definitive screaming queen") made sure the public knew he was only acting. As a *New York Times* reporter explained in an interview entitled, "You Don't Have to Be One to Play One," it's "not exactly the kind of part you'd imagine for a

---

[5] Thirty years after the film appeared, writer Jewelle Gomez reminisced, "In 1968 I saw a film, *The Killing of Sister George*, from which I identified as a lesbian for the first time, even though it contained no black women. . . . It contained the first fully developed (not to be confused with saintly) lesbian character I'd ever seen on the screen. Some critics and lesbians condemned it as stereotypical, but it actually worked for me because it took the archetype of a hard-drinking, butch lesbian and gave her dimension, emotion, vulnerability. . . . Most importantly for me, I saw lesbians within the context of a community, a possibility that was always being denied by the larger culture."

nice (married) Jewish boy." But then, "Cliff really needed the money," and was so broke he had even taken to "hocking his wife's silver candelabra." Elsewhere in the article we were shown Cliff popping open a cold beer, listening to country music (the only music "that really moves him"), and generally swaggering around the living room. In the accompanying photograph he clutched his "incredibly beautiful" wife.

The story of *Boys* focuses on a collection of assorted gay types who gather at a birthday party and proceed to savage—and comfort—each other in a drunken orgy combining self-hate and solidarity. After a behind-the-credits sequence that introduces the characters with a series of stereotype-evoking vignettes, the film, like the play, takes place entirely within the confines of the host's apartment, presumably conveying the claustrophobic isolation of the "gay world." Critics hailed it as "a landslide of truths," accepting both the stereotypical gay characters and their acute self-hatred. For gay people the film prompted a more complex set of responses. While stereotypical, the characters also rang true, and they weren't all unhappy or dysfunctional. The film allowed its gay characters to display a biting wit and a determination to survive despite the odds. As Vito Russo put it, *Boys* provided "the best and most potent argument for gay liberation ever offered in a popular art form. It supplied concrete and personalized examples of the negative effects of what homosexuals learn about themselves from the distortions of the media."

When the central character surveys the wreckage of his apartment at the end of the party and asks, "Who was it who said, 'You show me a happy homosexual and I'll show you a gay corpse?,'" he summarizes an entire genre of movies: out of thirty-two films between 1961 and 1976 with major lesbian or gay characters, thirteen feature gays who commit suicide and eighteen whose homosexual character are murdered. To gay protests about the film of *Boys in the Band*, director William Friedkin responded, "This film is not about homosexuality, it's about human problems. I hope there are happy homosexuals. They just don't happen to be in my film." Nor have they been in many other major American films.

While not yet presenting happy homosexuals, two films of the same period did mark an advance in the treatment of gay themes. Both *Midnight Cowboy* and *Sunday, Bloody Sunday* were made by gay, but still-closeted, British director John Schlesinger. *Midnight Cowboy* is a queer-inflected "buddy movie" about Joe Buck, cowboy from the sticks turned inept male hustler in New York (played by Jon Voight), and Ratso Rizzo, scuzzy crippled petty crook (played by Dustin Hoffman), who somehow end up offering each other friendship and comfort. The film's approach to homosexuality was ambivalent at best, typified by Joe Buck's hostile relations with gay male clients, and

Ratso's dismissal of Joe's cowboy getup as "faggy." Yet there was something about the film's acknowledgment of gay sexuality—however creepy—and its depiction of a male friendship that went beyond the jauntiness of Butch Cassidy and the Sundance Kid, that represented progress for Hollywood. This conclusion was shared by the industry, apparently, as *Midnight Cowboy* won the Best Picture Oscar for 1969.

Sunday, Bloody Sunday, released in 1971, was both more significant in its gay content and less successful at the box office. Even now, thirty years after it was made, *Sunday, Bloody Sunday* stands out as an unusually mature and sensitive film dealing with homosexuality. The story concerns two middle-aged Londoners: a physician, played by Peter Finch, and a career woman, played by Glenda Jackson, who are involved—and in love—with the same young man, played by Murray Head. Ultimately the young man leaves them both, going off to New York to pursue his artistic career, and they each, in their own way, philosophically accept their loneliness.[6] Peter Finch's doctor is far from a stereotype; if anything, he's so mature, articulate, and sensitive that he appears far too good for the callow young man he's in love with. The film is a landmark in another way: the relationship between Finch and Head is revealed to the audience through a totally unexpected and quite passionate kiss. According to Vito Russo, when they were about to shoot the kiss the cameraman asked, "Is this really necessary?" Finch was often asked by reporters how he felt doing the scene, to which he would reply, "I closed my eyes and thought of England." The kiss never failed to evoke gasps, giggles, and even jeers and walk-outs from audiences. To this day, an on-screen gay male kiss can be counted on to produce the same reactions, especially from young male audiences.[7]

FRIEDKIN DELIVERS GAY CORPSES

In 1979 William Friedkin shot another film in Greenwich Village with a gay plot, but this time it was based on a mystery novel written by a heterosexual *New York Times* editor, Gerald Walker. The novel, *Cruising*, used a plot device that has since become something of a cliché: someone is killing gay

---

[6] The bisexual character, not for the first, nor the last time, is presented as less worthy than either the heterosexual woman or the gay man: bisexuality, like promiscuity, is shown as inherently unfaithful. For a contemporary version, see *The Jerry Springer Show*, almost any week.

[7] In the 1995 film version of Paul Rudnick's stage success *Jeffrey*, this "problem" is handled by beginning with a passionate male-male kiss during the credit sequence, at which point the film "pans" out to a shot of two young couples sitting in the theater watching the scene. The girls swoon and sigh, while the guys hurl their popcorn in horrified disgust.

men and a police detective is assigned to go undercover to locate the killer in the seamy underworld of New York's S&M bars.[8] *Cruising* took the audience on a safari into the jungles of darkest Manhattan, as undercover cop Al Pacino tracks the psycho-killer who stabs gay men while fucking them. We learn that the killer is in some crazy way trying to placate his dead father by killing gay men—presumably thus killing the homosexuality that his father rejected in him. As Scott Tucker wrote in the *Body Politic*, "Friedkin does *not* have the killer dress up in the clothes of his long dead mother; he may have refrained only because Hitchcock's *Psycho* beat his psycho to it."

The killer isn't the only one with emotional problems: the undercover cop becomes psychologically caught up in the leather/S&M world he'd been sent to explore, possibly even to the point of becoming a killer himself. In the film's climactic scene Pacino and the killer cruise one another in Central Park, entering a dark tunnel (duh!) where they drop their pants and engage in some astounding dialogue: "How big are you?" "Party size." "Do me first." "Hips or lips?" Both men reach for their knives, and Pacino gets the killer first. In the final scenes, Pacino's gay next door neighbor—the only relatively happy gay man in the film—is killed and it appears that Pacino is the killer. The film ends with Pacino gazing in the mirror, leaving us to wonder whether he has been pulled into the psychotic world of gay sexuality. Homosexuality, it is strongly implied, is contagious as well as lethal.

Friedkin told the press that *he* didn't know who the real final murderer was, and that he wasn't necessarily homosexual, but the implication of the film is unmistakable. It was more likely that Friedkin was responding to the protests that engulfed Greenwich Village during the shooting of the film. Someone leaked the script to *Village Voice* columnist and gay activist Arthur Bell, who proceeded to raise hell in his column about what "promised to be the most oppressive, bigoted look at homosexuality ever presented on the screen," urging his readers "to give Friedkin and his production crew a terrible time if you spot them in your neighborhood." More than six hundred people gathered at a town meeting in response to Bell's columns, and activists subsequently asked the city to withdraw the film's shooting permit. City officials refused to intervene, citing free speech and asserting that "any-

---

[8] The same plot device was used around the same time by gay writer Felice Picano to somewhat better effect in *The Lure* (which at least was gay-positive), and more abysmally in 1982 in the asinine Hollywood film, *Partners*, in which super-straight cop Ryan O'Neal and closeted sissy cop John Hurt are sent to locate a killer preying on the Los Angeles gay community. In subsequent years several TV police shows have discovered this dramatic ploy, and in an even more bizarre variant, the 1992 film *A Stranger Among Us* features Melanie Griffith as a detective infiltrating New York's Hasidic community in search of a killer.

thing that brings this city seven million dollars is good." When the filming continued, the crew was met with hundreds of demonstrators blowing whistles, which carried far and loud enough to interfere with the shooting. A confrontation between demonstrators and police erupted when mounted police charged, and a group of protestors got close enough to engage in a tug-of-war over a camera cable before they were beaten back by police clubs.

The protests slowed the filming and added to its cost, but the show went on. In response to the protests Friedkin left the identity of the final killer unclear, thus making the film's conclusion more ambiguous than the script (and the novel) had suggested. Further, despite having told Vito Russo in an interview that "these scenes could be run as documentary footage," he inserted a disclaimer at the start: "This film is not intended as an indictment of the homosexual world. It is set in one small segment of that world, which is not meant to be representative of the whole." Of course, as Russo pointed out, this disclaimer is an admission of guilt: "What director would make such a statement if he truly believed that his film would not be taken to be representative of the whole?"

When *Cruising* opened in 1980 it was met by more protests, but this time the protestors were joined by the critics, who uniformly savaged the film. The film was largely ignored by audiences, despite full-page ads condemning the protestors as censors and urging citizens to exercise their First Amendment rights by seeing the film to judge it for themselves (nothing was said, however, about refunding their money if they disliked it). The protests over *Cruising* were paralleled by the gay community's response to another 1980 film, *Windows*, in which a psychotic lesbian (Elizabeth Ashley), in love with a straight woman (Talia Shire), hires a straight man to attack Shire so that she will reject men and turn to Ashley. As critic David Denby put it, "*Windows* exists only in the perverted fantasies of men who hate lesbians so much they will concoct any idiocy in order to slander them." Responding to such films, gay media activist Ron Gold emphasized, "We are not asking for censorship. We are asking Hollywood to use the same system of self-censorship they apply to other minorities. . . . We always find ourselves in the position of having to play civil libertarian to a bunch of bigots who want their constitutional right to express their hatred of us."

The leaflets protesting the filming of *Cruising* warned that the film "will encourage more violence against homosexuals. In the current climate of backlash against the gay rights movement this film is a genocidal act." The rhetoric might have seemed excessive at the time, but it was hauntingly recalled in November 1980 when the son of a Harlem minister drove up to the Ramrod bar, site of the filming of *Cruising*, and began firing a submachine gun. Ronald Crumpley, a 38-year-old former transit cop, married with two children, stole his father's car, drove to Virginia to buy guns, and set off, as he told the police, to kill gays: "They ruin everything." When it was over, six men were wounded and two gay men were dead.

GETTING THE WORD OUT

In the summer of 1966 anthropologist John Adair and filmmaker-turned-communications scholar Sol Worth embarked on an innovative research endeavor along with a group of Navajo men and women in Pine Springs, Arizona. Decades before, pioneering anthropologist Bronislaw Malinowski had written that "the final goal, of which an ethnographer should never lose sight . . . is, briefly, to grasp the native's point of view, his relation to life, to realize *his* vision of *his* world." Adair and Worth applied this principle by giving 16mm movie cameras to six Navajo people and encouraging them to make movies that would reflect their point of view, their vision of the world. The Navajo Film Themselves Project was recognized as a milestone in developing collaborative approaches to filmmaking.

Ten years later two of John Adair's children, Peter Adair and his sister Nancy, both gay, set out on another sort of collaborative film project: to record the stories of other gay and lesbian people, to let them speak for themselves. Their project became the Mariposa Film Group, comprising three lesbians and three gay men (one of them African American), assisted by several others, including Peter and Nancy's mother Casey, who worked on a book version of their project. Members of the group traveled the country, videotaping lesbians and gay men who were willing to tell their stories, and showing portions of the film-in-progress to obtain feedback and raise money, mostly from lesbian and gay audiences. From about 150 initial interviews the filmmakers eventually chose thirteen men and thirteen women to appear in the 16mm film. Months of editing reduced hundreds of hours of film to 135 minutes, giving each narrator approximately eight minutes of screen time (portions not included in the film were added to the book). The resulting film, *Word Is Out: Stories of Some of Our Lives* (1978), went on to successful runs and rave reviews in cities around the country. An edited one-hour version eventually played on PBS in October that same year.

The final group of narrators included a 77-year-old lesbian poet (who said, "If there was ever any problem with my being a lesbian, it was the loneliness, the fact that I didn't know anyone else like me"); a New Mexico Chicana couple; a San Francisco gender-fuck activist; a rural lesbian who talked about being committed to a state hospital as a teenager; a San Francisco gay lawyer who told of being forcibly committed by his in-laws and subjected to shock therapy; an African American college student contending with the pressures of being black and gay in an Ivy League school and the distance his school-ing was placing between him and his family; two divorced lesbians living with their kids in a suburb; and a young man who said that when he first fell in love with a man, "it meant I was a real person. I wasn't just a machine."

There were criticisms of the film for its focus on the personal stories of the narrators rather than on political issues of oppression and the gay liberation movement. But, in fact, woven through the accounts of individual lives were glimpses of lesbian and gay history not known to most viewers, gay or straight. The film's narrators included Mattachine Society founder Harry Hay, who talked about the early days of the movement.[9] George Menden-hall, a working-class San Francisco activist, was moved to tears—and so were many in the audience—when he talked about the Black Cat bar and its famous entertainer José Sarria, whose campaign for city supervisor in 1961 helped stimulate gay political organizing in San Francisco fifteen years before Harvey Milk.[10] For most viewers Pat Bond's stories of the comradeship she found while serving in the Women's Army Corps during World War II were a revelation, and her account of the repression and purges that followed the war was emotionally wrenching. San Francisco lesbian-feminist Sally Gearhart articulated the conflicts she experienced between feminism and gay liberation, "having to choose between . . . whether I was going to put my energy with my straight sisters, who in some cases were being very oppres-sive to lesbians, or with my gay brothers. . . . And it meant that a lot of times I was splitting myself up in ways that I didn't want to."

In story after story the personal and political intertwined, illuminating the narrators' lives and evoking laughter and tears in the spirit of the consciousness-raising groups that had emerged during the early 1970s. The echoing common-

[9] Hay's lover, John Burnside, summarized the conditions they faced: "When the first homophile movements began, a homosexual was placed in three categories: to the doctor you were sick; to the lawyer you were a criminal; to the minister you were wicked. These were con-tradictory categories, of course, because the minister implied that you had chosen your state by your freedom of will, while the doctor implied that you had caught it from somebody. I think that the founding of the [Mattachine] Society was the first step we all took in getting rid of these three categories."

[10] Mendenhall told how José Sarria's performances concluded with a political ritual: "At the end of every concert he would have everyone in the room stand, and we would put our arms around each other and sing, 'God Save Us Nelly Queens.' I get very emotional about this, and it sounds silly, but if you lived at that time and had the oppression coming down from the police department and from society, there was nowhere to turn . . . and to be able to put your arms around other gay men and to be able to stand up and sing, 'God Save Us Nelly Queens.' . . . We were really not saying, God Save Us Nelly Queens,' We were saying, 'We have our rights, too.'"

ality of the experiences recounted by the otherwise diverse cast of narrators—resonating with the lives of many viewers—served, in Richard Dyer's words, to "establish lesbian/gay identity and demonstrate the social dimension of personal experience." In its implicit insistence on the underlying shared experiences of lesbian and gay people, *Word Is Out* reflected the emergence of a political stance centered on what came to be called identity politics. The spirit of identity politics had been the implicit guiding principle in 1968 when Frank Kameny argued that "the ONLY people in all the world" who were trying to "instill in the homosexual community a sense of worth of the individual homosexual" were "the pitifully small number of us in the homophile movement." In their influential *Black Feminist Statement*, published in 1977, the Boston-based Combahee River Collective proclaimed that "the only people who care enough about us to work consistently for our liberation is us. . . . This focusing upon our own oppression is embodied in the concept of identity politics. We believe that the most profound and potentially the most radical politics come directly out of our own identity, as opposed to working to end somebody else's oppression."

The core narrative of lesbian and gay identity at that time—and it hasn't entirely changed—was that of coming out, to oneself, to other gay people, to family, friends, and the world at large. The theory and strategy of the post-Stonewall movement was centered on the ideology of public self-disclosure as the key to psychological health for individual gay people and to liberation from oppression for the gay community. Gay liberationists, in John D'Emilio's words, "recast coming out as a profoundly political act that could offer enormous personal benefits to an individual. The open avowal of one's sexual identity, whether at work, at school, at home, or before television cameras, symbolized the shedding of the self-hatred that gay men and women internalized, and consequently it promised an immediate improvement in one's life. To come out of the 'closet' quintessentially expressed the fusion of the personal and the political that the radicalism of the late 1960s exalted." Further, D'Emilio argued, "Visible lesbians and gay men also served as magnets that drew others in. . . . Once out of the closet, they could not easily fade back in. Coming out provided gay liberation with an army of permanent enlistees."[11]

---

[11] It is important, however, not to exaggerate the numbers: A few years into the era of gay liberation, an openly gay sociologist wrote about the homosexual community in Toronto. Assuming a total population of around 150,000 male homosexuals in metropolitan Toronto, John Lee estimated that perhaps 5,000 were "out at work," between 500 and 1,000 belonged to a gay liberation group, and possibly 50 were publicly identified in the media.

Or the political impact: Writing in 1991, John D'Emilio reflected with morning-after sobriety on the emotional intensity of the early post-Stonewall movement: "Coming out was a first step only. An openly gay banker is still a banker."

Coming out narratives connected individual experiences to shared experiences and thus solidified a sense of community and identity. *Word Is Out* was only the most widely distributed and ambitious example of the coming out documentary in which lesbian and gay people come out to the world by telling their stories. And, as Thomas Waugh noted, this telling was itself a political act: "The consent to declare oneself before the camera still has for every potential subject of a lesbian/gay documentary all the dimensions of an irreversible, life-changing political commitment."

Beyond the individual stories that gay people told each other in consciousness-raising groups and the world in documentary films, the 1970s also witnessed the rediscovery of stories from the past. In 1972 GAA member Jonathan Ned Katz created a theatrical docudrama, *Coming Out!*, that energized audiences. The Gay Academic Union was founded in 1973, and the following year John Lauritsen and David Thorstad's *The Early Homosexual Rights Movement* was published and the *Journal of Homosexuality* was launched. In 1976 Jonathan Katz followed his documentary play with a more influential project, the 700-page collection *Gay American History*. Following Katz's inspiring model, grassroots lesbian and gay history (and herstory) projects sprang up around the country—in Boston, Buffalo, Chicago, New York, San Francisco—and the results of their research began to appear in newspapers and journals created by the lesbian and gay liberation movement.[12] Jeffrey Weeks's *Coming Out: Homosexual Politics in Britain from the Nineteenth Century to the Present* was published in 1977 in Great Britain, introducing what came to be termed the social constructionist view of sexuality.[13] Gay history's first best-seller, John Boswell's *Christianity, Social Tolerance, and Homosexuality*, appeared in 1980, reinforcing the "essentialist" position opposing the rising tide of social constructionism.

Toronto's *The Body Politic* played a crucial role in the emergence of lesbian and gay studies, both by publishing the work of scholars who were pioneering what was then a far from respectable field, and by convening two key international conferences, in 1982 and 1985. These were crucial to the coalescing of lesbian and gay studies as an international "invisible college" of scholars in and

---

[12] An early vehicle for disseminating the fruits of the grassroots history projects was the "low-tech" slide show. I first encountered the research of Jonathan Katz and Allan Bérubé when they gave slide-illustrated lectures at Philadelphia's Gay and Lesbian Community Center in the late 1970s and early 1980s. Similarly, Vito Russo's 1981 book, *The Celluloid Closet*, was preceded by years of film-clip illustrated lectures around the country.

[13] Although it was then only a glimmer on the horizon in the English-speaking world, Michel Foucault's *The History of Sexuality*, vol. 1, *An Introduction*, appeared in translation in 1978.

out of the academy (two other influential conferences were held in Amsterdam, in 1983 and 1987). By the early 1980s the research of these community-based historians was feeding into the mainstream through the work of documentary filmmakers screened on public television. Historical documentaries such as *Silent Pioneers* (Lucy Winer, 1984), *Before Stonewall* (Greta Schiller, 1985), and especially the Oscar-winning *The Times of Harvey Milk* (Robert Epstein and Richard Schmiechen, 1984), were seen by audiences who would never have sought, found, or risked reading the *Body Politic* or *Gay Community News.*

GAY FILMS FOR STRAIGHT AUDIENCES

La Cage aux Folles was a surprise hit in 1978, far surpassing the typical run for a foreign-language film (it ran in one New York upper East Side theater for months). The film's success was even more surprising, however, when its subject matter is taken into account: this is a story about Renato and Albin, a middle-aged gay couple, the son they raised (the product of a one-night stand by one partner), and the son's rabidly right-wing prospective in-laws. The gay couple own a nightclub in which Albin is the headliner of a drag show. The plot of the film revolves around the son's efforts to hide the reality of his parents' lives from his prospective in-laws, at first by asking Albin to disappear. Albin refuses to cooperate and, after a failed attempt at learning to appear more masculine, greets the son's fiancée's parents in drag, as his "mother." Much farcical confusion ensues, with an appropriately satisfying comeuppance for the right-wing politico father of the fiancée.

The film's popularity with straight audiences can be explained in part by the perennial appeal of men in dresses, whether gay or straight, and the complete absence of any threat to what Christopher Isherwood called the heterosexual dictatorship. Renato and Albin are depicted as a loving, long-lasting couple, but we never see them kiss, nor express any other real physical affection; and they certainly never question "normal" masculinity as the appropriate standard of dress and behavior. Even more notable, however, is the film's refusal to condemn the son's abominable behavior: In order to avoid revealing the truth to his fiancée's parents, he is willing to repudiate the person who raised him as "her" child.[14] And, of course, he gets his way. By

[14] The sacrifice asked of (and offered by) a parent here is reminiscent of movie plots in which a mother from the wrong side of the tracks sacrifices everything so her daughter can live a rich girl's life, not knowing that her mother is even alive (e.g., *Stella Dallas*, in its various incarnations); or a black mother removes herself from the scene so that her light-skinned daughter can "pass" (e.g., *Pinky, Imitation of Life*).

making the fiancée's parents rabid right-wingers, the film creates a sort of see-saw, with the gay couple on one side and the prospective in-laws on the other, balanced by the heterosexual son as the "normal" figure in the middle with whom the straight audience can identify, thus even further insulating him from blame for his inexcusable behavior.

The success of *La Cage aux Folles* led to two sequels, in 1980 and 1985, and it inspired a Tony-award-winning Broadway musical by gay composer Jerry Herman and gay playwright Arthur Laurents. The story was remade by Hollywood in the 1990s as *The Birdcage*, with Robin Williams and Nathan Lane as the gay couple. The impact of *La Cage*'s success encouraged Hollywood producers to undertake gay-themed projects, especially ones in which effeminate queens turn out to be just as courageous as straights: *Zorro, the Gay Blade* (1981), inoffensive twaddle—the title tells you everything you need to know (once you also know George Hamilton plays Zorro); *Victor/Victoria* (1982), a female/male-impersonation farce in which James Garner can safely fall in love with Julie Andrews because (we know) he knows she's really a she; and the aforementioned *Partners* (1982), written by Francis Veber, who wrote *La Cage*, about a straight and a gay cop who go undercover as a gay couple to catch a murderer (the gay cop, played by John Hurt, is a mega-sissy, but he saves his macho partner's life in the end, while getting shot himself).[15]

Following a familiar pattern, the director of *Partners* was quoted assuring potential audiences that, "I don't see *Partners* as a gay film. It doesn't deal with the issue of gayness. It is a movie in which two people learn from each other." Somewhat less predictably, the coproducer of another film made at the same time made the same claim for his film: "We're not anxious to have *Making Love* defined as a gay movie." Allan Adler was talking about the story of a doctor who comes out of the closet and leaves his wife for another man: "We hope that it will be seen as a love story. It's not a slice of gay life."

The producer may have thought he was helping his film's box office chances by recycling this familiar rhetorical dodge, but he was fooling no one. Quite the opposite, as the making of *Making Love* had been much heralded in Hollywood and the media as the "breakthrough" gay film. Its birth depended on the convergence of many fortuitous circumstances. The proj-

---

[15] This is a classic example of the "Gunga Din" cliché, wherein a member of the lower orders—in the movie based on Kipling's poem, an Indian water-boy for the British army—sacrifices himself while saving the British officer hero, and is then accorded the tribute of being judged as good as us or, even, "you're a better man than I am Gunga Din!" Gunga Din was, however, also a dead man. *Partners* ends with the straight (previously homophobic) cop kneeling over the fallen queer, who may or may not be dying, and saying to the other police officers: "This is my partner," as the camera pulls back and the music swells.

ect was engineered by a successful agent, Arnold Steifel of International Creative Management. Written by a Steifel client, openly gay screenwriter Barry Sandler (based on a story idea by gay writer Scott Berg—whose brother was the president of ICM), the project was taken up by Daniel Melnick, a powerful (straight) producer with progressive views, and sold to Sherry Lansing, who had recently taken over as the first female head of production at a major studio. The director was Arthur Hiller, a solid industry performer with a record of successful but certainly not risk-taking movies. With a strong production team in place, the challenge they faced was casting the male leads. After being turned down by Michael Douglas, Harrison Ford, and William Hurt, among others, they succeeded in hiring two less established—but "certifiably heterosexual"—actors: Harry Hamlin and Michael Ontkean. Melnick reported that he persuaded them by asking, "If you played Adolf Hitler, would anyone think *you* were the most evil man of the 20th century? If you played the Boston Strangler, would anyone think *you* were a mass murderer?"

Making Love tells the story of a successful, handsome doctor (Ontkean) who must confess to his beautiful and loving wife (Kate Jackson) that he is in love with a man: a successful, handsome writer (Hamlin). When Hamlin makes it clear that he isn't the monogamous type, Ontkean finds a rich, handsome white architect and settles down with him in a Manhattan penthouse. The film's ending shows Ontkean visiting Jackson, settled with her new husband and her young son. Everyone is happy except the stubbornly promiscuous Hamlin, but we're not sure, as he's dropped out of the story by this point (if the film expresses any judgments about sexuality, it's to condemn the Hamlin character for his unrepentant nonmonogamy).

When the film opened, the studio ran two different ad campaigns: the ad for the straight-audience ad showed Ontkean and Hamlin together with Kate Jackson, who plays Ontkean's wife, and it's Ontkean and Jackson who are touching. In the gay-press ad Ontkean has his arm around a bare-chested Hamlin. For the film, the creators assiduously avoided melodrama: Ontkean's coming out is relatively lacking in anguish, and his breakup and divorce seem fairly painless. Jackson's character is a successful career woman who is not economically damaged by the divorce, and Ontkean's professional standing as a physician is unthreatened.[16] What they had succeeded in creating, how-

---

[16] The closest thing to a confrontation, though still well within the counterstereotypic tradition of Hollywood "message" films, is a scene where Ontkean comes out to his stuffy lawyer father: "I'm gay, Dad. A homosexual. That's right—your basketball star—class president—cub scout—doctor—son has sex with other men. And I'm not ashamed of it, either." The scene ended up on the cutting room floor.

ever, was a boring film that was too straight for gay audiences and too gay for straight audiences. It was a critical and commercial flop.

Despite the film's considerable drawbacks, it did contain one scene that left an impact on audiences: Hamlin and Ontkean kissing, undressing each other and, as the film's title promised, making love (although this last part wasn't exactly visible on screen). The scene set off the familiar jeers and cat-calls from straight audiences, but for gay (male) audiences it was the first time that two handsome male movie stars had appeared in a love scene. The film also has a happy ending—however Hollywoodish and white-washed. In this way the film might have fulfilled screenwriter Sandler's hope that it would reach a "17-year-old kid in Oklahoma City who's really confused about his sexuality," and that seeing a character choose a homosexual life and ulti-mately find happiness might make him think, "If it's okay for him, it's okay for me."

At the end of the 1960s, on the cusp of Stonewall, *Boys in the Band* and *Sister George* had offered straight audiences a matched pair of "backstage" glimpses of gay and lesbian life that were mixtures of misery and solidarity. In 1982, as Hollywood began cautiously opening a window onto gay and les-bian lives, *Making Love* had a lesbian counterpart in *Personal Best*, although in this case the writer-director, Robert Towne, was, in his words, boringly heterosexual. Towne's pitch to the media—and, likely, to the Warner Broth-ers executives—stressed the size of the homosexual audience: "We're talking about 35 or 40 million people . . . and if they hear a film is really interesting, you're going to get them out to see that film—not just a small percentage, but at least half of them." Towne also touted the edginess of the topic ("It gives us a taboo that we badly need for the sake of drama") in a way that dif-fered fundamentally from the goody-goody ambitions of *Making Love*. Yet if *Making Love* can be faulted for "normalizing" homosexuality into an all-male version of up-scale domesticity, *Personal Best* is another film about lesbianism as a temporary interruption in the flow of heterosexual life.

Personal Best tells the story of two women athletes, Chris (Mariel Hem-ingway) and Tory (Patrice Donnelly), who meet at the 1976 Olympic track trials, where they become friends and then lovers. They live together for sev-eral years, but their domineering (male) coach succeeds in turning them into competitors and they break up. Chris then begins an affair with a male swimmer. The film concludes at the 1980 track trials, where Chris deliberately sacrifices herself so that Tory can win a place on the 800-meter Olympic team—thus allowing feminine solidarity to triumph over the masculinist competitiveness represented by the coach (it doesn't hurt that Chris inde-pendently wins a place on the team in another track event). Yet, solidarity aside, the film keeps the dramatic focus firmly fixed on Chris, safely ensconced in heterosexuality while Tory recedes into a supporting role.

The film did not present a challenge to heterosexual supremacy. Once again, we are shown a single lesbian who has unsuccessfully loved—and lost—a woman who ends up as heterosexual. In Towne's words, "For some people, experimenting with homosexuality is a phase; for some people it is not a phase. In the film one girl [*sic*] discovers that her sexual preferences lie more in that direction; for the other girl [*sic*] that is not the case." And unlike the male-male kissing scene that disturbed straight (male) audiences of *Making Love*, *Personal Best* was easy on straight male eyes. As both lesbian and straight critics noted, the story permitted the camera to linger on the bodies of women athletes, in action and at rest, and in various states of undress.

Yet, as had been the case with *Sister George*, there were pleasures to be had by lesbian viewers of *Personal Best*. As feminist critic Elizabeth Ellsworth noted, lesbian feminist reviewers expressed pleasure in watching the dominant media "get it wrong," attempting but failing to colonize "real" lesbian space. Lesbian viewers also responded to Patrice Donnelly—in contrast to the official star, Mariel Hemingway. Lesbian reviewers noted the verisimilitude of Donnelly's performance, her "expression of desire and strength in the face of male heterosexual dominance." These reviewers, Ellsworth reports, celebrated the responses of lesbian audiences to these moments: "clapping, laughter, and feelings of validation in a context otherwise reserved for the reproduction of heterosexist romance."[17]

UNIVERSAL OR PARTICULAR?

During the late 1970s, as lesbian and gay filmmakers were able, with difficulty, to produce independent documentaries, there were stirrings of lesbian and gay fiction films as well, exhibited through mainstream (art) theaters and becoming accessible to a nationwide gay audience. Vito Russo described this budding genre as a homosexual cinema: "It neither concerns itself overtly

---

[17] Patrice Donnelly did not have an extensive film career after *Personal Best*, but she remained something of a lesbian icon, whether she liked this or not. As late as January 1998, she told the Los Angeles *Lesbian News*, "I love everybody. A lot of women assume that I'm a lesbian, and it's kind of a copout to say I'm bi. I'd rather say I'm sexual. I've had relationships with women and with men. I'm comfortable with my sexuality. I love the person, not the anatomy." Mariel Hemingway, generally assumed to be heterosexual, made headlines in 1994 when she played the lesbian who kissed Roseanne on a much discussed and heavily promoted episode of *Roseanne*.

with issues of gay politics nor does it present gay sexuality as society's perennial dirty secret. The key to gay films . . . is that they do not view the existence of gay people as controversial." Even more unusual, these films present gay characters as the central characters with whom audiences are invited to identify (in contrast, say, to the gay characters in *Sister George* or *Boys in the Band*, who are more specimens to be studied than characters to identify with).

Russo wrote in 1986, the year in which three of the most notable of these new films appeared: *Desert Hearts* and *Parting Glances* in the United States and *My Beautiful Laundrette* in Great Britain. All three did well with mainstream audiences, and they also evoked a powerful response among their primary audience, often becoming cult films. *Desert Hearts* is such a film. Made on a small budget raised in two and a half years of arduous grassroots efforts, and based on a novel by Canadian lesbian author Jane Rule, *Desert Hearts* achieved both crossover box office success and a cult following among lesbians.

"I've waited 25 years for this movie," a 47-year-old secretary in San Francisco told lesbian journalist Jan Husten. "I'm sick of seeing only heterosexual love stories. *Desert Hearts* is a movie I can finally identify with. It's like when I was little, we only had 'white dolls' to play with, as if all babies were white. Movie makers have done the same thing; they've generally ignored gays until the last few years. . . . I've seen it 22 times and am still not tired of it." The screenplay writer, Natalie Cooper, commented, "It isn't so much the content. It's a matter of the identification with it and the way it's been presented. I'm glad that it served—for anyone—no matter how small, something that could make people feel okay, instead of feeling peripheral or put down. Just to say, 'Hey, I dig it and I love it; I do that, too.' They can say, 'This is our movie, this is our thing.' It makes them feel, dare I say maybe, not proud but viable."

Desert Hearts is a "coming out" story in which a married woman staying in Reno in order to obtain a divorce falls in love with a young woman, experiencing both the joy (and sensual pleasure) of self-realization and the pain of hostile societal reactions. Audiences are presented with three primary characters: a woman who discovers her lesbianism in a relation with a younger, self-assured lover, and the younger woman's disapproving stepmother. Yet, for once, the heterosexual character's perspective does not dominate. The younger lesbian woman speaks the film's message when she says, "I don't act that way to change the world, I act that way so that the world doesn't change me." In the end, possibly to the audience's surprise, love wins out and the lovers go off together. As filmmaker Donna Deitch told *Ms.* magazine, "At the time I bought the rights to the book, there hadn't been a film about a relationship between two women that hadn't ended in suicide, like *The Children's Hour*, or in a bisexual triangle. I wanted to make just a love story, like any other love story between a man and a woman, handled in a frank and real way."

In contrast, *Parting Glances* is a film in which the homosexuality of the central characters is simply a fact, taken for granted by them, and others. Writer-director Bill Sherwood had moved to New York at eighteen, just months after the Stonewall riots, and he saw himself as among the first film-makers of the post-Stonewall generation, for whom gayness is assumed. In Sherwood's words, in this film, "Everyone's doing fine without the straights. They're completely on the periphery." A *Cincinnati Enquirer* critic said of *Parting Glances*, "The day may come when movies like this are part of the mainstream of American film—a time when people are treated as people, no matter what their sexual preference." But others faulted it for its concentration on gay characters. As Bill Sherwood put it, "Critics who were not sympathetic to *Parting Glances* would cite *My Beautiful Laundrette*, saying that it wasn't a film completely about gay people but also about issues which they consider more real or even more worthy. You get the opinion that it isn't entirely appropriate to have a film which is centered around gays."

The critical bind that Sherwood was caught in is a familiar one for minority artists facing mainstream critics: they are held to a standard of "universalism" that seems suspiciously modeled on the concerns of the critics themselves. The pattern was set by reviewers critiquing gay playwrights and novelists. Heterosexual critics find fault with gay artists for not rising above their parochial concerns, that is, for addressing themselves to the concerns of their fellow gay people. In a 1980 letter to the *New York Times Book Review*, justifying his negative review of Edmund White's *States of Desire: Travels in Gay America*, critic Paul Cowan asserted that "it's crucial to communicate across tribal lines. Good literature has always done that—it has transformed a particular subject into something universal. Mr. White didn't do that: in my opinion it's one of the reasons he failed to write a good book." Novelist David Leavitt was ground by the same ax, this time wielded by *New York Times* reviewer Christopher Lehmann-Haupt, when Leavitt published his first novel, *The Lost Language of Cranes*, in 1986. Lehmann-Haupt seemed quite sympathetic to the novel and congratulated Leavitt for creating explicitly homosexual characters (though he did this by dragging in the tired, and discredited, claim that Tennessee Williams and Edward Albee "were forced by convention to disguise homosexuals as heterosexuals"), thus enabling the critic to "discern a resolution to the old debate over whether or not homosexual art is inherently limited." In other words, parochial, not universal. And, no surprise, Leavitt didn't quite pass the test, perhaps because he was "subtly biased in favor of [a homosexual character's] outlook." Better luck next time.

In contrast, when a gay writer is praised, artistic success will be defined as having achieved universalism. Christopher Lehmann-Haupt, ever vigilant on the ramparts of literature, was more charitable toward Edmund White's 1988 novel, *The Beautiful Room Is Empty*, but no less focused on the main question. His review opened: "The subject is homosexuality in Edmund White's new novel. . . . There are in the book explicit scenes of lovemaking. So the question is immediately posed: Is this a novel of parochial appeal, or can anyone, regardless of sexual preference, appreciate it?" Fortunately for White, he passed the test, if only barely, as "there is much in [the novel] that makes one uncomfortable, if only because it is so specific in its sexual appeal."[18]

Time and again, when straight critics—and even some gay ones—wish to praise a queer writer they reach for the universalism button. In 1988 *Newsweek* recognized the growth in lesbian and gay publishing in a feature, "Out of the Closet Onto the Shelves." In discussing the growing body of AIDS-related writing, the critic Walter Clemons praised Paul Monette with the ultimate accolade: "The category of gay literature no longer applies: we enter the universal arena of human loss." Similarly, William Henry, writing in *Time*, commended Terence McNally's play, *The Lisbon Traviata*, for depicting a doomed affair "with specific detail and authentic, universal pain." Back at the *New York Times*, in 1993, Michiko Kakutani reviewed Dale Peck's "astonishing first novel," *Martin and John*, "an indelible portrait of gay life during the plague years," but, she seemed relieved, "it also opens out to become a universal story about love and loss and the redemptive powers of fiction."[19]

---

[18] The novel concludes with the narrator witnessing the Stonewall riots, and Lehmann-Haupt concluded his review: "Gay liberation has arrived; it is their Bastille day and we find ourselves cheering, even in the face of what we know is to come—and what Mr. White must surely write about in another sequel. Such is the subtlety and strength of [the novel] that we actually find ourselves cheering." Note that "we," who are cheering, are clearly *not* gay, even though some gays might read the *New York Times*. And note that "what we know is to come"—AIDS, of course—somehow in Lehmann-Haupt's mind casts the value of gay liberation in doubt.

[19] Speaking to the Australian gay paper *Capital Q* in May 1999, Peck himself bemoaned the niche marketing of fiction: "Critics take me very seriously but in terms of market I think I'm more or less sold and bought as a gay writer. It's terrible, because you don't sell any books. You sell a certain number and that's it. And you can't really run away from that without getting really atrociously self-hating, so you're sort of stuck. . . . It's a homophobic construction where people bend over backwards to accept you as a gay writer, but assume you're only of interest to gay people."

In 1993 playwright Tony Kushner astonished the theatrical world with the success of his epic, *Angels in America*, winning the Pulitzer and Tony awards and selling out theaters for this two-part, seven-hour "gay fantasia on national themes" (as *Angels* was subtitled). Critics were predictably quick to see Kushner's work in a broader, dare we say, universal light. Writing in the *Chicago Daily News* under the appropriate headline, "'Angels' Reaches Beyond Gay Issues," Richard Christiansen offered a representative sample: "Some of the reason for Kushner's success can be attributed to the strength of his voice as a member of the increasingly vocal gay community of this country. *Angels* springs directly from a gay political, social and sexual culture, and it expresses that culture with pride, force and eloquence. . . . But *Angels in America*, which roams across heaven and earth in its fantasy, is considerably more than a well-written gay play. For the first time in years, an American playwright has succeeded in painting on a broad canvas, exploring 'national themes' on a grand scale. . . . Much of its story is necessarily bleak, dealing with death by AIDS, but the play is also an amazingly vibrant and joyous work, celebrating not only the gay spirit but the eternal resilience of a confused and besieged humanity."

Perhaps good literature *has* always transformed a particular subject into something universal. But there is always a double standard in the application of the universalism criterion. And, needless to say, gay artists are not the first to have been put to the test. In an essay entitled "Colonialist Criticism," the Nigerian writer Chinua Achebe decried those Western critics who evaluate African literature on the basis of whether it overcomes parochialism and achieves universality: "It would never occur to them to doubt the universality of their own literature. In the nature of things, the work of a Western writer is automatically informed by universality. It is only others who must strive to achieve it." And, Achebe continued, they achieve it by taking on the coloring of European culture, "as though universality were some distant bend in the road which you may take if you travel out far enough in the direction of Europe or America, if you put adequate distance between you and your home."

In a particularly condescending example of the universalism ploy, critic Mary McCarthy wrote "A Memory of James Baldwin" in which she congratulated herself for appreciating Baldwin as her "first black *literary* intellectual." What she means by this is explained as follows: "Baldwin had read *everything*. Nor was his reading colored by his color—this was an unusual trait." Whether Baldwin thought McCarthy's readings were colored by her color we're not told. A similarly blatant example of racist universalism was reported by Michael Denneny, who "watched an almost classic liberal, Bill

Moyers, on his television show ask [Pulitzer prize-winning African American playwright] August Wilson, 'Don't you ever get tired of writing about the black experience?'" As Denneny says, this is a question of breathtaking stupidity that makes one wonder if Moyers would ask John Updike he ever tires of writing about the white experience. But, of course, we know the answer: Moyers probably equates "the white experience" with life itself, that is, it's universal.

Television Takes Over

NEW MEDIUM, OLD MESSAGE

In February 1971, just a few years after Stonewall, network television's first sympathetic portrait of a gay man appeared, when the controversial sitcom *All in the Family* aired an episode, "Judging Books by Covers," in which Archie Bunker discovered that a football-player pal was gay. Possibly because *All in the Family* wasn't yet the ratings giant it soon became, the gay-themed show received comparatively little attention (in subsequent shows Archie came to terms with a cross-dresser and a lesbian).[1]

The following year there was the more significant breakthrough of the ABC made-for-TV movie *That Certain Summer*, in which two gay men actually were shown touching (on the shoulder), and none of the gay characters had to die at the end of the story.[2] Still, the main character, a gay father who

---

[1] As we've recently learned, among those who did pay attention was then-President Richard Nixon, whose response was recorded by aide H. R. Haldeman: "The President wants a study done for his own knowledge. The baseball game was rained out last night. CBS . . . then put on a show to fill time. Star of show—square type—named Arch. Hippy son-in-law. This show was total glorification of homosex. Made Arch look bad—homo. look good. Is this common on TV? Destruction of civilization to build homos. Made the homos as the most attractive type. Followed Hee-Haw" (note jotted down by Haldeman during a meeting with Nixon on May 12, 1971). Journalist James Warren filled us in more recently, as access to the Nixon White House tapes was increased. The president tells his cronies: "I don't mind the homosexuality, I understand it. . . . Nevertheless, goddamn, I don't think you glorify it on public television, homosexuality, even more than you glorify whores. We all know we have weaknesses. But, goddamn it, what do you think that does to kids? You know what happened to the Greeks! Homosexuality destroyed them. Sure, Aristotle was a homo. We all know that so was Socrates." John Ehrlichman comments, "But he never had the influence television had," apparently referring to Socrates.

[2] The movie was championed by ABC executive Barry Diller, who is credited with creating the successful movie-of-the-week genre as well as with being one of Hollywood's most powerful closeted gays.

comes out to his son, says that if he were given a choice he would choose not to be homosexual.[3] This "breakthrough" was something of a false spring, however, as it did not herald the blooming of many other gay and lesbian characters. Yet gay and lesbian characters did turn up from time to time for one-shot appearances on network series (such as *Alice, Barney Miller,* and *The Nancy Walker Show*), and in 1978 two TV movies were based on real-life experiences of lesbian and gay people: *Sergeant Matlovich vs. the U.S. Air Force* told the story of the Vietnam vet who said, "They gave me a medal for killing two men and a discharge for loving one"; and *A Question of Love*, starring Jane Alexander and Gena Rowlands, recounted a lesbian mother's child custody case (the women never kiss, but one is shown tenderly drying her lover's hair).

The slight increase in gay (and less often lesbian) visibility in the mid-seventies was quickly seized upon by the right wing as a sign of media capitulation to what in the 1980s came to be called "special interests." The nastiness of the attacks on gay visibility on television was well represented in a nationally syndicated column by Nicholas Von Hoffman, who noted that the "old-style Chinese have the Year of the Tiger and the Year of the Pig," but the "new-style Americans are having the Year of the Fag" (11/4/76). Von Hoffman charted the decline of the American character as beginning with a "presentable gay" in the *Doonesbury* comic strip and, "from there it was but a hop, skip and a jump to television where the flits are swarming this year." Von Hoffman plaintively asked, "Is a new stereotype being born? Is network television about to kill off the bitchy, old-time outrageous fruit and replace him with a new type homo?" Among the horrors he foresaw were "the Six Million Dollar Queer or The Bionic Fruit."

Since the mid-1970s the gay movement and its enemies, mostly among the "religious right," have been constant antagonists (right-wing fund-raisers acknowledge that antihomosexual material is their best bet to get money from supporters), and television has often figured in the struggle. But although the right wing has attacked the networks for what it considers overly favorable attention to gay people, in fact gay people were mostly portrayed and used in news and dramatic media in ways that reinforced rather than challenged the prevailing images. As critic William Henry noted in an overview of TV's treatment of gays through the late 1980s,

[3] Gay media activist Ron Gold protested to ABC, "You wouldn't have a black character say, 'I don't know if I'm lazy and shiftless.'"

when TV does deal with gays it typically takes the point of view of straights struggling to understand. The central action is the progress of acceptance—not self-acceptance by the homosexual, but grief-stricken resignation to fate by his straight loved ones, who serve as surrogates for the audience. Homosexuality thus becomes not a fact of life, but a moral issue on which everyone in earshot is expected to voice some vehement opinion. Just as black characters were long expected to talk almost exclusively about being black, and handicapped characters (when seen at all) were expected to talk chiefly about their disabilities, so homosexual characters have been defined almost entirely by their "problem."

Being defined by their "problem," it is no surprise that gay characters were generally confined to television's favorite problem-of-the-week genre, the made-for-TV movie, with a very occasional one-shot appearance of a lesbian or gay character on a dramatic series. In a 1977 letter to a representative of the Unitarian Universalist Gay Caucus, an ABC official asserted that "the portrayal of homosexuals on television will not be a very common occurrence but when depicted and appropriate to a particular storyline or plot, such characterizations in ABC programs will be governed by standards of good taste." One standard of good taste that accorded with Hollywood's generally liberal values was writing gay characters (always male) who contradicted as many stereotypes as possible. The typical plot: a close friend of the juvenile lead in a "family" series, invariably a successful athlete and all-round great guy, comes out and everyone has to resolve their conflicting emotions in the appropriately liberal manner, accepting the gay as part of their world. An alternative "gay world" is never seen nor, really, mentioned.

Martin Sheen, who had played the gay father's young lover in *That Certain Summer*, switched roles in the high-profile 1985 TV movie *Consenting Adult*. This time Sheen is married to Marlo Thomas, and the story depicts the couple's reaction when their star athlete–medical student son comes out.[4] In the pattern already familiar to viewers, the father is horrified and hostile, while the mother is more accepting, although she first sends her son to a psychiatrist, hoping for a cure. The father's health is destroyed by the shock and he eventually dies, leaving a posthumous letter of reconciliation for his son. The movie ends with the mother tearfully inviting her son and his lover home for Thanksgiving.

---

[4] Both Sheen and Thomas are well-known as industry liberals. Thomas and her husband, Phil Donahue, are among the most visible media supporters of gay causes.

CBS produced a variant on this plot the following year with *Welcome Home, Bobby*, in which a suburban high school student questions his sexual orientation. Bobby sets off a furor at home and in his school when he ventures into Chicago on a voyage of exploration and is sent home by the police, apparently after they pick him up near a gay bar. The details of his search are discretely obscure but nonetheless obvious. His mother tells him she doesn't blame him, but doesn't specify what he'd done. His father puts it more bluntly: in their family men are men, and Bobby must abide by that rule or leave. Bobby leaves and lives by himself in a shack in the woods; although when his younger brother asks him, "Are you gay?" he replies, "I don't know." The movie insists on Bobby's right to decide his fate for himself, and it ends with the father driving out to the shack where he and Bobby embrace in the familiar cliché of father-son reconciliation. As usual, the gay character is isolated and a happy ending means acceptance by his heterosexual family.

Continuing gay male characters began to appear in the late 1970s and early 1980s (the very first was Peter, a gay set designer in ABC's short-lived 1972 sitcom *Grant's Tomb*, followed by the gay couple Gordon and George in the equally short-lived *Hot L Baltimore* of 1975) but they tended to be so subtle as to be readily misunderstood by the innocent (as in the case of Sidney in *Love, Sidney*, on NBC in 1981–82, whose homosexuality seemed to consist entirely of crying at Greta Garbo movies and having a photo of his dead lover on the mantelpiece), or confused about their sexuality and never seen in an ongoing romantic gay relationship.[5] Jody Dallas, played by Billy Crystal on the comedy series *Soap* (ABC, 1977–1981), began as a flamboyant gay character, toying with a sex-change operation: when he first appeared he was wearing his mother's dress. Shortly afterward, he attempted suicide when his closeted lover left him. The next season Jody realized he was actually bisexual, becoming involved with a woman and fathering a child. By the time the show was canceled Jody was embroiled in a custody fight and preparing to marry another woman.

The cast of the wildly successful prime-time soap *Dynasty* (ABC, 1981–1989) included the on-again, off-again, on-again Steven Carrington, who went from being gay to straight, accumulating two marriages and one

---

[5] There were frequent rumors around throughout the late 1970s that ABC was developing a sitcom about a gay couple, *Adam and Yves*. According to Steven Capsuto, ABC did order a pilot for such a series, but it was never made. However, perhaps because the title resonated with the favorite mantra of fundamentalist talk-show audiences ("God created Adam and Eve, not Adam and Steve"), the network received more than 100,000 letters protesting the nonexistent program.

child, and back to gay.[6] Worse still, Steven's male lovers had the unfortunate habit of getting killed, the first by Steven's father, series patriarch Blake Carrington, and the second by rebel soldiers who shot up a wedding in a Central European castle (don't ask). Toward the end of the series Steven's brother Adam outed Bart Falmont, the closeted son of Blake Carrington's political rival. In the 1991 *Dynasty: The Reunion* miniseries, Steven and Bart are lovers, living in Washington, D.C., where Blake visits them after he gets out of jail (you don't want to know), and he and Steven reconcile and, what else, embrace tearfully.

As the networks warily advanced across the minefields of American sexuality, it took a pay-television cable channel to put gay characters at the center of a series. In the summer of 1984 the cable channel Showtime premiered *Brothers*, a sit-com about three brothers. In the opening episode the youngest brother interrupts his wedding by announcing that he's gay and can't go through with the marriage. As the series unfolds, the newly gay brother is alternately chastised and supported by his brothers, but he never does much that might be seen as, well, gay. That was left to his friend Donald, an unabashedly flamboyant queen, who got all the best lines—and was frequently revealed as the source of true wisdom.[7] *Brothers* was sufficiently popular and, as a pay-television program, immune from sponsorship worries, to last five seasons.

NO SEX, PLEASE, WE'RE QUEER

In October 1981, CBS broadcast a made-for-TV movie starring *M*A*S*H* veteran Loretta Swit and newcomer Tyne Daly as a team of policewomen who become detectives. The movie was deliberately intended to present a

---

[6] After the first switch Armistead Maupin complained about "the love that dare not last another season." Maupin's criticism extended as well to the show's use of gay consultant Newton Deiter to ensure they were "technically accurate" about homosexuality: "It's a perfectly preposterous claim to be made by a company that owes its very life to a number of talented homosexuals. *Dynasty* hiring a gay consultant is like the Vatican hiring an Italian teacher." Deiter's response reveals much about the complexities of an activist becoming a semi-insider: "People make a mistake. They think that TV has an obligation to speak out for gay liberation. Television doesn't. Television is about selling product, and the people that run the networks are very nervous. The best you can hope for—and I don't mean just us, but any group—is that the point of view be expressed with some balance. And sometimes it's real tough for people to understand that."

[7] Any resemblance to NBC's late-nineties *Will & Grace* should surprise no one familiar with Hollywood.

contrast to the "jiggle TV" image of women in such TV hits as *Charlie's Angels*. It attracted the support of prominent feminists and was featured on the cover of *Ms.* magazine. The article ended with a message: "If you would like to see *Cagney and Lacey* expanded into a TV series, write to [an address in Los Angeles]." When the TV movie was a ratings smash, CBS moved quickly to develop it into a series. In the series version of *Cagney and Lacey* that premiered in March 1982, the role of Chris Cagney was played by Meg Foster, while Tyne Daley continued as Mary Beth Lacey.

Cagney and Lacey was a critical success and achieved respectable ratings, but CBS executives canceled the series. Producer Barney Rosenzweig was eventually told that the price of renewal was to replace Meg Foster as Cagney. Press accounts began to reveal the reasons behind CBS's hesitation when network vice president Harvey Shepard was quoted as saying that "the characterizations of both Cagney and Lacey were too tough." An article in *TV Guide* helped readers connect the dots: an unnamed CBS programmer had said that the characters were "too tough, too hard, and not feminine. . . . They were too harshly women's lib. . . . We perceived them as dykes." The network, clearly uncomfortable with the feminist stance of the series, focused its objections on the person of Meg Foster. Many thought that Foster was singled out because she had earlier played a lesbian character in the 1978 movie *A Different Story* (and not even a very positive portrayal: in the movie the lesbian and a gay man fall in love and get married).

When the series returned to the air in the fall of 1982, Chris Cagney was played by Sharon Gless, who was described by one reviewer as "blonde, single, and gorgeous." The character was also unmistakably heterosexual. The revised *Cagney and Lacey* continued to attract a faithful following among women viewers—including lesbians grateful for the rare example of female solidarity—but CBS canceled it once again. This cancellation brought about an avalanche of letters that, combined with the numerous Emmy nominations the series received, once again saved the program. Ultimately, *Cagney and Lacey* ran until 1988, garnering many awards along with high ratings and a large audience of lesbian viewers.

Although the lesbian character Dr. Lynne Carlson appeared for a few months in 1983 on the daytime serial *All My Children*, a regular lesbian character did not appear on prime-time television until the short-lived medical series *Heartbeat* in 1989. The role of the lesbian nurse practitioner Marilyn McGrath played by Gail Strickland on *Heartbeat* demonstrated that behind the superficial feminism of the program beat a familiar patriarchal heart. Although *Heartbeat* often presented detailed accounts and images of the heterosexual characters' romantic and sexual involvements, the lesbian character's lover was rarely shown, and they were never permitted to express desire or passion. As *People* magazine assured us (in an article titled "Is Prime Time Ready for Its First Lesbian? Gail Strickland Hopes So—And She's About to Find Out"), "On camera, physical intimacy between McGrath and her romantic partner, played by Gina Hecht, will be limited to eye contact and the occasional hug."

Apparently, for program executives progress means constructing images of lesbians and gays that are not threatening to heterosexuals by erasing any sign of lesbian and gay sexuality. This conclusion can be supported with examples of lesbian characters on other series. Except for the lesbian murderers in an episode of *Hunter*, none of the these lesbian characters is permitted to be sexual or even romantic. The desexualization of Marilyn McGrath did not, however, deflect the wrath of the Reverend Donald Wildmon's American Family Association, whose massive campaign against the program may have contributed to the cancellation of *Heartbeat* after one season.

Also in 1989, ABC broadcast a four-hour miniseries based on Gloria Naylor's novel, *The Women of Brewster Place*. The story traced the tales of a group of African American women over several decades while they all lived in tenements on a walled-off dead-end block. A major portion of the plot concerned a lesbian couple. In the words of the *New York Times*'s John O'Connor, the women "are portrayed with relative candor and sympathy in a plot development that turns into a condemnation of homophobia." But it is hardly subtle. As described by the *Philadelphia Inquirer*'s critic Ken Tucker, "When television wants to be didactic, the punishment inflicted upon homosexuals is out of all proportion to the drama." One of the women is gang-raped and nearly killed by a group of homophobic young men; but she, driven crazy with rage, then kills an innocent man she mistakes for one of her attackers. "Only then," Tucker notes, can the lesbians "take their place among the show's sympathetic characters." Earlier in the story the two women become the targets of the neighborhood busybody, who is horrified when she spies on them and, as she repeats to everyone in the vicinity, "I thought they was gonna kiss each other smack on the face." But despite the sympathetic representation of the couple (and despite the fact that the show's director, Donna Deitch, is openly lesbian), they do no such thing.

In this context no one should have been surprised at the furor aroused in February 1991 when two female attorneys on NBC's *L.A. Law* engaged in the first lesbian kiss on network television. Predictably, Reverend Wildmon geared up his fundamentalist letter-writing battalions to browbeat the networks and advertisers into censoring such acts by threatening them with product boycotts. Equally predictably, NBC began hedging its bets: "We were not attempting to create a lesbian character in that episode," said NBC spokeswoman Sue Binford. "It was much more of an attempt to add texture to C. J.'s character. It was a minor part of the overall story line."

Yet this minor texture added to the character of C. J. Lamb continued to attract attention from right-wing media watchdogs, lesbian and gay media viewers and activists, and the "infotainment" industry. In the last few episodes of the season the recipient of the famous kiss, Abby Perkins (played by Michele Green) seemed eager to push things even further. But now the bisexual C. J. Lamb (played by Amanda Donohoe) held back and declared that Abby wasn't really ready. Viewers realized they would have to wait till the fall to find out if network television was ready to permit two women to express sexual desire for each other. The answer never came, as Michele Green left the show over the summer. The bisexual C. J. was given a lesbian former lover in one fall 1991 episode, but at the end of the spring season she was embarking on an affair with a straight man. After the season ended, she too left the show, thus ending two years of frustration for lesbian and gay viewers.[8]

It wasn't only lesbian kisses that set off tremors in Hollywood. Similar waves were set off the previous season when the popular show *thirtysomething* ran an episode called "Strangers." The episode was written by openly gay series writer Richard Kramer, after he argued with the producers that the series, which took place in part in an advertising agency, was "just too fucking white and straight." "Strangers" focused on a series regular, played by David Marshall Grant, who meets and picks up another gay man, played by Peter Frechette. The episode showed the two men in bed, presumably after sex—but not touching, and certainly not kissing. The fundamentalist media activists responded in outrage, threatening to boycott sponsors, and ended up costing ABC over a million dollars in lost ad revenues. The network responded to the protests by pulling the episode from the rerun schedule.

In April 1993 David Kelley, who had written the "lesbian kiss" episode of *L.A. Law*, skated back out onto thin ice by writing an episode for his new

---

[8] Donahoe's departure from *L.A. Law* may have been spurred by more than her sexual ambiguity. In September 1991 the supermarket tabloid *Star* reported that she stirred "an even bigger outrage" by spitting on a crucifix in Ken Russell's film, *Lair of the White Worm*. Worse still, she was quoted saying that the act didn't offend her: "I'm an atheist, so it was actually a joy. Spitting on Christ was a lot of fun—especially for me, being a woman. Let's face it, the atrocities done in the name of Christ and Christianity to women throughout history are horrific." This predictably offended Phyllis Schlafly, who noted that "the bad people in the world defy God—she's one of those"; but it also upset NOW, whose spokesperson regretted "this business with the Cross—it sounds like a headache waiting to happen." More to the point, the magazine *Advertising Age* pointed out, "advertisers may hear about it and get upset."

series, *Picket Fences*, in which two high school girls "experiment" by kissing each other, and the parents of one girl panic over the possibility that their daughter might be a lesbian (she isn't). After negotiations with the network, the scene was aired with the screen darkened so that the actual kiss could not be seen.

In the early 1990s three successful network TV series made history of a sort by introducing lesbian or gay characters with continuing if secondary roles in which their sexuality was not the primary issue every time they appeared. In 1990 then-ratings queen Roseanne Barr brought into the circle of her top-rated show *Roseanne* (1988–1997) the character of Roseanne's openly gay boss (and later business partner), Leon Carp (played by Martin Mull), followed by her bisexual friend Nancy (Sandra Bernhard). The story of the founding of the fictional town of Cicely, Alaska, the setting of CBS's popular *Northern Exposure* (1990–1995), by lesbian lovers Roslyn and Cicely was told in the final episode of the 1992 season. The series had earlier introduced the secondary characters of Ron and Erick, a gay couple who own a bed-and-breakfast inn in Cicely. The twentysomething ensemble show *Melrose Place* (1992–1999) featured a gay man, Matt Fielding (Doug Savant), among the residents of a West Hollywood apartment complex. Matts's sexual orientation was mentioned in the pre-premiere publicity, but it was practically invisible in the show. Despite living in an area known colloquially as Boys' Town, Matt seemed hard-pressed to find other gay people with whom to socialize and apparently spent most of his time hanging out with his straight friends. In 1994 the *Advocate* put the actor on its cover with a headline asking the question many viewers wanted answered: "Why Can't This Man Get Laid?"

The 1993–94 television season was a landmark period for lesbian and gay visibility and the controversies it arouses. In an atmosphere shaped by President Clinton's betrayal of his promise to end military discrimination against gays and the mounting crusades of the religious right to repeal and prohibit civil rights protections for gay people, the television industry inched its cautious way forward through the cultural minefields.

On February 6, 1994, Tom Arnold, Roseanne's then-husband and executive producer of her number-one-rated show, announced that ABC had refused to air the episode scheduled for March 1 because it included a kiss between Roseanne and a lesbian character played by Mariel Hemingway. Arnold said he was told by ABC officials that "a woman cannot kiss a woman. It is bad for the kids to see," and besides, they would lose $1 million in advertising. The announcement set off a predictable storm of publicity and debate, leading many to suspect that the whole controversy was intended to build the audience for the episode, which was slated to air at the beginning of the spring "sweeps" month (a period critical in determining ratings standings). The issue occupied a great deal of attention in the familiar forums for national conversations—newspaper columns and editorials, TV and radio talk shows, supermarket tabloids—and certainly didn't hurt Roseanne's coincidental tour promoting her newly published memoirs. Among the points made repeatedly was that there was something amiss about an industry that routinely shows us women being beaten and shot but balks at showing two women kissing.

The suspense ended when ABC agreed to air the program and began to promote it heavily (for the few hermits who might not have heard about it already) as the "lesbian kiss" episode. When the show aired it was carried by all but two ABC affiliates, attracted an audience of 32 million, and resulted in about one hundred calls to the network, most of them positive. What did those 32 million viewers see? Before anything else, they saw and heard a parental advisory that the show "deals with mature sex themes and may not be appropriate for younger viewers." The program itself may well have been an anticlimax for those whose expectations had been built by the publicity. Roseanne, determined to show how cool she is, insists on accompanying Nancy and her new girlfriend (Hemingway) to a gay bar, and drags her sister Jackie along. The "climax" of the evening, as it were, occurs when the Mariel Hemingway character comes on to Roseanne and kisses her. The four-second kiss is obscured by the back of Hemingway's head, and we can see Roseanne's distaste as she rolls her eyes and wipes her mouth on her sleeve. The rest of the episode focuses on Roseanne's discomfort as she confronts the realization that she's not as cool as she thought she was.

The furor over Roseanne's kiss had barely subsided when the airwaves were roiled by the threat of yet another assault on traditional family values. Erick and Ron, the gay innkeepers on *Northern Exposure*, decide to get married—with a religious ceremony (within the peculiar definition of religion that obtained in Cicely), not a legal one—and the wedding occupies a large portion of an episode that aired May 2, 1994. The producers may have been cautious after the *Roseanne* flap, or perhaps they wished to avoid the copycat label, because the camera cuts away from the two men just as they are pronounced "married" and returns only after they apparently have embraced, thus pointedly not showing the one visual image virtually every media wedding can be expected to include. The producers said they avoided filming the kiss so it wouldn't become the focus of controversy and detract from the story; in fact, the result was markedly flat and lacking in feeling. The producers' decision did not prevent Reverend Wildmon from calling for a boycott, but only two stations (in Alabama and Louisiana) refused to broadcast the episode.

Television's "season of the kiss" came to an end on May 18 with the finale of *Melrose Place*. The Fox series had become highly popular, especially with younger viewers, because of its attractive young cast and complex soap opera plotlines full of sex and violence. In the final episode a visiting man (the best friend of main character Billy Campbell) falls for the gay character Matt Fielding. A scene was shot in which the two kiss before retiring to separate beds. As the producer told the press, the scene was included to show a gay man who has a well-rounded life. Weeks before the show was due to air, the predictable debate ensued. The Los Angeles chapter of GLAAD (Gay and Lesbian Alliance Against Defamation) expressed concern "that such a progressive network would be worried about this . . . a recurring gay character who happens to get kissed." On the other side, conservative critics chimed in with protests and boycott threats. Once again the industry blinked, and tried to split the difference. When the episode aired the two gay men were shown becoming attracted to each other. But when they stood saying goodnight, shaking hands, giving each other a meaningful look and moving toward one another, suddenly they are in slow motion and the shot cuts to Billy Campbell looking through the blinds of his apartment with a shocked expression (he hadn't known his best friend was gay). The scene then cuts back to the couple as they move apart. The audience's tender sensibilities had been spared the sight of two men exchanging a loving kiss, although the same episode offered promiscuous (heterosexual) sex, attempted murder, false accusations of (hetero)sexual harassment, and two daughters' recovered memories of childhood sexual abuse by their father; apparently, none of these required a parental advisory. It may not have been parents who were uppermost in the producers' minds, however. The president of the Fox Entertainment Group explained, "We're in a business. . . . We'd have lost up to a million dollars by airing that kiss."

In 1995 the NBC movie *Serving in Silence: The Grethe Cammermeyer Story* included a brief kiss between Glenn Close, playing the lesbian army colonel expelled from the service after coming out, and Judy Davis, as her lover. While filming the kiss scene, Close said, "I had a revelation of what it's like to be gay. . . . I thought, 'It's kind of nice to kiss a woman.'" Close, as Cammermeyer, hugs and kisses her sons, her staff, her nurses, her patients, even her lawyers, but, as Toronto TV critic Antonia Zerbisias noted, "it is not until the very last minute or so of this very stiflingly restrained TV movie that she kisses her lover." The inclusion of the lovers' kiss was probably a tribute to the clout of Barbra Streisand, who produced the TV movie. That same season the short-lived series *Courthouse* included an African American judge and her lover, who are seen in an intimate moment in their kitchen, but a kissing scene was eliminated before airing. TV producers weren't going entirely on instinct, either. An *Entertainment Weekly* survey revealed that 60 percent of their respondents said they'd be "turned off" by a same-sex kiss on a TV show.[9]

The 1995–96 TV season also featured two high-profile same-sex weddings.[10] The ratings smash *Friends* had long included secondary lesbian characters: the ex-wife of Ross, one of the core cast, and her lover. In earlier episodes Ross's ex-wife gave birth to a child—she had become pregnant with Ross just before she left him for her lover—and this had given the show an opportunity to be liberal about the changing landscape of American families. In 1996 the two women were married in a much-publicized episode, with a lot of the attention focused on the "guest star" minister, played by famous half-sister-turned-lesbian-activist, Candace Gingrich. Around the same time, as her long-running but running-out-of-steam show began throwing off plot sparks in all directions—such as having her mother (played by Estelle Parsons) suddenly realize she's a lesbian—Roseanne included a wedding show for her long-time gay character, played by Martin Mull. In neither of these two wedding episodes were viewers subjected to a kiss between the newlyweds.[11]

In the years since, same-sex kisses continue to be treated with all the delicacy and attention required for high-risk medical procedures. When teen-favorite *Party of Five* included a kiss between series regular Neve Campbell

[9] Lesbian kisses proved controversial in Britain as well as the United States. A kiss between two women characters on the British soap *Brookside* in 1995 provoked sufficient controversy that it was cut out of the program's rerun. At the same time, however, Channel Four aired a four-week series of *Dyke TV* that included both the *Brookside* kiss and a subsequent protest by the Lesbian Avengers against Channel Four's decision to cut it from the rerun. The following year a homosexual kiss on *East Enders* resulted in forty-one complaints to the Broadcasting Standards Council, but the council ruled that the BBC had "reflected contemporary themes in a realistic manner." At the same time, the council condemned the *Oprah Winfrey Show* for showing news footage of a murder (*Guardian*, 12/5/96).

[10] A 1991 wedding episode on the Fox series *Roc* did not evoke a great deal of attention, possibly because the show had an African American cast, but perhaps because the show also never attracted a crossover audience. In this wedding the dramatic tension focused on whether "gay uncle" Russell's brother would accept his sexuality and, equally controversial, his white partner. In the end, family wins and we get the traditional reconciling embrace.

[11] As the two "just married" men begin to clinch, the camera pans to the guests, focusing on Roseanne and her husband Dan (John Goodman), who fidgets and giggles, saying, "There's the kiss. I was wondering if they're gonna do it, and they're doing it. . . . Look at them going at it." Roseanne replies in a superior tone, "They're not 'going at it,' Dan. They just happen to be two people of the same sex kissing and there's nothing the matter with that." Just then Mariel Hemingway comes in and leans over from behind Roseanne, smiling in greeting. Roseanne see her, starts, and says, "Hi," with a smile, as the program ends.

(now a college student) and her lesbian writing teacher—scheduled during the spring 1999 sweeps month—the show occasioned lots of media attention and predictable outrage from the Christian Action Network. In the end, as with the earlier *Picket Fences* episode, the central character decides that this was just an experiment, and the lesbian character disappears after the three-episode story line. In contrast, same-sex kisses can be included with much less fanfare and self-congratulation, if it is clear that there is nothing romantic implied. In the ABC series, *Spin City*, the show's gay character (played by African American actor Michael Boatman) kisses the show's lead (Michael J. Fox), who is, if anything, excessively heterosexual, and it is clear to everyone that this is not a "real" kiss (it makes sense in the context of the plot).

In a November 1998 episode of the Fox hit *Ally McBeal*, in order to dissuade an unwanted suitor, Ally (Calista Flockhart) arranges for him to catch her and fellow lawyer Georgia engaged in a kiss. Unlike Roseanne and Mariel Hemingway, this kiss is given full screen visibility, but it attracted little attention and no hostile complaints. *Ally McBeal*'s creator David Kelley (author of the *L.A. Law* and *Picket Fences* "lesbian kiss" episodes) upped the ante for the November 1999 sweeps by having Ally and colleague Ling Woo (Lucy Liu) admit that they are intrigued by the idea of kissing each other, and of course they end up doing just that, at length.[12] Perhaps because the script makes quite clear that both women are, indeed, heterosexual, the kiss is shot in profile, locked lips clearly visible, rather than using the angle-of-choice for homosexual kisses, in which the back of one partner's head blocks our view of the actual contact. The episode won its time slot among the coveted young adult viewers, even beating Monday night football.

[12] The choice of Ling as the target of Ally's same-sex kiss was complicated by the exotic "dragon lady" aspect of her character. As one of the very few Asian American characters on television, Ling has been criticized for embodying familiar orientalist stereotypes.

AIDS and the Media

RUMORS OF A "GAY CANCER"

The most significant moments in history are often invisible at first. When a small group of gay men gathered in a living room in Los Angeles in 1951 to found the Mattachine Society, not even they could have foreseen the consequences of their courage. When the Stonewall riots erupted in Greenwich Village in June 1969 most lesbian and gay people could not know anything important had happened, because the media chose not to tell the story. And those who knew were not all pleased: the New York Mattachine Society deplored the disorder, little realizing that a new wave of militancy was about to sweep them aside. So, too, did few people notice the small stories about "a rare cancer" seen in homosexual men that first appeared in the press in the summer of 1981. But this cloud no bigger than a man's hand was soon to darken the skies.

At the end of the 1970's, America had been confronted with the specter of a seemingly incurable disease contracted through sexual contact: genital herpes. The media were quick to point out that the causes of the epidemic were to be found in the so-called sexual revolution. As the *New York Times Magazine* put it, "Health officials say that genital herpes became a growing problem only during the mid-1970's, after sexual codes had loosened in American society" (2/21/82:94). Media accounts were rife with thinly disguised moral judgments, mixing opinion with facts as they told us that, "Herpes could be an unpleasant fact of life for virtually an entire generation. The price, [health experts] say, of the sexual revolution" (CBS AM, 5/7/82). The sexual revolution, it was frequently emphasized, was characterized by permissiveness and promiscuity, and now the bills are coming due: "Spurred on by two decades of sexual permissiveness, the disease has cut swiftly through the ranks of the sexually active" (*Time*, 8/2/82).

Despite all the attention it received, the panic was short-lived and the fear of herpes did not ring down the curtain on the sexual revolution. Perhaps the extent of the "epidemic" was exaggerated, or perhaps herpes, while incurable, was not a sufficient deterrent to play the role it was assigned as the chief weapon of the emerging sexual counterrevolution of the 1980s. But the stage was set for the arrival of a much more potent and deadly threat: AIDS. AIDS provided society and the media with a double-edged opportunity and challenge, the truly frightening specter of a deadly disease that could be associated with sexual permissiveness, showing up among a group the media have consistently defined as being outside the mainstream.

In 1981 Lawrence Mass, a gay physician and writer, had begun a series of articles for the *New York Native*, a gay newspaper, in which he covered health-related issues of concern to gay men. It was in this context that he was struck by a conversation with Brent Harris, associate editor of the *Advocate*, in which Harris told him that he had been diagnosed with a rare form of cancer, Kaposi's sarcoma. "It was so rare, in fact," Mass later recalled, that "I had barely heard of it." Mass called health officials at the Centers for Disease Control in Atlanta, and they assured him that the rumors of a "gay cancer" were unfounded. On May 18, 1981, the *Native* published an article by Mass that was to be the first ever written about the disease that came to be called AIDS. Based on the assurances Mass received from the CDC, the article was far from alarming; its headline read "Disease Rumors Largely Unfounded." But it wasn't long before more frightening news began to appear.

In the June 5, 1981, issue of the CDC's *Morbidity and Mortality Weekly Report* there was an article about five gay men in Los Angeles diagnosed with a rare disease called pneumocystis carinii. The article noted that "the occurrence of pneumocystis in these five previously healthy individuals . . . is unusual. The fact that these patients were all homosexuals suggests an association between some aspect of a homosexual lifestyle or disease acquired through sexual contact." The CDC report was picked up by the Associated Press, and brief articles appeared in the *San Francisco Chronicle* and the *Los Angeles Times*. The first notice of AIDS in the *New York Times* came in a short piece that appeared on July 3, 1981, on page 20: "Rare Cancer Seen in 41 Homosexuals." At this point the newly emerging disease was being called GRID—Gay Related Immune Deficiency—and the name embodied the association between gay men and AIDS that has lasted ever since. In fact, many early press reports referred to a "gay plague."

The immediate response to the medical mystery that we know as AIDS was a deafening silence from the mainstream mass media, but even the gay press needed time to understand the magnitude of the crisis. Although one of its editors died of AIDS-related cancer in 1981, the *Advocate*'s first reference to the disease, in July of that year, quoted a CDC physician about pneumocystis. The relationships between the various opportunistic infections associated with AIDS would not become clear for some time. In the meantime, Dr. Lawrence Mass was writing articles in the *New York Native* that were the only accounts attempting to convey the seriousness of the situation. The *Native*, however, had a circulation of only about 14,000 readers, so Mass was relieved when the *Village Voice* commissioned an article from him. Mass delivered an article with the "most frightening headline" he could think of: "The Most Important New Public Health Problem in the United States," only to discover that the *Voice* would not run it. It seems likely that the editors were afraid the article would be seen by gay readers as too negative, but whatever their reasons it was not until December 1983 that the *Village Voice* published a major article on the epidemic.

The *New York Times* article on July 3, 1981, caught the attention of gay playwright Larry Kramer, who knew people suffering from Kaposi's sarcoma and suddenly became alarmed by the dimensions of the implied health crisis. Kramer assembled a group of friends, among them Lawrence Mass, and writers Nathan Fain and Edmund White, and together they established the first grassroots AIDS organization: the Gay Men's Health Crisis. One of their first goals was media exposure, to warn gay men of the risks they seemed to be facing, and to call for medical efforts to investigate and fight this new disease. The model in everyone's minds was Legionnaire's disease, the strange outbreak of a lethal infection that had killed twenty-nine people at an American Legion convention in 1976. But the example of Legionnaire's disease proved not to predict the media's response to AIDS. During the two months that the medical mystery persisted, the *New York Times* published sixty-two stories on Legionnaire's disease, eleven of them on the front page. In dramatic contrast, from July 1981 through the end of 1982, the *New York Times* ran a total of ten stories about AIDS, and none of them reached the front page. The television networks did not even mention AIDS on their nightly newscasts until 1982.

CIRCLING THE WAGONS

The AIDS epidemic has been widely interpreted as a challenge to the institutions and the values that typify the achievements of modern Western society: science and medicine, respect for the rights and concern for the welfare of all citizens. So far, the record of our societal and institutional response has been mixed at best, possibly because AIDS came upon us in ways that tested our motives and our institutions. By emerging among groups that are largely despised and rejected, AIDS proved once again the truism that the importance of an event may be determined less by what happened than to whom it happened.

In the early days of the AIDS epidemic (at a point when widespread educational efforts might have saved thousands of lives since lost), Congressman Henry Waxman of California made this point by contrasting public response to AIDS and to Legionnaire's disease: "Legionnaire's disease hit a group of predominately white, heterosexual, middle-aged members of the American Legion. The respectability of the victims brought them a degree of attention and funding for research and treatment far greater than that made available so far to the victims of Kaposi's sarcoma. . . . I want to emphasize that contrast, because the more popular Legionnaire's disease affected fewer people and proved to be less fatal. What society judged was not the severity of the disease but the social acceptability of the individuals affected with it."

The first accounts of AIDS in the mainstream media emphasized its apparent link to gay men's sexuality (there were also at that time two other outsider "risk groups," IV drug users and Haitians, and the first "innocent victims," hemophiliacs). The first story on AIDS aired by NBC News appeared in June 1982, and Tom Brokaw framed the issue in a fashion that remained constant throughout much subsequent coverage: "Scientists at the National Centers for Disease Control in Atlanta today released the results of a study that shows that the lifestyle of some male homosexuals has triggered an epidemic of a rare form of cancer."

The media alternated depictions that distanced AIDS as the fate befalling those gay men in the "fast lane" whose lifestyles have put them far outside the mainstream ("Investigators also believe that AIDS is principally a phenomenon of the raunchy subculture in large cities, where bars and bathhouses are literal hotbeds of sexual promiscuity," per *Rolling Stone*, 2/3/83,) with stories intimating that AIDS might also threaten the "general population." The media's mainstream orientation was reflected in their concern over the fate of the "general population" if and when AIDS spread beyond the deviant "risk groups" in which it mostly appeared. For example, although the *Philadelphia Inquirer* was an exception to the rule because it gave the epidemic serious attention in the early period, AIDS did not make the paper's front page until an article appeared headlined, "A Baffling Disease Turns Deadly to More Than Gays."[1] As media researcher Edward Albert put it,

> The press in some ways has circled the wagons. Outside are predominantly gay males subject no longer to opportunistic infections due to disease, but now to an opportunistic morality by which they are held at arm's length. Inside is a population reading about a progressive contagion that moves from homosexual males, IV-drug users, Haitians, and hemophiliacs to health-care workers, children, surgery patients, and heterosexual women (families), with the explicit implication that it will not stop there.

In a *CBS News* special titled, appropriately enough, "AIDS Hits Home" (10/22/86), correspondent Bernard Goldberg unwittingly spoke this premise when he commented: "For a very long time, heterosexuals, straight Americans, thought AIDS was somebody else's problem—that is, if they thought about AIDS at all. AIDS is what homosexuals got. But a scary reality is starting to hit home, that the AIDS virus is out there and it's not just gays who are catching it." In other words, one might say, real people are in danger.[2]

The initial flicker of attention in the mass media was not only late, it was also short-lived. There were merely five network television stories on AIDS in 1982 (and three of these focused on persons considered by the media to be "innocent victims"—hemophiliacs, children, and recipients of blood transfusions). In 1983 that number rose to thirty-nine, but the following year it dropped to twenty-five, even while the death rate continued to climb.

Between January and June of 1985 the *New York Times* published fifty-two articles about AIDS; from July to December of 1985 the *New York Times* ran 323 articles about AIDS. What reversed the trend? On July 25, 1985, Rock Hudson announced that he had AIDS; he died three months later. The *Times*

[1] The *Inquirer* was simultaneously running stories promulgating the identification of gays and AIDS that it was denying in its own coverage. The very issue that reported on the front page that "Homosexuals are not the only ones stricken," also included an article headed, "'Gay Plague' Has Instilled Fear of the Unknown," which opened by telling us that "a well-known gay activist in Philadelphia no longer hugs friends when he runs into them on the street, and seldom even shakes hands. 'It's probably stupid, but I can't help being leery,' explains Mark Segal, publisher of Philadelphia's Gay News."

[2] As late as 1992 a federal official, William Grigg of the Department of Health and Human Services, articulated an epidemiology of expendability that spelled out what had long been implicit in public responses to AIDS: "When you're fighting a fire, you control it from the outside and let the center burn. The same holds true for medicine."

was not unusual in this regard. The week after the announcement, Rock Hudson appeared on the covers of *Newsweek*, *People*, and *McLean's*, the largest Canadian newsweekly. Suddenly it seemed that everyone believed what *Life* magazine had warned in massive letters across its July cover: NOW NO ONE IS SAFE FROM AIDS. Ronald Milavsky, who was then a vice president at NBC, summarized the coverage of AIDS: "The most striking thing . . . is the low level of reporting until Rock Hudson's illness and the rather continuous high level after that. . . . Rock Hudson's illness, death, and his admission that he was indeed dying of AIDS was a very unusual combination that was big news and stimulated the public's interest. From July to December 1985, NBC broadcast over 200 stories on AIDS—three times as many as during the entire 1980 to 1984 period. The other news media reacted similarly." Note the implication that it was the low level of *public* interest that was responsible for the absence of sustained coverage before Rock Hudson.[3]

NATURAL SQUEAMISHNESS

There may still be uncertainty surrounding the causes and possible cures of AIDS, but there is little uncertain about the response of the media and other institutions to the epidemic. As many analysts have described and many news professionals have admitted, the homophobia of the press, combined with its assumption that audiences shared its biases, led it to ignore and downplay the story. There was, in addition, what NBC News science correspondent Robert Bazell termed "a natural squeamishness about most things sexual." Although our society is literally awash in sexual imagery, which is used as the lure in ads

---

[3] Rock Hudson's last acting role was on the ABC prime-time soap, *Dynasty*, where he played a romantic role with series star Linda Evans. After the revelation of Hudson's illness the media engaged in a retrospective frenzy of concern over the kisses Hudson and Evans had shared on screen. By 1986, when *Dynasty II: The Colbys* spun off, its star, Charlton Heston, successfully pressured the Screen Actors Guild to issue a ruling that its members do not have to tongue-kiss. Heston's fellow cast members differed in their responses to the kissing crisis. Emma Samms wasn't worried, "since we've been told by doctors that kissing does not transmit [AIDS]." John James, one of those kissing Emma Samms, was also calm: "I don't want to downplay the AIDS thing because I went to the benefit and I do think that a cure should be found, but it seems that in this country the press seems to get hysterical over things because it has nothing else to talk about. . . . As for me, I don't think about it." And Tracy Scoggins, who played Heston's daughter, was "not overly worried about it because you can tell a gay guy as soon as he kisses you. They're not out to stick their tongue down your throat and cop a feel, like straight guys. And, for another thing, usually they're more concerned about their makeup than you are, and they don't want to get it smeared all over their faces."

for hundreds of products, Americans are unusually prudish about any direct mention of sex or sex-related terms. Even when the medical community began to identify the ways in which HIV, the virus causing AIDS, is spread, the media were unwilling to use terminology that most people could readily understand. Robert Bazell noted that "there's a disparity at this point in this country between the moral values of certain groups. When you have a viewership that is the entire country, it becomes very difficult to know how to handle that." Most of the time television journalists opted for caution over public service.

In August 1982 Dan Rather on the *CBS Evening News* was blunt about the fact that the majority of people with AIDS were gay men, but not until May 1983 did CBS report that the major way AIDS is transmitted is through sexual contacts. Broadcast news media even today almost always use phrases like "bodily fluids" rather than use the word "semen" or vernacular terms such as "cum."

Public service announcements intended to educate the public about AIDS have tended to be tongue-tied by censorship and fear of political repercussions. After an initial effort at advertising condoms in the late 1980s was met with resistance from the networks, condom manufacturers backed off. As late as 1998 all the major television networks as well as Fox, UPN, and WB were unwilling to accept advertisements for condoms. As the amount of explicit sexual content in TV ads and programs increased, however, condom ads began appearing in the 1990s on cable channels such as MTV and Comedy Central, and some local network affiliates tentatively ventured into this territory, as when CBS affiliates in New York and Los Angeles ran a condom commercial during the August 1998 debut of the syndicated *Howard Stern Radio Show*.[4]

Print media have been considerably more forthcoming with accurate information. Harry Nelson could write an article for the *Los Angeles Times* in April 1983 reporting that the risk of AIDS "is associated with passive (receptive) anal intercourse" because of "the presence of the agent in the semen of the active partner." After a long period of sticking to the vague term "sexual

---

[4] European viewers see both condom ads and public service announcements that are inconceivably explicit by U.S. standards. In 1998 Britain's Channel Four ran a condom ad showing two men engaged in a sexual encounter, ending with the slogan: "be positive, stay negative." One might indeed wonder at this unusual example of capitalist reticence by American manufacturers in the face of a product for which there is both obvious demand and, well, sex appeal. This reluctance has even extended to the avoidance of the gay press. As late as February 2000, a gay marketer commented, "They're obvious naturals for the gay press. Even the most simplistic person in advertising should see that. But not one major condom company has ever done an ad campaign in the gay press."

contact," the *New York Times* published an article by Jane Brody, in the "Personal Health" column for February 12, 1986, which reported that "infected semen can spread AIDS through intercourse in which the virus comes in contact with broken blood vessels or lesions in the anus or vagina."

The media were not alone in their reluctance to deal with the topic of AIDS. President Ronald Reagan did not give a speech on this unprecedented health crisis until June 1987, by which point over 20,000 people had died of AIDS in the United States. But the media are not politicians, and they are expected to rise above their own prejudices. In fact, of course, much of the time they do not set aside their biases, and AIDS was no exception. As journalist James Kinsella has documented, homophobia among media personnel discouraged reporters and editors from tackling AIDS in the early years. Before it became an "official major story," any reporter suggesting an AIDS-related piece to his or her editor would be provoking the question, why are *you* interested? The implication that wouldn't need to be spelled out was, are you interested in something that affects gay men because you are gay yourself? Any reporter (or editor) came under suspicion of being gay if he or she seemed to take a personal interest in a story concerning the lives of gay people.[5] To be a suspect meant being subject to degrees of editorial exile, which few reporters (straight or gay) wished to risk. Further, reporters were professionally interested in getting their stories, and their bylines, in print and on the front page if possible. Proposing stories that editors aren't likely to run is not a good career move. Thus, it is not surprising that the most extensive AIDS coverage in the mainstream press was written by Randy Shilts for the *San Francisco Chronicle*; for Shilts was one of the few openly gay reporters in the country, and the first ever to be hired as an openly gay person.[6]

It was only after Rock Hudson had raised the status of AIDS to that of a front-page story that reporters could safely be associated with the topic. Even

[5] As James Kinsella noted, *Newsweek*'s Atlanta bureau writer Vincent Coppola became interested in AIDS when he learned that his brother suffered from the disease, and his interest and persistence led to *Newsweek*'s April 18, 1983, cover story: "The AIDS Epidemic: The Search for a Cure." This was the first major treatment of AIDS by a national general interest magazine and probably stimulated *Time*'s cover story three months later.

[6] Shilts was allied with certain political factions within San Francisco's gay and lesbian community, and he took sides on issues that he also reported on as a journalist. Shilts's partisan engagement with issues he covered was especially marked during the controversial movement to shut the bathhouses in San Francisco. His perspective favoring the closings influenced the outcome of the debate, and it also distinctly slanted the account in his book, *And the Band Played On*, in which Shilts's own involvement is not reported (nor did Shilts reveal his own HIV status until several years after the book was published).

then, media attention to AIDS seemed always to erupt whenever there was a dramatic story that involved heterosexuals. A young hemophiliac named Ryan White, harassed by schoolmates when they discovered he had AIDS, became a national figure after massive media exposure; a major AIDS funding bill was eventually named the Ryan White Act.[7]

In 1990 a Florida woman named Kimberly Bergalis claimed she contracted AIDS through a dental procedure (her dentist later died of AIDS) and became a media celebrity, featured on the cover of *People* magazine in October 1990. Sen. Jesse Helms (R-NC) sponsored legislation requiring health care workers to reveal their HIV status to patients, dismissing the statistical improbability of contracting AIDS from a health professional: "Don't tell that to Kimberly Bergalis!" After Helms's colleagues passed his bill by an 81 to 18 vote, gay activist Gregory King remarked, "we're seeing public policy as promulgated by *People* magazine."

That same year, AIDS-related coverage exploded again when basketball star "Magic" Johnson announced that he was HIV-positive. Six months later tennis legend Arthur Ashe announced that he was suffering from AIDS contracted through a blood transfusion years before, and yet another heterosexual AIDS story dominated the front pages for weeks. This time the homophobia implicit in the media's overreaction to heterosexual AIDS stories was barely hidden, as in a comment by *Philadelphia Inquirer* columnist Claude Lewis, who wrote about Ashe, "Because of you, AIDS is perhaps a bit more respectable today."

There was another drawback to the news media's handling of AIDS—the story simply went on too long. The news media like to focus on—what else?—news, and they find it difficult to stick with stories that develop slowly, without dramatic incidents. Because for years the media were indifferent to or afraid of the experiences of people with AIDS, their coverage focused almost entirely on the "medical mystery" or on supposed breakthroughs, most of which fizzled out.[8]

Despite the limitations of media coverage, by the late 1980s the AIDS epi-

---

[7] Ryan White also provided an opportunity for then-somewhat-out-of-the-closet celebrities, such as Elton John and Greg Louganis (who gave White one of his Olympic medals) to become involved in AIDS fund-raising. Somewhat similarly, Elizabeth Taylor's central role in fund-raising for AMFAR (the American Foundation for AIDS Research) gave convenient cover for many wealthy but closeted gay men, who could safely be photographed standing next to the world's most famous heterosexual woman.

[8] In a 1983 broadcast, Peter Jennings mentioned a plant fungus found in the blood of three AIDS patients that seemed to lower the body's resistance to the disease. "Doctors say their research is very preliminary but say they are very excited about it." As media analyst James Kinsella noted, there was no information on who the doctors were, or whether their study of three people was valid; and there was no follow-up.

demic had accomplished something that the lesbian and gay movement had not been able to achieve—the end of gay invisibility in the mass media. Even so, nearly all the attention to gay men was in the context of AIDS-related stories, and because this coverage seems to have exhausted the media's limited interest in gay people, lesbians became even less visible. AIDS also reinvigorated the two major mass media "roles" for gay people: victim and villain. The public image of gay men was becoming inescapably linked with the specter of plague.

What the news media could not be counted on to do was provide sustained, careful coverage and information vital to those actually suffering from HIV-related diseases.[9] As the story went from mystery to crisis to epidemic, seeming only to get worse and more horrifying, the gay press once again proved to be essential. Following Lawrence Mass's pioneering medical articles, Larry Kramer took to the pages of the *New York Native* with a series of thunderous calls to action. The most sensational and influential of these began with the headline emblazoned on the front page of the *Native* in March 1983: "1,112 and Counting." The article began even more dramatically: "If this article doesn't scare the shit out of you, we're in real trouble. If this article doesn't rouse you to anger, fury, rage, and action, gay men may have no future on this earth." The article did rouse gay men, lesbians, and their allies and helped to spur the growth of the political and service organizations within the gay community that have proved to be the primary vehicles for responding to the epidemic.

Although at first reluctant to accept the seriousness of the crisis, by mid-1983 the gay press was regularly covering the story, along with some of the alternative press, such as the *Village Voice*, where gay journalist Nathan Fain published important articles. That pattern has not changed over the years. Although the *Native* took itself out of consideration as a valuable source of AIDS information when it became obsessed by the conviction that HIV is not the primary cause of AIDS, the gay press in general, along with specialized newsletters and Web sites produced by AIDS organizations and activists, has become the essential lifeline of information and analysis about the major health crisis of the century.

MEDIA ACTIVISM IN A CRISIS

The AIDS epidemic is more than a health crisis. It is also a political crisis that exposed much of the hostility to gay people that was never far below the sur-

---

[9] An additional factor that inhibits adequate coverage of AIDS is the policy of leading science journals, such as the *New England Journal of Medicine*, not to publish anything that has already been reported in the press.

face. The specter of a "gay plague" was pointed to by preachers, politicians, and pundits eager to use a disease as a moral weapon in their crusade against "sexual permissiveness." Conservative columnist and perennial presidential candidate Patrick Buchanan was one of the first to latch onto AIDS as a political opportunity. In his syndicated column of May 24, 1983, Buchanan gloated, "The sexual revolution has begun to devour its children. And among the revolutionary vanguard, the Gay Rights activists, the mortality rate is highest and climbing." Buchanan went on to sound a theme that would soon be echoed in the sermons and speeches of the religious right: "The poor homosexuals—they have declared war upon nature, and now nature is exacting an awful retribution."[10] Buchanan was joined in his efforts by the Reverend Jerry Falwell, founder of the Moral Majority and a leading figure on the religious right, who had been relatively quiet about AIDS. But in July 1983 Falwell appeared on an ABC station in Virginia to debate with medical experts about AIDS, basing his arguments on the New Testament: "When you violate moral, health, and hygiene laws, you reap the whirlwind. You cannot shake your fist in God's face and get by with it." In October 1985 the American Coalition for Traditional Values held an organizing meeting on the topic, "How to Win an Election," at which an up-and-coming congressman named Newt Gingrich gave a keynote address. Introduced by the Reverend Tim LaHaye, a founder of the Moral Majority, as "a minister of God," Gingrich told his fellow traditionalists that AIDS was just what the doctor ordered for their crusade to take over Washington: "AIDS will do more to direct America back to the cost of violating traditional values, and to make America aware of the danger of certain behaviors than anything we've seen. For us it's a great rallying cry."

The attacks on gay men by religious and political figures did not stop at moral condemnation and gloating. Many proposed a quarantine of gay men as a public safety measure—a measure President Ronald Reagan was interested in until dissuaded by Surgeon General C. Everett Koop. Influential conservative writer William F. Buckley wrote a March 1986 op-ed column in the *New York Times*, "Crucial Steps in Combating the AIDS Epidemic," in which he urged that gay men testing positive for the HIV virus should have a warning sign tattooed on their buttocks. "Our society is generally threat-

---

[10] Buchanan might be said to be keeping company here with Larry Kramer, of all people. Kramer's rants against homosexual promiscuity antedated AIDS by several years, as in his vitriolic 1979 novel, *Faggots*. As late as 1997, reviewing Gabriel Rotello's *Sexual Ecology* in the *Advocate*, Kramer echoed Buchanan: "Nature always extracts a price for promiscuity."

ened, and in order to fight AIDS," he wrote, "we need the equivalent of universal military training."

The mainstream media were not only not helping solve the AIDS crisis, but in many instances they were part of the problem. One of the worst offenders was the reactionary *New York Post* (one of the oldest newspapers in the United States), which had become notorious for sleaze and sensationalism. AIDS proved no exception and the *Post* regularly infuriated the lesbian and gay community through its hostile headlines, slanted coverage, and negative editorials that characterized AIDS as fitting punishment for homosexual behavior. In the fall of 1985 New York City was embroiled in a controversy over plans to shut down the gay bathhouses. The baths had been closed in San Francisco the previous year after a lengthy and vociferous debate between those who believed the baths were a primary site for HIV transmission and those who argued that closing the baths would not stop sexual behavior but merely drive it elsewhere, where it would be more difficult to reach people with information and condoms. The issue in New York did not have the heat of the San Francisco debate, but it was lively and the *Post*'s articles and editorials were particularly homophobic.

The level of media activism in New York had died down by the early 1980s, and the decision of the National Gay and Lesbian Task Force to move to Washington merely confirmed that they were no longer engaged in serious media advocacy. A group of gay activists—Barry Adkins, Alan Barnett, Arnie Kantrowitz, Gregory Kolovakos, Jim Owles, Marty Robinson, Darryl Yates Rist, and Vito Russo—met to consider how the community might respond to the media. They decided to call a town meeting.

On November 14, 1985, more than seven hundred lesbians and gay men packed the pews of a Manhattan church to express their outrage at the media in general and the *New York Post* in particular. Vito Russo tackled the bathhouse issue directly: "This community is being divided over a smokescreen for what's really going on, which is that the AIDS epidemic is being used by right-wing fanatics and yellow journalists to create a witchhunt mentality against lesbians and gay men in the city." Writer Jewelle Gomez told the audience that she had been harassed on the street on her way to the meeting, and continued, "I hold two very specific groups responsible for this harassment. . . . The media of the city—the *New York Post*, the *New York Times*, the *Daily News*—I hold directly responsible. The other group I hold responsible is myself and all of us here tonight. We must take responsibility for what is being said about us . . . for our attitudes . . . for our images." Darryl Yates Rist then spoke: "Tonight is the final notice to the bigots! Tonight our tolerance has ended. We're no longer begging; we're no longer asking."

In the wake of the town meeting the organizing group established an organization to confront and educate the media about the concerns and the accomplishments of the lesbian and gay community. The Gay and Lesbian Alliance Against Defamation (GLAAD) was dedicated to "improving fairness, accuracy and inclusiveness in news coverage and media portrayals of all gay men and lesbians" and "to improve public attitudes about homosexuality in an effort to end violence and discrimination against lesbians and gay men and overcome their social isolation."

The first target of GLAAD's educational zeal was the *Post*. However, the editors not only refused to meet with GLAAD, they followed the town meeting with another hostile editorial on the bathhouse issue. It was time for direct action: a crowd numbering nearly seven hundred gathered outside the *Post* carrying posters and dirty rags to symbolize the paper. The *New York Post* did not undergo a change of heart because of the protest, although their coverage of lesbian and gay issues did show improvement for a period in the late 1980s. In 1991 *Post* editor Jerry Nachman told a group of activists, some of whom had thrown rags at his door in 1985, "Times have changed. . . . We've finally decided to take you guys seriously." The enlightenment of the *Post*, however temporary, can be credited in large part to the continuing efforts of GLAAD, which has made itself part of the New York and media landscape.

In 1988 GLAAD was able to appoint a full-time paid executive director, Craig Davidson, and in October of that year a second GLAAD chapter was founded in Los Angeles by activist Richard Jennings. The bicoastal presence of GLAAD/NY and GLAAD/LA gave the organization the ability to reach both news and entertainment media executives. GLAAD came to national attention in 1990, when its protest of homophobic comments made by *60 Minutes* commentator Andy Rooney led to his suspension by CBS.[11] Presumably, after the Andy Rooney incident, reporters and editors were more likely

---

[11] In Rooney's year-end "TV special," the CBS commentator said, "There was some recognition in 1989 of the fact that many of the ills which kill us are self-induced. Too much alcohol. Too much food, drugs, homosexual unions, cigarettes. They're all known to lead quite often to premature death." CBS responded to GLAAD's protests with a meeting, and Rooney apologized, saying that he had been "imprecise." Shortly afterwards, however, in an interview with the *Advocate*, Rooney was quoted as saying that "blacks have watered down their genes because the less intelligent ones are the ones that have the most children. They drop out of school early, do drugs and get pregnant." Rooney was also quoted saying, "maybe homosexuals have too many female hormones . . . and I think that homosexuality is inherently dangerous." The homophobic remarks alone wouldn't have done the trick, but the racist remarks (which Rooney denied making), led to a 90-day suspension by CBS. Public response, however, moved CBS to rescind the suspension within a few weeks. In the meantime, the supermarket tabloid *National Enquirer* (2/27/90) ran an "exclusive" interview: "The Gays Finally Got Me: They Set Me Up, Says Andy Rooney."

to read GLAAD's *Media Guide to the Lesbian and Gay Community.* GLAAD's efforts to promote visibility have ranged from placing 10,000 posters in the New York City subway system to producing a public service announcement featuring Bob Hope. Their annual New York and Los Angeles Media Award dinners are regularly attended by celebrities and media moguls; with the initiation of a third Media Award dinner in Washington, D.C., in 1999, that list expanded to include politicians. But possibly GLAAD's most important ongoing activity is the monitoring of media coverage of lesbian, gay, bisexual, and transgendered people. The results of the monitoring are communicated in GLAAD's "alerts" and newsletters, and in the gay press, as well as via the Internet, stimulating both positive and negative feedback to reporters, editors, writers, and producers. In 1992, GLAAD was named one of Hollywood's 100 most powerful entities by *Entertainment Weekly.*

Initially, GLAAD's chapters had been loosely coordinated, but in 1995 the two largest chapters, New York and Los Angeles, decided to merge into one organization to create a more coherent national organization. By 1999, in addition to New York and Los Angeles, there were GLAAD offices in Atlanta, Kansas City, San Francisco, and Washington, D.C. GLAAD's growing engagement with the Internet led to a 1998 merger with the pioneering Internet activist organization Digital Queers and in 1999, with the support of the Gill Foundation, GLAAD launched a Research and Analysis initiative to bridge the growing distance between the activist and academic realms.

Although GLAAD was launched in response to scurrilous media handling of AIDS-related stories, its later trajectory focused on gay and lesbian representations in the media, including but certainly not primarily in relation to AIDS. By 1987, however, as the AIDS toll continued to rise with little sustained response from the Reagan administration, activists once again looked for ways to break through the walls of public complacency and denial. A New York direct-action group, the Lavender Hill Mob, attracted media attention by demonstrating against the Supreme Court's 1986 *Bowers v. Hardwick* decision, upholding antisodomy laws, and zapping New York's Cardinal O'Connor to protest a Vatican statement opposing civil rights legislation to protect lesbian and gay rights. A group of gay artists calling itself the Silence = Death Project designed a poster that included that slogan in white letters on a black ground, below a pink triangle.[12] The Silence = Death posters were placed

[12] The pink triangle had long since become a gay liberation symbol, having been taken from the patch that homosexual prisoners were required to wear in Nazi concentration camps. However, whereas the Nazi triangle was worn point down, the Silence = Death triangle is pointed upwards.

around New York, but they quickly became identified with a new activist group that was formed in March 1987.

Following a rousing speech by Larry Kramer at New York's Lesbian and Gay Community Services Center, militant activists founded the AIDS Coalition to Unleash Power, widely known by its acronym, ACT UP. ACT UP, which described itself as a coalition of "diverse individuals united in anger and committed to direct action," grew quickly, drawing hundreds to its weekly meetings and grabbing public attention through media-savvy demonstrations and civil disobedience. ACT UP's trademark was the combination of homework and hell-raising—knowing the facts and using militant, media-attracting tactics to publicize them, as in its well-covered zap of the New York Stock Exchange to protest Burroughs Welcome's exorbitant pricing of the AIDS drug AZT, then costing around $10,000 per year (the drug company responded by lowering the price substantially). The Silence = Death group joined with ACT UP, lending its graphic arts skills to the creation of buttons, posters, and T-shirts that became an important fund-raising tool for the organization, while spreading ACT UP's message on billboards and bodies.[13]

By the end of the year ACT UP chapters were emerging all over the United States, and even as far as Paris and Tokyo. In October 1987 the second National March on Washington for Lesbian and Gay Rights attracted hundreds of thousands of marchers, and the ACT UP contingents were among the most visible and militant. The day after the march more than six hundred activists were arrested on the steps of the U.S. Supreme Court to protest *Bowers v. Hardwick*, the largest civil disobedience action since the Vietnam War demonstrations.

In contrast to the 1979 March, this time the media paid attention, and the story showed up on front pages around the country. Paying attention and giving credit are not the same thing, however. While ACT UP succeeded in raising issues and keeping them on the public agenda, the media often portrayed ACT UP as irrational extremists, falsely accused of acts like throwing blood and urine rather than acting as effective players in a world of media-dominated politics. When Peter Jennings ended a 1989 public television

---

[13] The art collective, now calling itself Gran Fury (after the Plymouth cars used by New York City undercover police), attracted attention from the art world for their innovative and powerful graphics. Still, when the Museum of Modern Art organized a show, "Committed to Print: Social and Political Themes in Recent American Printed Art," in 1988, no AIDS graphics were included. It would seem that the work of AIDS activists didn't pass the familiar universalism test. In the words of the MOMA catalogue: "In the final analysis it is not the specific issues or events that stand out. What we come away with is a shared sense of the human condition: rather than feeling set apart, we feel connected." Apparently, in 1988, MOMA's curators didn't feel connected to AIDS.

AIDS Quarterly with an optimistic note about treatment options: "So, for a change, at least all the news about AIDS is not all bad—in part because we have the financial resources in America, and also because there has been enormous pressure to mobilize those resources," he neglected to note just who it was who had been exerting that pressure.

Probably the most widely seen image of the 1987 March was the AIDS Memorial Quilt that was spread out over several blocks on the Washington Mall. Begun in San Francisco in 1985 by activist Cleve Jones, two years later the Names Project AIDS Memorial Quilt had grown to include thousands of three-by-six-foot panels. The Memorial Quilt offered a symbol of loss and mourning and was also an effective organizing tool, as local Names Project groups sprang up around the country, and portions of the quilt were exhibited in gymnasiums, armories, churches, and meeting halls to raise awareness and funds to fight AIDS. In 1990, *Common Threads: Stories from the Quilt*, a film by Rob Epstein that told the stories of several people with AIDS, won an Oscar for best documentary. In 1992, when the AIDS Memorial Quilt returned to Washington and was shown in its entirety, 22,000 panels covered more than fifteen acres.

Journalism's Closet Opens

When composer Aaron Copland died in December 1990, at the age of 90, the *New York Times* devoted almost a full page to his obituary. It is standard practice in such lengthy treatments to include extensive details about the person's private life. But this country's "newspaper of record" disposed of the great man's private life by tossing in, between commas, only three words: "a lifelong bachelor."

The obituary was written by senior *Times* critic John Rockwell, who also wrote a lengthy article on Copland as "the central figure in . . . American composition." Writing in the elaborate code that is part of the etiquette of "inning" (as opposed to "outing" the composer), Rockwell ventured to suggest that Copland's choice "to veil his private life in discretion" might have had consequences for his music as well. "One can regret that the decorous inhibition of his private life infused his public creativity."

The press was only slightly more honest in discussing the life of Leonard Bernstein, who died just a few months before Copland, but by then Bernstein's homosexuality had been written about in at least one "unauthorized" biography. Similar "discretion" was exercised by the press in writing obituaries for longtime civil rights leader Bayard Rustin (whose homosexuality had been used, behind the scenes, in an attempt to derail the 1963 March on Washington, which he coordinated), writer James Baldwin, and many other prominent figures who died outside the closet.

With the advent of AIDS it became more difficult to maintain the practice of denial about homosexuality, as more and more prominent men fell ill and died. But the media often cooperated in turning celebrity coffins into permanent closets. Despite the unprecedented publicity surrounding

Rock Hudson's involuntary coming out as the world's most famous person with AIDS, other famous "bachelors" preferred to die of other causes. Entertainer Liberace and fashion designers Perry Ellis and Halston were only the tip of an iceberg safely submerged by obituary policies. As sociologist Peter Nardi found, it is customary for many newspapers not to report any male lovers as survivors. When they *are* mentioned, they are typically referred to in the concealing language of "longtime companion." Not only is the stigma removed from the cause of death, but so is the stigma of a gay identity.

In 1986, when AIDS had claimed the lives of over eleven thousand Americans, the *Columbia Journalism Review* noted that the *New York Times* had cited AIDS as a cause of death in only a handful of obits. Similar patterns were found in most other large and small newspapers. The lone exception at that time was the *San Francisco Chronicle*, whose openly gay reporter Randy Shilts noted, "We had been running all these stories trying to remove the stigma from AIDS, and I think we all saw that not printing it in obituaries would utterly contradict our policy as a news organization."

Part of the reason for this posthumous euphemizing lies in the routines of newspaper obituary preparation. Most often it is the families of those who have died of AIDS who try to hide the true cause of death. In writing an obituary, reporters must call the deceased person's family to verify the cause of the death. Often forced to confront grieving parents, reporters say they usually take explanations at face value, even if their instincts tell them they are not getting the truth. When Tommy Lasorda Jr., a 33-year-old gay artist who was the son of Los Angeles Dodgers manager Tommy Lasorda, died of AIDS in 1991, the media reported that he died of pneumonia and severe dehydration.

By May 1992, when television actor Robert Reed died, his family was unable to keep the secret for long that AIDS contributed to the death of the *Brady Bunch*'s dad, or to suppress the related fact of his homosexuality. The changes that had begun to take place in media practice over the decade of the AIDS epidemic can best be seen in the response of openly gay *New York Times* editor, Jeffrey Schmalz: "It's important that people know that someone like this died of AIDS." Schmalz, who suspected Reed had died of AIDS, said he was angry when he saw that his own newspaper's obituary writer had accepted the family's story apparently without question. "An obituary is a news article; it's not an article written to please the survivors; it's not written for any other reason than to tell the truth."

By the early 1990s it was commonplace for newspapers, including the *Times*, to include mention of a "companion" among the survivors listed in obituaries for lesbian and gay people.[1] But burying is one thing, marrying is yet another.

In 1989 the *Brattleboro (Vt.) Reformer* broke a journalistic barrier by beginning to accept and publish notices of lesbian and gay "weddings"—commitment ceremonies conducted by members of the clergy or by couples wishing to commemorate their relationship. In the summer of 1992 the *Austin (Tex.) American-Statesman* printed commitment service announcements of two lesbian couples, complete with photographs, in its wedding section. All hell broke loose. A local conservative radio host held a press conference and tore up the paper saying, "This is an outright frontal attack on the most holy institution—the institution of marriage." The paper's publisher replied, "The times they are a-changing. Gays and lesbians are part of society; they are certainly part of the diversity of Austin." The paper maintained its policy, making it one of only about a dozen mainstream papers in the United States, at the time, that printed lesbian and gay wedding announcements. On January 24, 1993, the *Salina (Kan.) Journal* ran an announcement of the wedding of two gay men by a local minister; they accompanied it with a full page of articles on the couple, and the legal, psychological, and religious ramifications of their action, along with a photograph of the pair standing next to their wedding cake. There was some negative response but also a lot of praise.[2]

The two largest papers to do so were the *Seattle Times* and the *Minneapolis Tribune*, which began the practice after the city enacted a domestic partnership ordinance in 1991. The *El Paso Times*, a member of the Gannett Group, ran a gay wedding announcement on June 26, 1984, and the paper's editor explained in a commentary, "As we produce the *Times*, we strive to be fair and inclusive. . . . On most days we succeed. I strongly believe the *Times* succeeded today. If we erred, it was that we did not respond in a more timely fashion."

In September 1999 the *New York Times* published a story, "Why Is This Wedding Different from All Other Weddings?" in which the writer describes his sister's wedding to another woman, but the paper wouldn't run an

---

[1] Commonplace, but not invariable. When famed actor Sir John Gielgud died at the age of 96, the *Washington Post* ran a lengthy obituary on May 23, 2000, informing readers that Gielgud never learned to drive a car, and that he read trashy novels, but not that he had lived with Martin Hensler for forty years, let alone that he had been the center of a scandal when he was arrested for "soliciting" in the early 1950s.

[2] Seven years later, in June 2000, when the *St. Louis Post-Dispatch* published a photo of two gay men kissing "at their wedding reception after a ceremony at a local church," it received numerous letters, some praising the paper, but more expressing anger and disgust. One reader noted that "God is coming soon. I want to cry over this photograph and the idea of same-sex marriages and homosexuality."

announcement of the wedding. The same month, *Times* editorial writer Brent Staples wrote that "legitimacy for same-sex unions is the heart of the matter. By denying that legitimacy, we declare gay love less valid than heterosexual love and gay people less human. We cut them off from the rituals of family and marriage that bind us together as a culture."

When the State of Vermont instituted same-sex civil unions in July 2000, there were front-page stories across the country. Many Vermont newspaper editors, even at papers that had editorialized against the civil union legislation, said they would run civil union notices. "Of course we would treat them the same," said Annette Sharon, managing editor of the *Manchester (Vt.) Journal.* "If they want to make that announcement to their neighbors, the newspaper is the place for that to happen."

Ten years after Aaron Copland's death, on the eve of a yearlong centenary of his birth, the *New York Times* once again devoted a lengthy article to the man they called America's greatest composer. In contrast to the circumlocutions of his 1990 obituaries, the *Times* noted that, "For a homosexual man coming of age in the America of the 1910's, Copland was remarkably well adjusted."[3]

ALL THE NEWS NOT FIT TO PRINT

The *New York Times* is not just another newspaper. In the words of former *Times* columnist Sydney Schanberg, it is "the newspaper that interprets the establishment to the establishment; that tells the establishment what it is doing and how it should be done." The *Times* sees itself as the leader that other news media follow, and for good reason. The immense power of the *Times* generally has made the paper fairly slow to notice or respond to changes in society, as the paper seems to feel it has a responsibility to serve as a brake rather than a locomotive. At least this was the case in the 1960s as gay people began to become more visible in American society. The *Times*'s well-

---

[3] By this point, of course, the musical closet was a lot emptier than it had been earlier in the decade. In 1994 the *New York Times* published an extended article by musicologist K. Robert Schwarz that asked, "What effect might sexual orientation have on the music a composer creates?" In addressing this question Schwartz listed, or mentioned in passing, a "virtual pantheon of [American] gay composers," including Copland along with Samuel Barber, Leonard Bernstein, Mark Blitzstein, John Cage, John Corigliano, Henry Cowell, David Del Tredici, David Diamond, Lou Harrison, Cole Porter, Ned Rorem, and Virgil Thomson. The article provoked Copland's cousin, Rodney Clurman, to write indignantly, "Who cares [about the sexuality of Copland and other American composers]? Does that make Aaron and the others less good musicians? I grew up with Aaron. His sexuality was never discussed" (*NYT*, 7/31/94:H5).

known motto is "All the News That's Fit to Print" and for a long time it was clear that gay people's stories were unfit.

The news media are well known for not having clearly stated rules of procedure but rather for relying on an instinct known as "news judgment"— knowing what is and is not a "story," whether a story deserves front-page or back-page placement, and how a story should be presented. In fact, of course, there are rules. Some are written down in the guidelines that most media organizations maintain, but the most important rules are those learned by editors and reporters by observing what happens when someone breaks one. Such critical incidents provide everyone in a news organization with dramatic evidence that an unwritten rule exists and must be observed, and it was in this way that editors and reporters at the *New York Times* learned that the topic of homosexuality was not popular with the higher-ups. Two critical incidents in particular left long shadows on the *Times* newsroom.

In January 1966, three years after the landmark front-page article headlined "Growth of Overt Homosexuality in City Provokes Wide Concern," the *Times*'s theater critic Stanley Kauffmann wrote an article for the front page of the Sunday "Culture" section on "Homosexual Drama and Its Disguises" that decried the presence of disguised homosexuality in the theater. Referring in thinly veiled terms to "three of the most successful American playwrights of the last twenty years [who] are (reputed) to be homosexual"—most readers knew he was writing about Tennessee Williams, Edward Albee, and William Inge—Kauffmann said that he, "like many others," was "weary of disguised homosexual influence."

Kauffmann's article drew a barrage of response, both praise and criticism, and he followed it with a second piece two weeks later, under the bold headline, "On the Acceptability of the Homosexual."[4] However, by far the most influential response came from inside the *Times*'s own family. Iphigene Sulzberger was in her mid-70s in 1966, but as chair of the paper's board of directors and mother of publisher Arthur "Punch" Sulzberger, she wielded considerable power. Iphigene Sulzberger's tastes and preferences had long been a factor in steering the paper toward, or away from, certain topics or styles. She is credited by many for the *Times*'s steadfast refusal to run comic strips, and she made no secret of her unease with the newly "liberated" attitudes toward sexuality that characterized the 1960s. When she saw the

---

[4] In his second article, Kauffman expanded on his earlier point: "The homosexual dramatist ought to have the same freedom that the heterosexual has. While we deny him that freedom, we have no grounds for complaint when he uses disguises in order to write." This is, among other things, the presumption behind the oft-repeated claim that Albee's *Who's Afraid of Virginia Woolf?* is really about two gay couples—a claim Albee vociferously and convincingly denies.

Kauffmann article she wrote a note to her son that began, "I thought that you agreed with me that while homosexuality, like prostitution and social diseases, was now legitimate news, it should not be played on the front page of a section . . . . Why not put the article on an inside page with a headline not saying 'acceptability of the homosexuals'? Haven't we enough troubles with the young without giving them this encouragement?" The publisher's response to the note from his mother was swift and unambiguous. Executive editor Turner Catledge was summoned and told that the article was a mistake, and Catledge obediently wrote to Mrs. Sulzberger, apologizing for the breach: "I must say that I do not disagree with your point."

Mrs. Sulzberger's point was not lost on the rest of the paper's editors and writers, either, and the lesson they learned in 1966 was still in force when the *Times* decided to pay little attention to the Stonewall riots and the subsequent emergence of the lesbian and gay liberation movement.[5] However, there were limits to the paper's ability to ignore what was happening around it, and there were moments, such as the 1971 *New York Times Magazine* article by Merle Miller, when the *Times* actually seemed to be moving with the times.[6]

---

[5] *New York Times* reporter Albin Krebs later described the night of the Stonewall riots in the *Times* newsroom to Edward Alwood. Krebs recalled the night editor's disinclination to devote serious attention to the story, and continued, "I remember I very much wanted to say something, but at that time you didn't say anything if you wanted to keep your job. I don't think they would have fired me over it, but anyone who was 'suspect' would be marooned to the Family Style section, the women's news page, or to Culture Gulch—the arts section—places where people couldn't cause trouble." Of course, it was precisely in Culture Gulch that Stanley Kauffman had caused the trouble that clarified the unwritten rules for everyone. Albin Krebs himself wrote an article on the 1973 zap of ABC by the Gay Activists Alliance (GAA) in response to an offensive *Marcus Welby, M.D.* episode, and the headline read: "'Welby' Is Scored by Gay Activists"—one of the rare times the term gay slipped past the editorial watchdogs (*NYT*, 2/17/73).

[6] Articles like Miller's were more the exception than the rule, however. Shortly after his article appeared, two articles by *Times* "health reporter" Jane Brody promoted the views of reactionary psychiatrists like Lawrence Hatterer, who was quoted as tracing the supposed rise in homosexuality to pornography and the "growing public tolerance of homosexuality, which may make some men feel, 'Maybe it's easier, and why not?'" The headline of Brody's second article seems to have catapulted it onto the front page: "More Homosexuals Aided to Become Heterosexual." The article begins with a famous line from *Boys in the Band* ("You are a sad and pathetic man. . . . You're a homosexual and you don't want to be") and goes on to bring the Good News from the shrinks, describing psychiatric conversion methods, ranging from *Playboy* nudes to electric shock. As late as 1996, Brody defended these articles to journalist Charles Kaiser, despite their lack of balancing perspectives from happy homosexuals or psychiatrists with differing viewpoints. Although these articles appeared only three years before the American Psychiatric Association removed homosexuality from its list of mental illnesses, Brody still views them as "ahead of their time."

Then, in 1975, came another critical incident. The Sunday travel section ran an article that was certainly unusual for the *New York Times*. Not only was the article open about sexuality in a fashion that was not typical of the *Times*—the paper did not print the word *penis* until 1976, when it appeared in a "Personal Health" column about impotence—but the sexuality it was open about was homosexuality. The article was called "The All-Gay Cruise: Prejudice and Pride," by a freelancer named Cliff Jahr, and it described a week-long ocean cruise taken by three hundred gay men and lesbians. The article was hip and sexy in a most un-*Times*-like fashion—Jahr quotes one man boasting, "I've met three Mister Rights before lunch"—it was also imbued with an awareness of the gay experience, noting that the cruise gave the passengers a respite from the oppression of closeted lives.

There is no record of whether Iphigene Sulzberger read the Sunday travel piece, but her son the publisher did, and he was furious. According to some accounts, travel section editor Robert Stock and Sunday editor Max Frankel were nearly fired over the incident. Another person who was angered by the piece was managing editor Abe Rosenthal, whose reign as executive editor was to last from 1977 to 1986. Rosenthal was the metropolitan editor who assigned Robert Doty to prepare the paper's first front-page story on homosexuality back in 1963—motivated, apparently, by his surprise, upon returning to New York from nine years abroad, at seeing visibly gay men on the streets of Manhattan. As Rosenthal ascended to the top of the *Times* ladder, his prejudices defined the unspoken but nevertheless unmistakable rules for deciding what was fit to print. As journalist and writer Charles Kaiser, who worked at the *Times* under Rosenthal, put it, "Everyone below Rosenthal spent all of their time trying to figure out what to do to cater to his prejudices. One of these widely perceived prejudices was Abe's homophobia. So editors throughout the paper would keep stories concerning gays out of the paper."

One such story happened in November 1980, when a homophobic gunman went on a rampage in Greenwich Village, killing two gay men and wounding seven others with machine-gun fire. The story was front-page news in the *Post* and the *Daily News* but not in the *New York Times*. The metropolitan editor knew Rosenthal's feelings about gays and knew, as he later said, that "you had to be careful with the subject." At the *New York Post* the shootings had a dramatically different impact: they moved a longtime *Post* reporter to become the first reporter on a mainstream newspaper to come out on the job. Joe Nicholson went to the metropolitan editor and asked, "Would you be interested in me writing my reaction as a gay man?" The editor was startled, stammering "You're letting us know a new dimension of yourself," but quickly became enthusiastic, urging Nicholson to "Bleed a bit. And don't hesitate to say, 'I work in a city room with a lot of tough guys and a nasty city editor.'" Nicholson's article was not printed—the editors decided it was more of an opinion piece than a news story—but the result was that the *Post* now had an openly gay reporter. Still, one swallow does not a summer make, as Nicholson was to realize with sadness as he stood in the city room five years later and watched seven hundred lesbians and gay men demonstrating against the newspaper's homophobic AIDS coverage.

Abe Rosenthal's homophobia was felt at the *Times* in two ways: by ensuring that lesbian and gay reporters stayed firmly in the closet, and by making sure that the word *gay* was not used in the paper to describe gay people.[7] The furor over the travel section article was the critical incident inscribed in the paper's unwritten rule book. As *Times* editor Jeffrey Schmalz later recalled, "There was a lot of shouting about it. Abe thought it was a mistake and that we never should have done it. And we'd used the word *gay*. He said we could never use that word again." And, for the most part, they didn't. The word crept into news stories and headlines from time to time, but the paper's official policy ruled the word *gay* out of order, while at the same time the gay liberation movement was exploding all around it.[8] Rosenthal was not limited in his biases to antigay prejudice—he also refused to allow the word *Ms.* to be used until 1986—but his homophobia proved tragic when the AIDS crisis erupted on his watch.

As the AIDS epidemic began to emerge, the silence of the media in gen-

[7] The *Times* was not alone in its resistance to the word *gay*. The editor of the *Toronto Star* wrote to the Ontario Press Council in 1980 that "we do not admit gay as a description of homosexuals. To do so is to use the wrong word where the right word exists. . . . It may be that in time, gay will have lost its historic meaning and acquired another. If that happens, the language will be poorer. We do not intend to assist in its impoverishment." Other papers, however, were more accommodating, if equally disapproving, as evidenced by a 1978 memo from the style editor of the *Toronto Globe and Mail*: "The style guide [entry] dealing with the words gay and homosexual must yield to reality. A once precise word has been bastardized beyond recall and stolen. We yield to progress, if that's what it is, and relax the ban on gay, particularly in feature and entertainment stories."

[8] Rosenthal was certainly not alone in his aversion to the word *gay*. Complaints about the word became a minor journalistic genre by the 1980s. For example, in 1982 an Illinois state senator, "Name Withheld on Request," wrote "Dear Abby" that "it galls me that sexual deviates are called 'gays.' . . . Wouldn't you join me in an effort to retrieve the word 'gay' from ignominy." "Dear Abby" gave him a history lesson, pointing out that the term *gay* had been used for homosexuals longer than the term *homosexual*, which was coined in 1869. As recently as 1993, National Public Radio commentator Daniel Schorr lamented "words that become endangered species because of the way people misuse them. I have long mourned the loss of 'gay,' and the time one would quote, 'When our hearts were young and gay' without getting involved in a Pentagon battle."

eral, and the *New York Times* in particular, contributed to the magnitude of the unfolding tragedy. Although the death toll mounted in the early 1980s, the *Times* maintained a disdainful distance. As gay journalist Michelangelo Signorile put it, "Rosenthal, who attacks anti-Semitism in the media, never realized that the way he was treating the AIDS epidemic wasn't much different from the way that news organizations treated the Holocaust early on."

Ironically, the media blackout that broke the patience of many gay activists was not the report of a medical breakthrough but a fund-raiser. In April 1983 the Gay Men's Health Crisis arranged a circus benefit that sold out Madison Square Garden, filling it with 18,000 lesbians, gay men, and others. The arena was not only jam-packed; it was star-studded: Leonard Bernstein led the "Star Spangled Banner." The event was covered by television and the newspapers, but not the *New York Times*.

A group of lesbian and gay activists wrote to the publisher demanding a meeting and were offered an "off the record" meeting with a *Times* vice president. The meeting was not successful in obtaining changes in policy but it did result in a second meeting, this time with Executive Editor Abe Rosenthal. Rosenthal admitted that not covering the circus benefit had been a mistake, and even agreed that the paper should do more to cover AIDS. But he was unwilling to budge on the use of the word *gay* or to move very far in any direction toward meeting the demands of the lesbian and gay community. Yet even this small opening permitted some fresh air to penetrate the *Times*'s closeted atmosphere, and several people from the paper called to thank the activists for their efforts. The real changes at the *Times* did not come until there was a changing of the guard on 43rd Street.

THE GRAY LADY GOES GAY

In the years between 1986 and 1992 a series of changes took place that transformed the Gray Lady of 43rd Street, as the *New York Times* has long been called in the trade. The first of these changes may have been the most dramatic for most of the *Times* writers and editors. As journalist Sam Anson later put it, "The relief that swept through the newsroom the morning of October 16, 1986, was palpable, almost giddy." Abe Rosenthal had reached the mandatory retirement age of 65 and was replaced as executive editor by Max Frankel. Rosenthal's reign was described by many as a period of paranoia and terror at the *Times*—one reporter said, "He was like the Czar; people would get gulaged at the drop of a hat." But if the feeling of relief was general, it was especially felt by lesbian and gay employees. Max Frankel lost little time in letting people know that times had indeed changed, and that included the paper's attitude toward gay people and stories affecting them.

One of the first areas in which Frankel's piloting of the *Times* became apparent was in the coverage of AIDS. Within a few months of his taking over, the paper published its first serious articles on the impact of AIDS on New York—a four-part series in which each installment began on the front page. Within a year a media writer for the *Los Angeles Times* quoted medical authorities and other journalists as rating the *Times*'s AIDS coverage as some of the best then appearing anywhere.

In the summer of 1987 Frankel made a second major change by authorizing a memo from the managing editor: "Starting immediately, we will accept the word 'gay' as an adjective meaning homosexual, in references to social or cultural patterns and political issues." According to a former *Times* staffer, Frankel sent a memo to publisher Sulzberger: "Punch, you're going to have to swallow hard on this one: We're going to start using the word *gay*." Frankel was aware of the impact this change would have on the morale of the lesbian and gay employees at the paper "I knew they'd had a hard time, and I knew they weren't comfortable identifying themselves as gay"—but he may not have been aware of the extent to which the change signaled the start of a new era in the *Times*'s coverage of gay issues.[9]

The new realities at the *Times* were dramatized by two critical incidents that occurred within a few years of Frankel's policy changes. In January 1989 Urvashi Vaid, then media director of the National Gay and Lesbian Task Force, met with *Times* reporter Gina Kolata and urged her to write a story about the lesbian "baby boom" around the country. The story that Kolata submitted to the editors, after speaking with many parents, legal advocates, and experts, was not the story that appeared on January 30. Without notifying Kolata, editors had added a paragraph which contained negative and biased statements about lesbians and the children they raised. The story was

[9] Frankel may have heartened lesbian and gay *Times* staffers, but Joseph Epstein wasn't impressed. Epstein, who earned his place in gay history with his 1970 *Harper's* homophobic classic (which provoked a zap by the GAA), later became editor of the *American Scholar*. In the late 1980s philosophers Edward Stein and Paul Bloom submitted a review of a work on homosexuality to the *American Scholar* and found themselves locked in a battle with Epstein over their use of the words "lesbian" and "gay," which he wished to replace with "female homosexual" and "homosexual." When told that even the *New York Times* used lesbian and gay, Epstein replied, "I am sure that you will understand that we do not look to the *New York Times* for leadership in this, or indeed any other matter." As their dialogue continued, Epstein opined that "in these febrile and volatile times, [the word *gay*] may not be around that long," and cited the style of the London *Times* as his preferred model. This led Stein to wonder why the *American Scholar* would scorn the *New York Times* in favor of the London *Times*.

also rearranged to give prominence to the antigay views of a sociologist at a Catholic college, and misquoted a psychiatrist. The most offensive paragraph in the story, not written by Kolata, read: "Some clinicians, however, speculate that in the long term, girls might have difficulty in intimate relationships with men, and boys might be uncomfortable with their roles as males. If lesbian parents are openly hostile toward men, these difficulties could be worsened."

The article, sent out through the *Times*'s wire service to hundreds of newspapers around the United States and abroad, set off a storm of protest, led by Vaid at NGLTF, along with the ACLU's Gay and Lesbian Rights Project and GLAAD (Gay and Lesbian Alliance Against Defamation). The *Times*'s response to the protests, while insufficient to correct the damage done by the article, nevertheless was an unprecedented admission by the paper. On February 3, four days after the original article, a small box at the bottom of page eight labeled "Editors' Note" acknowledged the errors and the fact that "these comments were added to the article during editing" and "did not fairly reflect a spectrum of views."

On an afternoon in 1991 during the Persian Gulf War, foreign news editor Barnard Gwertzman set off an explosion of his own during the regular afternoon "page one" editorial meeting. Describing a story he received about the elaborate display of multicolored tents of the U.S. troops stationed in the desert, he said, laughing, "I told the reporter to change it because he made the soldiers look like a bunch of faggots." According to some present, a silence fell over the room before the meeting continued. After the meeting several gay people who had been present told Gwertzman of their objections to his remark (their openness was itself a sign of the changes at the paper). But the more important change was the response by Frankel and managing editor Joseph Lelyveld, who took Gwertzman aside and bawled him out. In a 1992 interview with Charles Kaiser, Frankel acknowledged that it might have been best to respond to the comment on the spot; still, the event left a clear imprint on the paper's collective consciousness.

The replacement of Rosenthal by Frankel was only one of two personnel changes that signaled a seismic shift at the *Times*. In 1990 the matriarch of the Sulzberger clan, Iphigene, died at 97, removing a force for conservatism that had been palpable at the paper for decades. Much more important, however, was the ascension of her grandson, Arthur Sulzberger Jr., to the role of publisher in January 1992.

Even before he took over the helm of the family paper, Arthur Jr. had begun to make his presence felt as a harbinger of a generational shift at the *Times*. After several years at the Washington bureau, Sulzberger Jr. joined the metropolitan staff in New York at age 28, as an assignment editor, part of the process of learning the ropes at the ship he was destined to captain. Working under Rosenthal he soon recognized the impact of the executive editor's tyrannical style, and he was sensitive to the anxieties suffered by the lesbian and gay employees. A child of the sixties, who grew up during the civil rights and antiwar struggles of that decade, Sulzberger junior was particularly sensitive to what he referred to as "diversity," and for him that included gay people. Deciding to explore the problems facing gays at the *Times*, he began to approach the journalists he knew to be gay, inviting them to lunch. He started with Jeffrey Schmalz, with whom he shared a desk ("He took me to lunch and asked, 'So when are you going to tell me that you're gay?'"). As Sulzberger described the lunches, "I was just tired of having this code of silence. . . . I didn't recognize the degree of pressure they were under as individuals and, therefore, didn't recognize the degree of relief this might hold. I knew there was pressure, I knew it was an unnecessary pressure. But I didn't realize that they, by living with it day by day, were so affected by it."

Even Sulzberger's openness and encouragement, however, could not change the atmosphere at the *Times* in the early 1980s; but when Frankel took over as executive editor, Sulzberger began to exercise more influence. Frankel later told Charles Kaiser that his initial discussions about using the word *gay* had been with Sulzberger. When Sulzberger junior replaced his father in 1992, he began putting his ideas into practice.

The new publisher's devotion to diversity was not merely a matter of principle; it was also a matter of shrewd business sense. The *Times* is facing a shrinking readership among the straight, white, middle-aged, upper-middle-class and increasingly suburban population that is less interested in a metropolitan paper. Part of the paper's response has been to appeal to younger readers, and gay and lesbian readers (a group much less likely to flee to the suburbs) are prominent among those it is trying to reach. Under the new publisher's reign, and with the engagement of executive editors Max Frankel and then Joseph Lelyveld, the *Times* began to pay more serious and more continuing attention to issues and events of concern to lesbian and gay people, as well as to African Americans and other groups previously ill-attended by the paper (it was around this time that an African American, Gerald Boyd, was brought on board as metropolitan editor).

In 1992 Robert Bray, then communications director for NGLTF, articulated an important demand: "I don't want more articles about gays specifically. I'd rather see our visibility permeate the paper at all levels. I want to see the gay rodeo on the Sports pages. I want to see gays included in the stories about Valentine's Day." In fact, what Bray wanted is happening at the *New York Times* and at many other big city newspapers. Some (almost random) examples from the *Times* can illustrate the astounding changes wrought in the early 90s:

April 6, 1991: an article about the dramatic shifts in gay activism runs under the headline, "'Gay' Fades as Militants Pick 'Queer.'" The article by Alessandra Stanley is lengthy, well-researched, and quite on target.

May 24, 1991: Robert Lipsyte's column in the Sports section laments the reality that "Gay Bias Moves Off the Sidelines," lambasting professional and college sports for their homophobia.

July 31, 1991: the "About New York" column is devoted to a story about lesbians and gays organizing in Queens, in response to the killing of a gay man.

November 29, 1992: a feature on a Washington establishment that is "one part bookstore, one part restaurant and perhaps one part singles bar" includes several vignettes, including one of two young men who might be interested in each other. The manager is quoted, "This is definitely a pickup spot—if you're gay, straight, whatever, this is the place."

November 28, 1993: the Sunday "Arts & Leisure" column by Herbert Muschamp focuses on a new building of the Metropolitan Community Church. "A new church in Washington for lesbians and gay men reflects the congregation's belief in the value of being visibly who you are," was the call-out quote in bold letters.

December 26, 1993: the "Ideas and Trends" column of the Sunday News and Review section is titled "Bias Against Gay People: Hatred of a Special Kind." The article quotes representatives of two major lesbian and gay rights organizations; a spokesperson for the Gay Men's Health Crisis; John DeCecco, a gay psychologist and editor of the *Journal of Homosexuality*; a prominent lesbian historian; and the leader of a gay church in Dallas. There are references to the fact that "many straight Americans still feel queasy about homosexuality," but writer Natalie Angier didn't feel the need—or was not required—to elicit hostile statements from right-wing figures.

The "About Men" and "Hers" columns of the Sunday *Times Magazine* feature several notable columns: in November 1992 journalist and author William MacLeish writes about coming to terms with his daughter's lesbianism; in October 1993 Ellen Graf writes about small moments of coming out, such as cashing a check at the local super-market with her and her lover's names on it; in January 1994 author David Masiello writes about his difficulties in coming out to his eld-erly father.

Although the *Times* still declines to run wedding announcements for lesbian or gay couples, the daily "Chronicle" column—the *Times*'s genteel version of a gossip column—has included accounts of gay commitment ceremonies and weddings. On February 10, 1994, the "Chronicle" column reported the birth of a daughter to "Gerri Wells and Brigitte Weil [who] met on the barricades of ACT UP, the AIDS protest group. . . . 'This is the second generation of ACT UP,' said Ms. Wells, 39, a building contractor, who gave birth to the child, conceived by artificial insemination through an anonymous donor."

April 17, 1994: "Shared Lives Won't Accept Eternity Apart" tells about a gay couple who were fighting for the right to a family burial plot in their Long Island town.

May 22, 1994: "Two White Sport Coats, Two Pink Carnations: One Couple for a Prom" tells of the special citywide lesbian and gay prom sponsored by the Los Angeles school district, but paid for by private donations. The article includes contextual information as well: "There are roughly two million gay and lesbian adolescents in the United States, a recent Harris poll found. They have high suicide rates, and alcohol and drug abuse are common, with the problem most acute in areas isolated from support services like those found in Los Angeles."

In the spirit of Robert Bray's wish for a gay Valentine story, in a Janu-ary 1999 article on "The Role E-Mail Can Play in Matters of the Heart," one of the vignettes about e-romance described a gay rela-tionship: "Michael Kaminer, 32, president of a public relations firm in New York, has broken up via e-mail but said he regretted it. . . . 'I put together a very terse e-mail and sent it over to him,' he said."

This is the journalistic equivalent of "mainstreaming," and it signifies a major shift in societal definitions. On the one hand, the media are paying more attention to issues of primary concern to gay people, such as the ongo-ing struggle to live one's life unburdened by special discrimination. On the other hand, gay people are becoming a part of the landscape that does not require special justification to be included in news stories that do not directly concern homosexuality. To be sure, such inclusions tend to be in "lifestyle" or "culture" stories rather than in "hard" news. By now it is unremarkable to find the homes of gay (rarely lesbian) couples featured in the *Times*'s "Home" section, and coverage of the arts is more forthcoming about the lives of artists, writers, and performers. In contrast, when Charles Kaiser interviewed Frankel in 1992 for the gay weekly *NYQ*, he rattled off a list of "foreign news" stories about gay-related developments that were not covered in the *Times*—the explosion of a post-1989 gay movement in Eastern Europe, the repeal of Israel's sodomy law, the execution of gay men in Iran, the passage of the antigay Clause 28 by Margaret Thatcher's government—despite having been brought to the foreign editor's attention by GLAAD. Kaiser reports GLAAD's view that the lack of attention to such stories is due to the reporters who end up as foreign correspondents. Frankel disagrees, but the fact remains that the changes in coverage have occurred selectively in terms of which news domains have been affected. According to *Times* editor Jeffrey Schmalz, this factor came into play in 1993 when the "gays in the military" story was handled by the "Pentagon beat" reporters, who predictably saw things from the military's perspective.

The editorial pages of the *Times* have become one of the gay-friendliest locations in American media, running strongly worded editorials in favor of full equality for lesbian and gay people. The op-ed page runs frequent pieces by lesbian and gay writers, and several regular columnists, Frank Rich in particular, have written eloquently in support of lesbian and gay concerns.

Quite possibly, the moment that most dramatically marked the gaying of the Gray Lady was the column of November 15, 1991, by former editor Abe Rosenthal, titled "Hidden Harassment." The column, inspired by Anita Hill's accusations against Clarence Thomas and the press furor over Magic Johnson's announcement of his HIV status, expresses wonder that the country was unaware of sexual harassment or the dangers of AIDS. Gay people and AIDS activists all over the country must have choked on their morning coffee as they read Rosenthal's words: "Harassment and assault of gays and lesbians is an illness in our society. What will it take to recognize it and try to treat it by legal medicine?"

When even Abe Rosenthal was undergoing a late conversion, it should come as no surprise that the *Times*'s "lavender enlightenment" (as gay journalist Michelangelo Signorile labeled it) would draw fire from the right. Writing in the very conservative *American Spectator* in 1993, former *Times* critic John Corry bemoaned the "new moral canon" that defines homosexuality as "widespread, healthy and even endearing." Corry's ire is particularly aimed at "America's most prestigious newspaper," which, "unfortunately . . . has embraced the new canon. Indeed, it seems to want to expand it. The aggressively trendy—and increasingly incomprehensible—Sunday *Styles* section appears determined to legitimize all aberrant lifestyles, while the editorial page sees homophobia, sexism, or racism at the root of most problems. . . . There are days when the *Times* seems to be edited by ACT UP and Larry Kramer." Seemingly echoing the same point, but from a different perspective, the *Times*'s national political correspondent, Richard Berke, was quoted by the conservative *Washington Times* on July 28, 2000, as telling the National Lesbian and Gay Journalists Association that "the pro-homosexual metamorphosis at the *New York Times* has advanced so far that on any given day, three-quarters of the people who decide what goes on the front page are 'not-so-closeted' homosexuals."

COMING OUT IN THE NEWSROOM

In 1990 two veteran news editors came out and, although the circumstances were vastly different, each had a profound impact on American journalism. On December 21, Jeffrey Schmalz was at his desk in the *New York Times* newsroom when he realized that a vision problem he'd been experiencing was getting much worse. Scared that he might be having a stroke, he stood up, took a few steps, and collapsed on the floor in the grip of a grand mal seizure. "As I was waking up," Schmalz later recalled, "a crowd was gathered around me, and Max [Frankel] was holding my hand." Although Schmalz had discussed his gayness at that memorable lunch with Arthur Sulzberger Jr. years before, most of his colleagues were unaware of his sexuality and no one, including Schmalz himself, realized that he had AIDS. Schmalz's coming out simultaneously as gay and as a person with AIDS gave the *Times* something it had never had before: a highly placed and well-respected editor who could—now—speak with personal authority on two topics the paper was trying to come to terms with. In an unprecedented move the editors agreed to assign Schmalz to write stories about AIDS and about the issue of gays in the 1990 political season.

Schmalz's assignment evoked a long-standing question in journalism about who should cover which issues. In a profession dominated by straight white males, it is well known that editors worry about whether the nonwhite, nonmale, and/or nonstraight journalist can be "objective" in writing about people who share their distinctive attributes. Presumably, conventional wisdom implies, straight white men are capable of objectivity in all circumstances. Because Schmalz's proposal came from a longtime, trusted reporter and editor, the *Times* was taking a step long advocated by lesbian and gay activists and resisted by the paper: it was creating a "gay beat" and assigning an openly gay reporter to it. "I think the feeling was that if you say I can't write about AIDS, then you have to say that blacks can't write about blacks, that Jews can't write about Israel," Schmalz said.

In the two years that remained before Schmalz died, in November 1993, he wrote many articles for the *Times* about AIDS and politics. In October 1992 he wrote a cover story for the *New York Times Magazine* that exemplified the intersections of these topics, focusing on the roles played by lesbians and gay men in the presidential election campaign. His last article, also published in the magazine, three weeks after his death, was a mixture of cynicism and despair about the failure of the Clinton administration to fulfill its promises regarding AIDS policies. When Schmalz died he was eulogized in the *Times* by Frankel in terms that revealed an awareness of the challenge Schmalz represented to the ideology of journalistic objectivity: "The healthy Jeff was an outstanding correspondent and editor. . . . Jeff in illness plumbed the depth of his experience and applied it brilliantly to his coverage of the plague, producing a remarkable bequest to American journalism." A final ironic footnote to the story was that Schmalz's obituary was written by Richard Meislin, a longtime *Times* reporter who had been pushed off the paper's fast track when Abe Rosenthal discovered that he was gay. In 1994 the *Times* appointed veteran David Dunlop—the second gay reporter whom Sulzberger had invited, over lunch, to come out—to what was now explicitly defined as the gay beat.

The second dramatic journalistic coming out in the 1990s happened at the April meeting of the American Society of Newspaper Editors (ASNE). Leroy Aarons, executive editor of the *Oakland Tribune*, had spearheaded a survey of newspapers across the country to gauge tolerance of gays in the newsrooms as well as coverage of lesbian and gay issues. The findings were discouraging. While most papers tolerated gay employees in nonnews departments such as the arts, they reported rampant homophobia and few efforts to change by editors or management. Most of the 205 lesbian and gay journalists responding felt isolated and vulnerable. When Aarons spoke at the ASNE meeting to report the results of the survey, he went farther than anyone expected: he came out as a gay man.

When Aarons came out of the newsroom closet he inspired hundreds of journalists to follow him, and his speech sowed the seeds of what soon became the National Lesbian and Gay Journalists Association (NLGJA). Aarons retired from the *Oakland Tribune* to devote himself to building NLGJA and spent the following year as a kind of Johnny Appleseed of gay journalism, traveling around the country speaking to lesbian and gay jour-

nalists and media activists. By the time the first NLGJA newsletter was pub-
lished in September 1991, there were chapters functioning in Chicago, Los
Angeles, San Francisco, and Washington, D.C., and forming in Boston, New
York, Philadelphia, Seattle, and Texas. Issues of the NLGJA's newsletter,
Alternatives, provided dramatic and emotional reading, printing stories of
coming out experiences by lesbian and gay journalists around the country:

> *Houston Post* columnist Juan Palomo came out in a column discussing
> the murder of a gay man and was told by his editors he couldn't
> come out. When the story was picked up by an alternative paper,
> Palomo was fired, only to be rehired the next week following
> protests from activists.
>
> Gordon Smith, assistant executive editor of the *Providence Journal-
> Bulletin*, felt he was putting thirty-one years of experience on the
> line when he told his boss that he was gay, but in fact the reaction
> was overwhelmingly positive.
>
> Linda Villarosa, senior editor at *Essence* magazine, was out to her col-
> leagues, but she took a giant step further out when she coauthored
> with her mother a first-person conversation about their relationship
> as mother and lesbian daughter.
>
> Loraine Anderson, the 44-year-old city editor of the *Traverse City
> Record Eagle* in Michigan, came out in a March 1992 column under
> the headline, "I've Heard My Last Homophobic Remark," because
> she could no longer sit by silently and say nothing.
>
> In May 1992 the *Detroit News*'s Washington Bureau news editor Deb
> Price suddenly became the most widely read openly gay journalist in
> the world, with an audience upwards of 2 million, when the *Detroit
> News* gave her a regular weekly column devoted to lesbian and gay
> issues. Deb Price's column is syndicated via the Gannett newspaper
> chain and appears in papers around the country as well as in *USA
> Today*.[10] In Philadelphia the *Daily News* began weekly alternating
> columns by lesbian writer Victoria Brownworth and gay writer
> Mubarik Dahir (after several years Dahir moved, and the *Daily News*
> replaced Brownworth with lesbian columnist Debbie Woodell).

---

[10] Price's columns evoked predictable angry letters from readers of the *Detroit News*, and
other papers it appeared in, but relatively few subscription cancellations, and many letters of support. Price received letters from grateful teenagers, and from a 73-year-old retired teacher, who
asked, "Please keep my secret. I do not have the courage to come out of the closet yet." In 1995
Price published a collection of her columns, interspersed with an account of their experiences by
her lover, *Washington Post* editor Joyce Murdoch.

When the New York chapter held its first public forum the panel included *New York Times* managing (later executive) editor Joseph Lelyveld, who began his remarks, "I'm really delighted to be here and to have the opportunity to show solidarity with my gay colleagues at the *Times*, but, more importantly, to deepen my own awareness of your concerns."

At the first NLGJA conference, in San Francisco in June 1992, over 300 members watched *New York Times* publisher Arthur Sulzberger Jr. in a videotaped speech: "We can no longer offer our readers a predominately white, straight, male version of events and say that we are doing our job. As a white, straight male, let me quickly add that I don't think that particular vision is any better or worse than a gay or lesbian vision, a black or Hispanic vision, or any other. But in a world as diverse as ours it is simply not complete and therefore not sufficient."

The second NLGJA conference was held in New York, and the six hundred journalists who attended listened to an opening panel comprising television news stars Tom Brokaw, Robert MacNeil, Dan Rather, and Judy Woodruff. The panel was not only a dramatic demonstration of the legitimacy the media were granting to NLGJA and its issues, but it also put the spotlight on the difference between print and broadcast journalism.

In 1993 NLGJA, together with the Radio and Television News Directors Foundation, conducted a survey of broadcast news directors and of lesbian and gay broadcast journalists. The survey, similar to the 1990 ASNE study, revealed that there is much work to be done before newsrooms are comfortable environments for lesbian and gay journalists and before the news media live up to their responsibilities in covering issues of concern to lesbian and gay people.

The majority of NLGJA's members are print journalists, and there are strikingly few members who are on-air radio or television reporters (somewhat more "behind the camera" broadcast journalists are involved). This pattern doesn't stop at the NLGJA, of course; there are far fewer openly lesbian or gay on-air radio or TV journalists than there are openly gay reporters or columnists. Even that is an overstatement, as the number of openly gay on-air journalists can be counted on the fingers of one hand (one of the very few is Hank Plante of KPIX in San Francisco, who came out as a print journalist before switching to broadcast). Broadcast executives are ambivalent about the prospect of openly gay reporters, although in big cities at least they are aware that this is an inevitable development. CBS News chief Eric Ober, in an interview with Charles Kaiser in the NLGJA newsletter, insisted he would have no difficulty with a correspondent who came out, but this was a hypothetical case. It is not entirely hypothetical, however. In July 1993 Steve Gendel, the chief science and medical correspondent for the CNBC cable channel, became the first gay newsman to come out on national television. At the opening of CNBC's *Real Personal,* he got real personal, telling viewers he was gay before launching a discussion of research indicating that homosexuality has a genetic link: "As you know," he told host Bob Berkowitz, "and as our audience is about to find out, I am a gay man."

Gendel said that he was encouraged in his decision to come out by his bosses at CNBC. "It's my understanding that I'm the first mainstream reporter to do this. As a reporter, I'm a little embarrassed to be the focus of the story. Other than that, I've been surprised at how positive the reaction has been." Gendel said he was also pleasantly surprised by colleagues and behind-the-scenes camera and studio crews. "There are people who I thought would have been indifferent, but they've all come up to me and wanted to talk about it. I'm not trying to make too big a political statement. But if we're going to further our own position in society in any way, then we're going to have to let people know."

When Garret Glaser, entertainment reporter at KNBC-TV in Los Angeles and a member of the NLGJA's board, told his boss he planned to come out on the air, the station said that he would be allowed to declare his sexual orientation on air, but only if he did it during the February or May "sweeps"—one of those periods of intense audience measurement used to set local ad rates. As it happened, however, *Los Angeles Times* TV critic Howard Rosenberg spilled the beans about Glaser in his column, and Glaser then came out on air in December 1994, speaking "as a gay man who has lost many friends to AIDS."

The ranks of openly gay on-air journalists, besides being thin, are also all male. NLGJA member Barbara Raab, an NBC news executive, told journalist Keith Eddings that "the aura of availability" that surrounds women reporters would be shattered if they were known to be lesbian. "There are lesbians on the air, but there are no open lesbians on the air," Raab maintained.

In journalism, as in other professions, AIDS has occasionally provided the impetus for coming out. A CNN vice president, speaking at the 1994 NLJGA conference, said that the only two reporters who had come out at CNN did so after they were diagnosed with AIDS. Tom Cassidy, who anchored a program about business leaders, came out in 1990, three years after being diagnosed and fourteen months before his death at age 41.[11] One of the more

---

[11] Not that AIDS has invariably propelled a journalist toward candor. The 1988 death of Max Robinson, who in 1978 became the first black news anchor on network television, occasioned a flurry of defensive maneuvering. Robinson himself had kept his AIDS-related illness a secret, but he was later reported to have wanted his death to "emphasize the need for AIDS awareness among black people." However, as Phillip Harper argued, the palpable desire on the part of Robinson's friends to distance their late friend from any suspicion of homosexuality worked to the detriment of their attempts to make factual statements about the nature of HIV transmission.

dramatic instances occurred in Boston in fall 1994 when popular right-wing radio talk show personality David Brudnoy came out after he collapsed on the air with AIDS-related pneumonia. Contrary to what he might have expected, given his vehemently expressed right-wing views, Brudnoy's coming out was greeted with expressions of support and sympathy from across the political spectrum. Brudnoy happily told reporters about the positive "response I've gotten from people who are significant conservatives, friends of mine across the land, Bill Buckley of *National Review*, and a variety of other people . . . all responding with warmth and affection" (*CBS This Morning*, 1/10/95). One of the few dissenting perspectives came from GLAAD, which faulted the media for ignoring the contradictions between Brudnoy's political ideology and his sexual orientation: "Brudnoy—a media professional who should know better—is suggesting that public hate is irrelevant; let homophobes rant all they want out loud as long as they say (or at least act like) they 'love' you in private. Because he and William F. Buckley are private 'friends,' for example, Brudnoy excuses Buckley's public homophobia."

Breaking the Code of Silence

According to the *New York Times*, when the National Lesbian and Gay Journalists Association met for its first convention in 1992, "the morality of identifying secretly gay public officials, a practice known as 'outing,' was the question discussed most often." The issue of outing burst onto the journalistic scene in 1990, but the concept—if not the term—arose at the very dawn of modern gay consciousness at the end of the nineteenth century. The idea that homosexuals constitute a "people" set apart from the society in which they live, however invisibly, has led inevitably to the question of what obligations they have to this "community." While outing has been a constant temptation, until recently lesbian and gay journalists, like gay people in general, abided by a social contract they never actually signed but were informed about when they came out into the gay community: we keep each other's secrets. But after nearly ten years and more than a hundred thousand deaths from AIDS, this contract was becoming frayed.

The AIDS Coalition to Unleash Power, or ACT UP, came into being in March 1987 and quickly infused a new burst of militant energy into the AIDS and gay movements. ACT UP combined streetwise activists and newly radicalized middle-class professionals who had been propelled into politics by their experience with the AIDS epidemic. It was a group of men and women, largely lesbian and gay, who believed in doing its homework and in using outrageous media-attracting tactics that successfully dramatized the issues of AIDS research, treatment, and health care.

The journalists who tore up the fraying social contract are members of the ACT UP generation. This is also a generation that has lived its entire life in the age of mass media gossip and infotainment. From *People* magazine to Liz

Smith, from Jay Leno and David Letterman to Oprah and Jerry Springer, from the *National Enquirer* and the *Globe* to the *Philadelphia Inquirer* and the *Boston Globe*, we have become a society drenched in gossip and "news" about celebrities of all sorts. Whether it's the fifteen minutes of fame haphazardly awarded to random individuals catapulted by events onto the public stage, or the perennial allure of Liz Taylor or Madonna on the cover of a magazine, we have come to expect that anyone hit by the media spotlight will share his or her private life with us.

Despite the explosion of lesbian and gay visibility since the late 1960s, the near total absence of openly gay celebrities insures the continuing importance of gossip in the crafting of gay subcultural identity. Insider gay gossip has always focused heavily on the exchange of names of famous people who are secretly gay, just as Jews have told each other with pride about rich and famous people who are, but not generally known to be, Jewish.[1] The denial and erasure of lesbians and gay men from the formal curricula of our schools and from the informal but even more influential curriculum of our mass media leads to the understandable desire to discover and celebrate the contributions of lesbian and gay figures. Just as African American activists and educators have brought out the often obscured achievements of people of color, and just as feminist art historians have uncovered the accomplishments of women artists whose work had been misattributed to men, so too have lesbian and gay scholars assembled lists of famous people who were homosexual.

In such a climate it should not surprise us that some gay journalists became increasingly impatient with the code that bound the media in a conspiracy of silence and deception about the real lives of lesbian and gay celebrities. Not only do the media draw the line of discretion much farther from home when writing about gay people than when writing about nongay figures; they actively engage in obfuscation and collude in outright lies—what some have called "inning." Outing was adopted as a tactic in opposition to the tacit agreement by which gay private lives were granted an exemption from the public's "right to know," thus protecting the closets of the rich and famous and leaving unchallenged the distaste of the media—and the public—for facing the reality of lesbian and gay existence.

---

[1] Ralph Schoenstein recalled his uncle's hobby of "ferreting out which mainstream American celebrities were Jewish, members of the 'tinseled Hebraic underground.'" The studios often played to this interest with niche-targeted messages: John Garfield (whose name was cosmetically altered from Jacob Garfinkle to Jules Garfield for the Broadway stage, only to discover that Jules wouldn't pass muster at Warner Brothers) was routinely referred to as a Jewish actor in releases to the Jewish press, and celebrated in articles such as "Another Jewish Actor Rises to Stardom" in the Los Angeles *Bnai Brith Messenger*.

Michelangelo Signorile is a member of this generation that came of age after the explosion of gay liberation—he was born in 1960—but who scarcely knew the gay world in its brief "golden age" between Stonewall and AIDS. After studying journalism in college Signorile landed a job with a Broadway press agent and quickly learned the difference between the "rules" of journalism and the practice of gossip writing: "Some of my anger about the media came from seeing these people. It was so corrupted." Around this time he became involved with ACT UP and was soon politically engaged in AIDS activism. In June 1989, *OutWeek*, a new lesbian and gay weekly news magazine, signed Signorile as features editor and columnist. His disillusionment with the ethics of gossip journalists, fueled by his newly militant gay politics and AIDS activism, turned to anger which he unleashed in his "Gossip Watch" column.

The names that appeared in Signorile's columns were likely to be those of the targets of his ire; for this was not the usual gossipy listing of who had been seen where and with whom. This weekly dissection of New York's and Hollywood's celebrity and gossip elite attacked the media for failing to pay enough attention to AIDS, pretending that lesbian and gay celebrities are heterosexual, and flattering politicians "who are keeping us down at best, murdering us at worst." Signorile's most frequent targets were the gossip writers who reported on the doings of the "elite," flattering their egos and, in many cases, reporting on their nonexistent heterosexual romances.

Around the same time, gay author Armistead Maupin began spicing up book tour interviews with the gay press by naming names and challenging them to print them: "If the gay press has any function at all," Maupin believes, "it's to tweak the conscience of famous people who are in the closet; and certainly we shouldn't continue to lionize those among us who are making a success of themselves in the mainstream while remaining so determinedly in the closet. . . . I'm taking the hard line on it and saying homophobia is homophobia."

Maupin's disclosures were printed in many gay papers and periodicals, but the mainstream press ignored this novelty, just as they had earlier declined to specify precisely what ACT UP demonstrators were saying about Illinois governor James Thompson. Within a few months, however, the mainstream media had joined the gay press in playing the game while simultaneously debating the rules. An article on the ethics of outing by media critic William Henry in *Time* described the new developments without naming any names (Governor Thompson became "an outing victim [who] had endorsed legislation allowing hospitals to test patients for AIDS without their consent") and posed the ethical conflict between the right to privacy and the importance of coming out. Henry came down against outing: "it claims an unjustifiable right to sacrifice the lives of others."

In February 1990 billionaire publisher Malcolm Forbes died and the outing season was soon to be in full swing. The March 18, 1990, cover of *OutWeek* showed a photo of Malcolm Forbes on his motorcycle, with the bold headline: "The Secret Gay Life of Malcolm Forbes." The article, by Signorile, began with Forbes's funeral, noting the presence among the mourners of many prominent homophobes, including Richard Nixon and William F. Buckley, and asked whether they knew "that they were coming to pay homage to someone who embodied what they ultimately detested?" Signorile described a pattern of sexual behavior that was attested to by many young men. "People talked and, in quite a few segments of the gay male community at least, it seemed that *everyone* knew *someone* who'd done it with Malcolm Forbes. He was also quite showy, liking to ride around with his 'dates' on his motorcycle." Among those who were aware of these stories were New York's gossip columnists—the very writers who were major perpetrators of the false Malcolm Forbes/Liz Taylor romance, trying to convince readers that they were a hot item.

Signorile concluded his article with a defense of outing Forbes. First, he noted that, "All too often history is distorted," and the fact that one of the most influential men in America was gay should be recorded. Second, "it sends a clear message to the public at large that we are everywhere."

Although several papers outside New York picked up the Forbes story, the New York press ignored it until reports from other places made it difficult to avoid. The stories that began appearing all carried headlines that focused on the issue of conflict between privacy and the tactics of outing. The next round of mainstream newspaper analyses focused as well on the dilemma outing posed for the media. The *Sunday (Portland) Oregonian* titled its thoughtful article on outing, "Controversial Tactic to Expose Alleged Closet Homosexuals Just One Example of New Militancy Splitting AIDS Lobby," and accompanied it with a sidebar: "Practice puts press on spot," quoting the editor's determination to make decisions about whether to publish such allegations on a case-by-case basis.

When it came to the articles they printed, however, the papers were not always as consistent in their unwillingness to name any names. The *San Francisco Chronicle*, which editorialized against outing the day after running its article on the subject, cited not only Forbes and deceased California publisher C. K. McClatchy as outing victims (in the latter's case, it was a newspaper, not gay activists, that revealed that he had AIDS, after he died of a heart attack), but also named living outing targets Ed Koch, Calvin Klein, and Cher's daughter Chastity Bono (who had been the subject of front-page stories in the supermarket tabloids). *Chronicle* city editor Dan Rosenheim did not see a contradiction between the paper's policy not to out people and the printing of these names: "it was our feeling that the information had been distributed sufficiently widely that it had become part of the general public awareness."

When gay activists Michael Petrelis and Carl Goodman held a press conference in May 1990 on the Capitol steps and read the names of twelve men and women in politics and music whom they described as secretly gay, the press showed up but no major news organization published or broadcast the names. Writing about the press conference, the Capitol Hill newspaper *Roll Call* noted that the list included "three Senators, five House members, two governors, one official of a Northeastern city, and, inexplicably, one leading figure in the entertainment industry." *Roll Call*'s "Press Gallery" columnists posed the hypothetical question of whether the press should report that a member of Congress with an *antigay* voting record was gay, if they were provided with evidence for this claim. Their answer, citing a spokesman for the gay lobby Human Rights Campaign (HRC) in addition to the publisher of Washington's gay paper, the *Blade*, was "a resounding no," although they might report the fact that someone else had accused such a person of "being a homosexual hypocrite."

The alternative and gay press joined the debate over outing, but in these cases the articles were written by openly gay people who presented the issues in a longer historical context and with a more complex awareness of the arguments on both sides. In the letters column of the *Village Voice* of April 24, 1990, two leading gay writers responded to some of the central arguments of the outing controversy. Lesbian novelist Sarah Schulman, while admitting her ambivalence over the morality of outing, objected to the characterization of the tactic as an invasion of privacy: "Most gay people stay in the closet— i.e., dishonor their relationships—because to do so is a prerequisite for employment. Having to hide the way you live because of fear of punishment isn't a 'right,' nor is it 'privacy.' Being in the closet is not an objective, neutral, or value-free condition. It is maintained by force, not choice."

In the same issue longtime gay activist and writer Vito Russo noted that to say someone is gay is to talk "about *sexual orientation*, not their sexual activity." But, most critically, he pointed out, "Signorile is saying that if being gay is *not* disgusting, is *not* awful, then why can't we talk about it? After all, it's not an insult to call someone gay. Is it?"

OUTING THE PENTAGON

Michelangelo Signorile had long been receiving tips about Assistant Secretary of Defense Pete Williams from people angry over the Department of Defense's policy of excluding lesbian and gay people from the military, but with Williams's sudden media visibility during the 1991 Persian Gulf War "[I] got a tidal wave of information about the topic once again as well as a lot of pressure from colleagues urging me to expose the truth." Signorile was well aware of the severity and the cost—in dollars and in human suffering—of the military's discriminatory policies. In fact, despite the gay movement's dramatic gains in securing protection against discrimination in cities and states around the country, under the Reagan and Bush administrations the Pentagon's antigay efforts had intensified.

In June 1991, Air Force harassment of Charles Greeley, a captain who had marched in a Gay Pride parade the day before he was to be discharged, proved to be the spark that exploded Pete Williams's closet door. Michael Petrelis called a press conference at which he announced that "Pete Williams, an openly closeted gay man, hypocritically remains silent in his job as Pentagon spokesman while the Department of Defense continues its irrational policy of ejecting thousands of gays and lesbians from the armed services." Petrelis and his associates in Washington's Queer Nation chapter also put up posters around town, showing Pete Williams surrounded by large print: ABSOLUTELY QUEER. PETE WILLIAMS. PENTAGON SPOKESMAN, TAP DANCER. CONSUMMATE QUEER.[2] In somewhat smaller print it read, "Gay Bush appointee sits by while gay servicemen and women are burned." The posters were quickly torn down, but the town was electric with the news, which had become the chatter of Washington dinner parties, the buzz in gay and right-wing circles, and, according to insiders, the hottest gossip in every boardroom at the Pentagon itself.

Already at work on an article about Williams, Signorile had completed the bulk of the research by the time the Greeley incident turned Pete Williams into the latest Queer Nation poster boy. But before it could be published, Signorile's story hit a snag of a totally different kind. *OutWeek*, the magazine that had launched outing and given Signorile a platform, was shut down by a fight among its owners. Signorile's story about Pete Williams, scheduled as the cover story for the next issue of *OutWeek*, then found a home at the

---

[2] This tactic was inspired by OutPost, a spiritual lovechild of *OutWeek* and Queer Nation, which had begun to put posters up around Manhattan in the spring of 1991 with large photographs of celebrities over large type reading: ABSOLUTELY QUEER. The phrase was an obvious reference to the ads featuring art work with the tag "Absolut [artist's name]" that were very familiar to gay people because Absolut Vodka had long been one of the few mainstream products to advertise regularly in the gay press. The first group of anonymous posters—they were "signed" with the words: "OutPost—Cleaner Closets Today Mean a Better Tomorrow"—featured rich and famous folks already familiar to gossip and outing circles: Jodie Foster and Merv Griffin (Griffin had been outed by a lawsuit filed by an alleged former lover, but this was not news to gay gossip circles, despite his well-publicized "romance" with Eva Gabor).

Advocate, which set it as the cover story for the August 27 issue. Aware that mainstream media had ducked the story when Queer Nation outed Williams in Washington, the *Advocate* decided to build an irresistible groundswell by distributing advance copies of the article and by linking the outing of Williams to the military's increasingly violent exclusion of gays and lesbians from the armed forces.

The *Advocate*'s strategy paid off, because this time the story broke through the resistance of the media's gatekeepers who had squelched the June outing. Jack Anderson's syndicated column for August 3 was headlined "Gay Group Tries to 'Out' Pentagon Spokesman." Anderson's column is syndicated in approximately eight hundred newspapers around the country, but some of the largest, such as the *Washington Post* and the *San Francisco Chronicle*, declined to run this installment. Still, the story did run in hundreds of papers, and many more picked up the lead and ran their own stories. The majority of the articles, whether they included Pete Williams's name (e.g., *Detroit News*, *Detroit Free Press*, *New York Daily News*, *Oakland Tribune*, *Philadelphia Inquirer*, and Williams's home state *Saturday Wyoming Tribune-Eagle*) or declined to print the name (e.g., *New York Newsday*, *New York Post*, *New York Times*, *Los Angeles Times*), clearly framed the issue in terms of hypocrisy and discrimination, as when *New York Newsday* coyly referred to "a prominent, high-ranking civilian official of the Department of Defense, an agency that routinely discharges members of the armed forces for being gay or lesbian."

The exposure of Pete Williams's homosexuality at the same time that the Pentagon was booting out lesbian and gay Gulf War veterans put the military on the defensive. Defense Secretary Dick Cheney was squarely on the hot seat because Pete Williams was his protégé, a Wyoming journalist who had joined Cheney's staff when Cheney was a congressman and moved with him to the Defense Department. The *New York Times* reported that the Secretary "defended the right of homosexuals to hold civilian jobs at the Pentagon, saying that as long as they fulfilled their professional responsibilities their private lives were their own business." But though Cheney stood by the basic policy of exclusion, repeating the mantra that "homosexuality is incompatible with military service," the magical powers of this phrase had been seriously weakened by the exposure of the hypocrisy embodied by Pete Williams. Within weeks of the *Advocate*'s article both the *New York Times* and the *Washington Post* ran editorials attacking the military's antigay policy, and *Time* magazine published a lengthy account of the controversy surrounding the issue that was clearly sympathetic to the gay cause.

The outing of Pete Williams was a prime exhibit for the defense of outing as a political strategy: it placed the issue of the military's antigay discrimination squarely on the public agenda. The late Thomas Stoddard, then executive director of the Lambda Legal Defense and Education Fund, who had previously criticized outing, said that the Pete Williams story was "the *only* example in which outing has advanced the interests of gay people." Some writers in the mainstream media agreed with this judgment, such as openly gay *Detroit News* media critic Michael McWilliams, who argued that "outing should be used only in extreme cases . . . some cause-and-effect relationship must be established between a gay person doing his or her job and doing damage to other gay people."

In the *Los Angeles Times*, Marshall Alan Phillips focused on the double standard of the media when it comes to gay people: "If a public figure is Jewish or Jehovah's Witness or Hindu, divorced or married or single, Asian or Icelandic or Kenyan, those personal and private facts, if adequately verified, may be duly reported. No need for an on-the-record admission. Only in the case of gays does this silly rule of invisibility apply. It is based on the hackneyed straight assumption that, somehow, being a gay person is innately bad."

Marjorie Williams, a *Washington Post* reporter, published an article in the *Washington Monthly* of September 1991, which reviewed such episodes as the Gary Hart adultery case and the many uncovered stories of Washington alcoholics. She also briefly mentioned "a radical outing publication . . . trying to interest the major media in a civilian Pentagon official who is gay." Williams gave her vote to those who decided to preserve his privacy: "It does terrible violence to the ideal of a common interest to carry too far the insistence that a particular person, by virtue of gender or sexual orientation or color or any other index, has a greater responsibility than others to address a particular issue."

But this is precisely the heart of the issue of outing as considered by gay people. While the mainstream media have been preoccupied with the question of political hypocrisy, calibrating their measuring instruments to determine whether a particular case reaches their threshold of outrage, lesbian and gay activists and journalists are more likely to factor into their calculations the question of communal responsibility.[3]

The involuntary exposure of closeted homosexuals was long a favored tac-

[3] Gay legal activist and scholar William Rubenstein applied a concept of communal responsibility first articulated by African American law professor David Wilkins as the obligation thesis. Wilkins, drawing on the example of Thurgood Marshall, argued that black attorneys must recognize that they have moral obligations running to the black community. Rubenstein extended the concept to posit that "successful gay people have a duty to consider the interests of other gay people when performing their new roles . . . to ensure that the progress of the individual lesbians, gay men, and bisexuals will not unduly impede the advancements of the gay community as a whole." While Wilkins and Rubenstein are explicitly focusing on the moral obligations of attorneys, their analysis can clearly be extended to other professions.

tic used as a form of social control by the enemies of gays.[4] Now, the adoption of outing as a political tactic challenges their ability to determine the meaning of gay identity and the consequences of its visibility. While the Pete Williams story did not resolve the debate over outing, neither did it destroy the life or career of its target. After the Democratic victory in the 1992 elections, Pete Williams lost his Pentagon job but was quickly hired by NBC News as a Washington correspondent. Thus, although Williams has never publicly affirmed his homosexuality, there is at least one on-air network reporter who is known to be gay.

KINDA ASK, SORTA TELL

The furor over outing shifted the line toward more equal treatment of public figures by the news media and a greater willingness to include someone's homosexuality when it is relevant to a story. One of Michael Petrelis's targets had been Wisconsin Congressman Steve Gunderson, a Republican who had never supported any gay causes in his eleven years in office. After Petrelis and other activists made his homosexuality public, Gunderson began to be more supportive of gay issues and more open about his sexuality. In October 1994 he was the subject of a profile by gay journalist Chandler Burr in the *New York Times Magazine*, with the headline "Congressman (R) Wisconsin. Fiscal Conservative. Social Moderate. Gay." By 1996 Gunderson, who decided not to run for reelection, had published a memoir together with his lover, architect Rob Morse, and become active in gay Republican circles, as well as serving on the board of the Human Rights Campaign, the nation's largest lesbian-gay political organization.

In March 1995 the *Wall Street Journal* ran a front-page article reporting that *Rolling Stone* founder Jann Wenner "left the home he shared with his wife and three young children and began a relationship with a young male staffer at Calvin Klein." As former *OutWeek* editor Gabriel Rotello put it, "If *OutWeek*'s Forbes article ignited the outing war with a bang, the *Journal*'s piece on Wenner—and follow-up articles in *Newsweek*, the *Washington Post*, and elsewhere—symbolically ends it with a whimper."

---

[4] The use of outing by right-wing homophobes hasn't ended with the adoption of the tactic by gay activists. In 1995 columnist Cal Thomas wrote an attack of what he considered the news media's pro-gay bias in covering "gay gene" research. Among Thomas's arguments was the failure of the press to "report on [geneticist Dean] Hamer's own homosexuality, which might indicate to some readers that Hamer has a bias in favor of discovering a biological cause for homosexual behavior."

The war might have ended, but outing remains a tactic in activists' arsenals, as closeted legislators Sen. Barbara Mikulski (D-MD) and Congressman Jim Kolbe (R-AZ) discovered after they voted for the Defense of Marriage Act in 1996 (Kolbe had previously voted to maintain the military's antigay policies). Kolbe beat the *Advocate* to the punch by coming out himself, telling a reporter, "I feel a tremendous burden lifted. It's a relief." Like Gunderson, Kolbe has become a supporter of the Log Cabin Gay Republicans. After confronting Mikulski at a New York book-signing, Signorile and media activist Ann Northrop proposed National Outing Day. "From this day forward, the day before National Coming Out Day will be National Outing Day," Signorile said. "It's a day to out a favorite public figure to everyone you know, through e-mail messages, voice mail messages, notes and letters in the mail, and in casual conversation throughout the day. And if there happens to be an elected official who voted anti-gay and who is making a public appearance, it's a day to go and confront that person."[5]

By the end of the decade the status of outing remained ambiguous, as positions shifted in the political breeze. Speaking to the International Network of Lesbian and Gay Officials in November 1999, Signorile defended the outing of public figures as responsible journalism—telling the truth—"when someone's orientation is relevant, it [should be] looked at and it's not something used as a blackmailing tool." And, in fact, public figures coming out and being identified as gay in the media is becoming more common and even less newsworthy.

When longtime L.A. city councilman and mayoral candidate Joel Wachs came out the same week that Signorile spoke, the *Los Angeles Times* ran an op-ed piece on "The Yawn Heard 'Round Los Angeles." At the same time, however, there was a thunderous silence from the lesbian and gay movement when Vice President Al Gore appointed Donna Brazile as his presidential campaign manager in October 1999. Brazile's appointment attracted media attention because, as the *Washington Post* put it, "everyone took note that Brazile, 39, is the first black woman to hold such a high post in a major-party campaign." The lengthy *Post* profile, like a similar article in the *New York Times*, went into great detail about Brazile's history of political organizing—including her well-publicized firing from Michael Dukasis's 1988 campaign after she urged journalists to cover George Bush's alleged adultery. But while

---

[5] In November 1999 a Web page falsely attributed to Chris Bull (the political reporter for the "officially" anti-outing *Advocate*) detailed the antigay voting records of two Republican congressmen alleged to be gay (www.geocities.com/WestHollywood/Chelsea/5392). By late 2000, the letter page on the Web site, which had been updated to include more recent antigay votes, had garnered scores of responses, almost all endorsing the outing strategy.

the *Post* noted Brazile's involvement in the lesbian and gay rights movement, including her membership on "the board of the Millennium March on Washington—a gay rights event planned for April" (Brazile resigned from the board after she was appointed to the Gore campaign), her personal life was deftly ushered offstage. "The last time I talked about someone's personal life, I got fired. I'm not about to make my personal life public," she says. "I'm single and available. If I had a personal life, I'd have a sexual orientation."[6]

U.S. News and World Report was puzzled by the silence of the Human Rights Campaign, the major sponsor of the Millennium March, which might have been expected to herald the appointment of a leading activist to head Gore's campaign. Yet according to the Human Rights Campaign, "It's just not news," while *U.S. News* quoted a gay rights activist as saying the Gore campaign wanted "the spotlight to shine instead on the fact that Brazile is the first black woman to run a presidential campaign." The Human Rights Campaign, which organizes the National Coming Out Day every October, seemed desperate to avoid what most observers thought was a notable story. The HRC's communications director David Smith told the *Atlanta Southern Voice*, a gay paper, "I have no idea about her sexual orientation," a statement the paper characterized as "false, if not an intentional lie."

Yet if HRC was in the dark about Brazile's sexuality, conservative gay writer Andrew Sullivan was not. Writing in 1995, Sullivan had denounced outing as the tyrannical enforcement of ideology, traumatizing individuals by obliterating their "complex negotiations of self-disclosure," invading their autonomy and sacrificing their dignity. Sullivan criticized the outing of Pete Williams— whom he referred to, rather quaintly by that point, as "a civilian in the Defense Department"—and as "a man . . . for whom there was no proof of his hostility to homosexuals, and some evidence that he may have been doing good." If Pete Williams could be so described, what description would fit someone who had long worked for lesbian and gay rights? But in Donna Brazile's case, Sullivan sounded more like Signorile in 1991 than Sullivan in 1995 (when he published his autobiography, *Virtually Normal*), except that he was writing in the *New York Times Magazine*, not the *Advocate*.

In an article with the unambiguous subhead, "When It Comes to Public Figures Disclosing Their Sexuality, the New Rule Is Kinda Ask, Sorta Tell," Sullivan leads off with an account of the Brazile appointment and subsequent obfuscation, concluding that, "Of course, Brazile has every right to say noth-

---

[6] Connoisseurs of closet coverage might have been reminded of a *New York Times* profile of Pete Williams that attributed his bachelorhood to his workaholic schedule, quoting friends and relations to make the point that "he always put his energy into his job, and in Washington all he does is work. Frankly, I've never seen him make room in his life for a woman."

ing if she wants to, even to the point of seeming ridiculous." Sullivan's article, which makes points all-too-familiar to the activists he labeled as tyrants a few years back, goes on to talk about—one might even say out, if any of this were really news—politicians Ed Koch, Janet Reno, and Donna Shalala (all Democrats, by coincidence?), and entertainers Rosie O'Donnell, Ricky Martin, and Richard Simmons. Sullivan's conclusion? "I don't believe in 'outing' people. But I don't believe in 'inning' them, either. . . . There comes a point, surely, at which the diminishing public stigmatization of homosexuality makes this kind of coyness not so much understandably defensive as simply feeble: insulting to homosexuals, who know better, and condescending to heterosexuals, who deserve better."[7]

The *New York Times*, which had consistently criticized outing and refused even to name Malcolm Forbes and Pete Williams when reporting on their outing, responded to questions about Sullivan's piece by noting that he was a columnist expressing his own views and not the paper's. It added, "He is not invading anyone's privacy. He is dealing with how people portray themselves."

---

[7] Definitely not amused were openly gay actor Rupert Everett and his close friend Madonna, who were quoted on the subject in the March 2000 *Vanity Fair* cover story (coinciding with the release of a movie in which he plays, surprise, her gay best friend): "Despite his own moral victory [Everett's] not the type to urge other gay actors to come out. Neither he nor Madonna take kindly to a recent article in the *New York Times Magazine*, in which writer Andrew Sullivan pressured certain public figures, such as former New York City Mayor Ed Koch, Ricky Martin, and Rosie O'Donnell, to define their sexuality. 'I hate that type of person,' Everett says, referring to outers of all stripes. 'I don't think you should be defined by your sexual preference,' Madonna says. 'I can't stand those hideous people, trying to call people out' (Everett referring to Sullivan). 'That's really fascist behavior. Horrible.' 'Right.' Madonna puts down her fork. "Ed Koch is gay?!' she asks."

9

Hollywood Under Pressure

AIDS VICTIMS AND VILLAINS

AIDS revived the two familiar roles the mass media offer to members of minority groups: victim and villain. Victims, as in the family-centered television movies *An Early Frost* (NBC, 1985) and *Our Sons* (ABC, 1991), are objects of pity, and when treated well by the authors they end by being tearfully reconciled with their families. Television dramatists have presented the plight of (white, middle-class) gay men with AIDS, but their particular concern is the agony of the families/friends who have to face the awful truth: their son (brother, boyfriend, husband, etc.) is gay. But, even with AIDS, not too gay, mind you. Villains—real or imagined—are those who carelessly, or worse, deliberately, place others at risk by continuing to practice unsafe sex, or health professionals who, through negligence or malevolence, infect their patients.[1]

In the first network made-for-TV movie on AIDS, NBC's *An Early Frost*, a young, rich, white, handsome lawyer is forced out of the closet by AIDS. As lesbian critic Andrea Weiss put it, "We know he is gay because he tells his disbelieving parents so, but his lack of a gay sensibility, politics and sense of community make him one of those homosexuals heterosexuals love." NBC was quoted as "anxious that [*An Early Frost*] not be seen as a 'gay' story,"

---

[1] The most notorious AIDS villain was Gaetan Dugas, a Canadian airline steward who was featured in Randy Shilts's 1987 account of the AIDS epidemic, *And the Band Played On*, as Patient Zero. Despite the fact that the supposed "patient zero" factor in spreading HIV had been discredited by the time Shilts completed his book, Dugas is described as a one-man infection squad, sleeping with men and then telling them they would die. It was the Patient Zero angle that attracted the most media attention when St. Martin's Press was trying to publicize the book. Editor Michael Denneny later took the credit—or blame—for pushing the most sensational part of Shilts's book, claiming "that book would have been stillborn without using the 'Patient Zero' ploy."

and its star, Aiden Quinn, was featured in a *TV Guide* article titled, "Why This Young Hunk Risked Playing an AIDS Victim," in which we learn that his friends warned, "You've got to be courageous to play a fag." The TV movie followed the typical pattern of focusing primarily on the heterosexual family and their response to the gay person in their midst, carefully avoiding any depiction of the gay "families of choice" that so many lesbian and gay people have created and from which they derive support. While *An Early Frost*, which aired shortly after Rock Hudson's death, dutifully included basic AIDS information, circa 1985, it also showed the Aiden Quinn character sleeping in a separate bed from his lover: "I just don't think we should take any chances."[2] In contrast to the ostentatious absence of physical affection between the lovers—scenes originally written in were edited out—after extensive deliberations that included consultation with Dr. James Curran, head of the CDC's AIDS program, the producers included a kiss between Quinn and his grandmother. When Quinn resists her initiative, she says "It's a disease, not a disgrace—come on, give your old grandmother a kiss."

It took the networks six years to return to the subject of gay men with AIDS (if we exclude TV bio-pics about Liberace and Rock Hudson), and when ABC broadcast *Our Sons* in April 1991, some things had changed, but much remained the same.[3] This time the gay couple (played by Hugh Grant and Zeliko Ivanek) are both out of the closet, and Grant's mother (played by Julie Andrews) is a sophisticated Hollywood executive who knows about her son and his lover. The dramatic interest of the film, then, centers on Julie Andrews's role in fetching Ivanek's "trailer-trash" mother (played by Ann Margaret) from Arkansas and helping to reunite her with her son before he dies. Once more, although the gay lovers are allowed to exhibit a mite more affection and are more visibly gay—the dying lover is a successful decorator—there is no acknowledgment of a supportive gay community or an AIDS activist movement.

---

[2] NBC promoted the film's educational content, mailing advance informational material to over 200,000 organizations, and scheduling an AIDS special hosted by Tom Brokaw to follow the program.

[3] AIDS did figure in network programming between 1985 and 1991, but it tended to affect white people with bad luck. In the 1987 ABC *Afterschool Special*, "Just a Regular Kid: An AIDS Story," Paul, a white, middle-class high school student, is faced with a moral dilemma. As he prepares to make a speech urging that AIDS carriers be barred from his school, he learns that his best friend Kevin has contracted AIDS through a blood transfusion. The program dramatizes the ostracism suffered by Kevin, while imparting medical facts, and ends with a predictable show of support by Paul for his friend. As *New York Times* TV critic John O'Connor pointed out, however, " it is difficult to realize from this sort of television exercise that the vast majority of AIDS victims are homosexuals and drug addicts, with an alarming number of blacks and Hispanics represented in the totals. But these groups, it seems, don't lend themselves as easily to inspirational tracts."

Television's repetition compulsion where AIDS is concerned was evidenced in 1997 on the cable channel HBO (Home Box Office). *In the Gloaming,* Christopher Reeve's directorial debut (after suffering neck injuries that rendered him paraplegic—and thus nearly immune to criticism), is the story of a young gay man who returns to his upper-class Westchester home so that his saintly mother (played by Glenn Close) can care for him as he dies from AIDS. Once more, the gay man, whose lover deserted him when the going got rough, finds support and love in the arms of his mother (fans of trite psychiatric theories no doubt appreciated the distant father, and the sister who believes that their mother made her brother gay).

Programs that are less family-centered are more likely to show us the AIDS carrier as villain, threatening the health of innocent victims. An egregious example of the villain scenario occurred on an episode of the NBC series *Midnight Caller* in December 1988. The story focused on Mike Barnes, a bisexual man who knows he is infected with HIV but continues to engage in unprotected sex with numerous partners. The hero of the series, a San Francisco radio talk show host, learns that a former lover (a woman) has tested HIV-positive after an affair with the man, and he uses his radio show to track the man down. In the original script the woman kills the bisexual man at the end, but after protests from AIDS groups who saw the script, he is saved by the hero, and some conciliatory additions were made to the script. These include a brief scene in a gay bar which carefully lets the bartender emphasize that "Mike Barnes is an exception, an aberrant" in sexually active circles.

The other concession was more interesting. As John O'Connor of the *New York Times* put it, "one of the most sympathetic characters" turns out to be Ross Parker, Barnes's abandoned lover, who is dying of AIDS. "It's nice just to talk to somebody. I don't get a lot of company these days," he says to the hero, who visits him while hunting for Barnes. O'Connor ends his review with the thought that, "Perhaps a future episode can focus primarily on a character like Ross, a decent person with AIDS who finds himself abandoned by friends, family and society." Here O'Connor unwittingly touches upon a truly important point: the AIDS stories that television has assiduously avoided. But these aren't the stories of pathetic abandonment that O'Connor urged on programmers.

There are truly dramatic and important AIDS stories that we never see enacted or even reflected glancingly in TV drama, but they aren't stories of villainous AIDS carriers or abandoned victims who may finally be accepted back into the arms of their families. These are stories of how the gay *community* responded to an unparalleled health crisis with an unprecedented grassroots movement of social service and medical organizing. They are stories of public health information and sex education; of research-backed militant agitation for reforms in the testing and approval of drugs; of coalition-building with other marginalized groups suffering disproportionately from the AIDS risk.

The consistent feature of all TV dramatic programming on AIDS (and most news, public affairs, and documentary programming as well) has been to focus on *individual* people suffering from AIDS and, if the angle of vision is widened at all, it will then include (straight) family members and possibly a lover (as long as they barely touch) and perhaps one or two friends (more likely to be straight than gay). What is wrong with this picture? What's wrong is that it not only leaves out all of the important—and dramatic—achievements of the gay community noted above, but that it falsely suggests that gay people with AIDS *are* alone and abandoned, unless and until they are taken back into the bosom of their family. Even the best of the TV AIDS stories fall into this pattern.

An episode of *L.A. Law* (May 16, 1991) included a gay lawyer dying of AIDS who sues his health insurance company to obtain payment for an experimental drug that might prolong his life (he wins, with the assistance of *L.A. Law* star Jimmy Smits). The ailing lawyer is shown as a strong and principled person who is willing to fight for his rights, and for the rights of others in his situation. But viewers of the program would never know—from this episode, or from any other prime-time TV drama—about the significant efforts and dramatic achievements of the militant organization ACT UP in forcing the medical establishment, the FDA, and drug companies to deal more equitably and openly with patients. It has been widely acknowledged by medical scientists such as Anthony Fauci of the National Institutes of Health that ACT UP wrought substantial changes in the way the medical community relates to the populations it serves. These successes were not brought about by lone individuals, however courageous and eloquent; yet the *L.A. Law* episode, for all its good intentions, continues the tradition of isolating the gay person as a lone victim.

The pattern of portraying people with AIDS outside the context of the gay community and the service organizations created in response to AIDS was dramatically reinforced in Hollywood's first major film centering on the epidemic, Jonathan Demme's *Philadelphia* (1993). Once again we meet a white gay man who lives an upper-middle-class life as a closeted lawyer—although he has a lover and he is out to his family—until he is stricken with AIDS, whereupon he is promptly fired from the big-time law firm where he had been a rising star. Shortly afterwards, he shows up in the office of a (black) homophobic ambulance-chasing lawyer and asks him to represent him in suing his old law firm, because he has been turned down by other lawyers. The ambulance chaser refuses but later reconsiders, takes the case, and wins it, while at the same time undergoing a conversion to tolerance and accept-ance of at least one person (we have no reason to think that the character would not be horrified were he later to learn that his newborn child was gay). The film was presented and largely received as a landmark of progress in Hol-lywood's approach to AIDS and gay people, and there is no question that it did bring the realities of AIDS home to many who had not yet gotten the message (Tom Hanks's Oscar-winning performance as the gay lawyer also helped diminish the fear of "gay roles"). Still, as an account of the realities of AIDS, or gay life, it was mired in the same-old same-old.

While the protagonist is supported by his incredibly accepting family, in most ways the film continues the familiar practice of marginalization and denial. The homophobic lawyer is shown repeatedly in intimate scenes with his wife and children, but the gay lawyer and his lover are barely allowed to touch, and their only (brief) kiss is obscured by the back of the lover's head. A scene showing the two of them talking in bed was reportedly shot but not used. The gay couple seems to have gay friends, but those friends have few lines and are mostly confined to a costume party, presumably representing the true image of gay life. Most dishonest, however, is the erasure of the organized response to AIDS. The only acknowledgment of the AIDS activist movement is a very brief glimpse of ACT UP–style demonstrators seen out-side the courthouse, but they are juxtaposed with a group of antigay funda-mentalists also demonstrating, thus creating a visual parallel of the two groups as equal and opposing "radical extremists" who can safely be dis-missed as irrational.

The biggest lie in the movie is told when the gay lawyer fired because he has AIDS says that he was turned down by many lawyers before ending up in the office of the ambulance-chasing homophobe. In Philadelphia, as in many other large cities, a person in his position would have been able to avail him-self of lesbian and gay legal services or even ones especially created to deal with AIDS-related cases. In other words, a key dramatic premise of the film—the victimized person with AIDS ends up at the mercy of a homophobe who can then be converted to tolerance—requires the erasure of the accomplish-ments of the gay community, just as the fear of heterosexual audiences' sen-sibilities requires the denial of the realities of gay life.

A KINDER, GENTLER HOLLYWOOD

Three months before *Philadelphia* opened to box-office success and Oscar-winning critical acclaim, the cable network HBO aired a two-and-a-half-hour version of Randy Shilts's 1987 600-page best-seller, *And the Band Played On*. Although considered by a movie studio and optioned for television by NBC, the book spent years in limbo. In 1991 Shilts blamed Hollywood's homophobia and closeted executives for the delays: "Gays are so terrified of being exposed, they'll get in the way of a project." Ironically, therefore, it was perhaps the advent of outing that propelled Shilts's book—as well as *Philadelphia*—onto the screen.

"Nineteen ninety-one will be known as the year that altered Hollywood's relationship with gay and lesbian people as never before," wrote gay journalist Doug Sadownick. The year began with the rage surrounding *The Silence of the Lambs* because of the portrayal of its psychotic serial killer as a stereotypical gay man, and the fires were further fueled when GLAAD/SF obtained copies of the script of the film *Basic Instinct*, due to be shot in San Francisco that spring. The activists were outraged by the depiction of every one of the female characters as a psycho-lesbian or psycho-bisexual killer, and demanded changes. After unsuccessful negotiations with the producers, protestors disrupted the filming.[4] The producers obtained a restraining order and demonstrators were subsequently arrested, as both filming and protesting continued for several weeks.

Coming on the heels of the opening of *Silence of the Lambs*, the anger over *Basic Instinct* led Michelangelo Signorile and other activists to call for a March on Hollywood in 1992 that would hold accountable celebrities and gay and lesbian showbiz power holders. The march never took place, but the outrage expressed in the gay press began to have an impact.

The 1991–92 television season gave more evidence that Hollywood was listening to lesbian and gay voices. Gay characters and themes appeared on many series (*L.A. Law, Coach, Roseanne, Designing Women, Seinfeld, Dear John*, among others), and producer Esther Shapiro claimed that "awareness about AIDS has made the sleeping liberals more awake, creating a more relaxed attitude about gay themes." But movie studios were still resisting lesbian and gay stories. Despite the critical and even financial success of independent films made by and for lesbian and gay people, such as Donna

---

[4] Screenwriter Joe Eszterhas, who had been paid a record $3 million for the screenplay, told the press that, after a two-hour meeting with San Francisco gay leaders, he "realized that there were insensitivities in the script which could be corrected while also improving its artistic and thematic structure." When the producers countered that "the changes compromised the integrity of the script," Eszterhas said, "There is simply no reason to allow a powerful actor like Michael Douglas to say things that can perpetuate hate when it would be just as easy for him to say something else. I didn't know that before I wrote the script. I do now." The producers, however, had the final say, and the script was not changed.

Deitch's *Desert Hearts* and Bill Sherwood's *Parting Glances*, both in 1986, Hollywood executives were still "looking for good scripts." In 1990, *Longtime Companion*, a story about a group of gay men dealing with and dying from AIDS, which had been financed by public television's *American Playhouse* series, was picked up for theatrical distribution by an independent company.[5] While not a smash, the film, which cost $1.5 million, brought in over $4 million and garnered a Golden Globe award and an Oscar nomination for actor Bruce Davison.

As March 1992 rolled around, Hollywood began bracing for an onslaught of gay activism. *Basic Instinct* was due to open around the country on March 20, and lesbian and gay groups from coast to coast were planning demonstrations at which they promised to loudly reveal the thriller's ending in order to discourage potential audiences. At the same time, activists were also angry at the obscuring of the lesbian relationship at the heart of *Fried Green Tomatoes*, an unexpected hit at the box office. As GLAAD and Queer Nation saw it, Hollywood was happy to be explicit about psycho-lesbian killers but became coy when it came to loving and happy lesbians. A third cause for gay outrage was the depiction of a cabal of degenerate gays at the heart of the conspiracy to kill Kennedy in Oliver Stone's *JFK*, their sleaziness accentuated in contrast to the (fictionalized) portrayal of New Orleans district attorney Jim Garrison's wholesome nuclear family.

Neither protests nor negative reviews dissuaded audiences attracted by the flood of hype publicizing *Basic Instinct*'s graphic sex. But they did have an impact on the news media, which devoted an unprecedented amount of attention to the questions raised about the portrayals of lesbian women and gay men in movies and television. Major feature stories were run in newspapers—the *New York Times* even commissioned gay novelist and ACT UP member John Weir to write a lengthy piece on "Gay Bashing, Villainy and the Oscars" for the Sunday Arts and Leisure section—as well as on CNN, *NBC Nightly News*, and *Entertainment Tonight*.

One reason for all the media attention to Hollywood homophobia was the

---

[5] *Longtime Companion* differed from other AIDS-related films because it centers around the experience of the gay characters—both those who live with, and die from, AIDS—and their lovers and friends. In an ironic twist, the film, which was written and directed by openly gay men, was criticized by reviewers, such as Vincent Canby in the *New York Times*, for focusing on white, middle-class men. GLAAD queried, "When was the last time he criticized, say, a Woody Allen movie for dealing only with intellectual Jewish New Yorkers? . . . In short, he recognizes that there is nothing inherently invalid about a movie focusing on a precise social milieu; he is simply uncomfortable with this particular milieu—the company of gay people who loved, fought for, and have taken care of each other during the epidemic."

Academy Awards ceremony that shortly followed the opening of *Basic Instinct*. This annual orgy of movie-mania became the focus of queer action. By early March word had spread that Oscar night would see all sorts of protests. The producers promised tight security and said they would cut to a commercial if an interruption occurred on the air.

The Silence of the Lambs had been nominated for most of the major awards, and the movie and its star Jodie Foster were the focus of both protests and media handwringing. The *Star* brought the news to supermarket aisles around the country that "gays plot to 'out' 60 stars at Oscars," and that "militants smear Best Actress Nominee Jodie Foster," thus making sure that few were unaware that Jodie Foster had been outed. The *National Enquirer* alerted its readers to the fact that "Hollywood celebrities are scared out of their wits because a gay terrorist group is plotting to destroy the Academy Awards by exposing stars they claim are secret homosexuals and lesbians."

The night of March 30 came, and the Academy Award ceremonies went off with a minimum of disruption from the protesters demonstrating outside—kept far away by a phalanx of mounted police. None at all appeared inside. *The Silence of the Lambs* swept the top honors, and Jodie Foster accepted her second Best Actress Oscar with a speech full of heavily coded language, thanking "all the people in this industry who have respected my choices and have not been afraid of the power and dignity that that entitled me to." Still, there were visible signs of the changes that had been going on during the past year. Nearly every lapel sported a red ribbon, the new symbol of AIDS awareness, which host Billy Crystal and presenter Richard Gere explained to the audience. Short Documentary award-winner Debra Chasnoff thanked her "life partner Kim Klausner" in her acceptance speech, and the lover of deceased composer Howard Ashman accepted his award for Best Song.

The threatened outings never happened, but Hollywood's lesbian and gay closet door stood a bit more ajar than ever before. Suddenly, it seemed that good scripts were being found, and by some of the very people who had been in the queer spotlight: *Silence of the Lambs* director Jonathan Demme announced plans for *Philadelphia* and HBO agreed to produce *And the Band Played On*.

QUEERING THE "STRAIGHT" TEXT

Gay novelist Ethan Mordden wrote that "gays invariably comprehend straights, because, whatever our sexuality, we all grow up within the straight culture. . . . Gays understand straights; but straights don't understand gays any more than whites understand blacks or Christians understand Jews, however good their intentions." Reflecting on the "misreading" of gay films by straight critics, Richard Goldstein noted, "We don't live in the same world. I know their society but they still don't know mine." This is a common experience of ethnic, racial, and sexual minorities.

The experience of minorities in mass society will always include a cultural diet dominated by images created for the majorities whose experiences and interests they reflect. Minorities will invariably be culturally bilingual, while members of the dominant majority will have no such burden, or opportunity. In fact, of course, media images consumed by majority audiences often are produced by minority group members, as long as the telltale labels are safely removed or hidden from sight. There is indeed traffic that moves from the minority to the majority, but this crossover commerce requires careful and often deceptive packaging if its cargo is to be palatable to the majority.

British cultural critics Kobena Mercer and Isaac Julien remark on the "immense popularity of black music among whites in modern societies . . . always associated with dance and the erotic potentialities of the dance floor." In this they join Stuart Hall in recognizing "silenced and unacknowledged, the fact of American popular culture itself, which has always contained within it, whether silenced or not, black American popular vernacular traditions." In her account of black images in American popular culture, Patricia Turner notes the genre of films inaugurated by George Lucas's 1973 *American Graffiti*, that turn "nostalgia for the late 1950s and 1960s into movie-making success in the 1970s, 1980s and 1990s." Citing such films as *Animal House* (1978), *Diner* (1982), *The Big Chill* (1983), *Back to the Future* (1985), and *Stand by Me* (1986), she points out that the producers "re-create the environments of their youth or idealized projections of one. Period music becomes an essential component. Each of these movies boasts a soundtrack true to the era it reflects. Most of the musical selections are, in fact, classic rhythm and blues or early rock and roll." Turner goes on to remind us that "although the characters in these films identify black music as a significant reminder of their coming of age, their social groups don't reflect any impulses to integrate." The cliques that are sentimentally recalled or reunited in these movies are all white, even as they re-create "the good old days when blacks could be relied on to supply good dance music without intruding into the social situation."

In an analysis of ways that "gay men have been creating culture which in turn has been assimilated into the mainstream," critic Michael Bronski characterizes the contributions of "this culture and sensibility, in addition to being one of the most important forces shaping Western culture," as also "one of the most progressive, liberating, and visionary." And just as many have noted the powerful influence of African Americans on mainstream culture through style and the physical, sexualized body (whether in music, fashion, or sports), so Bronski notes a similar influence of gays.

> The association of homosexuality with the sexual and the cry of "sex obsession" have been used to attack homosexuals but it is precisely this quality, this "obsession with sex" which is at the basis of the liberation offered by the gay sensibility. Gay artists have constantly argued in favor of an open imagination, sought to present images of beauty to a culture which has demanded only the most utilitarian necessities, and portrayed alternative worlds as a release from an oppressive reality. Freeing sexuality and eroticism is an impulse everyone feels on some level, no matter how much they consciously support the existing system. And this has always been the potent threat of the gay sensibility. A threat which the mainstream culture constantly attempts to co-opt and defuse by assimilation.[6]

In a highly influential article on "camp," Susan Sontag opened a critical Pandora's box by claiming that "Jews and homosexuals are the outstanding creative minorities in contemporary urban culture. Creative that is, in the truest sense: they are creators of sensibilities." Years later George Steiner echoed Sontag: "Judaism and homosexuality (most intensely where they overlap, as in a Proust or a Wittgenstein) can be seen to have been the two main generators of the entire fabric and savor of urban modernity in the West."

But, as with the soundtracks of the nostalgic films Turner cites, the contributions of gays have almost always been enjoyed without acknowledgment of their creators. In this context lesbians and gays might again be closer to

---

[6] Bronski cites the example of men's fashions since the 1950s. Beginning with the fifties' "gay look" of sneakers and chinos and continuing through the adoption of blue jeans as a gay style, "what eventually happened was that the straight world was drawn to the erotic and psychological freedom that these gay clothes represented and they, in time, became an accepted staple of U.S. apparel. . . . Each of these [successive] looks started in urban gay male communities and were quickly taken up by the fashion industry and marketed as the 'new look' for the heterosexual male. Each 'look' is progressively more sexual and more open—the 'tough' Levi outside covers willingly suggestive sexual undergarments. These looks became commonplace to U.S. culture: the Marlboro Man and the Calvin Klein underwear man—to choose the most obvious and mythical examples—peered out of almost every magazine and newspaper, down from billboards, out of televisions. American men were discovering that they were sexual and they were learning it from queers."

Jews than to blacks. David Van Leer discusses the relations of minority cultural contributions to visibility, noting that "Ralph Ellison locates a black man's invisibility in the refusal of white culture to look at him; gay invisibility seems an effect not only of straight culture's inability to see, but also of homosexuals' unwillingness to make themselves visible through coming out." Thus, not surprisingly, the emergence of the homosexual subcultural identity proclaimed by Daniel Webster Cory in 1951—"a minority that cannot accept the outlook, customs, and laws of the dominant group"—owed much to the efforts of lesbians and gay men to pierce the veils of secrecy, to ask and to tell each other's secrets, at least within the security of the ghettoes of gay bars.

The crystallizing of lesbian and gay identities is somewhat akin to the rediscovery of their "ethnic roots" by third-generation Americans whose parents had successfully assimilated into the mainstream. But for gay people there were no grandparents to visit, and the stars and stories of popular culture often took the place of the "old country"; as Andrea Weiss put it: "Rumor and gossip constitute the unrecorded history of the gay subculture." Writing about the emergence of lesbian identities in the 1930s, Weiss cites Patricia Spacks's analysis of gossip as an alternative discourse through which "those who are otherwise powerless can assign meanings and assume the power of representation, reinterpreting materials from the dominant culture into shared private meanings."

If gossip and outing are exercises in unmasking the minority authors responsible for images seemingly produced *by* as well as *of* and *for* the majority, there are also reading strategies that deliberately go "against the grain" even when neither the text nor the author is necessarily a candidate for outing. In instances of what Michel de Certeau called cultural "poaching," minority audiences "appropriate" majority images and read them "as if" they had been intended for the minority.[7] Gay cultural critic Alexander Doty advances an extended argument for such "queer readings," going far beyond the familiar terrain of gossip to claim a much wider cultural territory for oppositional and resistant readings. "Within cultural production and reception, queer erotics are already part of culture's erotic center, both as a necessary construct by which to define the heterosexual and the straight (as 'not queer'), and as a position that can be and is occupied in various ways by otherwise heterosexual and straight-identifying people."

Doty's map of queer readings takes us through a veritable Cook's Tour of

---

[7] Of course, given the general awareness of the sexual *marranos* scattered throughout Hollywood, gay audiences might well have imagined that they were being winked at from the closet.

television history, placing such classic pairings as Lucy and Ethel, Jack Benny and Rochester, Laverne and Shirley, in the company of more transparently gay figures like Pee Wee Herman (who, nevertheless, was accepted as a popular kid's show host until he, as it were, exposed himself as a queer). In a less imperialistic mode, critic Mimi White cites the frequent televisual premise of *homosocial* groupings as an opening to oppositionally *homoerotic* readings. The successful TV comedy series *Golden Girls, Kate and Allie*, and, to a lesser degree, *Designing Women*, "validate women's bonding as a form of social stability, a viable and attractive alternative to the traditional family, and even hint at the possibility of lesbian lifestyles—at least as far as possible within dominant ideology."

One of the most extensive opportunities for queer reading of a televisual text was provided by the CBS police series *Cagney and Lacey*. This long-running (1982–1988), award-winning series about two women police detectives garnered a large and loyal following of lesbians who were able to read the women as lesbian despite the characters' explicit heterosexuality.[8]

In a study utilizing the 1994 TV film *Cagney & Lacey: The Return*, Tanya Hands explored the interpretations and recollections of lesbian viewers, many of whom had recorded and kept the original series programs. These women had no difficulty reading the detectives as lesbians. As one respondent put it, "I always thought Cagney was a dyke, but they would have her with a guy once in a while. . . . I just didn't ever see her as a straight woman." Some of the older women recalled planning social events around the program: "We, a bunch of my friends, would get together each week at each other's houses. We'd have dinner, or whatever. Or we would just call each other during the commercials if we weren't together. Sometimes each of us would be on the phone with someone else during the length of the whole show."

Jane Feuer wrote about a more public version of such queer readings, describing the "*Dynasty* Nights" at many gay bars on Wednesday evenings, drawing an audience of gay men who were interested in the fate of (sometimes) gay Steven Carrington as well as the dramatic excesses (and costumes) of Alexis Carrington (Joan Collins). In her 1995 study Tanya Hands visited a lesbian bar in Philadelphia for the Wednesday night screenings of the ABC hit, *Ellen*, starring former standup comedienne Ellen DeGeneres who, along with her character, Ellen Morgan, was still in the closet. DeGeneres's lesbianism had long been a staple of gay gossip, and Hands's respondents

---

[8] In fact, as we've already noted, Meg Foster, the first Cagney, was replaced after one season because CBS executives thought she looked "too dykey."

explained that much of their enjoyment derived from reading Ellen as a lesbian: "*We* know her character is gay. I just wish it was apparent to other people." Hands's lesbian respondents, while disappointed over DeGeneres's early evasiveness in discussing her sexual orientation, were understanding: "I would prefer if she was just an out lesbian on the show, but in the mindset of ratings, immediately I think, well, that would never happen. . . . I think if she actually did do it as an out lesbian, it would be great, but the fact that she knows lesbian people are chuckling and getting it is probably enough for her to keep going. And for now, it's enough for us."

In the late 1990s the New Zealand-based mythological-fantasy TV show *Xena, Warrior Princess* became a cult favorite among lesbians. Linda Birner, editor of the Sacramento gay paper, *Mom Guess What*, told the *Sacramento Bee* (8/27/97), "Lesbians don't go out anymore on Saturday nights. Everyone's home watching *Xena*."

The powerful heroine, played by Lucy Lawless, and her companion Gabrielle (Renee O'Connor), did little to discourage the readings their lesbian viewers preferred, and the producers seemed to deliberately infuse the show with barely hidden erotic overtones. Lucy Lawless, while clearly marked as heterosexual—complete with husband and baby—has steadily refused to distance herself from her lesbian fans, although she has also given in to the inevitable universalizing ploy, as when she told *US* magazine in October 1997:

At first it was a surprise to hear that people were throwing a loopy slant on it just because two women were traveling around together with no visible means of male support. We kind of laughed and played along with it. That was a long time ago, and since, we've moved on. I think the characters transcend labeling, just like gay people don't want to be identified solely by their sexuality. They contribute so many things to society that to limit it to their sexuality is unimaginative.

10

Hollywood's Gay Nineties

In the spring of 1995 Joyce Millman, TV critic for the *San Francisco Examiner*, wrote a prescient column on "The Sitcom That Dare Not Speak Its Name." The program was ABC's *Ellen*, which, while performing well in the all-important ratings contest, was having difficulty finding its identity. Based on the wry, self-deprecating persona Ellen DeGeneres had developed as a standup comedian, *Ellen* was one of many sitcoms spawned by the success of comedy club circuit graduates Roseanne and Jerry Seinfeld. Along with Asian American Margaret Cho (*All American Girl*) and southern working-class Brett Butler (*Grace Under Fire*), DeGeneres was swept into prime time by television's unquenchable thirst for imitation. *Seinfeld* and fellow NBC hit *Friends* were also models for the bunch-of-twentysomething-friends-hanging-around format of *Ellen* (originally titled *These Friends of Mine*). But as Millman perceptively noted, something was off-key in the lead character's ambivalence toward those staples of sitcom plotting, dating and romance. "As a single gal sitcom, *Ellen* doesn't make any sense at all, until you view it through the looking glass where the unspoken subtext becomes the main point. Then *Ellen* is transformed into one of TV's savviest, funniest, slyest shows. Ellen Morgan is a closet lesbian."

Millman's insight was likely shared by many in the media, as well as in the audience, but she also wondered, "If *Ellen* were to lay all its cards on the table, so to speak, could it still be a hit? Well, the pro-gay attitude of *Roseanne* hasn't hurt that show. The pressure to be a role model, though, coupled with the inevitable conservative protests, might squeeze the life out of an up-front *Ellen*."

For her part, Ellen DeGeneres (who noted in a November 1995 interview with *Entertainment Weekly* that she wanted more women writers on *Ellen*, because the male writers were "focusing on me dating all the time. . . . There are lots of women who don't date this much") stubbornly refused to be drawn out on her private life. Even though the publicity for her best-selling book, *My Point. . . And I Do Have One*, promised "strange but true stories from her own life," she insisted that "the book was never intended to be confessional. I never talked about my personal life in standup. I never talked about it before. And suddenly, it's become this huge issue. And I don't have anything to say about it anymore. I really don't."

Others were not necessarily as discrete. Rumors about DeGeneres's lesbianism, long familiar in gay circles, began to break through the media's veil. In January 1996 *New York* magazine's "Intelligencer Column" snickered at the coyness of New York's *Daily News* gossip columnist, who "oddly neglected to mention" that the fan Ellen DeGeneres was spotted "soul-kissing and pawing" was a woman. In the summer of 1996 DeGeneres began conferring with her publicist regarding the implications of coming out. Pat Kingsley, president of PMK, the powerful Hollywood PR firm that represents Tom Cruise and Jodie Foster, told her that she "didn't know because it hadn't been done before." What followed was viewed by many PR professionals as a triumph of placement, and by much of the public as a feeding frenzy of hype.

The story began with a press release from *TV Guide* in advance of its September 28, 1996, issue, reporting that the producers of *Ellen*, as well as ABC-TV and Disney Television (which owns ABC), discussed having Ellen Morgan come out during the 1996–97 season. While that story, and others, noted that no decision had been made by the network, DeGeneres and the producers were loading the dice by dropping hints throughout the season's opening episodes (which ran, by strange coincidence, just as the story broke). In the very first show, Ellen Morgan serenades herself in the bathroom mirror as she prepares to brush her teeth: "I feel pretty, I feel pretty, I feel pretty and witty and . . ."—at which point she notices that the faucet isn't working and instead of completing the lyric as written—"gay"—she says "Hey!" Other moments were even less subtle, as when Ellen Morgan steps out of a closet in her new house, saying "Yeah, there's plenty of room, but it's not very comfortable."

The flood of publicity that followed *TV Guide*'s press release demonstrated both the appeal and volatility of the issue. Although Disney Television's response was a tight-lipped, "We don't comment on rumors and speculation," neither gay organizations nor their enemies were restrained in their responses. Alan Klein, communications director for GLAAD, said, "If the character Ellen does come out, it would be a milestone for network television because never before has a lead character been out of the closet." In the other corner, Pat Robertson promised protests by religious groups and expressed skepticism at the idea of Ellen as a lesbian, "because she's such an attractive actress." Donald Wildmon's American Family Association warned that advertisers on a show with a gay lead would "reveal their true allegiances to themes which gnaw at traditional family values" (*AFA Action Alert*, 10/2/96).

As the season progressed, the story continued to build. Ellen DeGeneres fueled the flames with appearances on *Regis and Kathie Lee* and David Letterman's and Rosie O'Donnell's talk shows, joking that her character would be revealed to be Lebanese or that they were adding a new character, Les Behan, to the show.[1] As newspaper and magazine stories proliferated, complete with polling data—*Entertainment Weekly* commissioned a survey, reporting that 72 percent of respondents would not be "personally offended if a lead character on a TV program were gay" but that only 31 percent thought that "the trend towards more gay characters on TV" is good, while 44 percent thought it was bad—the real question for ABC and Disney was probably the reaction of advertisers. In a widely quoted assessment, network advertising buyer Paul Schulman advised, "I don't think they would have any sort of major problem if she comes out of the closet and has a girlfriend. But if the two of them are in bed together, I think that would cause some advertisers to be squeamish."

Pressure from lesbian and gay viewers and organizations—egged on by GLAAD's "Ellen Watch" Web site—and media curiosity kept the issue on the public agenda. ABC executives admitted a coming out episode was in the works but remained publicly uncommitted to airing it. In the words of ABC Entertainment president Jamie Tarses, "We are very seriously considering about going in the direction that everyone's speculating on." Meanwhile, as Ellen Morgan's sexuality was being debated in ABC's and Disney's executive offices, Ellen DeGeneres was facing a similar question: If Ellen Morgan came out, could Ellen DeGeneres continue to refuse to discuss her private life? As lesbian comedian Lea DeLaria asked, "What, is she going to say 'I'm not a lesbian, but I play one on TV'?"

From the start of DeGeneres's conversations with her publicist, it was obvious to them that both Ellens would have to come out, and it was here

---

[1] In one especially in-jokey moment, Rosie O'Donnell, noting her own penchant for Middle Eastern food, said "I could be Lebanese myself," to which DeGeneres added, "Half of Hollywood is Lebanese."

that the PR campaign orchestrated by PMK and ABC was especially effective. Once the decision was made to proceed with the coming out—and the flood of publicity unleashed back in September 1996 really left the network no choice—ABC set the date for the episode for the spring sweeps and began to organize the publicity (it also moved the program from its early prime-time slot to a later hour). As the taping date neared, stories appeared with clockwork regularity, heralding the growing list of guest appearances on the hour-long episode: the roster eventually included Oprah Winfrey as Ellen's therapist (who better to ease audiences across this emotional threshold than our national media empath?), Laura Dern as the woman Ellen falls for, and cameos by k. d. lang, Melissa Etheridge, Demi Moore, Billy Bob Thornton, and Dwight Yoakum. At the same time, DeGeneres's publicists at PMK executed a spectacular media coming out for the star, limiting her to three interviews, but what interviews! Beginning with a cover story in *Time*—a photo of DeGeneres with the bold headline, "Yep, I'm gay"—and continuing with a two-part interview with Diane Sawyer on ABC's *20/20*, one segment airing the week before and one immediately following the coming out episode.[2] The publicity grand slam was completed with an appearance on *Oprah* the afternoon of the coming out episode.

The *Oprah* appearance was more than just another round in the PR barrage; it opened a whole new front in the cultural war that Ellen/*Ellen* had come to represent. In a sidebar interview accompanying the *Time* article, DeGeneres answered a question, "Are you involved with anybody now?" saying "I just met somebody. This appears to be something I want to last forever, if it can." As viewers tuned in to *Oprah* on April 30 learned, that somebody was rising Hollywood star Anne Heche.

Anne Heche's coming out had not been foreshadowed in the flood of publicity surrounding Ellen/*Ellen*, and it was a first of a different kind for Hollywood: the coming out of a female star (or star-in-the-making) who was identified with romantic roles. Ellen DeGeneres had never been typed as a romantic lead—critics had often noted her "studied absence of man-catching glamour"—but Heche had recently been seen sexually entangled with Alec Baldwin and Johnny Depp, and was about to appear in the big-budget Hollywood film *Volcano*, playing a scientist with a romantic interest in Tommy Lee Jones.

---

[2] Ellen's coming out party was also a demonstration of media "synergy"—in addition to *20/20*, ABC's *World News Tonight* on the day of the episode did two segments, totaling five minutes, relating to Ellen and lesbianism while *Good Morning America* did segments that day and the next; neither CBS nor NBC covered the story.

Previous comings out—or exposures—had occurred after a star was past his or her "media prime," as in the case of a 1955 *Confidential* exposé of Marlene Dietrich, Johnny Mathis's 1982 coming out interview in *US* magazine, or the later revelations by or about TV actors Raymond Burr, Nancy Kulp, Dick Sargent, Dack Rambo, among others.[3] But Heche was just entering the ranks of Hollywood's A-list as an attractive, (hetero)sexual young woman and had recently been signed to play opposite box-office heavyweight Harrison Ford. The director of that movie, Ivan Reitman, at first seemed worried but quickly backed down: "Harrison and I want to emphasize that Anne is definitely in the film . . . and that both of us are enthusiastically looking forward to working with her." The journalistic consensus seemed to be that Heche's career could survive coming out because she somehow wouldn't threaten women and would appeal to male viewers' fascination with lesbian sexuality, as long as she eventually ended up with a male lover.

Heche's declaration that she hadn't ever considered herself a lesbian until she spotted Ellen DeGeneres across a crowded room also unsettled the lesson that Oprah and her audience had been taught by previous queer guests. As one woman in the audience put it, "We're led to believe that people who are gay tend to know from birth, and you kind of disputed that." Oprah quickly scheduled an emergency session the following week, bringing on a pack of scholars and lesbian/gay activists of all persuasions, attempting (unsuccessfully) to regain a secure position on the issue.

What seemed to go unnoticed in the commotion was the eerie resemblance between Anne Heche's revelation that she loved Ellen DeGeneres and Ellen Morgan's discovery that she loved the character played by Laura Dern on *Ellen*: fiction and real life converge on the road to Damascus. In some ways the *nouveau dyke* experiences of Ellen Morgan would necessarily be more familiar to Heche than to DeGeneres, who had, after all, come out nearly twenty years earlier. Ellen Morgan, in turn, deflected attention from a question that might have dimmed the glowing adulation DeGeneres was basking in: why had it taken her so long to come out publicly? As columnist Dan Savage pointed out, Oprah and Diane Sawyer seemed to be interviewing Ellen Morgan, not Ellen Degeneres.

The coming out episode of *Ellen* drew the largest audience of the week and, along with the *20/20* interview, propelled ABC to the top of sweeps

---

[3] Entertainment writer Boze Hadleigh has pioneered an entire genre of "confessional" interviews with Hollywood gay and lesbian celebrities, always published posthumously and thus conveniently immune from both libel suits and denials by the interviewees. Caveat lector!

heap. Across the country *Ellen* parties were held in homes and fund-raisers filled halls from Manhattan to Kansas City to West Hollywood. In Birmingham, Alabama, where the local ABC affiliate refused to carry the episode, a local group sold two thousand tickets for a closed-circuit showing at an auditorium. Although some regular *Ellen* advertisers (Chrysler, McDonald's, Coca-Cola and Domino's Pizza, among others) stayed away, ABC easily sold the commercial slots for upwards of $300,000 per thirty-second spot (up from the usual $150,000 to $200,000) to such sponsors as Volkswagen, the Gap, Warner Brothers, and Burlington Coat Factory. Treading warily, ABC refused to sell air time to Olivia Cruise Lines, a lesbian travel company. The Human Rights Campaign (HRC) produced an ad explaining that lesbians and gay men were vulnerable to employment discrimination in forty-one states, but ABC turned them down. However, HRC did succeed in placing the ad on approximately thirty ABC affiliates around the country.

Critical reaction to the episode was enthusiastic—it eventually won a screenwriting Emmy and a Peabody award—spilling out of the media columns into the news and editorial pages. The *New York Times* ran an editorial (May 1, 1997), praising the show's "wit and poignancy" and the star's "brave decision," but also chastising DeGeneres and Heche for their "ostentatious display of affection . . . in front of President Clinton at the White House Correspondents Dinner" (the "display" apparently consisted of hand-holding that would have been unremarkable for a straight couple) and sternly warning that, "As the first openly gay lead character on and off television, Ms DeGeneres faces a special challenge—keeping her show fresh, funny and free of special pleading."

The next episodes of *Ellen* didn't come close to the blockbuster ratings of the coming out show, but it still led its time slot. However, ABC waited until the last moment before renewing the program for the 1997–98 season. The network, like the *New York Times*, seemed uneasy at the prospect of a sitcom that might be accused of "special pleading." By the start of the 1998 fall season, Ellen DeGeneres and ABC were conducting a semipublic tug-of-war over the direction Ellen Morgan's new life would take.

In her coming out interviews DeGeneres emphasized that she did not wish to be an activist: "I never wanted to be 'the lesbian actress.' I never wanted to be the spokesperson for the gay community. Ever. I did it for my own truth."[4] Yet, quite predictably, caught in the headlights of unrelenting

---

[4] Pushing her "nonpolitical" image in her interview with Diane Sawyer, DeGeneres also noted her dislike for the term *lesbian* ("It sounds like a cult or something . . . It just sounds like you've got some kind of disease") and her displeasure with the sight of "dykes on bikes or these men dressed as women" in parades ("It's like saying Joey Buttafuco represents the heterosexual population").

media attention, attracting both adulation and hostility, forced to negotiate every script line with corporate executives concerned with boycotts and bottom lines, Ellen DeGeneres found herself sucked into a public role.[5] Being catapulted into the public arena as a famous lesbian did not, however, transform the long-closeted performer into a politically astute activist. In April 1998, appearing in England to promote the U.K. broadcast of the coming out episode, she was still insisting, "I don't see it as being political, but everyone else does. I was just searching for my own personal freedom."[6]

Despite earlier disclaimers that *Ellen* would not become the "lesbian dating show," the new episodes did focus on Ellen Morgan's exploration of her new identity, eventually falling in love with another woman, kissing her, and heading off with her to the bedroom at the close of a November show. ABC countered by placing parental advisories before these episodes and giving them a TV-14 rating ("Parents Strongly Cautioned") under the new television rating system introduced in 1997. Ellen objected over the advisories, as did GLAAD and other gay organizations, noting that no such cautions were placed on programs with much more explicit, but hetero, sexual content. Both ABC and DeGeneres were willing to use the conflict to promote the show, however, as when a promo aired during *Monday Night Football* (10/28/97) featured the star saying, "Hi, I'm Ellen DeGeneres. I can't tell you the plot of this week's show, but it's titled 'Ellen Kisses a Girl and Upsets the Network.'"

The "new" *Ellen* was popular with gay audiences, and the critics generally approved of the direction taken—especially successful was an episode in which Emma Thompson "comes out" as a lesbian (and an Ohioan)—but the ratings were not high enough to protect the show from accusations of being "too gay." The issue erupted in flames when GLAAD's entertainment director Chastity Bono told an interviewer from *Daily Variety* that she felt *Ellen* was in ratings trouble because, as she later put it, "the subject matter had become too gay-specific for Middle America." *Variety*'s front-page headline, "*Ellen* Is Too Gay," probably cost Bono her job at GLAAD, and it certainly

---

[5] Her mother, Betty, who was introduced to the public in Diane Sawyer's second *20/20* interview, was soon drafted as a spokesperson for PFLAG (Parents and Friends of Lesbians and Gays), joining Candace Gingrich (of the Human Rights Campaign) and Chastity Bono (then at GLAAD), in the ranks of "celebrities by virtue of being the relative of a famous person."

[6] One thing Ellen DeGeneres and Ellen Morgan had in common was their aversion to seeing their situation in a political light. When Ellen's gay friend Peter introduces her to some lesbian and gay activists—depicted as humorless, PC enforcers—she complains about the "bumper stickers and the flags," with much the same tone as Ellen DeGeneres talking with Diane Sawyer.

helped grease the skids on which *Ellen* was sliding toward cancellation by the end of the 1997–98 season.

Ellen Morgan didn't survive as a lesbian lead character on prime-time television, but her coming out was a milestone in American cultural history: a narrative punctuated by media events that represented and reinforced transformations in the social climate. Despite Gil Scott-Heron's 1960s-era pronouncement that the revolution would not be televised, it has long been clear that television serves as the platform on which the drama of our common culture is played out. Social change is a gradual and uneven process, which may be why highlighting signifying moments is attractive. As different groups demand their place in society, their claim is partly demonstrated through media representation, even fictional depictions.

The drama of white America's reluctant embrace of African Americans can be traced from the caricatures of *Amos 'n' Andy* in the 1950s, and the flap when British singer Petula Clark touched Harry Belafonte's arm in the early 1960s, to Diahann Carroll as *Julia* (long before she got to play a "soap opera bitch" opposite Joan Collins in *Dynasty*), and culminating in the career of Bill Cosby. Long before *The Cosby Show* topped the ratings, Cosby broke new ground as the first African American to star in a TV series, as Robert Culp's partner on *I Spy* in the mid-1960s.

Norman Lear's *All in the Family* introduced a variety of hot-button topics throughout the 1970s, and its spinoff, *Maude*, featured the first—and still the only—lead character to have an abortion. When Dan Quayle focused on the fictional Murphy Brown in order to criticize single mothers, the story, complete with a photo of "Murphy Brown" (as opposed to Candace Bergen), ran on the front page of the *New York Times*.

Thus, Ellen Morgan took her place in a long line of television firsts, frightening the horses of the Christian Right; heartening the spirits of many, such as the woman who wrote to a *New York Times* reporter that "Ellen's decision to come out has indeed spurred me to tiptoe out of my own closet"; and evoking ambivalence in others, such as lesbian cartoonist Alison Bechdel, who told the Los Angeles *Lesbian News*,

> The Ellen thing's got me all in a twist. I feel like if you take this quest for visibility to its logical extreme and we end up on network TV and in every other book, people won't have the same need for this rich subculture that we've built. . . . That's kind of sad to me, even though in a way it's progress. It's sad because I like being on the margins. I think you have a richer life that way. I don't want to see queer life turned into a commodity on network TV.

STILL VILLAINOUS AFTER ALL THESE YEARS

Just as the saga of Ellen's coming out was reaching its climax in late April 1997, a vastly different sort of story began its journey to the headlines. A gay man named Jeffrey Trail was killed in a Minneapolis apartment, followed within a few days by the discovery of the body of another gay man, David Madson, near Chicago, and then the stabbed body of Lee Miglin, a wealthy Chicago businessman, was discovered in his garage. Almost immediately, the suspected killer of all three men was identified as Andrew Cunanan of San Diego, who had known both Trail and Madsen. The multiple killings set off a manhunt for Cunanan, who apparently fled East in Miglin's car, which he abandoned in New Jersey after killing a cemetary caretaker and stealing his truck. At this point the trail went cold, and although the FBI issued alerts there was no visible trace of the suspected killer. Although *America's Most Wanted* labeled Cunanan "Public Enemy Number One," and the gay press ran stories with Cunanan's picture to warn that a killer was on the loose, the manhunt seemed stalled until July 15, when Andrew Cunanan burst onto the world's front pages by shooting and killing renowned fashion designer Gianni Versace on the front steps of his South Beach, Florida, mansion.

The killing of Gianni Versace turned the previously obscure story into one of the biggest news events of the year, putting Andrew Cunanan at the top of network news and on the cover of *Newsweek*.[7] The tidal wave of the story swept aside lessons slowly learned by the news media, as they rushed to judgment about the killer, the victim, and the circumstances of the tragic events. When a normally careful journalist like Tom Brokaw refers to the "homicidal homosexual" who killed Versace, it's hardly surprising that the sleazy ones, like the *New York Post*, kept using phrases such as "bloodthirsty gay serial killer" and engaged in homophobic speculation.[8] The saga of Andrew Cunanan, entangled after the killing of Gianni Versace with the glamorous world of high fashion and the South Beach party scene, triggered journalistic conditioned reflexes that associate gay with sex, and especially with promiscuity, decadence, and AIDS.

Within a day of the Versace murder the media were promoting the the-

---

[7] A Lexis-Nexis search for the four months following Cunanan's first murder turned up 994 stories; in contrast, for the year following the first stories about the possibility that Ellen Degeneres's character would come out—and including the hype surrounding the actual coming out—the total number of stories was 641.

[8] Some of the offenders did not have the excuse that they were caught up in the excitement of the moment. The September 1997 issue of *Vanity Fair* promoted an article by Maureen Orth with the cover line, "On the Trail of the Gay Serial Killer."

ory—soon taken for granted as fact—that Cunanan was HIV-positive and that, as a *New York Post* headline put it, "AIDS Fuels His Fury" (a hypothesis disputed by Joel Achenbach in the *Washington Post*). As it turned out, when an autopsy was conducted on Cunanan's body (he committed suicide the week after shooting Versace), he was not HIV-positive and we will probably never know what motivated his murders. The media and the police also elaborated the hypothesis that Cunanan had escaped from Miami dressed as a woman. Reported sightings of a cross-dressing Cunanan were encouraged by broadcast and printed images of what he might look like in a wig and makeup.

Many media accounts delved into Cunanan's past in an attempt to explain what had turned a shallow young man into a cold-blooded killer. Almost without exception the stories depicted Cunanan as a prostitute, whether an amateur gigolo or, as his mother was reported to have termed him, a "high-class homosexual prostitute" (his father told reporters that this was not true: "he was an altar boy"). In any case, there was no evidence that Cunanan was turning tricks, though it is quite possible that he was—or wanted to be—a "trophy boy." Other stories, equally unsupported by real evidence, speculated that Cunanan was part of a sexual underworld of drugs and kinky sex. Journalist Maureen Orth, who wrote a long article on Cunanan for *Vanity Fair* and then a book on the case, told CNN's Larry King that Cunanan "traversed a gay parallel universe in America today—traveling from the seamy, drug-addled underbelly of the demimonde to the cultured and privileged world of the rich and the closeted." Orth allowed her imagination to take her even farther when she reported that Cunanan and Versace were acquainted—a claim that was never supported by evidence—with the implication that this somehow explained the murder.

If Cunanan was fair game for homophobic media speculation, it might have been expected that his victims would receive better treatment. But Gianni Versace was not exactly left in peace after his death. *New York Post* gossip columnist Cindy Adams lost no time in playing blame-the-victim, writing that Versace frequented "what the uptight might term dens of iniquity," and the TV tabloid *Hard Copy* followed suit, showing topless men dancing in Miami, and promising to explore "Versace's private playland . . . a world some say may have led to his untimely death." According to *Hard Copy* of July 16, 1997, Versace threw "the kinds of parties that Cunanan reportedly trolled for fresh victims." *Newsweek* even reported the (soon discredited) claim that Cunanan had attended a "small party" at Versace's house two days before the killing. Maureen Orth also alleged in her book that Versace was HIV-positive, although his family denies this and, even if true, its relevance to his killing is nonexistent.

When it came to reporting Versace's celebrity-studded funeral, the media went into great detail, offering pictures and descriptions of the mourners, with Princess Diana and Elton John receiving the most elaborate coverage, along with Versace's sister, brother, and his nieces. Almost completely unmentioned was Antonio D'Amico, his lover of eleven years (also overlooked was Elton John's lover, David Furman, who was clearly visible, but never identified, in numerous photographs of the funeral). Not only did the media erase D'Amico, failing to mention him in obituaries or coverage of the funeral, but some went further in their eagerness to "in" a man who had never hidden his homosexuality. The wire services devoted much space to the funeral, informing us that "the men closest to the designer—his brother Santo, Sting and Elton John—all wore black crew necks rather than a tie under dark jackets. . . . Elton John stood in silence for 15 minutes. Then he burst into tears and had to be coaxed away by Versace's brother" (*St. Louis Post-Dispatch*, 7/23/97). The *London Daily Telegraph*'s obituary (7/16/97) concluded, "Versace never married. 'As a person, he is not very sexual,' a woman colleague explained, 'but there is plenty of suggestion.'"

The media do not require the drama of a serial killer as a pretext for lapses into homophobic coverage of gay men. Unearthing a tactic that was used by police before being curtailed in the 1960s, local TV stations in 1998 began sneaking cameras into public toilets in the hope of catching men engaged in sex.[9] A Seattle TV station did a story concerning a Web site that lists places across the country where men meet for sex, and followed up by sending a reporter into a local mensroom with a hidden camera. The Seattle story was quickly imitated by ABC's San Diego affiliate, in time for the February sweeps period, and the ploy was quickly picked up by other ABC affiliates. The standard practice in these stories is to electronically scramble the image to obscure the faces of the men depicted, but in at least one instance a San Antonio station screwed up and clearly broadcast the faces of two men. Also, as *Detroit Free Press* reporter John Smyntek noted (5/28/98), it is not known what happens to the original tapes; station executives might assume that all hidden camera footage is erased after the broadcast but, in fact, copies might well be kept by station personnel. The *San Diego Union-Tribune*, writing about the local angle, pointed out that the station in question appeared to

---

[9] In one of the most publicized instances of police surveillance, LBJ aide Walter Jenkins, a middle-aged Catholic with six children, was arrested in October 1964 in a YMCA restroom a few blocks from the White House. The White House and the FBI attributed Jenkins's behavior to "fatigue, alcohol, physical illness and lack of food." Jenkins quickly resigned, and when presidential candidate Barry Goldwater refused to make a campaign issue out of the story, the scandal quickly subsided.

violate California state law, which forbids such hidden filming in bathrooms, but also noted that "there will be no action taken against Channel 10 unless someone who was taped comes forward and complains to police that their privacy was invaded, said a spokeswoman for the City Attorney."[10] The newspaper also revealed that portions of the San Diego station's report were taken verbatim from the earlier story broadcast by the Seattle station.

By the time the May sweeps loomed, the story gimmick had been written up in the *Rundown*, a weekly eight-page trade paper and tip sheet for TV stations, and spread across the country as local news directors exchanged ideas for audience-attracting sweeps stories. "If a station in a market finds a story that does really well, that story will make the rounds in every market," the news director for two stations in Florida told a reporter. By November 1998, local TV stations in more than forty cities, including Boston, Charlotte, Cincinnati, Columbus, Detroit, Houston, Las Vegas, Miami, New York, Oklahoma City, Philadelphia, Pittsburgh, San Antonio, and Syracuse, all ran such stories, heavily hyped—usually during sweeps periods. As the new general manager of New York's Fox TV station admitted to the *Village Voice*'s Richard Goldstein, he was under orders to improve their ratings: "I'm here to stem the downturning tide," and toilet-tryst TV might do the trick. WSOC in Charlotte, North Carolina, offered their videotapes to the local vice squad, who subsequently arrested eleven men.[11]

Gay leaders responding to the TV tabloid sensationalism were often eager to condemn public sex while decrying the media's tactics. Karen Boothe, then president of the National Lesbian and Gay Journalists Association said in a May 11, 1998, press release that "NLGJA in no way condones illegal sexual activity in public places, but nor do we condone exploitative coverage that

---

[10] California Penal Code Section 647(k) makes the following conduct a misdemeanor: "Anyone who looks through a hole or opening, into, or otherwise views, by means of any instrumentality, including, but not limited to, a periscope, telescope, binoculars, camera, or camcorder, the interior of a bathroom, changing room, fitting room, dressing room, or tanning booth, or the interior of any other area in which the occupant has a reasonable expectation of privacy, with the intent to invade the privacy of a person or persons inside." A violation of 647(k) is punishable by a fine of $1,000 and/or six months in jail.

[11] The police do not necessarily depend on TV news crews to do their work. Oakland County, Michigan, police installed a camera in an Oakland University men's bathroom after "officers verified there were unusually high numbers of people going in and out of the bathroom during the summer, when enrollment is at its lowest," and subsequently arrested two men, whose names were then printed in the local paper. And then there are the entrepreneurs: in July 1999 the AP reported that "athletes at eight universities say they were secretly videotaped in locker rooms and the tapes were sold through Internet sites advertising 'hot young dudes.'" Other Internet sites offer videos purportedly shot in women's rest rooms or health club locker rooms.

panders to sexual curiosity as a way of pumping up ratings." Mark Segal, publisher of the *Philadelphia Gay News*, said he was "opposed to heterosexuals or gay men or anybody having public sex," but that the local TV story was a "scare story," not an investigation of public sex. At the same time, other gay leaders pointed out the double standard that views public sex between men and women, in parked cars or on beaches, as romantic and even amusing, while public (though much less visible) sex between men is seen as horrible and perverted.[12]

Although the stations typically focused on the so-called threat to children who might stumble on men engaged in sex, none ever turned up evidence of this happening. New York's Fox station ran ads for several days that were typical of stations across the country: "Sexual deviants are roaming our local stores and malls, places that you shop, with your children. . . . Could you or your child be an innocent victim of cruising for sex?" In fact, as has been known at least since sociologist Laud Humphreys' 1970 study, *Tearoom Trade*, "outsiders" rarely stumble onto such scenes, as the activities typically cease when newcomers enter the space, and only resume when the person either leaves or indicates an interest in watching or participating. Vice cops succeed in apprehending men engaging in "public sex" in restrooms only by giving clear signals that they are interested themselves—whether in watching or participating—and then arresting men who respond positively to their signals, as George Michael learned in a Los Angeles park restroom in April 1998.[13] The reporters who fearlessly caught men in the act in shopping mall restrooms must have also "played by the rules," in order not to have caused their targets to cease their activities.

When Philadelphia's NBC affiliate WCAU-TV was preparing to air its version of this exposé during the November 1998 sweeps, local activists sought to persuade the station that its "Hidden Camera Investigation" was exposing a nonexistent problem: none of the places where the footage was shot

---

[12] An article in the *UCLA Daily Bruin* pointed out the hypocrisy inherent in the differential response to heterosexual and homosexual "public sex," noting that an episode of the ABC sitcom *Dharma and Greg* broadcast the same day as a news report about gay public sex featured the two lead characters "pondering where they would like to have sex in public." The article also recalled a *Daily Bruin* interview with graduating seniors in which one cited as his fondest memory having sex with his girlfriend in the library.

[13] News reports made it fairly clear that George Michael had been masturbating in front of a vice cop, who was giving encouraging signals. As Michael described the event during a live interview on MTV, "I got followed into the restroom and then this cop—I didn't know it was a cop, obviously—he started playing this game, which I think is called, 'I'll show you mine, you show me yours, and then when you show me yours, I'm going to nick you.'" Following his arrest Michael quickly made an appearance on CNN in which he came out as a gay man, surprising no one who had paid any attention to the singer's career, but successfully defusing the arrest scandal.

had ever recorded even a single complaint about children encountering sexual activity in their bathrooms. In discussions with the station news director and the reporter who prepared the story, they kept asking, "What if a child walked in and saw these men?" It was explained that such activities cease when outsiders enter—and certainly if a child entered—and would only resume if the newcomer indicated interest. The reporter protested, "Well, they didn't stop when I was there," to which an activist replied, "You were showing interest!" The reporter, a good-looking young man, was wearing a pair of eyeglasses with a camera built into the nosepiece, which meant that in order to capture the shocking behavior on video he had to be looking directly and steadily at the men who were engaging in whatever it was—which certainly passes for interest and encouragement, under the familiar "rules of the game" for tearoom sex. One might well describe the reporter's actions as video-entrapment. The local media establishment felt differently, apparently, as the series won a mid-Atlantic Emmy Award for "Outstanding Service News."

Print media, which occasionally decry the sensationalism of tabloid TV, are nonetheless often willing to print the names and addresses of men arrested in "sting operations" by vice cops who stake out public parks and restrooms. In January 1998 the *Arkansas Democrat-Gazette* listed the names and addresses of twenty-four men arrested in a "3-day park sting" (in contrast to the paper's discretion in not revealing the names of men arrested in an earlier heterosexual prostitution sting), and one of the men subsequently committed suicide. His suicide note said, "my name and everything is in the paper this morning." The *Columbus Dispatch* followed suit in November 1999, reporting on "Dozens Charged with Indecency in City Park" and listing the names, ages, and addresses of forty-three men. The article singled out several clergymen, teachers, and a school board member, who promptly resigned his position. Sometimes the sting operations bite their instigators, as when an Elkhart, Indiana, vice cop arrested the president of the City Park Board, "the man who helped lead a task force charged with cleaning up lewd acts at Elliot Park," when he "behaved in an indecent manner with an undercover male police officer."

SAD YOUNG MEN

Writing about the 1950s and 1960s, Richard Dyer described the figure of the sad young man commonly employed to represent male homosexuality in popular culture. The image of a handsome young man poised on the brink of adulthood is here painted not with the glow of optimism, facing a bright future of possibilities, but tinged with a melancholy foreshadowing the sad fate in store for those condemned to the gay life. The sad young man is a very different image than the familiar stereotype of the lonely, aging queer, facing the bleak prospect of old age without the comfort and support of family and children. As Dyer notes, the sad young man is marked in terms of transition, "moving between normal and queer worlds, always caught at the moment of exploration and discovery."

On American television the figure of the sad young man has become a favorite vehicle for writers and producers venturing onto the thin ice of gay-related characters and stories. The early 1990s saw a sudden spurt in gay-related episodes (two men on *thirtysomething*, a "lesbian" kiss on *L.A. Law*), and even in continuing gay characters (a central lesbian character on the short-lived *Heartbeat*, and secondary gay characters on *Roseanne* and *North-ern Exposure*). Prominent in this flowering of gay themes was a veritable bouquet of sad young men. As an unambiguously out gay man, Matt Fielding in *Melrose Place* doesn't quite fit the stereotype, although his inability to get laid might qualify him for the sad label. But there were plenty of others whose claims to the title aren't in question.[14]

In January 1992 the NBC science fiction series, *Quantum Leap*, ran an episode by openly gay writer Bobby Duncan, in which the hero "leaps" into the body of a mid-sixties military cadet who must save a gay fellow cadet driven to the verge of suicide by homophobic harassment. Later that spring Fox-TV aired a movie of the week, *Doing Time on Maple Drive*, that might be described as a dysfunctional family Olympics. The Carter family, headed by a military officer martinet and a social-climbing bitch, includes three children: the older son, an alcoholic ne'er-do-well; a daughter who has disappointed her father by marrying a medical student who can't afford the lifestyle daddy expects; and the younger son, star athlete and Yale student, who is engaged to marry a member of what seems very much like the Kennedy clan. The plot is predictable: golden boy brings his fiancé home to meet the family, she discovers that he's gay (when she reads a note he's left in a jacket pocket) and leaves after breaking off the engagement, whereupon he drives his car into a tree. He survives, but when he returns home, arm in a cast, his mother has found out that the engagement is broken—"How can

---

[14] Of course, the story of a sad young man's discovery of his sexuality and enduring the pain of coming out to family and friends was already familiar to television audiences. The TV movies *Consenting Adult* and *Welcome Home, Bobby*, the ABC *Afterschool Special* "What If I'm Gay?" and even the long-running character of Steven Carrington on *Dynasty* would fit the pattern.

you do this to me? The invitations have gone out!" He comes out to everyone, denouncing his mother (who already knew but denied it), and the movie ends on a somewhat uncertain note of possible reconciliation (with the father), but certainly nothing to deflect the sad young man label.

If still beset by melancholy and the hostility of parents and peers, the sad young man *was* growing a bit more militant, as demonstrated through the summer of 1992 by Billy Douglas on the soap opera *One Life to Live* (and several years later by another openly gay teen on *All My Children*). But in 1994 two young gay Hispanic men brought together real life and popular culture, redefining the image of the sad young man.

A new series in the fall of 1994 on ABC, *My So-Called Life*, centered on a 15-year-old high school student and her circle of friends. It didn't take long for critical and audience attention to note one friend in particular, Rickie Vasquez, half black, half Hispanic, and bisexual on the way to coming out as gay. Rickie, who hangs out in the girls' bathroom and wears eyeliner, encounters verbal and physical hostility from schoolmates and family that was both realistic and familiar to the young actor, Wilson Cruz, who played him. In an episode that aired just before Christmas, Rickie is beaten and thrown out of his house, and the actor recalled being kicked out by his own father after he came out to him on Christmas Eve.[15] The actor quickly came out in interviews, and much of the publicity highlighted the similarities between the actor and the character. Cruz himself noted, "I can play him as honestly as I can to what I went through, how I reacted to these things." He recalled the lack of support he found in the media: "I would turn on the TV and think, *Please, give me a sign that I fit in somewhere, that I'm not alone out here*," and concluded, "I hope I can help kids see that they're not the only ones in the world." Despite critical acclaim and a cult following, *My So-Called Life* did not survive in the ratings jungle and was canceled after one season. It was picked up for replay, however, on another frontier of popular culture that has proven open to lesbian and gay realities, the rock-and-roll cable channel MTV.

In one of its most successful innovations, MTV introduced a series called *The Real World* that brings together a group of twentysomething strangers to live in a house and have their lives filmed by a documentary crew. From its beginning the program (one of whose producers, Jon Murray, is openly gay) has included gay cast members. The very first season, filmed in New York,

---

[15] On this Christmas episode, in a most unusual (for television) example of support, Rickie rings the doorbell of a sympathetic teacher—shown to be gay (we see his lover in the background)—who takes him in.

included a gay man, and lesbian and gay housemates participated in six of the first eight seasons. The third season, set in San Francisco, quickly became the most dramatic of all, with the intrusion of a very real tragedy. One of the participants chosen for the San Francisco group was a charismatic 22-year-old Cuban American from Miami, Pedro Zamora, who was diagnosed with HIV at 17 and had been an AIDS activist and educator ever since. The series began with some of the housemates being put off and upset by Zamora's HIV status and ultimately changing their attitudes. The show not only provided Zamora with a national platform for AIDS education but also chronicled his budding relationship with an African American gay man, Sean Sasser. The two exchanged rings in a marriage ceremony during one episode, bringing an actual gay relationship to television audiences. And, yes, they kissed, many times.

As the series progressed, however, Pedro's health worsened. "My friend is dying and I don't know what to do," one of his roommates wept at one point. The fact that Pedro Zamora was a real person, his health monitored by the media from CNN to the *Wall Street Journal* (which ran a front-page article noting a phone call to Zamora in the hospital from President Clinton), made the final episodes powerfully moving to audiences who had come to know him and knew that he was dying.[16] On November 10, 1994, millions of viewers watched as Pedro Zamora left *The Real World* at the end of the final episode, filmed months before in San Francisco. The next day, in a Miami hospital, Pedro Zamora died at age 22.

Four years after Pedro Zamora's death, the death of another young gay man captured the attention of the nation, but instead of AIDS, it was anti-gay violence that was now in the spotlight. One morning in early October 1998, a cyclist out for a morning ride on the outskirts of Laramie, Wyoming, spotted what looked at first like a scarecrow hanging from a barbed-wire fence. When he realized that the figure was that of a young man, beaten and tied to the fence, the story of Matthew Shepard was on its way to the headlines. By the time Matthew Shepard died, two local young men were in jail, soon to be charged with first-degree murder. Although the local paper reported the assault, it was after two gay friends of Shepard's at the University of Wyoming alerted the larger *Casper Star-Tribune* that the story made its way to the Associated Press as a hate crime attack on a gay student. The news media had been primed for the hate crime angle by the recent murder of James Byrd, an African American man dragged to death behind a car in Texas a few months earlier. Journalists descended on Laramie, covering

---

[16] The series is heavily edited after the five-month period during which the cast live together, and the edited episodes air long after they were actually filmed.

Shepard's death and funeral, delving into his short life and brutal killing, and the story leapt onto front pages around the world, dominating headlines for more than a week, even briefly eclipsing the presidential sex scandal.[17]

The attack on Shepard occurred just before October's National Coming Out Day, and it was quickly drawn into the ongoing public debate over hate crimes legislation. A candlelight vigil on the steps of the Capitol in Washington featured Sen. Ted Kennedy (D-MA) and Congressman Barney Frank (D-MA), as well as Ellen DeGeneres and Anne Heche, among others. President Clinton condemned the murder and called on Congress to pass federal legislation increasing penalties for bias-motivated crimes, and the governor of Wyoming asked the state legislature to "have a renewed discussion of what we might do to strengthen our laws." In the end, however, neither the Wyoming legislature nor Congress would pass hate crime measures.

The media may have been united in outrage, and most politicians might have taken the opportunity to condemn murder, but not everyone was moved. As Matthew Shepard lay in a coma, members of a Colorado State University fraternity marched in a homecoming parade with a scarecrow tied to a fencepost, wearing a sign that read, "I'm Gay," and the words "Up My Ass," painted on its back. The incident was greeted by outrage and led to disciplinary action against members of the fraternity. To no one's surprise, antigay crusader Rev. Fred Phelps, proprietor of the "God Hates Fags" Web site, showed up on the day of the funeral to gloat over the death of another fag.[18]

---

[17] The Internet played a major role in the rapid dissemination of the story, alerting activists around the world to the unfolding events, and providing information that was used by gay organizations elsewhere to inform media and organize hundreds of vigils across the country. A "Matthew Shepard Online Resources" Web site contained links to organizations working on media, education, and hate-crime campaigns.

[18] Phelps's "God Hates Fags" Web site contains a "Perpetual Gospel Memorial to Matthew Shepard," featuring an image of Shepard surrounded by the flames of hell, and the following text: "When Matthew Shepard died on October 12, 1998, every pervert in this country (from Bill Clinton on down) used his death as a soap box to promote so-called 'gay rights.' In religious protest of this, WBC [Westboro Baptist Church] picketed the funeral of Matthew Shepard, to inject a little truth and sanity into the irrational orgy of lies consuming this world. WBC does not support the murder of Matthew Shepard, and we believe that his murderers are in violation of God's commandment that 'thou shalt not kill.' Unless they repent, they will receive the same sentence that Matthew Shepard received—eternal fire. However, the truth about Matthew Shepard needs to be known. He lived a Satanic lifestyle. He got himself killed trolling for anonymous homosexual sex in a bar at midnight. Unless he repented in the final hours of his life, he is in hell. He will be in hell for all eternity, 'where their worm dieth not, and the fire is not quenched.' Mark 9:44. For each day that passes, he has only eternity to look forward to. All the candlelight vigils, all the tributes, all the acts of Congress, all the rulings by the Supreme Court of the United States, will not shorten his sentence by so much as one day. And all the riches of the world will not buy him one drop of water to cool his tongue."

The cover of *Time* magazine for October 26, 1998, showed an image of the fence where Matthew Shepard had been tied, with the headline, "The War Over Gays." The coverage there, as elsewhere, related the murder to larger issues surrounding the situation of gay people in America. Within a few months of the Shepard killing, the brutal murder of Billy Jack Gaither, a gay man in rural Alabama, garnered national media attention—and another statement of "grief and outrage" from the president, once more calling for passage of the Hate Crimes Prevention Act—and nearly all the coverage explicitly tied the story to the killing of Matthew Shepard.

Shepard might have been typecast for the role of a sad young man. Although he had come out to his family and his friends, his mother insisted "he didn't put a sign around his neck saying I'M GAY. He was fearful." And he had reason to be. Short and slight, he had been gang-raped in Morocco while on a trip during his senior year in high school, and had been beaten outside a Wyoming bar only a few months prior to his killing. But by most accounts Shepard was also outgoing and friendly, and it is known that he willingly left the Fireside bar with the two men who proceeded to rob and beat him. Although the truth will probably never be known—whether they approached him, implying or stating that they were gay, or he approached them, making a pass and triggering their murderous rage—most accounts of the killing erased any implication that Shepard might have had a sexual motive in going off with Russell Henderson and Aaron McKinney. The media, and the lesbian and gay organizations that understandably used the murder as a platform for raising the issue of antigay violence, preferred to concentrate on the image of a somewhat wistful and sad young man captured in an endlessly reproduced snapshot that became an icon of innocent victimhood.[19]

Matthew Shepard was not only a symbol for murderous hate crimes; he also represented the dangers that are all too familiar to young lesbians and gay men who encounter the enmity of their classmates and peers. At a time of steadily increasing visibility of gay people throughout society, in high school and college classrooms as well as on the news and in TV programs, young people also seem more open in expressing prejudice and hostility. The month after Shepard's killing, *Who's Who Among American High School Stu-*

---

[19] The sexual angle did make an appearance at the trial of Aaron McKinney in October 1999 (Russell Henderson pleaded guilty in March 1999), when his lawyer tried to introduce a "homosexual panic" defense. The lawyer said that McKinney bashed Matthew Shepard's skull through his brain stem because he was "humiliated in front of his friend" by a sexual advance. After the judge disallowed the "homosexual panic" argument, the defense agreed to accept two consecutive life sentences rather than risk the death penalty (and the plea bargain also included an unprecedented and disturbing gag order forbidding McKinney or his lawyers from speaking with the press about the case).

dents published its annual survey of attitudes based on a poll of 3,123 high-achieving teenagers. The results included much that was shocking to adults, such as 80 percent admitting cheating; but the news stories headlined the increase in intolerance, especially of homosexuality: 48 percent said they were "very" or "somewhat" prejudiced against homosexuality, up nearly 20 percent over the previous year. Males admitted greater intolerance, with 24 percent claiming to be "very" prejudiced, versus 11 percent of females. And it is young men in their teens and early twenties—like the 21-year-old killers of Matthew Shepard—who commit most antigay violence.

The survey would not have been news to a young man named Jamie Nabozny, but he made news of his own in 1996, when he successfully sued a Wisconsin school district for failing to stop the antigay abuse he had suffered for years. Other pupils realized Nabozny was gay when he was in the seventh grade. In later years a classmate pushed him to the floor and simulated raping him as other pupils watched; another time he was knocked into a urinal by one boy while another urinated on him. When he sought help from the principal, he was told "boys will be boys." After the bathroom incident, the principal advised him to go home and change clothes. During another assault ten students surrounded Nabozny while a student wearing boots repeatedly kicked him in the stomach. Nabozny attempted suicide several times and, like many gay teenagers in similar situations, he dropped out of high school. But Jamie Nabozny also fought back in federal court, and won. The school district agreed to a $900,000 settlement.

The attacks on Jamie Nabozny and on many other lesbian and gay teenagers are not the whole story, because they also reflect the increasing willingness of gay teens to come out. In 1997 *Time* reported that up to 10 percent of U.S. teens tell pollsters that they are gay, lesbian, bisexual, or "questioning" their orientation, and Gay-Straight Alliances are springing up in schools across the country. The new openness is spurred by the solidarity and support provided through the Internet by Web zines and online chatrooms.

It did not take long for the new visibility of gay teens to be reflected on the TV screen. As the television networks began to eagerly seek high school and college-age audiences—the hot new demographic of the late 1990s—a slew of programs began appearing on the up-and-coming Fox and WB networks that focused on high school settings.[20] After the success of Fox's *Beverly Hills 90210* in 1990 (still running in 1999), Fox introduced *Party of*

[20] According to one theory, advertisers were drawn to these shows because young people are among the lowest TV viewers, and thus these offered a rare opportunity to attract their attention, unlike their couch potato elders, who could be counted on to see commercials on many other programs.

Five, and WB launched *Dawson's Creek* in 1998 and *Felicity* in 1999. These programs featured younger casts than previous programs, and their plots centered on the joys and pain—lots of pain—of the teenage years. Among the facts of life for these TV teens are the existence and experiences of gay people.

"It's happening on TV because it happens in real life," P. K. Simonds, a coexecutive producer of *Party of Five*, told *TV Guide*. "Kids who go to high school know kids who deal with this issue. Issues of identity are very important to young people: figuring who they are, what they are inside and how they fit in. These stories are especially relevant to young audiences because they're about young people like themselves who are learning about themselves."[21]

One character on *Beverly Hills* discovered that his mother was a lesbian, but that occurred many years into the show (an earlier episode included a gay friend coming out to a series regular, who got over it). *Party of Five* included a gay secondary character, played by openly gay actor Mitchell Anderson, and a brief appearance by a lesbian writing teacher. *Felicity* included a minor character, the gay brother of Felicity's dorm adviser, in an early episode. But it was *Dawson's Creek* that included a gay character among the main cast during its second season. Jack arrives at Capeside High School and takes up with Joey, former girlfriend of lead character Dawson. But soon enough Jack begins to realize that his true feelings lie elsewhere. When Jack reads a poem in his high school class that hints at an attraction to men, he quickly becomes a target for harassment, and someone spray-paints an antigay epithet on his locker. Jack wrestles with his feelings, first denying them to Joey and others, and finally declaring his homosexuality to his outraged father.

Jack is in many ways a familiar sad young man, accepting his homosexuality, but struggling and far from happy about it. But he is not alone—although his father reacts with hostility, his sister and his friends are supportive.[22] What he did not have was a boyfriend, although Kevin Williams, the program's openly gay creator, intimated that this would happen. When it does, it can be counted on to evoke controversy that the program had been spared. The Parents Television Council, a conservative media watchdog group, didn't

[21] In 1994 HBO brought real life to the screen in *More Than Friends; The Coming Out of Heidi Leiter*, recounting the story of a high school student who took her girlfriend to the prom, and then appeared on *The Phil Donahue Show*.

[22] When members of an opposing football team focus on attacking the openly gay player, his teammates all put on makeup under their helmets and, jeering "Try to find the homo now!" they proceed to win the game.

alert its members to the story. "To bring up the fact that there are homosexuals in society is not something to rant and rave about at this point," said Mark Honig, its executive director, although he also noted that the group may feel differently if Jack starts dating men.

In the 1999–2000 season Jack met Ethan, an openly gay college student, and spent much of the year battling indecision over how far he could go. When, in the season's final show, he finally got up the nerve to kiss Ethan, he discovered that Ethan had "made up" with his ex-boyfriend and he ended up crying on the kitchen floor, comforted by his newly supportive father. The season closed with the figure of a classic sad young man, leaving viewers to hope for joy and romance next fall.[23]

SOME OF MY BEST FRIENDS ARE CELIBATE

In the 1981 movie *Only When I Laugh*, James Coco played the best friend of the star, Marsha Mason. At one point she asks, "Why don't we get married?" and he answers, "Because I'm gay and you're an alcoholic, and we'd have trouble getting our kids into a decent school." Around that time the TV sitcom *Love, Sidney* gave us an implicitly gay Tony Randall who takes in single mother Swoozie Kurtz and her daughter, thus creating a nonsexual nuclear family. The asexual gay best friend is a variant on familiar movie and TV standbys, such as the effeminate sidekicks played by Edward Everett Horton and Franklin Pangborn in the 1930s, and the wise-cracking but romantically unlinked women played by Eve Arden in the movies and on television, and it became a dramatic staple of films in the early 1990s—with the gay man often played by actors known for comedic roles, such as George Carlin in *Prince of Tides* and Nathan Lane in *Frankie and Johnny* (both 1991).[24]

Another favorite variant on the desexualized gay man appeared in the mid-1990s cross-dressing films *To Wong Foo, Thanks for Everything, Julie Newmar* (1995, on the heels of the Australian *Adventures of Priscilla, Queen of the*

---

[23] The following season also ended with Jack kissing another male, and this time he kisses his new boyfriend at the high school prom. This kiss, which lasts about five seconds, is reciprocated, but audiences shouldn't get their hopes up. As reported in *Entertainment Weekly* magazine (5/11/01), actor Kerr Smith draws the line at once-a-year: "That's as far as I'm going to take it. I don't think teenagers need to see two guys kissing on a weekly basis."

[24] The asexual gay friend is also reminiscent of the Asian bachelors who served as houseboy/cook/butler on such TV series as *Bachelor Father* (1957–1962), *Bonanza* (1959–1973), and *Falcon Crest* (1981–1990), among others. The Asian family retainer generally offers wise advice to his employers, while remaining single and apparently celibate.

Desert) and in Hollywood's remake of *La Cage aux Folles*, *The Birdcage*, which topped the box office for several weeks in 1996. As *Newsweek* critic David Ansen put it, "Drag queens are the cinema's favorite naughty pets, harmless if not quite housebroken." Robin Williams and Nathan Lane play familiar versions of the swishy queens of earlier movies, and they are not required—or permitted—to show affection in any direct, physical form (they are portrayed, however, as a loving couple who have successfully raised a son). The three drag queens in *To Wong Foo* (played by certifiably straight John Leguizamo, Wesley Snipes, and Patrick Swayze) transform the lives of the residents of a small midwestern town, performing miracles of the sort wrought by (typically effeminate) angels in the Hollywood *It's a Wonderful Life* genre.

In the late 1990s, however, the gay man–straight woman platonic romance suddenly seemed to be popping up all over. Three Hollywood movies in a row mined this familiar vein: the runaway box office success *My Best Friend's Wedding*, in which (openly gay actor) Rupert Everett steals the show, dancing and wise-cracking with best friend Julia Roberts; then gay artist Greg Kinnear offers Helen Hunt the emotional support she can't get from possible boyfriend Jack Nicholson in the Oscar-winning *As Good As It Gets*; and in *The Object of My Affection*, Jennifer Aniston and Paul Rudd are best friends even though they have sex with other people (and *almost* with each other on one occasion). A little lower on Hollywood's radar screen, the Showtime cable channel broadcast the second installment of Armistead Maupin's *Tales of the City*, which had lots of gay sex but also had a friendship between a straight woman and a gay man close to its dramatic center.

After the cancellation of *Ellen*, the networks were caught between the desire to capitalize on the newly available chic of gay characters and the fear of falling into the parental advisory quicksand that swallowed *Ellen*. They were also feeling pressure from the growing number of openly gay writers and producers who wanted to march through the doors opened by *Ellen*, as well as *Roseanne* and *Melrose Place*. At this moment, apparently, the gay man–straight woman relationship was ready for prime time.

Conventional wisdom, as purveyed by journalists and even by then-GLAAD official Chastity Bono, was that *Ellen* became "too gay" after the momentous coming out episode. Despite Ellen DeGeneres's own insistence that she wasn't an activist, and despite the program's unflattering depiction of gay activists as humorless PC-Stalinoids, it seems that a program centering on the experience of a newly hatched lesbian *was* too gay for TV. In the words of gay conservative columnist Dale Carpenter, DeGeneres forgot that "a serious discussion of gay issues has no intrinsic interest for mainstream

Americans." And Carpenter, for one, prefers "not forcing the issue on the unwilling masses."

Enter *Will & Grace*. Packaged by a gay (Max Mutchnick)-straight (David Kohan) team of producers, *Will & Grace* combines familiar elements from TV's armory of sure-fire devices with a new twist. An "odd couple" for the 1990s, Will and Grace are best friends who share an apartment, end each other's sentences, commiserate over their recently ended relationships with other people, and generally center their lives around each other. But they're not romantically involved. Unlike previous variations on the theme, they are not separated by distance, or class, or even other partners, but by sexual orientation. The dramatic "will they or won't they?" tension of *Moonlighting*, *Lois and Clark*, and *The X-Files* is here dissolved in the sitcom laugh track possibilities of both chasing the same attractive man, or persuading her mother that he isn't her daughter's Mr. Right. Both attractive, professional Manhattan thirtysomethings, Grace is played by tall redhead Debra Messing with something of a Lucy flair for physical comedy; Will, the straight-acting lawyer, is played by straight actor Eric McCormack. But Will and Grace are graced with a matched pair of sidekicks, who provide the id to their ego (there's no super-ego function in sitcom-land) and raise the outrageousness ante.

Will's other best friend is Jack (Sean Hayes, who is evasive about his sexual orientation),[25] the flamboyant yang to Will's yin, who provides the otherwise missing evidence that Will is indeed gay: focus-groups on whom the program was tested often failed to identify Will as gay, but never misread Jack. The quartet is completed by Grace's dippy socialite "assistant" Karen (Megan Mullaly), whose rude, lewd self-absorption makes her a perfect match for Jack.[26] When they first meet, he erupts, "Peter, Paul, and Mary, you *are* fabulous! Loving the boobs! Let's touch stomachs!" whereupon they lift their shirts and do.

[25] Hayes, whose first showbiz break came playing a gay photographer in the indie movie *Billy's Hollywood Screen Kiss* (1998), responded to *Entertainment Weekly*": "Right now I'm just starting. If I was 40 and had $8 billion and nothing to worry about, I'd tell people when I go number two on the toilet."

[26] The characterization of Karen went a bit too far in September 1999, when she called her Salvadoran maid Rosario "Tamale." This was also a feat of bad timing, as the episode was due to air just as African American and Hispanic groups were staging a boycott to protest the lack of minority characters on TV. By the time the show was aired the word had been changed to "honey," but when the episode reran later that season, the original "Tamale" was back. A spokeswoman for NBC commented: "We felt that we overreacted when we edited out the remark in the original airing. Karen and Rosario have a loving relationship and often trade barbs with each other, and the word is used in context of that relationship."

Jack's over-the-top exuberance takes the weight of being *the* gay character off of Will, although Jack's whirling dervish energy doesn't quite disguise the fact that both Will and Jack are living in an essentially straight society, not visibly engaged in a gay community. However, with or without Jack's campy bona fides the inescapable question all along has been, will Will have a love life or even a sex life? Sitcom characters aren't generally known for steamy romance, even in the 1990s, but they certainly do date, and kiss, and have sex, if generally offscreen. In the post-*Ellen* era that gave birth to *Will & Grace*, the issue pervaded discussions of the program. When journalist Stacey D'Erasmo set out to write about the new show in the fall of 1998, a publicist with whom she was arranging for interviews fairly screamed into the phone, "Just don't ask me when anyone's going to kiss! That's so boring!" Despite the publicist's efforts, what *Entertainment Weekly* described as "the burning question, What *about* Will's sex life—as in, will he ever have one?" could not be avoided. NBC president Warren Littlefield said, "We'll cross that bridge when we come to it." The producers were quoted as hoping for "fireworks by the end of the first season," though McCormack (who plays Will) demurred innocently that he didn't want it to happen as a sweeps-week stunt. After the first season ended without that bridge being crossed, the tension (or hype) focused on the second season. McCormack told *TV Guide*, "We showed we could do a funny show without a boyfriend and be funny. To be true to what we started, Will's got to go out there, get a really good dinner with a guy at least." McCormack wasn't the only one expressing impatience. GLAAD's Scott Seomin told *USA Today*, "If Will doesn't have some semblance of a romantic life in the second season, then the network has failed to realistically deliver the show's premise of a life of a gay man. However, I have been told by the producers that GLAAD has nothing to worry about."

As a new century dawned, audiences were still waiting for Will's love interest to appear, but the cast of *Will & Grace* did make history of another sort when they taped a 30-second TV spot denouncing a California ballot initiative prohibiting same-sex marriage. The mingling of entertainment and politics is a familiar staple of our time, but it is unprecedented for the cast of a top-rated TV show to take such a public position, especially on a controversial topic. The network was quick to assert that this was "something that the cast chose to do personally and does not reflect NBC's beliefs at all," and an NBC executive said the network wouldn't run the ad. The program's gay producer, Max Mutchnick, who thought up the spot, noted, "I would imagine that people who support this initiative wouldn't be big fans of the show."

While American viewers were wondering when Will would get a date, let alone get laid, Britain's Channel Four was making television history with something completely different. *Queer as Folk*, an eight-part series that began in February 1999 and was quickly set for a sequel, centers on three gay men in Manchester who spend most of their nonworking hours in the bars of Manchester's trendy gay neighborhood. The three men include two 29-year-olds—Stuart, a sexy, heartless Don Juan who wants to "die shagging," and Vince, his shy best friend, hopelessly yearning to shag Stuart—and Nathan, a golden-haired 15-year-old who is bursting out of the closet. In the first episode Nathan is picked up (or vice versa) by Stuart, and we are shown the boy being introduced to rimming and anal sex.

Although the show did provoke some outcries from conservatives, and from some established gay organizations—Angela Mason, director of the lobbying group Stonewall, thought "the explicit sex scenes with a youthful 15-year-old did smack of sensationalism"—the protests subsided as the hit series continued. Matthew Parris, openly gay columnist for the *London Times*, noted as a sign of progress that gay people had the self-confidence to "take representations that are not positive," and went on, "It was widely suspected that the program makers made [Nathan] 15 to cause a row. . . . So there was a disinclination on the part of the press to give them the row they wanted." Another London columnist even advised, "There is lots of homosexual rumpy-pumpy for those who like that sort of thing."

At least as much as the explicit sex, *Queer as Folk* was a novelty for mainstream media because the dramatic lens was trained on the gay characters and their world, with only token straight characters, and no effort was made to explain things to, or wink at the audience. "Most of the gay drama we've had on British television has dealt with big statements: victimization, the political agenda, AIDS," Channel Four's head of drama Gub Neal said to the *New York Times*. "But this group of characters doesn't think they're victims at all. They're not even aware that they're a minority. They simply exist and say, 'Hey, we don't have to make any apologies, and we're not going away.' The series has given us a chance to simply reveal gay life, to some extent, in its ordinariness."

Ordinary or not, *Queer as Folk*, in the words of gay writer-producer Richard Kramer, "jumps right past the border patrol that, basically, the American entertainment monolith sets up"—something Kramer knows about, as the author of the notorious *thirtysomething* episode in which two men were shown in bed. Kramer went on: "Tolerance and acceptance were never interesting points or subjects for drama. That's the most interesting thing about *Queer as Folk*. It presupposes that tolerance and acceptance were achieved a long time ago."

It didn't take long for the series to attract Hollywood's attention, and the Showtime cable channel entered into a deal to produce an American version, set in Pittsburgh.[27] Showtime, whose advertising slogan is "No Limits," was looking for ways to compete with the success that rival HBO was having with such adventurous and racy series as *The Sopranos*, *Oz*, and *Sex and the City*. Executives at Showtime told the *New York Times* that *Queer as Folk* would be as explicit in the United States as it was in Britain. "I thought this show was unique," said Jerry Offsay, Showtime's president of programming. "I had never seen characters like these on television. The characters were unapologetic, they lived their lives the way they wanted to. There were great twists and turns and reverses in the storytelling. This show will be as edgy as any television series has ever been in America." Edginess has its limits, however. Unlike the British Nathan, who is 15, in the American version Justin is nearly 18. "The boy is on the cusp of being the legal age," said Tony Jonas, one of the executive producers of the series. "The idea is, kids who are seniors in high school are being sexual. We can't deny that. It's the reality."

Backed by a massive promotional budget, largely aimed at gay audiences, *Queer as Folk* attracted an enormous amount of mostly favorable critical attention and brought many new subscribers to the cable channel. The American version of the series, stretched from eight hours to twenty-two 45-minute episodes, faithfully reproduced the queer-centered, sex-drenched ambience of the original. Once again, a group of gay men occupy the center of attention while their attention mainly seems occupied by various sexual exploits, although these are mostly performed by "alpha gay" Brian (i.e., Stuart) and 17-year-old Justin.[28] The resemblances to *Boys in the Band* are striking—another collection of friends with little in common besides gayness—but the differences are more important. These are not tortured, self-loathing

---

[27] The name proved daunting to Showtime as well as the content. Where the British producers assumed familiarity with the old Yorkshire saying, "There's nowt as queer as folk," nearly every press release on the Showtime series seemed obliged to explain the origin of the series title.

[28] In a notable deviation from the British version, the most explicit visual sexual action depicted in the first episode was between two lesbian women (the mother of Brian's son and her lover)—perhaps a move to attract straight male viewers otherwise put off by the pervasive gay male sexuality? Meanwhile, in the early episodes AIDS is mostly obtrusive by its absence, although Justin's initiation into anal sex is dramatized as a condom-sheathed "demonstration" of safe sex.

gay men trading barbed witticisms; their plentiful angst has more to do with success or failure in the gay singles scene.

Daniel Lipman, openly gay executive producer (along with his longtime life and work partner Ron Cowen), said their goal was to "keep the integrity for the initial core audience while going after a more general audience." Whether this more general audience would be there was a question posed by many critics. Although few reviewers predicted the series would appeal to many straight viewers, *TV Guide* warned those irked by the magazine's favorable notice, "They're here. They're queer. Get used to it."

11

Beyond Prime Time

ADAM AND STEVE AND PHIL AND OPRAH

The sexual revolution of the 1960s, that favorite target of the cultural right wing, was well under way before Dwight Eisenhower passed the torch to the new generation's representative, John F. Kennedy. After two decades of depression and war, America in the 1950s was ripe for an explosion of hedonism. As the United States moved from a war to a peacetime economy (though not abandoning the Cold War alliance of government and defense industries), the celebration of consumerism became a central theme of American culture. In the words of market researcher Ernest Dichter, it was necessary to persuade the average American that "the hedonistic approach to his life is a moral, not an immoral one."

The Kinsey reports on male (1948) and female (1953) sexuality might be seen as the curtain-raisers for a radically transformed public perspective on private behavior. The new gospel of consumerism found one its most effective prophets in *Playboy*, the magazine begun in December 1953 by Hugh Hefner. *Playboy* was an immediate success, promoting a lifestyle of sexual indulgence—for men—that was opposed to marriage, family, monogamy.[1] Women, whose sexual independence—and availability—was increased by the arrival of the birth control pill, began to demand speaking roles in the morality tale unfolding on the public stage. By the mid-1960s Helen Gurley Brown's *Cosmopolitan* offered a tamer counterpart to *Playboy* and Betty Friedan's *The Feminine Mystique* had sparked the prairie fire of women's liberation.

---

[1] Moreover, as Barbara Ehrenreich explained, *Playboy* presented a model of bachelorhood uncontaminated by the suspicion of homosexuality: "The playboy didn't avoid marriage because he was a little bit 'queer,' but on the contrary, because he was so ebulliently, even compulsively heterosexual."

As the 1960s progressed there seemed to be fewer limits on what could be talked about, whether in the relative privacy of women's consciousness-raising groups or on the public stages of rock concerts and political demonstrations. Thus, it was probably inevitable that the new openness would pierce the veil of gentility that cloaked the relatively new medium of television.

One of the earliest programming genres on television was the talk show, a relatively inexpensive way to fill much of the available screen time by scheduling guests with agendas to push and axes to grind. In the mid-1960s such high-minded, politically oriented talk show hosts as David Susskind (who famously, and controversially, hosted Soviet premier Nikita Krushchev) were joined by the edgier and more aggressive likes of Alan Burke and Joe Pyne, who would attack and insult their guests. At the other extreme were the polite, celebrity-oriented show hosts such as Mike Douglas, who would entertain daytime studio and home audiences of women. In 1967 a Columbus, Ohio, daytime host named Phil Donahue revolutionized the talk show, almost by accident, when he took the microphone out into the studio and brought the audience into the act. The response was immediate and irreversible—the audience was now part of the show—and Donahue, who relocated first to Chicago and then to New York, became the king of daytime television. Donahue rode the crest of the second wave of the sexual revolution, offering women a place at the media table, discussing topics previously reserved for men, or simply off-limits for public discussion. As Heaton and Wilson put it, *The Phil Donahue Show* afforded women "the opportunity to voice their opinions about everything from politics to sex, and even the politics of sex."

Donahue's arrival on the national media scene coincided with the emergence of the lesbian and gay liberation movement, and it wasn't long before he opened his stage to people who had few if any opportunities to speak for themselves. Queer guests generally had to contend with hostile audiences, especially in the earlier years—by the mid-1980s Donahue had taken to asking, almost plaintively, why his audiences seemed so accepting of sexual nonconformity—and they generally found themselves being "explained" by experts. For a long time it seemed necessary to producers to "balance" gay guests with homophobes, often clergy or conservative medical professionals.[2]

---

[2] As late as 1994, *Donahue Show* producers included reactionary psychologist Paul Cameron on a program ostensibly about female impersonation, alongside the stars of the Australian film *Priscilla, Queen of the Desert*, lesbian anthropologist Esther Newton, author of the classic study of drag, *Mother Camp*, and a prominent New York drag queen. Despite a promise from staffers that Donahue would note Cameron's 1983 expulsion from the American Psychological Association, he did no such thing and this task was left to Esther Newton.

But even in such circumstances, Donahue offered an unprecedented opportunity for sexual minorities to represent their own lives. In between the mantra of "God created Adam and Eve, not Adam and Steve," repeated endlessly by fundamentalist audience members, and the sympathetic incomprehension of many middle-Americans, lesbian, gay, bisexual, and transgendered people took the stage to talk about coming out in high school, or as a married man, or as a grandmother; about being a gay parent or the child of a gay parent, or the parent of a gay child; about being a woman trapped in a man's body or about the experience of transitioning from one bodily status to another. When the AIDS epidemic exploded in the early 1980s, *Donahue*, along with its more sensation-oriented rival *Geraldo*, offered one of the earliest national platforms for discussion and information on a topic the news media were inexcusably slow to address.

Throughout the 1980s and early 1990s Donahue and his imitators continued to provide a steady stream of queer themes for increasingly sophisticated audiences. Donahue often said that if he was truly successful he would be replaced by a black woman and, of course, he was. Oprah Winfrey arrived on the talk show scene in 1986, and her more emotional, empathetic style quickly catapulted her to the top of the daytime ratings. For the next decade Oprah and Phil, joined by numerous others, injected multiple daily doses of public celebrity and private emotion into the nation's bloodstream. In the mid-1990s the heated competition among nearly thirty syndicated talk shows, and the growing interest in attracting a younger demographic audience slice, was capped by the runaway success of Ricki Lake. Lake, who started in showbiz in John Waters's sleaze-celebrating movies, opened the doors to a new style of daytime TV, abandoning the expert-oriented high-toned seriousness of Phil and Oprah, or even its more tabloid versions in *Geraldo* and *Sally Jesse Raphael*, in favor of rowdy audience engagement more reminiscent of professional wrestling. The final step toward what many critics decried as freak-show television came with the success of *The Jerry Springer Show*. Springer, a former Cincinnati politician and TV newsman, was a standard-issue Donahue imitator when his producers saw the writing on the studio wall and turned toward outrageousness, moving the show from "issues to relationships. We younged it up. We made it contemporary. And we raised the rating about 30 to 35 percent."

The newer style of talk show quickly dominated the ratings, driving Donahue into retirement in 1996 and leaving Oprah as the undisputed queen of the high road. On the crowded low road, programmers recruited guests with on-air 800-numbers, filling their schedule with squabbling family members and current or former lovers. These programs typically scheduled many more guests than was standard on Phil or Oprah—producers were always worried, and often rightly so, that guests would back out, so they overbooked—and frequently they added lesbian, gay, and bisexual guests into the mix, without identifying the program as gay-themed. This form of mainstreaming—gay teens could also squabble with their parents, siblings, and former lovers, just like anyone else—reflected and perhaps encouraged a kind of tacit acceptance of queerness on the part of studio and home audiences.

In the late 1990s it became clear that audiences were more hostile to bisexuals than to gay or lesbian guests, because bisexuals seem either confused or unfaithful. Studio audiences apparently have learned the lessons taught so long by Phil and Oprah, and accept gay people as a fact of life—the liberal talk show hosts are quite stubbornly devoted to the position that "gays are born, not made"—but bisexuals are infuriatingly indecisive. Bisexuals are also seen as promiscuous, by definition, and condemned for this in a way that gays and lesbians are not. But if bisexuals strain audiences' newly acquired sophistication, transgendered people arouse endless fascination and evoke mixed emotional responses. TV talk shows have been obsessed with topics concerning transsexualism since the early 1980s, when cross-dressing was considered a fairly daring topic—Phil Donahue never tired of congratulating himself for wearing a skirt on a 1988 program—and there is probably no topic more alluring to programmers. As Joshua Gamson has noted, these programs, for all their sensationalism and insult-tossing on stage and from the audience, "turn out to be gound-level versions of high-academic theories of gender 'performativity' and gender construction." For activists the talk shows offer an opportunity to reach people who might never otherwise encounter a gay or transgendered person speaking about their lives, and they are, therefore, often willing to put up with hostile audiences and sanctimonious hosts. Trans-activist Angela Gardner described her experience on the *Mort Downey Jr. Show* as "a root canal without the anasthetic." But, she added, "we got more membership response from that show than anything we ever did. . . . From all over the country we were getting phone calls for information."

One format favored by the new crop of talk shows invites guests to meet someone who harbors a "secret crush" on them. After the person with the crush tells the host and audience about their fantasy—while we see the object of desire sitting backstage—the "star" is brought out and we see his or her face as they see who it is who has the crush on them. This is a format used by *Ricki Lake*, *Jerry Springer*, and *Jenny Jones*, among others, and they mixed gay and straight crushers and crushees. On one *Jenny Jones* "secret crush" program from 1994, a straight-identified man reveals a crush on his straight best friend, who responds with interest, saying that he's "try-sexual—I'll try anything once." The two men's mutual sexual interest is then seen, and raised, by the crush-holder's girlfriend, who reveals her desire for a "three-way" with both men: after all, men always fantasize about having two women at once, so why shouldn't she have two men? A woman in the audience jumps up and cheers, "You go, girl!"

In 1995 a *Jenny Jones* "secret crush" program confronted Jonathan Schmitz with acquaintance Scott Amedure's secret lust, and he was clearly not interested in reciprocating. A few days later, back home in Michigan, Schmitz bought a shotgun and killed Amedure—the episode was never aired. The murder led to an outpouring of public condemnation of the *Jenny Jones* program and "trash TV" in general, but the truth was more complicated. It did appear that Schmitz had been misled by the producers into thinking his secret admirer was a woman, and he clearly felt humiliated by the public revelation that he was desired by another man. Yet these are hardly grounds for murder—despite the longtime appeal to judges and juries of the now generally discredited "homosexual panic" defense—and Schmitz was convicted of second-degree murder (his "public humiliation" defense apparently saved him from a first-degree conviction). The family of the victim, Scott Amedure, sued Warner Brothers, owner of the *Jenny Jones* show, claiming that they were negligent in not realizing that Schmitz was mentally unstable and that publicly confronting him with a homosexual admirer risked a violent outcome. Despite programmers' claims that they had not misled Schmitz, and Jones's testimony that she knew practically nothing whatever about how her own show was put together, the jury sided with the plaintiff's argument that "the *Jenny Jones* show and what it does to people is unsafe at any speed," and awarded the family more than $25 million in damages. As the judgment against Warner Brothers wound its way through the lengthy appeals process, pundits piled more criticism on "trash TV," and talk show excesses were briefly reined in. But as the memory of the murder and the law suit faded, the ratings once more took precedence over moralism. The race for the bottom resumed.

THE TONGUE-TIED PUBLIC SQUARE

The Public Broadcasting System (PBS) was mandated by Congress to fulfill a mission first stated by a 1967 Carnegie Commission report, to "help us see America whole, in all its diversity" and "provide a voice for groups in the community that might otherwise be unheard." In adopting (some of) the recommendations of the Carnegie Commission and establishing

PBS, Congress failed to specify the term "public" beyond its being "non-commercial," thus leaving open the question of "what is public about public television."

In 1988 the U.S. Congress created the Independent Television Service (ITVS), mandated to "develop, produce and package independent work that addresses the needs of underserved communities," and in the same year PBS launched the series *P.O.V.* (for Point of View) in order to "provide visibility and support for compelling personal visions of nonfiction film and video producers." *P.O.V.* stood out within the framework of American broadcasting, even PBS, by virtue of the intention—built into its name—to show documentaries that openly reflected the views of their makers, avoiding the familiar trappings of "objectivity" and proclaimed neutrality. In the words of the series' "Call for Entries," it sought "films made because the filmmaker had something to say—to a large audience—in his or her own way." The series was an immediate success, showing films such as *Gates of Heaven* by Errol Morris, about a pet cemetery, and *Twinsburg, OH: Some Kind of Weird Twin Thing* by Sue Marcoux, about an annual twins convention. Things heated up quite a bit when the series scheduled Marlon Riggs's *Tongues Untied* to air on July 16, 1991.

Marlon Riggs had not expected *Tongues Untied* to air on PBS, despite his 1987 Emmy Award–winning film *Ethnic Notions*, because he didn't think "TV would have the courage to show" a film that openly explored the experiences of black gay men. Still, *P.O.V.* decided to schedule the film, which had won awards at fourteen international film festivals and had already been shown on the BBC and on public broadcasting stations in New York, San Francisco, and Los Angeles. But how would it play in Peoria? As it turned out, *P.O.V.* was stepping into the middle of a cultural war that was already raging in the United States—a war that was being fought over control of the public sphere.

As the 1980s drew to a close, the right wing had shifted the focus of the political counterrevolution they were mounting against the gains of minorities and women to encompass the domain of elite culture. Although the political struggles of the 1980s had often been fought on the field of culture, it was the lowlands of mass and even marginal media—commercial television, rock and roll, pornography—that drew the attention of moral enforcers. Signaling the opening of a new front, right-wing columnist and frequent presidential candidate Patrick Buchanan called for "a cultural revolution in the '90s as sweeping as the political revolution in the '80s." In terms that feminist writer Carole Vance analogized to Nazi cultural metaphors, Buchanan warned that, "Just as a poisoned land will yield up poisonous fruits, so a polluted culture, left to fester and stink, can destroy a nation's soul." In the ensuing skirmishes the forces of counterrevolution laid siege to art and public broadcasting agencies that dared to exhibit the work of uppity gays and blacks.

Most notorious was the series of attacks in 1989 on the National Endowment for the Arts (NEA) for funding arts programs that included Andres Serrano's photograph, "Piss Christ," and Robert Mapplethorpe's explicitly sexual photographs of gay men. Capitalizing on the momentum built up by the attacks on "Piss Christ" and by the Corcoran Gallery's (Washington, D.C.) craven cancellation of the Mapplethorpe show scheduled for July 1989, Jesse Helms successfully passed an amendment to severely curtail the funding options of the NEA. The Helms amendment was eventually "compromised" in House-Senate conference, and opponents had to pretend that they achieved a victory by whittling down Helms's wording to a ban of NEA funding for anything that would be considered obscene under current Supreme Court rulings. The larger impact extended beyond the precise wording of the legislation, as it achieved its intended effect by confusing and intimidating cultural institutions.

Although *Tongues Untied* had received no direct funding from the NEA, and of its entire $175,000 budget, only $5,000 could be seen as indirectly derived from the NEA (through the Rocky Mountain Film Center), its appearance on the *P.O.V.* schedule drew the series into the fray. Rev. Donald Wildmon of the American Family Association (AFA) attacked the film, *P.O.V.*, and the NEA. Wildmon issued a release claiming that PBS stations "are showing an inordinately high number of programs dealing with homosexuality," and recommended that viewers first protest the screening to their local PBS stations and then be sure to watch it "to see for themselves how their tax dollars are being spent." The AFA was joined in the attack by Pat Robertson and his Christian Coalition. On July 3, Robertson's TV show, the *700 Club*, ran a report on Riggs that began, "He's black, he's homosexual, he's got AIDS, and he could be this summer's version of the Mapplethorpe controversy." *P.O.V.* later estimated that nearly two-thirds of the 284 stations that normally carry the series declined to air *Tongues Untied*, an unusually high number of cancellations that included many of the nation's largest markets. But the story didn't end there.

Shortly after the *Tongues Untied* screening, *P.O.V.* canceled its planned broadcast of *Stop the Church*, a film about ACT UP's 1989 demonstration at St. Patrick's Cathedral in New York City protesting Cardinal O'Connor and the Catholic Church's positions on AIDS. The schedule for the broadcast had been set months before, but suddenly PBS executives discovered that the film "crossed the line of being responsible programming into being ridicule." *P.O.V.* president David Davis felt that, after the recent problems with the Riggs film, it would be "irresponsible, with as little notice, to expect stations to handle the level of press interest and viewer response *Stop the Church* is likely to generate." As journalism historian James Ledbetter commented, this may have been the first time in television history that a program was canceled because viewers might have been too interested in it.

In the winter of 1992, as Patrick Buchanan challenged President Bush for the Republican presidential nomination, he ran a television commercial that featured scenes from *Tongues Untied* with the following text narrated and superimposed on images of leather-clad white gay men: "In the last three years the Bush administration has invested our tax dollars in pornographic and blasphemous art too shocking to show. This so called art has glorified homosexuality, exploited children, and perverted the image of Jesus Christ. Even after good people protested, Bush continued to fund this kind of art."

Shortly after Buchanan began airing the ads, NEA chair John Frohnmayer was told to resign, and the reverberations continued to feed the right wing's criticisms of the NEA and PBS. The pattern was repeated on several later occasions when public television broadcast programming that addressed lesbian and gay concerns. When a public TV station in New York scheduled a new lesbian/gay TV series, *In the Life,* then-senator (and later presidential candidate) Bob Dole took to the Senate floor to denounce the program, which he had never seen—it had yet to be aired—falsely asserting that it had been produced with taxpayers' money (the funds were raised privately)—as if lesbian and gay citizens did not pay taxes. Dole sarcastically described PBS "apologists [who] are hiding behind Big Bird, Mister Rogers, and *Masterpiece Theatre,* laying down their quality smokescreen while they shovel out funding for gay and lesbian shows, all those doom and gloom reports about what is wrong with America, and all the liberal cheerleading we see on public television" (*Congressional Record,* 6/12/92).

In the fall of 1992 the liberal media watchdog group Fairness and Accuracy in Media issued a study of public television that countered right-wing claims of liberal bias and "pro-homosexual" bias. After examining the types of people who appear as sources in a wide range of public TV programs (1,644 sources, appearing in 423 segments in 114 programs, such as the *McNeil-Lehrer News Hour*), the researchers could not find a single representative of a gay or lesbian organization.

In 1997 *P.O.V.* and PBS struck again, refusing to air *Out at Work,* a documentary illustrating workplace discrimination through the stories of three lesbian and gay workers.[3] PBS claimed that 23 percent of the film's $65,000 financing was problematic because it was derived from labor unions and the lesbian Astrea Foundation. PBS executive Sandra Heberer explained, somewhat contradictorily, that "PBS guidelines prohibit funding that might lead to an assumption that individual underwriters might have exercised editorial control over program content—even if, as it is clear in this case, those underwriters did not." What she did not explain, however, was why PBS was not similarly disturbed when the *New York Times* funded a documentary on its history, or when PBS's money series are underwritten by insurance and financial corporations, and the flagship *News Hour* program is underwritten by such corporate giants as Archer Daniels Midland and Citicorp.

When PBS scheduled a BBC production of gay author David Leavitt's *The Lost Language of Cranes* as part of the *Great Performances* series in June 1992, the gay themes set off a predictable outcry from the right, and the Texaco Oil Company withdrew its corporate sponsorship from the PBS series. In January 1994, PBS's *American Playhouse* series scored its biggest ratings success with the six-hour miniseries *Tales of the City*, coproduced by Channel Four. The story, based on gay author Armistead Maupin's popular serial-novel about San Francisco, impressed most viewers by faithfully capturing the flavor of the original. It also included two man-to-man kisses, one fairly romantic and viewed from the side without one man's head blocking our view.[4] Reverend Wildmon was also attracted to the series, and in March he sent every member of Congress a "12-minutes bootleg videotape darkly highlighting the series' four-letter words, fleeting nudity, pot-smoking and one prolonged gay kiss." The American Family Association's March "Action! Page" mailing was headlined "Your Tax Dollars Used to Air Pornographic, Profane, Homosexual TV Series." While listing several programs that "presented homosexuality in a very favorable light," it mostly focused on *Tales of the City*: "Those are your tax dollars PBS used to air this pro-homosexual propaganda. And it's our Judeo-Christian values PBS continues to attack and defame. . . . PBS can rightly be called the Homosexual Pride Taxpayer-Funded TV Network." The Georgia State Senate passed a resolution direct-

---

[3] *P.O.V.* did not have a consistent stance on lesbian and gay-related films, but they preferred the more narrow focus of, say, Tom Joslin and Peter Friedman's *Silverlake Life: The View from Here* (1993), the personal account, shot on home video, of two filmmakers dying of AIDS.

[4] Around the same time, HBO produced a six-hour version of Randy Shilts's *And the Band Played On*. Ian Mckellan, who played gay activist Bill Kraus, told Maupin, "It was decided that Kraus should be seen in a tender domestic moment with his lover, so I was called back for additional footage. But when B. D. Wong and I kissed, it was too much for HBO, so they cut it. An executive on the set said he personally had no problem with the kiss, but it was his responsibility to see to it that viewers—and this is a direct quote—not be grossed out."

ing the local public TV station to cease airing *Tales of the City* and never air it again. Within a few weeks PBS announced that it was abandoning plans to coproduce a sequel for which the scripts had already been completed, and the budget for *American Playhouse* was cut by two thirds.

More Tales of the City did make it to U.S. television screens in June 1998 but not to public television. The cable channel Showtime replaced PBS as producer of the series, and Maupin happily noted that "cable allows you the opportunity to tell grown-up stories without restrictions." Reviewing the sequel in the *New York Times*, gay novelist Stephen McCauley was relieved: "Fortunately, Showtime has increased the casual drug use and made the nudity less fleeting, and the same-sex relationships happier and more passionate."

The growing willingness of cable channels to tackle projects considered too controversial for pubic television has raised serious questions about the need for public television now that movie channels, Art & Entertainment, Discovery, the Learning Channel, Bravo, etc., have taken over much of the territory previously monopolized by PBS. As most Americans enter the promised 500-channel cable environment, it will become more difficult to defend the need for a PBS that, in critic James Ledbetter's words, "is engaged in duplicating, in content and in form, benign programming that most American television viewers already watch elsewhere." If public television is to live up to the vision of its creators by providing a voice for groups in the community that might otherwise be unheard, it will have to find the courage to withstand criticism, and even to court rather than avoid controversy.

In 1995 the Independent Television Service (ITVS) presented a four-part series, *The Question of Equality*, in keeping with ITVS's congressional mandate "to develop, produce and package independent work that addresses the needs of underserved communities." The series, timed to air on public television stations during October's National Lesbian and Gay History Month, included programs on Stonewall and its immediate aftermath; the political culture wars of the early 1990s and the fight over Oregon's antigay Ballot Measure 9 (the measure lost); anti-lesbian and gay discrimination in the military and the flaws in the "don't ask, don't tell" policy; and the experiences of openly lesbian and gay teenagers. The series was well received—the *Los Angeles Times* referred to it as an "epochal . . . television breakthrough"— and it demonstrated the continuing potential of public television to serve as a venue hospitable to minority perspectives. Beginning with *Word Is Out: Stories of Some of Our Lives* and later with *Before Stonewall, Silent Pioneers, Common Threads: Stories from the Quilt, Coming Out Under Fire, License to Kill,* and *After Stonewall*, public television has provided the only (relatively) nationwide exposure for documentaries in which lesbian and gay people tell their own stories and trace their own history.

The public square represented by public television, however eroded by cable-carried competition and however challenged by right-wing campaigns, remains an important sector of the cultural landscape. Lesbian and gay people continue to make claims on this public resource, and the struggle for access to the public airwaves remains an important site of struggle for equality.

In the spring of 1999 the issue was joined again when San Francisco's KQED stepped in after PBS declined to distribute *It's Elementary: Talking About Gay Issues in School* by Oscar-winning documentarian Debra Chasnoff. The film focuses on ways of introducing children to issues of diversity and acceptance of lesbian and gay people, showing what Chasnoff termed "age appropriate" lessons taking place in first- through eighth-grade classrooms across the country.

The film opens with Sen. Robert Smith (R-NH) protesting gay and lesbian "filth" in the schools, waving documents and warning about such "trash" as a symptom of moral decay, thundering, "You wonder what's wrong with America?" The film cuts to a third-grade classroom, where the children are discussing the same topic, and one small boy asks, "Who, like, really cares if you're gay? It's like barely nobody knows in the world. It's, like, what's the big whoop?" Of course, for Senator Smith and his allies, the big whoop is precisely the lack of hysteria that characterizes the classroom discussions shown in the film. *It's Elementary* shows these students neither revulsed nor signing up to march in Gay Pride parades—but curious and matter-of-fact. In perhaps the first film ever to explore children's reactions so thoroughly, the contrast between venomous adults and tolerant children is startling.

The armies of counterrevolution were quick to mobilize against the broadcasting of *It's Elementary*. Donald Wildmon's American Family Association rushed out a fund-raising letter, decrying the "pro-homosexuality bombshell fired into our children's elementary schools," and Beverly LaHaye of Concerned Women for America, in her fund-raising letter, called the film a "major new effort to recruit innocent children into the tragically destructive homosexual lifestyle." A more recent arrival on the cultural battlefield, conservative radio counselor Dr. Laura Schlessinger, made the film a major target, calling it an "agenda piece" that teaches kids that gay is okay. "I think pedophilia is next," she warned her listeners.

The film was ultimately broadcast by approximately 100 out of 347 public television stations nationwide. Some stations responded to protests by following the broadcast with a counter-video, *Suffer the Children*, produced by Wildmon's American Family Association. As program director Brad Fay of KIXE in Chico-Redding, California, explained to the *San Francisco Examiner*: "It's terrible. It's a rebuttal nonetheless. I feel if there's this much controversy, the more you can educate people the better—even if it is a right-wing reactionary view." In contrast, Leta Powell Drake, program director for Nebraska Education Television, said, "Part of our mission is to educate our viewers, and even sometimes challenge them. You wonder about this deep-rooted hatred for people who are different—where does that come from?"

GETTING OVER THE RAINBOW

Lesbian archivist Joan Nestle cites the recollections of a lesbian musician about the Moody Garden Gang, a butch-femme working-class lesbian community centered around a bar in Lowell, Massachusetts, in the 1950s:

> It was our Mecca, we were family, and we had found a home. . . . So many of the kids ask what's so special about Moody Gardens. To us it was our world, a small world, yes, but if you were starving you didn't refuse a slice of bread, and we were starving just for the feeling of having others around us. We were kings of the hill. We were the *Moody Gardens*. . . . If there hadn't been little Moody Gardens all over the world, we wouldn't even be allowed to get together as we do today and feel, in a small way, we are being accepted and we are not alone.

The gay community in the decades before Stonewall came together in the restricted and vulnerable spaces of the bars and baths in order, in Nestle's words, "to breathe the life we could not anywhere else." The bars were also the crucibles of resistance that eventually exploded into riots, first in Los Angeles and then, famously, at the Stonewall. Gathered in the smoke-filled dimly lit bars, gay lives fantasized to the soundtrack provided by jukebox selections. Gay men famously idolized Judy Garland, identifying with her survivor's grit and determination, and a long-lived myth attributes the Stonewall riots to the emotional fervor created by Judy Garland's funeral earlier that day.[5]

[5] Probably the most famous pre-Stonewall code phrase—besides the term *gay* itself—was to ask if someone was a "friend of Dorothy," a reference to Garland's most famous movie role.

In the euphoria of the post-Stonewall period the Gay Activists Alliance's first gathering spot was a former firehouse in SoHo, where Saturday night dances drew enormous crowds, offering the movement's young recruits a revolution they could dance to. These were heady times, as men danced with men and women danced with women in large, loud spaces that were neither owned by the Mafia nor raided by the police.

The decade of the 1970s witnessed the birth and diffusion of a visible, unmistakably eroticized gay male culture, and its heart beat with a disco pulse. Even before Stonewall, gay disk jockeys and impresarios were creating the late-night dance venues that gave birth to disco, and by the early 1970s disco clubs were springing up everywhere, Dionysiac pleasure palaces for the newly liberated urban gay male. Very likely as an unconscious tribute to the power of gay male sexual energy represented by disco, the early 1970s witnessed the odd phenomenon of pseudo-gay Glam Rock in Britain, where David Bowie "came out" as gay—or bisexual—in a perversely successful attention-grabbing career move. Bowie's ambiguous forays into sexual perversity raised his public profile and made him a hero to many gays—the *Gay News* of London saw him as a "potent spokesman" for gay rock. Even his critics, such as John Gill, acknowledge that Bowie's "clever (if ultimately meaningless) packaging of sexual outrage created a safe space where many of us, gay, bi or straight, could play out games and experiment with difference," much as *The Rocky Horror Picture Show*'s late-night screenings functioned for many young people around the same time.[6]

If David Bowie and fellow faux-queer Glam rockers Marc Bolan, Brian Eno, and Lou Reed were hitching a ride on the notoriety of gay sexuality, others were engaged in hijacking the energy of disco for resale to straight audiences. The hit movie *Saturday Night Fever* (1977) translated disco to a working-class Brooklyn neighborhood where John Travolta's Tony Manero ruled the dance floor and gay men were hassled on the basketball court. Studio 54 became the most glamorous dance club in the country, attracting straight and closeted gay glitterati, along with hordes of wannabes crowding

---

[6] Cult movies like *The Rocky Horror Picture Show* (1975) provided occasions for meeting others who shared a common perspective, turning a media product into the pretext for communal interaction. In a 1981 study of patrons waiting to see *Rocky Horror*, it was learned that, excluding the first-timers, the mean number of times the movie had been seen was eleven. The audience members were there to participate in a ritual and a social event that created and reinforced a solidarity of nonmainstream identification. The *Rocky Horror* cult served all over the United States as an opportunity for lesbian and gay teenagers to meet and support each other in the coming out process. Twenty years later, the kitsch classic *The Sound of Music* became a gay sing-along hit in London and New York, with audience members dressing as nuns, Nazis, and Swiss youths.

the ropes and hoping the doorman would smile on them. Impresario Jacques Morali recruited a band-full of gay stereotypes to become the Village People, whose barely disguised gay anthems managed to fly under America's radar screens.

But even voguish and disguised, disco was clearly not territory in which straight white males felt at home. Disco has been described as "an extended conversation between black female divas and gay men" (and even, in the case of Sylvester, a black male diva), and thus straight white men rightly felt that they were being decentered. By the late 1970s the backlash against disco had become unmistakable, as "Disco Sucks!" became the war cry of the angry white male, and disk jockeys organized disco demolition rallies. By the dawn of the 1980s, Reagan was in the White House, rumors of a "gay cancer" were beginning to surface, and disco was all but dead.

If disco was the soundtrack for gay male culture of the 1970s, it wasn't the only flowering of queer music in those heady days. Lesbian musicians were creating their own musical world, inspired by the twin passions of feminism and lesbian liberation. Alix Dobkin was a folk singer who grew up in the world of leftist causes, and when she came out as a lesbian feminist she began writing songs that reflected her new identity: "I was bowled over that whatever I wrote about being a lesbian was going to be utterly original and unique." It wasn't only her songs that were original; she also pioneered self-production and distribution, pressing copies of her first album, *Lavender Jane Loves Women*, and selling them through classified ads in feminist publications, at concerts, and at the important and influential Michigan Womyn's Music Festival that, since the mid-seventies, has brought together thousands of women each summer. Dobkin's example was soon followed by Holly Near and her Redwood Records, and Olivia Records, whose album *The Changer and the Changed*, by Meg Williamson, eventually sold over a quarter of a million copies.[7] The Michigan festival became a platform for launching other lesbian and bisexual musicians, as such varied performers as Janis Ian (in her new, lesbian persona), Tracy Chapman, Michelle Shocked, Two Nice Girls, the Indigo Girls, Ferron, and Melissa Etheridge benefited from the exposure it provided.

The popular music scene in the United States was transformed in the early 1980s with the arrival of MTV, which quickly took on a role hitherto only approached by *American Bandstand* as a national forum for launching trends

---

[7] The tradition of self-produced and distributed music has continued ever since the early 1970s, with such notable examples as the gay male a cappella group the Flirtations, and bisexual singer Ani DiFranco.

and careers. MTV's visual energy and production values greatly amplified the reach and power of newly emerging talents, and turned media-savvy performers such as Michael Jackson (who "broke" MTV's color barrier) and Madonna into true superstars. MTV was shrewdly in touch with the youthful audiences whose tastes it was molding as well as reflecting, first promoting a new crop of British bands and later providing the bridge that hip-hop traveled from the urban ghettos to the white suburbs.

MTV was a vehicle for sexually ambiguous singers making their (often tortuous) way out of the closet: Elton John, the only one among the original Glam Rock bisexuals who finally landed on gay; Boy George, who never really fooled anyone, but dithered for a while; the Pet Shop Boys and R.E.M.'s Michael Stipe, who stayed coy longer than was really necessary; and George Michael, who waited until he was entrapped in a Beverly Hills restroom to tell us what we already knew. And then there were the polymorphously perverse, such as Madonna and Prince, who kept the sexual lines blurred without ever quite crossing over into queer (Madonna told a concert audience in 1994 that she was a gay man trapped inside a woman's body). MTV has also hosted gay-inclusive nonmusical content, such as the *Real World* series and the more recent college dorm serial-soap, *Undressed*, which includes both lesbian and gay characters among its perpetually sexually active cast. Yet, lest anyone mistake MTV for entirely gay-friendly territory, it also provided a platform for the homophobic and misogynist posturings of angry-white-male heavy metal and angry-black-male gangsta rap.[8] In 2000 race was transcended by the success of white rapper Eminem, but unfortunately, misogyny and homophobia remained intact: "My words are like a dagger with a jagged edge / That'll stab you in the head / Whether you're a fag or a lez / Or the homosex, hermaph or a trans-a-vest / Pants or dress / Hate Fags? The answer's yes."[9]

The reign of heavy metal's homophobia was ended or at least diluted by the unexpected advent of grunge, surging out of the Northwest with the success of Seattle's Nirvana. The group's lead singer, Kurt Cobain, wrote in the liner notes of their CD, *Insecticide*: "If any of you [fans] in any way hate

[8] Possibly the most notorious examples of homophobia were the wildly successful heavy metal band Guns 'N' Roses, whose lead singer Axl Rose sang, "Faggots they make no sense to me / They . . . spread some fucking disease," and rapper Buju Banton's *Boom Bye Bye*: "Faggots have to run / Or get a bullet in the head / Bang-bang, [shots] in a faggot's head / Homeboys don't condone nasty men / They must die / Two men necking / Lying in a bed / Hugging each other / And caressing one another's legs / Get an automatic or an Uzi instead / Shoot them now, let us shoot them [gunshot]."

[9] Proving the power of profit over solidarity, Eminem is produced by Interscope Geffen, which reminded many of David Geffen's earlier role in promoting Guns 'N' Roses.

homosexuals, people of different color, or women, please do this one favor for us—leave us the fuck alone! Don't come to our shows and don't buy our records!" Grunge helped ease the way for "homocore" bands like Pansy Division that pushed beyond a critical barrier by writing openly queer lyrics—Pansy Division paid tribute to Nirvana with their song "Smells like Queer Spirit."

The increasing openness of some performers—although notably, the most flamboyant queers, such as Culture Club's Boy George, Bronski Beat's Jimmy Somerville, Erasure's Andy Bell, were all British—began to simultaneously raise the audience's expectations and strain its patience. Performers who scrupulously stuck to gender-vague lyrics, refused to talk about their personal lives, and dithered about avoiding labels and identities, began to feel the pressure from their fans. As lesbian critic Lily Braindrop put it in 1991, responding to performers who ask, "Who cares about that stuff anyway?": "Millions of queers in this country who are aching to see a mainstream performer stand up and say, 'Yes, I am!'"

The first mainstream star to take up the challenge, although only after a protracted period of teasing, was k. d. lang, the Canadian singer who combines country and cabaret or, to quote an album title, torch and twang.[10] Lang, a multiple Grammy-winner who has been variously compared to Patsy Cline and Judy Garland, came out in a July 1992 *Advocate* cover story which helped set off a flurry of "lesbian chic" in the publishing world. In addition to appearing on the cover of *New York* magazine, lang posed for *Vanity Fair* sitting in a barber's chair and being "shaved" by supermodel Cindy Crawford. Coming out certainly didn't harm lang's career—she won a best female pop vocal Grammy the following year—and may have been the stimulus for her friend, rocker Melissa Etheridge, who came out onstage at a Clinton Inaugural Ball in January 1993. Etheridge also followed lang by winning a Grammy for her aptly titled *Yes I Am* and went on to greater visibility when her then-lover, director Julie Cypher, bore two children (in January 2000 the identity of the father was revealed: veteran rocker David Crosby).

[10] Pioneering a routine later employed by Ellen DeGeneres, who told Rosie O'Donnell that she was rumored to be Lebanese, lang would tell audiences that the rumors were true, she was a La . . . , La . . . , Lawrence Welk fan. After she came out, lang attributed her discretion to her mother's concerns about the reactions of the small town of Consort, Alberta, where she was born: "I want to be out. I want to be out! Man, if I didn't worry about my mother, I'd be the biggest parader in the whole world." As it turned out, her mother's fears may have been exaggerated; when asked about lang's announcement, the mayor of Consort replied, "She's done more to put us on the map than anybody and we are extremely pleased with her. She's still personable and very approachable, and her preferred lifestyle is insignificant to me."

In the summer of 2000 another female pop star made a move out of the closet, in this case someone who had not been widely rumored to be gay. The cover of the June issue of the national lesbian magazine *Curve* announced "Sinéad Comes Out" next to a picture of the Irish singer who had first exploded onto the pop scene in the late 1980s with a bald head and controversial lyrics about racism, war, and child abuse. Sinéad O'Connor's notoriety hit its peak when she tore up a picture of the pope on *Saturday Night Live*, but since then she has been ordained as a priest in the tiny splinter Latin Tridentine Church. Speaking to *Curve*, O'Connor said, "I'm a lesbian . . . although I haven't been very open about that and throughout most of my life I've gone out with blokes because I haven't necessarily been terribly comfortable about being a lesbian. But I actually am a lesbian. . . . I don't think I necessarily paved the way for anyone, but other people paved the way for me."[11]

Melissa Etheridge and k. d. lang came out, taking on the responsibilities that come with the territory, and their careers moved to new heights. But once again, as with other branches of show business, their male counterparts were still hesitating behind their closet doors. True, there are openly gay British pop stars, complementing the openly gay British actors—there are even matching gay knights: Sir Ian McKellen and Sir Elton John. In the United States, heavy metal rocker Rob Halford, former lead singer of Judas Priest, came out in an *Advocate* cover story, but little notice was taken. Rufus Wainwright may have been out from the beginning of his career, but he's still at the start of that career, and still working the alternative music niche (and, he says, he keeps falling in love with straight men). RuPaul may have had a cable talk show and a hit song, but even 6-foot-plus African American drag queens don't break the showbiz mold. But when Puerto Rican ex-Menudo singer Ricky Martin exploded into superstardom at the 1999 Grammy Awards, the massive press coverage—ranging from the covers of *Time* and *TV Guide* to the supermarket tabloids—seemed fixated on the rumors about the star's sexuality. *Billboard*'s talent editor, Larry Flick, commented, "We've gotten to the point where people aren't so shocked by the gay thing, and the media is feeling those questions aren't as taboo." For his part, however, Ricky Martin remains elusive. Speaking to his friend Gloria Estefan for *Interview* magazine, he limited himself to, "What I say

[11] That O'Connor may still be uncomfortable about being a lesbian is suggested by a lengthy feature on her new album that appeared at the same time as word about her upcoming *Curve* cover story. In the *Philadelphia Inquirer* feature, while discussing her work, her spirituality, and her children—including details about custody fights and struggles with depression—there is no mention whatever of the lesbianism that she revealed in *Curve*.

about sexuality is, I leave it for my room and lock the door. I go back to my culture. It's something you don't talk about."

LOCKER-ROOM CLOSETS

In 1975, after David Kopay read an article in the *Washington Star* by sports-writer Lynn Rosellini about gay professional athletes, he called Rosellini and offered to become the first major league athlete to come out publicly. Kopay, a recently retired NFL running back, was the only gay athlete featured by name in Rosellini's series and in 1977 he published *The David Kopay Story*. In the quarter century since Kopay came out, only a handful of athletes have joined what remains a very exclusive club. The membership rolls in the club reveal some striking patterns: male athletes tend to come out after they have retired from active play; lesbians are more likely to be out while still competing; team players are less likely than individual competitors to come out.

Athletic competition plays a central role in most human societies, often as training for military combat or as a substitute for it. Americans place sports near the top of the hierarchy of skills to be cultivated and admired, and a cult of athletics often seems to permeate the institutions of secondary education. And like the military—another institution focused on physicality and cohesiveness—institutionalized sports, from high school locker rooms to big-league dugouts, is hostile to any signs of homosexuality. In a culture where coaches routinely berate poor performance by accusing boys of being sissies, and where famed Penn State women's basketball coach Rene Portland boasted that no lesbians could play for her, it should surprise no one that most athletes stay closeted. Even sociologist Harry Edwards, who became famous as an advocate for racial equality in professional sports, condemned athletes who discuss their sexual orientation openly: "Whoever makes it a public or political issue is wrong. There is nothing professional sports teams can do with it. It's not something I would ever raise with a team. I take issue with anyone who tries to make it an issue on either side." In other words, don't ask, don't tell.

Sports in American society is more than a high school and college obsession; it's a very big business. Sports coverage is a central component of journalism—many local news audiences tune in for sports reports and many newspaper readers turn to the sports section first—and sports programming comprises a major portion of broadcast revenues. For athletes, as for other show business stars, coming out, however psychologically liberating, involves financial and professional costs. After David Kopay came out, even as a retired NFL player, he was unable to obtain a coaching job. Other openly gay athletes, such as tennis great Martina Navratilova, and even some only rumored to be gay, such as multi-Olympic gold medal–winning track star Carl Lewis, have been denied many of the big-money endorsements their straight colleagues have received.

Kopay was all alone in the gay athlete's club for quite a while, and when he was joined it wasn't entirely a voluntary act. In 1981 women's professional tennis star, and former Wimbledon champion, Billie Jean King was outed when a former secretary filed a "galimony" suit, claiming that they had been lovers and that King had promised to support her. King, who was then married, at first denied the charge, then admitted the affair, which she labeled a mistake. Ultimately, King divorced and came out as a lesbian. The media furor over King's sexuality was amplified by her high profile as a fighter for gender equity in sports. Her 1973 "Battle of the Sexes" victory over Bobby Riggs before a TV audience of 50 million made her a symbol of women's athletics, but she went beyond symbolism by organizing a walkout of women from a national tournament because their prize money was a tenth of the men's. Shortly afterwards, she initiated the Women's Tennis Federation, which led a separate women's tennis circuit. The scandal didn't last very long, and the WTF survived the episode with some loss of sponsors. Billie Jean King was variously defended by some who were willing to overlook "her confessed period of lesbianism away from the courts," and attacked by those, like Philadelphia sportswriter Rosemarie Ross, who seemed to have been waiting for an opportunity to gloat, "King's career is pretty much over."

Shortly after the Billie Jean King lawsuit story broke, Martina Navratilova made history by coming out while still at the height of her career. After denying the rumors swirling around her relationship with lesbian author Rita Mae Brown, the Czech émigré star came out in a newspaper interview.[12] In the years since coming out Navratilova continued to blaze a trail, as she went on to amass an unsurpassed record of tournament victories, becoming the most visible openly lesbian athlete in the world. Asked in the early 1990s if she was

---

[12] Just before she came out, Martina seemed to be kowtowing to the sports world's prejudices by playing straight. A 1981 article headlined "Women's Tennis Stays in Shape: Tour Has Withstood Backlash of King-Navratilova Revelations" disclosed that she "had ended her lesbian relationship with novelist Rita Mae Brown," and that "she dresses more femininely, on and off court." We are informed that much of the credit for Martina's rehabilitation goes to former women's basketball star Nancy Lieberman, who "is in charge of shaping Marina up socially." When Lieberman invited Martina to share her Dallas home—the invitation was accepted—she said she wanted to "introduce Martina to the heterosexual lifestyle. . . . Now that I've gotten to know her, she's a gentle person and not as masculine as they said."

setting an example that encouraged other gay athletes to come out, Navratilova turned around and said, "I don't see any line forming behind me." But in 1993 Gigi Fernandez came out when she appeared with Navratilova on stage at the March on Washington. By 1999, when openly lesbian French junior world champion Amélie Mauresmo was criticized by opponents Martina Hingis and Lindsay Davenport in unmistakably homophobic fashion—Lindsay complained after losing to Mauresmo, "I thought I was playing a guy," and Hingis called her "half a man"—it was Hingis and Davenport who were caught up in a media storm, forced to backtrack and defend themselves.

On the men's side of the aisle, the highest profile gay athlete is probably diver Greg Louganis, whose back-to-back Olympic double gold medals defined him as the world's greatest diver. Louganis electrified audiences when he hit his head on the diving board during the 1988 Olympic preliminaries, then went on to win the gold.[13] Despite his medals Louganis was offered few endorsements—a Wheaties box picture was considered but dropped—and by the early 1990s he retired from diving and tried a career in acting. Taking the role of a gay chorus boy in Paul Rudnick's play *Jeffrey* was understandably taken as a coming out gesture, and *New York Times* sports columnist Robert Lipsyte took him up on it, asking, "So, does this mean you're out?" While Louganis preferred to say that he was "working on things," by the following summer he opened the Gay Games in New York, saying, "It's great to be out and proud."[14]

[13] When Louganis published his memoirs (*Breaking the Surface*) in 1995, this incident was the centerpiece of the media publicity— and the highlight of his ABC-TV interview with Barbara Walters, in which he revealed that he is HIV-positive and had been in 1988—including a *People* magazine cover story excerpted from the book. Despite the fact that the chlorinated water in the pool would have killed any virus, there was some danger to the doctor who closed the stitches in Louganis's head, but the media hype over the story missed the opportunity to educate, or to illuminate the pressures that kept Louganis in the closet.

[14] The Gay Games were reported as a news story by the New York and national media but fared less well in the sports pages. This was not surprising to most lesbian and gay media watchers. As NLGJA president Leroy Aarons put it, "Sports departments are generally very macho places." Straight *Denver Post* sportswriter Mike Monroe concurs: "Most people drawn to cover sports have the same skewed values jocks do. They're not particularly socially conscious or openminded." Los Angeles gay activist Rick Valdivia discovered this when he called the *L.A. Times* to complain about the lack of Gay Games coverage in the sports pages. He was told by the sports editor that it wasn't covered because they didn't consider it an athletic event because the level of competition was not professional (in fact several Olympic athletes participated in the Gay Games). When Valdivia asked why, then, they devoted a full page to a story about night-fishing off the coast of L.A., he was told that was because the paper didn't have a recreational sports section. Valdivia concluded, "Apparently, it's a Catch-22. The Gay Games aren't professional enough to be considered a real sports event, but neither are they a recreational sports event."

In 1995 figure skater Rudy Galindo, whose career was seemingly in decline after the death of two of his coaches, and a brother, from AIDS-related causes, attracted little attention when he came out in an interview with sportswriter Christine Brennan. This all changed in 1996 when the 28-year-old Galindo surprised everyone by winning the U.S. Figure Skating title, thus becoming one of the very first openly gay stars in a sport widely considered to be rife with gay men. Galindo rapidly became a willing role model for gay athletes, speaking at gay events and AIDS fund-raisers, and writing the obligatory autobiography with Eric Marcus.

Louganis and Galindo were both stars in individual competition, as were Olympic swimming medalist Bruce Hayes, divers David Pilcher and Patrick Jeffrey, and skater Doug Mattis. Gay team sports players have not been counted among the out crowd.[15] *Advocate* editor Judy Weider has acknowledged that "there are several prominent athletes in team sports who, to the best of our knowledge, are gay," and that she and her staff check in with "selected gay male athletes in the big U.S. team sports, to see if they are ready to come out." So far, none has, and big-time sports agent Leigh Steinberg says, "Frankly, it would be easier for someone convicted of bank robbery to get a job in the NFL than an overtly gay player."[16]

The ranks of openly gay team-sports stars are limited to those few, like David Kopay and former New York Giants tackle Ron Simmons, who came out after their careers ended. Baseball player Glenn Burke, released from the Oakland A's in 1979, later recounted how his career was destroyed by homophobic managers, although he only came out publicly in 1993, the year before he died of AIDS. More recently, center fielder Billy Bean, who played for three major league teams during his nine-year career, came out in 1999 after leaving baseball. During his playing days, he revealed, he had hidden his relationship with his first lover, who would hide in his car if Bean's teammates dropped by. After his lover died suddenly, of a ruptured pancreas, he had to play the next day and could not attend the funeral.

---

[15] The preponderance of individual versus team sports players among openly gay athletes may be rooted in more than culture. Anthropologists Frederick Whitam and Robin Mathy studied [mostly male] homosexuals in four countries and found consistent patterns of preference and aversion for types of athletic activities. Across Brazil, the Philippines, and the United States, "Heterosexual males and lesbians prefer physically aggressive sports, football, baseball, and basketball, while homosexual males and heterosexual females prefer less physically aggressive sports, such as gymnastics and swimming."

[16] In contrast, after Australian soccer star Ian Roberts not only came out but posed nude for a gay magazine, his endorsement opportunities increased. In Brazil, where soccer great Pelé revealed that he—and many of his teammates—had been sexually initiated by older men, and in Argentina, many leading players are known to be gay.

Even an umpire known to be gay could not be tolerated in major league baseball, as Dave Pallone learned when he was fired in 1988. When Pallone wrote *Behind The Mask: My Double Life in Baseball*, he claimed that an all-star team of gay baseball players could be assembled and, whether he was entirely serious or not, the tremors he set off must have been a satisfying bit of revenge. San Francisco Giants manager Dusty Baker recalled, "That started kind of like a witch hunt. Even some of the wives were asking their husbands, 'Are you one of them?' That was a heavy time."

Just as most people assume, rightly or not, that male figure skaters are likely to be gay—and certainly many of their male fans are—so it has been widely assumed that women's golf and basketball include many lesbians in the ranks of both players and fans. The prime exhibit here would be the annual Dinah Shore women's golf tournament in Palm Springs each March. The large number of lesbians who congregate in the desert resort every spring has led to estimates that dwarf the attendance at the Michigan Womyn's Music Festival and even Provincetown's ultra-gay Women's Week. As a *San Jose Mercury News* sportswriter noted, "Dinah Shore Week is a chance for many to get away from hometowns where their sexual orientation may be secret. Palm Springs becomes a place to enjoy the rare feeling of being open and in a majority."

However openly lesbian many in the audience might be, the Ladies Professional Golf Association is, as its name suggests, both conservative and reticent about matters of sexuality. That there was a backlash against the increasing openness of lesbian golfers, and their fans, was revealed in the comments attributed to CBS golf commentator Ben Wright in May 1995. As reported by a Wilmington, Delaware, reporter, Wright said that women golfers are handicapped by their breasts, which get in the way of their swing, and that "lesbians in the sport hurt women's golf. . . . Lesbianism on the tour is not reticent. It's paraded. There's a defiance in them in the last decade." There was an immediate uproar, as LPGA commissioner Charles Mechem rushed to defend the sport from "an unfair attack—a cheap shot—on a group of talented professional women . . . a way of demeaning or trivializing their performance and their accomplishments." Mechem insisted that lesbianism does not exist on the LPGA tour, and that "lifestyle issues are private matters." At the same time, women athletes condemned Wright's homophobia, and Martina Navratilova asked how Wright could putt "with that big stomach?" CBS briefly suspended Wright and then reinstated him after he denied having made the statements attributed to him.

Ben Wright's putative comments aside, the ranks of women—or lady—golfers does not include legions of open lesbians. In 1996 pro golfer Muffin

Spencer-Devlin was profiled in *Sports Illustrated* and discussed her marriage ceremony with musician Lynda Roth, at their Laguna Beach home. Spencer-Devlin was not followed out of the LPGA closet by any other golfers, and other lesbian golfers have mostly kept their distance from her (in March 1998, however, Patty Sheehan came out in a *Golf World* magazine column). On the other hand, sponsors didn't flee from the LPGA or from Spencer-Devlin, and the organization did agree to replace the "Spousal Badge"—an access pass previously given to players' husbands—with a "buddy clip" that can be given to a significant other.

Women's basketball is experiencing rapid expansion and success, fueled by the U.S. team's Olympic achievement in 1996 and the support of a generation of post-Title IX women. And it's not called Lady's Basketball. The fans at the Dinah Shore are an older and generally more restrained group than the growing legions of lesbian fans of the WNBA. Former pro basketball player Mariah Burton Nelson, a Washington Mystics season-ticket holder, told the *Washington Post* that "there's a lot of anger on the part of lesbians for being left out of society in general and having to deal with homophobia in sports." Resentment at efforts to heterosexualize the sport and gloss over the large lesbian fan base led the Lesbian Avengers protest group to stage a "visibility action" at an August 1998 Mystics game: buying a block of sixty seats and wearing the group's T-shirts. The following summer a group of "Lesbians for Liberty" staged a "Lesbian Visibility Action" at the Liberty basketball game in New York's Madison Square Garden. In the spring of 2001 the WNBA's Los Angeles Sparks deviated from its family-oriented marketing program by holding a pep rally at the lesbian Girl Bar in West Hollywood. The team's general manager noted, "This isn't about marketing to sexual lifestyles, it's about marketing to a group of people we think will buy tickets." *Philadelphia Daily News* lesbian columnist Debbie Woodell bemoaned the fact that there are no openly lesbian WNBA players, noting, "Most of us who are out know how hard it was to take those first steps. And we'll be there when the first big name in basketball takes that huge first step. (Hint to anyone who's reading: It feels like making a game-winning shot.)"

As the 1990s drew to a close, the playing fields of American professional sports remained a major battleground in the ongoing cultural wars. The popularity of the U.S. women's soccer team in the 1999 World Cup competition was due to their spectacular success in winning games, but their media images were also heavily focused on their heterosexual credentials as wives and mothers. The crowds that cheered when Brandi Chastain ripped off her jersey top (and promoted her Nike sports bra) were comfortable in the knowledge that she's straight. When Green Bay Packers star Reggie White—

an ordained minister—was invited to address the Wisconsin state legislature in March 1998 and mixed ethnic stereotypes ("Hispanics are gifted in family structure. . . . Asians can turn a television into a watch") with homophobic ranting about sinners who are "like liars, cheaters, backstabbers and malicious people," there was an outcry, but his career was secure. White was condemned by gay groups, and by many journalists and public figures, but not by the NFL.

Atlanta Braves pitcher John Rocker didn't get off quite as easily after he gave an interview to *Sports Illustrated* in December 1999. Rocker, who was known for mouthing off, told the reporter that he wouldn't play for a New York team: "Imagine having to take the (No.) 7 train to [Shea Stadium] looking like you're in Beirut next to some kid with purple hair, next to some queer with AIDS, right next to some 20-year-old mom with four kids. It's depressing. The biggest thing I don't like about New York are the foreigners." Rocker managed to offend enough groups that he was quickly forced to apologize. As New Orleans sportswriter Mark Purdy wrote, "Major League Baseball is, at heart, a service entertainment industry. And when you have a high profile player from a World Series team who goes off and insults immigrants, gay people and minorities . . . well, that doesn't help sell many tickets to immigrants, gay people and minorities. As well as to their friends, relatives, lovers and anyone else who doesn't appreciate irrational hate." Baseball commissioner Bud Selig sentenced him to "sensitivity training" sessions and levied a $20,000 fine and a 30-day suspension. Within a few days an arbitrator reduced the fine to $500 and cut the suspension in half; Rocker returned to training camp and resumed playing.

12

Morning Papers, Afternoon Soaps

COMING OUT IN THE COMICS

When 17-year-old Lawrence Poirier told his parents in April 1993 that he was gay, it was not an especially remarkable event (although it is always a significant moment when a teenager comes out to his or her parents). Neither was the outcome all that unusual: Lawrence's parents threw him out of the house, then relented and decided to accept his homosexuality. But Lawrence Poirier is not a typical teenager; he is a character in a comic strip, *For Better or For Worse*, that was then running in over 1,400 newspapers in the United States and Canada. Canadian artist Lynn Johnston had been drawing the daily strip for thirteen years when she decided to include the five-week story line about Lawrence's coming out. She based her story in part on the experience of her own family when her brother-in-law came out.

For Better or For Worse is a notable success story among syndicated newspaper comic strips, having grown from 250 papers in 1981. Widely praised in her field, Lynn Johnston is the first woman cartoonist to win the Reuben, the National Cartoonist Society's Cartoonist of the Year award. Working within the genre of domestic comedy, Johnston was credited with combining gentle humor and sharp observation as she chronicled the lives of a suburban Toronto family and their friends and neighbors. *For Better or For Worse* is unusual in that its characters have aged more or less in real time as the series continues, including the mother's pregnancy and birth of another child since the strip began. Introduced as a little boy in 1981, Lawrence Poirer became a close friend of Michael, the son of the central Patterson family, and regularly appeared as he, Michael, and their other friends grew into teenagers. Thus, when Lawrence came out to Michael, and then to his parents, readers were learning something new about a young man they had come to know and, presumably, feel kindly toward.

The story line about Lawrence hit the comic pages with the force of a small earthquake, sending shockwaves through many normally placid newsrooms. Approximately forty papers suspended the strip for the duration of the sequence and sixteen canceled for good. Many newspapers ran editorials or articles, warning readers of what was about to break loose on the comics page—the newspaper equivalent of a "parental advisory" before a TV program—and explaining why they decided to run, or not run, the "coming out" episodes. The editor of the *Las Vegas Review-Journal* explained his refusal to run the story: "It's not offensive at all, but it was condoning homosexuality almost to the point of advocacy." Others went farther: Nackey Loeb, publisher of the *Union Leader*, New Hampshire's notoriously far-right newspaper, ran a front-page editorial denouncing the comic strip as "political propaganda . . . to promote homosexuality as a normal, acceptable and morally justified lifestyle."

On the other hand, there was also an unprecedented growth in new newspapers subscribing to the strip, and a flood of mail: nearly two thousand letters sent to Johnston and hundreds more to the newspapers. Approximately one-third of the letters were hostile, with many readers threatening to cancel their subscriptions to the offending newspaper. Some expressed themselves more forcefully, like the writer who asked, "When are you and your lying perverts going to quit your bullshit?" Another writer, seemingly under the impression that the strip featured explicit sexual depictions, wrote that "the comics page is no place for homosexual relations!" Repeatedly, letter writers objected to the episodes' presumed departure from the comics' previous "value neutrality" in order to "send a message" and provide "a political forum for a liberal agenda."[1] The large majority of the writers were favorable, thanking Lynn Johnston for the story line and often recounting experiences of their own. One man wrote, "Last week I had a call from a cousin of mine in Toronto. We were very close friends but had not spoken in many years. When he found out I was gay he just would have nothing to do with me. He has been reading your strip and felt the need to call me to re-establish, if possible, our friendship."

---

[1] It shouldn't be necessary to point out that the supposedly "value neutral" comic strips that these readers prefer are, in fact, carriers of an ideology that is transparent to those who already share it. This is, after all, what cultural theorists mean by hegemony, and comic strips have never been immune from its effects. As Lee Daniels has noted, "Somehow it was decided that what the people needed was reassurance . . . that what should be going into millions of homes all over the United States was a comforting and conformist version of the lives that were lived in these homes."

Lawrence disappeared from *For Better or For Worse* after the five-week story line and returned briefly for two days the following June, when he showed up at his high school prom with his boyfriend. When his friend Mike expressed surprise, he declared, "I decided . . . No matter what anybody says, you gotta stand up for yourself, stand up for your freedom, stand up for . . . " Mike interrupts, "Lawrence—sit down and eat!!"

In the summer of 1997 Johnston brought Lawrence back for another brief gay-related appearance (he had been seen from time to time in episodes that did not touch on sexuality). Over four days Lawrence confided in Mrs. Patterson that his "partner, Ben, is moving to Paris" to take up a piano scholarship. Mrs. Patterson comforts Lawrence, assuring him that "Ben isn't leaving forever," and besides, "you have to be prepared to feel pain if you're going to fall in love." The week ends with Lawrence expressing his gratitude to Michael that "being gay has never changed our friendship." Once again the opposing forces lined up. After the Universal Press Syndicate warned the 1,700 papers carrying the strip about the impending episodes, at least thirty papers requested past strips to run instead, and the Christian Family Network called on its members to decline the papers during that week. In response, the Gay and Lesbian Alliance Against Defamation (GLAAD) suggested that gay-friendly readers buy three copies of their local paper and mail the extras to the Christian Family Network and the American Family Association.[2]

But Lawrence wasn't the first gay character in a newspaper comic strip. That honor goes to Andy Lippincott, referred to disparagingly by columnist Nicholas von Hoffman in 1976 as a "presentable gay" on *Doonesbury*, Gary Trudeau's politically oriented strip. Andy Lippincott first appeared as a fellow law school student of series regular Joanie Caucus. In a variant of the familiar "all the good men are married or gay" trope, Joanie falls in love with the handsome, intelligent and, above all, sensitive, Andy—their first conversation is about sexual harassment law. When Andy tells her that he loves her, but that he's gay, she is flummoxed: "I mean, I know I still have a good friend in Andy, but it's kind of a setback when your boyfriend tells you he's gay." Andy then disappeared from *Doonesbury* for six years, reappearing for a brief moment in 1982 as "one of the organizers of the Bay Area Gay Alliance" hosting Joanie's boss, Congresswoman Lacey Davenport. Andy

---

[2] Supporters of the strip did not, however, register a complaint that, as on TV shows, the gay character is presented as a disturbance in the field of heterosexual normality, who can expect at best to be accepted by his family and friends. At least Lawrence was given a boyfriend, even if they never so much as hold hands.

Lippincott's most extensive presence on *Doonesbury* was as the series' Person With AIDS, once again paired with Joanie Caucus, who discovers Andy's condition in April 1989. For the next year Andy made many appearances, in gradually worsening health but never losing his sense of humor. After his death in May 1990, readers saw his memorial service, featuring a video-taped Andy as Master of Ceremonies—"No words of pity, OK? I'm doing fine now. It's a little hard to tell from the décor, but I think I made it into heaven!"—and visited the AIDS Memorial Quilt with Joanie and Lacey Davenport.

In fall 1993 Andy made an appearance—this time in a dream—to help another *Doonesbury* character, Mark Slackmeyer, the antiwar activist turned NPR radio talk show DJ, realize that he is gay. Subsequently, Mark comes out to his friends (who take it well) and his parents (who take it badly), and then comes out on his NPR radio show. In a brief June 1994 sequence, Mark tries unsuccessfully to pick up another man—who turns out to be a "deeply religious married man"—and ends up explaining the thesis of Yale historian John Boswell's book about the existence of the Catholic Church's rites for same-sex ceremonies in the early Christian era. Because Mark is one of the series' central characters, his frequent appearances are not necessarily related to his sexuality. However, in keeping with *Doonesbury*'s political focus (some papers carry it on the editorial page for this reason), Mark's gayness intersects with his politics. In a June 1994 radio interview with former Vice President Dan Quayle (represented on *Doonesbury* by a feather), Mark continued his discussion of Boswell's book on early Catholic gay marriages. The Quayle feather responds to Mark's question about same-sex marriages: "If you have a man, and then you have another man, well then you have two men and no women that are married to these men. So right off the bat, they don't have family-style values. Also, what if they then produce children?" To which Mark replied, "Well, I imagine there'd be a Nobel in it for them." Eventually Mark finds true love with conservative commentator Chase Talbott III (his father approves of his choice in this instance), and they decide to get married. This gave them—and us—the opportunity to learn how uneasy the prospect of a gay marriage makes *Doonesbury*'s liberal minister character, and so, in the summer of 1999, they flew to Pago Pago to exchange wedding vows on the beach.

The stormy response to Lawrence's coming out in the comic pages pales, however, in comparison with the public panic over comic books that raged in the late 1940s and early 1950s, culminating in hearings before a U.S. Senate subcommittee on juvenile delinquency. Comic books had become a lucrative business by the mid-1930s, and they became even more popular in the 1940s. In 1941, 10 million copies sold each month; by 1947 that figure had risen to 60 million. Contributing to the astounding success of the comic books were the action, crime, and horror genres, featuring superheroes (Superman, Batman, Captain Marvel, and Wonder Woman most prominent among them), as well as gory depictions of blood and guts. Critics of the comics were quick to attack, raising the sorts of arguments now more familiar in debates about the effects of television and video games. Comics were accused of instigating violent and criminal behavior by children—a classic instance being that of a young boy in a "Superman" cape, who supposedly jumped to his death from a window—as well as undermining literacy and good taste. By far the most prominent and influential of the critics was psychiatrist Frederic Wertham, whose 1954 book *Seduction of the Innocent* captured public attention and helped prod the Senate into holding hearings on comic books. The hearings resulted in the comic book industry adopting a "voluntary" Code, similar to the Motion Picture Production Code introduced in the 1930s, and spelled the doom of the worst offenders in the crime and horror genres.

Among the charges leveled against comic books was that they contributed to homosexuality. Wertham wrote that "only someone ignorant of the fundamentals of psychiatry and of the psychopathology of sex can fail to realize a subtle atmosphere of homoerotism which pervades the adventures of the mature Batman and his young friend Robin."[3] Similarly, Wonder Woman and her "Holiday Girl" followers were "anti-masculine" and likely to encourage lesbianism among girls. The comic book industry responded to such accusations much as the movie industry did, by scrupulously avoiding any acknowledgment of homosexuality, and vigorously defending "truth, justice, and the American way." The Motion Picture Code was swept away by the 1960s, but comic books took decades longer to recognize changing cultural conditions.

"The Comics Break New Ground Again" was the surprising headline of an editorial in the *New York Times* in January 1992. The staid establishment newspaper demonstrated its newfound awareness of gay issues by proclaiming that "comic book hero Northstar has revealed to the 100,000 or so people who follow his exploits that he is gay." Northstar, the *Times* helpfully informed its readers, appears in *Alpha Flight*, a series produced by Marvel Comics. Northstar revealed his sexual orientation in a story about his adop-

---

[3] As my childhood recollections clearly demonstrate, it didn't take psychiatric training to detect, or appreciate, the homoerotic overtones in Batman.

tion of an HIV-infected baby.[4] Noting that Marvel Comics had long been a pioneer in diversifying popular culture, having introduced female and disabled superheroes, the *Times* welcomed these revelations as an indicator of social change, evidence that "gay Americans are gradually being accepted in mainstream popular culture."[5]

The *Times* also noted that DC Comics had introduced a gay character and AIDS-related themes in its *Flash* series. In 1995 DC Comics published a four-book miniseries, *Metropolis S.C.U.* (Special Crimes Unit), in which the main character, Capt. Maggie Sawyer, is a lesbian superhero with a lover. Sawyer had previously appeared as a supporting character in *Superman* comics, but in the *Metropolis S.C.U.* series she protects the planet herself, fighting off a variety of supervillains as well as facing the "real-life" challenges of juggling a career, a relationship, and motherhood. As media activist Al Kielwasser put it, the miniseries, which earned the Comics Code Authority's Seal of Approval, struck an admirable blow against one of reality's deadlier supervillains.

Also in 1995, Shadowhawk, a heroic African American crime fighter from Image Comics, dies of AIDS. Bad guys had injected the superhero with HIV earlier in the series. "Why did it have to be me?" ShadowHawk wonders, between the THUKS and CRAKS of bashing evil perpetrators. "I wasn't at risk . . . I don't DESERVE this!!" "Who does?" asks the next panel.

One step beyond DC Comics sits Vertigo, a line of comics labeled "For Mature Readers" because of its adult themes, sci-fi, horror, and occult titles. When the Vertigo line spun off from DC in the early 1990s, what it intended was a place for comic book fans to find complex fiction told in comic-book

[4] Northstar is urged to come out by another Canadian superhero, Major Mapleleaf, whose gay son died of AIDS: "Don't you realize the good that you can do? By not talking about your lifestyle—by closeting yourself—you're as responsible for my son's death as the homophobic politicians who refuse to address the AIDS crisis." Shortly afterwards we see the front page of the *Daily Mail*: "Alpha Flight's Northstar Proclaims Homosexuality: 'It has been said Silence Equals Death. I no longer wish to be part of the Death that is the AIDS crisis,' said Jean-Paul Beaubier, the former Olympic athlete better known as Northstar of Alpha Flight."

[5] Despite the *New York Times*'s praise for its positive contributions to cultural diversity, Marvel Comics has not always been so enlightened about gay people. In October 1980, before the advent of AIDS might have raised the company's consciousness, the then-popular Hulk went on a mad rampage after his alter ego, Dr. Bruce Banner, is threatened with rape in a YMCA shower. In the story, "A Very Personal Hell," the mild-mannered Banner is staying at the New York YMCA and, as he is shown heading for the shower, we see two sinister figures lurking. The two, a white man and a black man, enter the shower and begin threatening rape. The black man, pushing Banner against the wall: "Umm, you're *soft*! And all pearly white—and you've got the cutest little cheeks! Think he'll whine, Dewey?" "Yeah, Luellen—an' I like it when they whine," replies his friend and, taking off his shirt, Dewey tells Banner, "You won't like it this time, but I will!" Banner scares off his assailants by turning into the Hulk.

form. Vertigo is one of the most critically acclaimed lines of comic books, and nearly every Vertigo title has had either a gay character or had one gay story. Vertigo's most ambitious gay story is *Seven Miles a Second*, a 60-page comic published in 1996, chronicling the life of controversial artist and writer David Wojnarowicz. Taken from Wojnarowicz's own writing, the work portrays Wojnarowicz's adolescence as a hustler and his death from AIDS. Elizabeth Hess of the *Village Voice* said it "is destined to become one of the major auto-biographical works from the decade."

In March 2000 the DC Comics series *The Authority* broke new ground by revealing that two of its 21st-century superheroes, Apollo and Midnighter, were lovers. Mark Miller, author of the series, told the *London Times*, "The whole idea of a superhero is that he or she fights for the underdog, so I don't see why we shouldn't have superheroes who are gay."

The more unconventional comics of the 1980s and 1990s have often been willing and able to include lesbian and gay characters, and with much less fanfare and controversy than either the conventional newspaper comic strips or the comic books' superhero series. Matt Groening's *Life in Hell* strip, appearing in dozens rather than hundreds of (mostly alternative) papers, has long featured Akbar and Jeff, the identical gay couple whose love-hate relationship has beguiled many readers and offended others. Groening says he is particularly pleased when people with homophobic attitudes start to like the characters and then realize they're a gay couple: "They feel upset. How can they reconcile liking these characters with knowing their sexual orientation?" Groening's TV animated series *The Simpsons* has frequently included gay themes and characters, winning an Emmy for an episode in which openly gay movie director John Waters (*Pink Flamingos, Hairspray, Serial Mom, Polyester*) teaches Homer and Bart a lesson about homophobia.

The envelope *The Simpsons* pushed was ripped open in 1997 when cable channel's Comedy Central began running *South Park*. The show centers on four foul-mouthed third-graders, their families and neighbors in the mythical small town of South Park, Colorado, a cold, snowy place where the elementary school cafeteria cook is a soul-crooning African American and their teacher talks to them through a hand-puppet. Among *South Park*'s most notorious episodes was one in which Stan, one of the kids, learns that his pet dog is gay (don't ask). The dog runs away because everyone is making fun of him, and Stan goes searching, finding him at Big Gay Al's Big Gay Animal Retreat. Big Gay Al—flouncily lovable with a heart of gold—takes Stan on "Big Gay Al's Big Gay Boatride," where dioramas of gay people through the ages are depicted as benign and their oppressors, mainly the religious right, are the ride's scary parts. Stan learns his lesson, and when he returns to South Park he announces that "Gay is OK!" and brings his neighbors to Big Gay Al's, where many find pets they thought they had lost forever. Big Gay Al was among the milder of *South Park*'s forays into territory previously off-limits to "family" entertainment. In the spring of 1998 another of the main characters, Cartman, discovers that his father is actually his mother: she's a "hermaphrodite" who fathered Cartman with an unknown woman. Before that, when Cartman and his friends tried to become lesbians in order to be attractive to their substitute teacher, Ms. Ellen, they tried licking his carpet and eating cardboard because his mother told him lesbians "lick carpet" and "eat box." Predictably, *South Park* occasioned much editorial concern and pundit hand-wringing, and Comedy Central was careful to schedule the program in later prime-time. However, the creators of *South Park* went on to produce a movie version in 1999 that featured a sexual relationship between Satan and Sadam Hussein.[6]

In the late 1990s many cartoonists who flourished in the confines of the lesbian and gay press, such as Howard Cruse, whose *Wendel* series ran for years in the *Advocate*, and Alison Bechdel, creator of the widely syndicated *Dykes to Watch Out For*, have also found a home on the Internet. Self-publishing on the Internet is rapid and inexpensive and also provides opportunities to sell book collections (Bechdel's books are steady best-sellers in lesbian/gay and feminist bookstores).

In January 1999 Chris Cooper, a former Marvel writer and editor, launched *Queer Nation*, an online gay comic strip, featuring gay and lesbian superheroes doing battle with the newly elected fundamentalist President Pat, and his league of Patzis.[7] Reflecting on his years at Marvel, Cooper said, "I became exasperated with the [X-Men's] premise that there's a group of people who look like everybody else but have this secret they discover at adolescence about themselves." Cooper's impatience with seeing the experiences of gay teens—coming out yet having to remain hidden—mined so thoroughly, yet never seeing a gay X-Man, motivated him to create *Queer Nation*. "There isn't a lot of mythmaking in our culture these days," Cooper noted. "Hopefully, I'll be able to give our community some archetypes that encapsulate all the things we aspire to."

---

[6] When the watchdogs for the Motion Picture Association of America rejected the original title, *South Park: All Hell Breaks Loose*, because of the objectionable word "hell," the producers came back with *South Park: Bigger, Longer, and Uncut*. This time it was approved without difficulty: "They just didn't get it," chuckled the directors.

[7] *Queer Nation*'s superheroes are variants on the familiar genre: Shy, mild-mannered accountant, Fred Flagg, after massive exposure to Lambda rays from Comet Q, becomes "massively muscled Adonis—Hunk—whenever he's sexually aroused."

YOU'RE THE FIRST PERSON I HAVE EVER TOLD

August 31, 1992

Dear Ryan,

First of all, I want to thank you for the courage you have shown playing the part of a homosexual teenager. Especially in this day and age when discrimination and violence against gays is on the rise.

As you act on *One Life to Live* as a gay teenager, I also act. I act as a straight, normal twenty one year old. It has become routine to act like the perfect son or brother. You are the first person I have ever told and may be the last, that I am gay. I don't think I will ever be able to tell anyone the truth. Had not your portrayal and this story line of a gay teen hit me so deeply, I probably would not be telling you. Your character is so realistic and you do such a great job portraying how gay teens really feel.

Recently, I saw phone numbers for gay youth. For those who are troubled about their sexuality. I honestly don't feel I have enough courage to call any of these places. For some reason, I think somehow, someone will find out. If my family or friends find out, I'm afraid they wouldn't look at me the same or would never love me as much as they do now.

I feel that way because of things I hear my family say about homosexuals. Until recently, I would laugh at jokes about gays or would pretend to dislike the way they were. I cannot and will not do that anymore. Now I just stay silent and try to ignore things that are said about gays and even AIDS itself. I overheard my father say that faggots started AIDS and normal people like Magic Johnson have to suffer for what gays have done. Well do you think I could ever tell him that I am one of those who he thinks have caused normal people to suffer and die from AIDS. It's something I could never foresee.

I know this is just your job and I'm sorry for throwing all of my problems at you like this. I certainly don't expect you to solve any of them but it feels good just to tell someone. . . . Thank you for your time.

In the summer of 1992 the daytime TV serial *One Life to Live* began what was to be one of the longest and most complex television narratives to deal with a lesbian or gay character. Billy Douglas is a high school student who has recently moved to Llanview (the fictional small town outside Philadelphia where *One Life* takes place), and becomes a star athlete and class president. When Billy confides, first to his best friends and then to his minister, that he is gay, he sets off a series of plot twists that differ from the usual soap opera complications in that they expose homophobia and AIDS-phobia among the residents of Llanview and thus offer the characters—and the audience—an opportunity to address topics that soap operas have generally preferred to ignore.

Earlier, in the fall of 1983, ABC's *All My Children* had included Lynn, a lesbian psychologist played by Donna Pescow, for an eight-week plotline in which she helps her friend Devon, who needs a place to stay, thus providing many opportunities for Devon (as the audience's surrogate) to ask questions and to learn that, "It's not a disease; it's not contagious." The show's producer boasted, "It's a small miracle that we got as far as we did," predicting that viewers would see gay characters on other soaps. But it proved to be a long wait.

Eighteen months before "The Accusation" appeared on *One Life to Live*, an article in *Soap Opera Weekly* explained "Why Daytime Isn't Gaytime," concluding that "homosexuals seem forever doomed to reside in the daytime's dark and lonely off-screen closet, deprived of light by narrow-mindedness and bigotry, kept there by ignorance and intolerance." The article may have been excessively pessimistic about the willingness of a soap's producers and network to introduce a gay character, but it was accurate on another score: the difficulty of having a regular character turn out gay. A writer for *One Life* is quoted, "It's difficult to maintain a homosexual character as a hero over a period of time"—certainly true as long as such a character is not permitted to engage in numerous romantic couplings with other characters. As *One Life*'s head writer Michael Malone explained at a University of Pennsylvania symposium in 1993, they decided to introduce a new character—Billy Douglas—to be the centerpiece of "The Accusation" because they didn't want to have a regular long-term teenage character turn out to be gay.

The plotline featuring Billy Douglas was the dominant thread of *One Life to Live* from July through early September 1992, after which Billy appeared less frequently until he left Llanview for Yale the following spring. Billy Douglas was played by Ryan Phillippe, in his first professional role, and he found himself at the center of a great deal of media and audience attention. He received an unusually large amount of mail even for a good-looking young soap opera actor. Even more unusual was the fact that the majority of the nearly five hundred letters he received during the months that he appeared on *One Life* came from young men, most of whom identified themselves as gay. Many of the young gay men—and several of the older men—wrote that they were particularly moved by and grateful for Ryan's sensitive portrayal of an experience much like their own, being isolated and vulnerable in a society that would prefer not to know they existed.

For many of the fans who wrote to Ryan Phillippe, just as for thousands of lesbians and gay youth growing up today, the lesbian/gay movement appears unknown, or perhaps irrelevant or unreachable—the fear of exposure is so great. And so, in 1992, after nearly a quarter century of lesbian and gay activism, a straight actor playing a gay teenager on TV seemed their best hope for support, advice, and sometimes even friendship. For many, he was also their first confidante for stories of isolation and terror.

While it is not difficult to imagine that an African American, Asian American, Latina or Latino actor would get letters from teenagers who identify with and appreciate any appearance of their underrepresented group on the public media stage, it is hard to imagine that they would receive letters like the one quoted above, let alone similar letters from adults:

Dear Ryan:

Your performance has been "right on." I am a happily married, successful father of two teenagers (one, your age, equally good looking as you). I am fifty-five years old, and have kept my sexual preference (gay) a secret, except for a few very close friends, all my life. . . . Have I been successful? Yes. Has my life been a torture chamber of lies and deceit? Yes . . .

You see, I lived the character you are playing, and still live it, although in the "closet." I've never been a victim of homophobia, because no one knows I'm a life-long, born-that-way homosexual, comfortable with who I am, but not comfortable with living as a gay person. Still your character has created an empathy in me, because I can relate so well to your character.

You are doing a service to millions of people, whether you know it or not, just by bringing the subject to a mass audience. Keep up the good work.

Sorry, I can't sign this letter.

Somewhat surprisingly, there were literally no negative or hostile letters received by Phillippe or the show's producers in response to the gay teenager or the other elements of the plotline focusing on homophobia and AIDS-phobia. It was only later, in December 1992, when Billy Douglas (who by then had a much smaller role overall) met and began a friendship with another gay youth, that the program began to receive negative letters. The relationship between Billy and his friend was never developed, however, and by the time Billy "left for Yale," the viewers—and the producers—had been spared the question of whether soap opera's first gay teenagers would be allowed to kiss.

How can we understand the nature of the relationships these letter-writers feel that they had with Ryan Phillippe, an actor they had seen in a single role and, possibly, in TV and magazine interviews; or did Billy Douglas, the troubled but courageous gay teenager, seem so real he reminded them of themselves or of a friend or relative? Most of the writers seemed well aware that Ryan Phillippe is an actor and that Billy Douglas is a character. Why, then, did these writers, both the isolated and fearful gay teens as well as the adults haunted by unhappy memories, feel that a young actor known to be straight, but portraying a confused and troubled youth, was an appropriate target for their confessions, their overtures, and their pleas for help?

Back in the 1950s, psychiatrists Donald Horton and Richard Wohl introduced the term "para-social interaction" to describe an audience's unrealistic sense of pseudo-familiarity with media celebrities. They defined such responses as pathological only when they are a "substitute for autonomous social participation, when [they proceed] in absolute defiance of objective reality." As Joli Jensen (critically) summarized their view, "Para-social interaction is an attempt by the socially excluded (and thus psychologically needy) to compensate for the absence of 'authentic' relationships in their lives." Apparently in the 1990s many teenagers and even adults who confronted the choice between the stifling agony of the closet and the possibility—even certainty—of familial and societal rejection did not have the option of authentic relationships with anyone to help them deal with their emotional crises. Thus an inexperienced but sincere young heterosexual actor found himself playing not only role model but also confessor and phantom friend to people in great pain and need.

After Billy Douglas left for Yale in 1993, soap-land was devoid of gay characters until November 1995 when Michael Delaney (Chris Bruno), the popular high school history teacher in *All My Children*'s Pine Valley, came out to his class during a lesson on the Holocaust and soon found himself at the center of a firestorm.[8] The parents of some of his students go ballistic and

---

[8] Michael Delaney's coming out was modeled on the real-life experience of Missouri teacher Rodney Wilson, who came out to his students in 1994 and ended up embroiled in a public controversy. Wilson ultimately kept his job and was instrumental in establishing October as Gay History Month.

demand that the school board fire the teacher, which they do. His students rally to his defense, and he ultimately is victorious in a lawsuit and is reinstated.[9] At this point the focus shifts to the travails of his gay student, Kevin (Ben Jorgenson), whom his parents try to save through "conversion therapy." Kevin's struggle with his parents, and the quack psychiatrist they employ, played out over many months, along with his friend Kelsey's attempts to seduce him into heterosexuality. Although Kevin continued to maintain a gay identity, the show's producers didn't give him any friends, let alone a boyfriend.[10] Michael Delaney did find a boyfriend, but neither appeared very often—and certainly they were not shown engaged in physical contact. Chris Bruno did not renew his contract as Michael Delaney, and Kevin gradually drifted out of sight by the end of 1997, leaving Pine Valley, like the rest of soap opera land, without any queer inhabitants. But it didn't stay that way.

In the middle of 2000 a new actress, Eden Riegel, was hired to play Bianca Montgomery, the teenaged daughter of soap legend Erica Kane (Susan Lucci) in *All My Children*, and soon viewers noticed that Bianca had a secret. Over the next few months Bianca gradually revealed to several other characters that she is gay, culminating in a tearful coming out to her mother just before Christmas. Fans of the soap had filled Web chatrooms for months with speculation about how Erica Kane would take the news, although few doubted that eventually a mother's love would endure. Whatever the outcome, new ground had been broken, because, as Riegel put it, "The audience has watched Bianca grow up and they've learned to love her. The character is integral to the show. . . . They're in it for the long haul."

[9] In the course of these events his sister is shot and killed by the homophobic brother of a student who comes out while defending the teacher—all of this on the set of a local TV talk show which is airing a program on the controversy. Michael Delaney is then represented in his lawsuit against the school board by his previously homophobic, now widowed-but-wiser brother-in-law. Thus the world turns in Pine Valley.

[10] The August 19, 1997, issue of *Soap Opera Magazine* featured a readers' poll on Kevin's future: "During the process of self-discovery, what conclusion would you like to see Kevin reach?" OPTION NO. 1: "I hope *AMC* uses this story line to illustrate the point that you can't change what people are. If Kevin is gay, then no amount of therapy is going to change that. I hope Kevin's parents (and viewers) will learn this important lesson." OPTION NO. 2: "If the powers-that-be aren't willing to go full speed ahead and give Kevin a boyfriend, I'd much rather see Kevin realize he's straight and find a love interest in someone like [his best friend] Kelsey than stay on the back burner forever. Ben Jorgensen is much too talented an actor to be used merely as a coffee-pourer."

13

Old Stories and New Technologies

THE GOOD PARTS

Whenever a new communications technology arrives on the scene it can safely be predicted that among its earliest users will be churches spreading the Christian Gospel, and the creators and purveyors of explicit sexual imagery. Those with the strongest, if not necessarily the purest, motives will be the ones to explore the possibilities inherent in each medium to capture words and images and to convey them to those hungering for their messages. In the case of pornography, sexual images and stories have generally been officially condemned while privately enjoyed. They also have offered channels for the vicarious expression and satisfaction of minority interests that are difficult, embarrassing, and occasionally illegal to indulge in reality. For lesbians and gay men, whose sexuality is officially denied and erased, pornography often provided a vital message: "For isolated gays porn can be an important means of saying 'other gays exist.'"

Lesbian writer Dorothy Allison recalls her first encounter with "hard-core" paperbacks she found under her parents' mattress when she was a child:

> What the books did contribute was a word—the word *Lesbian*. When she finally appeared . . . I knew her immediately . . . When she pulled the frightened girl close after thirty pages, I got damp all down my legs. That's what it was, and I wasn't the only one even if none had turned up in the neighborhood yet. Details aside, the desire matched up. She wanted women; I wanted my girlfriends. The word was *Lesbian*. After that, I started looking for it.

The pornography Dorothy Allison found was (most likely) written by and for straight men, who have always appreciated a bit of lesbian spice in their erotic menu; an appetizer before the main course. For gay men, however, heterosexual pornography has never been a welcoming venue. Still, as Thomas Waugh has documented, since the invention of photography gay men have created, collected, and enjoyed their own pornography.

In the 1940s and 1950s, photographers such as Bruce of Los Angeles and Bob Mizer of the Athletic Model Guild expanded the genre of "physique" magazines aimed, implicitly but successfully, at gay men. The physique magazines were sold mostly through mail order, but were also carried by newsstands in some urban locations. In the late 1950s *Grecian Guild Pictorial*, one of the gayest of these magazines, estimated a circulation of nearly 75 thousand, and estimates for the entire group reached 750,000. Waugh claims that "the exponential expansion of 'physique culture' constitutes the most significant gay cultural achievement during the formative quarter-century following World War II." The pinup publications were an early form of community-building that provided, along with the bars, a rare venue for the cohesion of gay identity and the sense of community.[1]

Even so, only in recent decades has it become possible for most gay youth and adults to explore this narrow-cast channel of imagery created for and by queers. John Burger's account of gay male video pornography illustrates several ways these videos serve as history texts of the gay male experience: "First, many of them resituate gay men into past and present social conditions in which they have mostly been hidden (such as the California gold rush, the U.S. Armed Forces, and college fraternities). Second, the videos also document current gay-specific social conditions, such as bar life, nightclubs, bathhouses, and so on." Burger continues: "These videos . . . are important documents not only of the all-gay environment, real or invented, but of the gay male psyche which so desperately envisions such spaces where they can be free from the social oppressions encountered daily. . . . If we must be marginalized, let us at least create enjoyable spaces on the fringe—whether in imaginary representations or in reality, like the bathhouses."

Similar accounts of pornography produced for and by lesbians (certainly a more recent and limited genre) note its importance for those, in Lisa Henderson's words, "for whom sexual imagery is one link in a social and cultural

---

[1] The Grecian Guild was not oblivious to the ideological climate of the Cold War, however, and promulgated a patriotic Grecian Guild creed along with the pinup photos of muscular young men: "I pledge allegiance to my native land, ever willing to serve the cause of my country whenever and wherever she may need me. I seek a sound mind in a sound body that I may be a complete man; I am a Grecian."

lifeline, a link emblematic of their refusal to accept established sexual hierar-
chies and their will to make their own place." It must be acknowledged, however, that minority cultural production is not immune from contagion by the
racism and sexism endemic to our culture.

The existence of these sexual images is a threat to those who guard the
ramparts of the sexual reservation. Visible lesbian or gay (or any unconventional) sexuality undermines the unquestioned normalcy of the status quo
and opens up the possibility of making choices that people might never have
otherwise considered. The fight to keep sexuality invisible (especially in its
"deviant" forms) is part of an ancient battle waged by the forces of established order against the subversive potential of powerful images and the way-
ward impulses they might inspire in the vulnerable. The vulnerable, it is
important to recognize, are rarely if ever the holders of established power
themselves, but rather those over whom that power is held: children, women,
and "lower classes" of all sorts.

Traditionally, the only acceptable storytellers outside the circle of family
and immediate community were those certified by religious institutions.
The emergence of schools intruded a new group of specialists between children and the world they grow up into. The arrival of mass media of communications fundamentally altered the situation: children were increasingly
open to influences that parents, priests, and teachers could neither monitor
nor control. Beginning with the widespread availability of printed materials
to the literate, increasing with media less dependent on literacy (photography, movies, radio, and even the telephone), and culminating with television's omnipresence (and newly creeping over the horizon, the Internet),
children have become more and more independent consumers of mass-pro-
duced stories.

The feared power of images—verbal or, even more powerfully, visual—
seems to reside in the representation of precisely those behaviors and options
which the holders of power wish to deny to those they control, protect, and
fear. Images of violence have remained ubiquitously available although
repeatedly denounced by moral authorities (and endlessly studied by media
researchers). Images of sexual behavior, in contrast, have been the targets of
more effective attack, and their availability has been generally hedged
through legal proscriptions. While parents, preachers, and politicians have
criticized violence in the movies, comic books, and television, they have succeeded in criminalizing many explicit sexual images and have prosecuted
those who produce or distribute and even, on occasion, those who consume
them.

The legal term for prohibited sexual representations (in words or images) is *obscenity*, and its most influential definition in Western law comes from Victorian England's Lord Chief Justice Cockburn, who ruled in 1868 (*Regina v. Hicklin*) that "the test of obscenity is this: whether the tendency of the matter charged as obscenity is to deprave and corrupt those who minds are open to such immoral influences, and into whose hands a publication of this sort may fall."[2] Just a few years later, in the United States, Anthony Comstock successfully lobbied for the passage of *An Act for the Suppression of Trade in, and Circulation of, Obscene Literature and Articles of immoral Use*, which President Grant signed in 1873 and which was widely referred to as the Comstock Law.

Comstock came to be a symbol of America's fear of uncontrolled sexuality, just as his unique position as Special Agent of the U.S. Post Office for over forty years made him its moral policeman. In his writing and in his crusades against immorality Comstock articulated a widespread obsession with the ubiquitous *Traps for the Young* (the title of his 1883 work) which lay in wait. "Newspapers, 'half-dime' novels, advertisements, theaters, saloons, lotteries, pool halls, postcards, photographs, even painting and sculpture— wherever the poor child turned, in Comstock's nightmarish America, something lurked, ready to debauch him."

In the 1970s, North American and Western European societies witnessed an explosion in sexual expression by gay men and, to a lesser extent, lesbians, that added a new chapter to the so-called sexual revolution of the 1960s. The convergence of post-Stonewall openness and the increasingly liberal legal climate of the late 1960s permitted the rapid growth of a gay-male-oriented porn film industry. By 1973 there were more than fifty gay hard-core theaters in the United States, at least twelve in New York City alone.[3] The era of theatrical gay porn was brought to a close by the emerging technology of home video. The video cassette recorder transformed the porn industry, just as porn was helping to popularize the VCR. In 1978 and 1979, before the major movie studios adopted the new video technology, more than 75 percent of the video cassettes sold were pornographic. For gay people the opportunity to view pornography in the privacy of the home was

---

[2] The U.S. Supreme Court has modified *Hicklin* in a series of decisions, most recently *Miller v. California* (1973), in which obscenity is defined by an appeal to "prurient interest," characterized as depicting, "in a patently offensive way, sexual conduct specifically defined by state law," violating contemporary community standards (thus moving the judgment to the local level), and, "taken as a whole, [lacking] serious literary, artistic, political or scientific value."

[3] In 1971 director Wakefield Poole made gay porn history with *Boys in the Sand*, an $8,000 hard-core feature that grossed $400,000 and earned reviews in *Variety* and the *New York Times*.

especially welcome, even before AIDS made porn the safest form of sex (except, unfortunately, for many performers).[4]

The same period also witnessed the emergence of the sexual and cultural counterrevolution that has come to play a large role in contemporary politics. At the same moment that lesbian and gay people joined to fight against the reactionary forces led by Anita Bryant in Florida and State Senator Briggs in California, many feminists were turning their attention to symbolic violence against women in media and advertising and its possible role in encouraging rape. By the late 1970s, Women Against Violence in Pornography and the Media, in California, and Women Against Pornography, in New York, used marches through "red light" districts to "take back the night." However, despite their claims, the antiporn crusaders did not speak for all feminists, and theirs were not the only voices being raised. When the San Francisco lesbian S/M group Samois emerged in 1979, a line was drawn and lesbian sexuality became a central battleground of what came to be called the "sex wars."

Lesbians resisting the antiporn arguments acknowledged the "deeply erotophobic" nature of Western culture but argued against the choice of primary targets. In Amber Hollibaugh's words, "Instead of traipsing through porn districts . . . we might be demanding better contraception, self-defense classes, and decent non-judgmental sex education. Then women would be strong enough to make our 'no's stick as well as our 'yes's." Further, and equally important, they were alarmed at the essentialist view of female sexuality implicit in the antiporn ideology:

> They state that power in sex is male, because it leads to dominance and submission which are in turn defined as exclusively masculine. They suggest that any arousal which is translated through images and expressions of power originates from a masculine and sexist kind of desire. Any similar arousal felt by women is simply false consciousness. In real life this forces many feminists to give up sex as they enjoy it, and forces an even larger group to go underground with their dreams. For many women who have no idea what they might eventually want it means

---

[4] The porn studios resisted depicting "safer sex" for a long time, and by the time they adopted the now ubiquitous condom in the late 1980s, many porn performers had died of AIDS-related causes, and many have died since. The porn studios' initial efforts at safer sex were somewhat awkward and even misleading, as in the guidelines included at the end of Falcon studio's films around 1989 that advised, "Don't engage in sexual contact with other persons wihout consulting your physician in advance," but neglected such basic information as the importance of using water-based lubricants with latex condoms.

silencing and fearing the unknown aspects of their passions, as they begin surfacing. Silence, hiding, fear, shame—these have always been imposed on women so that we should have no knowledge, let alone control, of what we want. Will we now impose these on ourselves?

The "sex wars" loosed a flood of debate with (mostly lesbian) feminists playing leading roles on both sides. But the issue moved beyond the level of even acrimonious debate when the leading antiporn activists, Andrea Dworkin and Catherine MacKinnon, entered the political and legislative arena. In 1983 they drafted an ordinance that was subsequently adopted by the Minneapolis City Council, but vetoed by the mayor. They were more successful in Indianapolis, where the mayor signed it into law. The ordinance never went into effect, however, as it was immediately challenged in the federal courts, where it was ultimately ruled unconstitutional.

The Dworkin/MacKinnon ordinance was not based on standard obscenity arguments. Pornography for Dworkin and MacKinnon is not a *representation* of harm against women, it *is* harm against women (in MacKinnon's words, "pornography amounts to terrorism" against women). At the very least it is the theory of which rape is the practice (to paraphrase a famous statement by feminist activist Robin Morgan). Among the more striking and troublesome features of their analysis and their ordinance is the claim that women *cannot* consent to perform in porn: "a woman's decision to pose for a sexual image should be treated as the product of coercion even under circumstances where a man's decision would be treated as voluntary and consensual." The logic of presumptive nonconsent makes adult women equivalent to minors.

However, these very features of the Dworkin/MacKinnon position also contained the seed of their eventual constitutional undoing (in the United States, though not in Canada, where their views were incorporated in the 1992 *Butler v. The Queen* Supreme Court decision). By arguing that pornography must be seen as a vehicle of sexist ideology, they confer on it the status of political thought, and thus render it worthy of constitutional protection. In the end, this was a major rationale in the federal courts' decisions striking down the Indianapolis ordinance.

By the mid-1990s it appeared that the sex wars had died down, and it was possible to agree with Heather Findlay that "sex-positive feminists—those of us who are generally in support of the philosophy and civil rights of pornographers, S/M activists and sex workers—have won the lesbian sex wars." Findlay's evidence consists of the abundance of "high quality, often experimental lesbian erotics" available in print, image, and video.

Some of the credit for this might even go to the antiporn feminists. As Victoria Brownworth put it, "Lesbian erotica was born out of . . . the antipornography wave—partially because it was being born anyway, and partially in retaliation. Some lesbians had waited a long time to have sex and have fun, and didn't want to be told what kind of sex was politically correct and what kind wasn't." However, much of the credit must go to the commercial opportunities and technological advances that have made the production and distribution of lesbian and especially gay male pornography financially viable. The free market *can* be a vehicle for free speech.

SOMEWHERE THERE'S A PLACE FOR US

In recent years new options have emerged that offer isolated members of a minority the opportunity to reach and communicate with like-minded fellows: scattered cable-TV and radio programs that are available to those lucky enough to live within their range,[5] and for those with access to cyberspace, the Internet and the World Wide Web.

New media create opportunities for the formation of new communities, and the Internet is no exception. In contrast to most other modern media, the Internet offers opportunities for individual engagement both as senders and receivers, permitting the coalescing of interest-based networks spanning vast distances. The potential for friendship and group formation provided by the Internet is particularly valuable for members of self-identified minorities who are scattered and often besieged in their home surroundings. A brief tour of the Web will reveal countless sites devoted to specialized interests that draw like-minded participants across national and international boundaries. Notable among the interests served by this (so far) uniquely egalitarian and open medium of communication are those represented by sexual minorities. Currently there are on-line forums, bulletin boards, home-page sites, and on-line "zines" addressed to lesbian and gay readers, such as the *Oasis*, a Web site dedicated to providing information and contacts for lesbian and gay teenagers.

"Does anyone else feel like you're the only gay guy on the planet, or at

---

[5] Los Angeles radio producer Greg Gordon, recalling his experience as a teenager ("I thought I was the only one"), "found a way to reach into the closets and countrysides where gays are painfully isolated: gay radio. He started *This Way Out*, a weekly half-hour show of news and commentary that now airs on seventy radio stations in six countries. . . . Those who tune in are often older gays in rural areas or young people who feel they can't talk to their parents or teachers about being gay"

least in Arlington, Texas?" When 17-year-old Ryan Matthew posted that question on AOL in 1995, he received more than one hundred supportive e-mail messages. Similar accounts abound, not only in the United States but in many other parts of the world. Lilach Nir interviewed Israeli gay teenagers who participate in on-line discussions unavailable to them in their "real" environments of smaller cities, rural villages, and kibbutzim.

The popularity of the Internet for gay men and lesbians isn't limited to teenagers. According to the Associated Press, in June 1996, "It's the unspoken secret of the online world that gay men and lesbians are among the most avid, loyal and plentiful commercial users of the Internet. On any given evening, one-third of all the member-created chat rooms on America Online are devoted to gay topics." As described by Tom Reilly, the Internet executive who created PlanetOut as the "gay global village of cyberspace. . . . Gays and lesbians don't have a high level of ownership of mainstream media properties. The Internet is the first medium where we can have equal footing with the big players."

While one of the clichés of computer-mediated communication is that one can hide one's true identity, so that nobody knows you're 15 and live in Montana and are gay, it is also true, as Nir's informants told her, that in their IRC conversations they "are *unmasking* the covers they are forced to wear in their straight daily lives." The opportunities for deceptive (as well as truthful) self-presentation on the Internet have featured in the alarms raised in response to the Internet's potential to disseminate that most volatile of media substances, sexually explicit words and images.

Consider 15-year-old Daniel Montgomery, for example. In June 1995 the Seattle papers reported that the teenager had been "lured" away from home by a stranger, but not someone "casing his neighborhood or hanging around outside his high school. . . . Instead, the mysterious character known to the Montgomerys only as 'Damien Star' was lurking in a place that has proven much more ominous: cyberspace." The encounter took place in a "gay chat room" on America Online—"it was there that the man apparently enticed Daniel Montgomery with secret promises" to run away from home and join him in San Francisco. Daniel's father believed his son was the victim of "an organized attempt by adults to recruit boys like Daniel." The vice principal of his school told the paper that "we've certainly had runaways before . . . but holy cow, this makes you sick." The police were sympathetic but not alarmed: "If a child is listed as a runaway, what we do is take a runaway report. . . . We don't go and actively seek them out."

Within a few days, however, it seemed that things were not quite as earlier reports had suggested. Daniel's father, identified with the religious right, acknowledged that "there are issues between him and the teenager," presumably because "Daniel may have been sexually confused." More important, it turned out that Damien Starr wasn't the pseudonym of a dirty old man who was infiltrating the Internet to lure innocent teenagers into a life of depravity. Damien Starr is the real name of a San Francisco teenager who met Daniel Montgomery in a gay America Online chat room and apparently responded sympathetically to accounts of his difficulties with his parents.

But the "unmasking" of Damien Starr did nothing to allay the fears of those who see in the Internet a threat to the innocent and vulnerable. The week after Daniel Montgomery returned home to his parents, the U.S. Senate voted to impose heavy fines and prison terms on those who distribute sexually explicit material over computer networks. Voting 84–16 in a session rife with lurid talk about child pornography and on-line descriptions of bestiality, advocates of tough regulation easily overwhelmed objections from a handful of lawmakers who said the measure would violate constitutional rights to free speech and threaten the growth of computer networks. "Take a look at this disgusting material, pictures which were copied for free off the Internet only this week," said Sen. Jim Exon (D-NE), the measure's chief sponsor, as he brandished a big blue binder with a bright red label: "Caution."

Senator Exon, like his predecessors back to Comstock, presented his role as protecting children, not as restricting expression. "I'm not trying to be a super censor. The first thing I was concerned with was kids being able to pull up pornography on their machines." Special Agent Comstock was present in more than spirit, however, as the U.S. Congress moved toward the inclusion of Senator Exon's Communications Decency Act (CDA) as part of the omnibus Telecommunications Reform Act signed by President Clinton on February 8, 1996. The CDA revived the provisions of the 1873 Comstock Act prohibiting mailing of abortion-related materials across state lines, which are still on the books, though essentially nullified by *Roe v. Wade*, and added them to the prohibition against making available to minors on-line materials that "in context, depicts or describes in terms patently offensive as measured by contemporary community standards, sexual or excretory activities or organs." The CDA was the target of an immediate lawsuit filed by the ACLU in the name of a group of plaintiffs that included Planned Parenthood, Critical Path AIDS Project, and an on-line publisher of writings by lesbian and gay teenagers.

In June 1996 a three-judge federal district court panel struck down the CDA. Judge Stewart Dalzell wrote that "the Internet may fairly be regarded as a never-ending worldwide conversation. The Government may not, through the CDA, interrupt that conversation. As the most participatory form of mass speech yet developed, the Internet deserves the highest protection from government intrusion" (*ACLU v. Reno*). The following year the U.S. Supreme Court voted 7 to 2 to affirm the lower court's decision, explicitly resisting the politically popular appeal of child protection rhetoric: "Regardless of the strength of the government's interest [in protecting children], the level of discourse reaching a mailbox simply cannot be limited to that which would be suitable for a sandbox."

Comstock's heirs are not easily discouraged, however, in their zeal to protect children from sexuality. In October 1998 the U.S. Congress passed a more narrowly drawn version of the CDA, the Child Online Protection Act (COPA), which President Clinton opposed but signed, relying on the courts to protect citizens from the legislative and executive branches. In the debate over COPA in the House Commerce Committee, Representative (now Speaker) Dennis Hastert articulated the familiar cry: "Even though our children may be at home with the doors locked that doesn't mean that they are safe. We must continue to be proactive in warding off pedophiles and other creeps who want to take advantage of our children. It's not infringing on our liberties, it's about protecting our kids." COPA was immediately challenged by the ACLU and seventeen plaintiffs, many of them lesbian and gay bookstores, publications, organizations, writers, and Internet activists. As PlanetOut founder Tom Reilly testified in federal court in January 1999: "Many people find just being gay to be 'harmful to minors.' . . . We operate a community of interest, rather than a community of geography, but based on our community standards no information on our site is offensive in any way" (*Yahoo News*, 1/22/99).

The drafters of COPA attempted to narrow its focus, thus hoping to avoid the fate of CDA, and they targeted commercial sites by requiring that they obtain credit card information before admitting users to so-called "adult" sites. The plaintiffs argued that these restrictions imposed an economic hardship and barrier both for providers and users, and that they also constituted a chilling effect that would lead providers to self-censorship. While the ultimate outcome of COPA and succeeding legislative efforts will remain in the hands of the courts—a federal appeals court struck down COPA in June 2000, and the Bush administration later announced plans to appeal to the Supreme Court—there is already ample evidence of the complications created by the imposition of related measures involving Internet "filtering software."

Having lost the battle of the CDA, congressional censors turned to a technological fix akin to the V-chip mandated for inclusion in future TV sets: the requirement that filtering software for the Internet be used by schools and libraries that receive federal funds for Internet access, in order to block material deemed inappropriate for children. The introduction of the Internet School Filtering Act in spring 1998 opened a door much wider than that of the local school and public library, however, as commercial providers rushed to offer parents a variety of filtering services. In the words of GLAAD's executive director Joan Garry, "We had gone from the frying pan of active censorship [the CDA] into the fire of censorship by passive omission."

Commercial filtering software works by blocking access to sites based on keywords presumed to signal sexual content, and this often includes the very words *gay, lesbian, homosexual,* or even *sexual orientation.* Parents—or schools and libraries—that install such filtering software thus prevent teenagers (and adults, in many instances) from gaining access to support groups, informational sites, and even the Association of Gay Square Dance Clubs. As a representative of CyberSitter put it, "I wouldn't even care to debate the issue if gay and lesbian issues are suitable for teenagers. . . . We filter anything that has to do with sex. Sexual orientation [is about sex] by virtue of the fact that it has sex in the name." Thus, sites offering safer sex information are routinely excluded by many filtering programs (along with sites focused on breast cancer). Some filter providers, such as SurfWatch and CyberPatrol, promised to permit access to informational, educational, and support sites, but GLAAD and its allies remain concerned about the implementation of these commitments in deciding on specific instances and keywords.

Even when filtering programs do not automatically exclude sites that address lesbian and gay people's concerns, they pose other dangers to gay teenagers. NetNanny, CyberSitter, and SafeSearch, among others, allow parents to set their own exclusionary criteria, and they make suggestions that some might find questionable. The president of Solid Oak, the provider of CyberSitter software, cited the National Organization for Women's Web site as a target: "The NOW site has a bunch of lesbian stuff on it, and our users don't want it." CyberSitter was at the time the filter recommended by the ultra-right Focus on the Family organization.

At the end of the 2000 legislative session, Congress passed another filtering mandate, the Children's Internet Protection Act, sponsored by Sen. John McCain (R-AZ), among others. Enthusiasm for the measure, which is likely to suffer the same constitutional fate as its predecessors, was diminished somewhat by the discovery that many popular filters, such as CyberPatrol, carried their blocking efforts too far, preventing access to the American Family Association's site, and even to the "Freedom Works" Web site of Republican Representative Dick Armey (presumably because of his first name).[6]

The filtering technology has another worrisome feature: an "audit trail" that allows parents (or librarians and school administrators) to trace which sites and newsgroups their children (or other users) have tried to access. As GLAAD points out, this auditing feature is particularly dangerous to youth, if it leads to the accidental disclosure of sexual orientation.[7] In the words of a 16-year-old lesbian, quoted in GLAAD's 1997 report, *Access Denied*:

> Living in a small town in South Carolina makes it almost an impossibility to be open about sexuality. Both emotional and physical safety is in the hands of those who are not primarily known for their open-mindedness and understanding. Through e-mail, I've created a support system for myself of different gay/lesbian listservs, and through people I could not have otherwise contacted. Coming to terms with my sexuality would have been so much harder if I had been alone. I owe a debt of gratitude to the people I've met, and who have supported me—the people who told me I was not "evil," or "immoral," or "sick" after these very things were drummed into my head. At 16, I am content with myself.

The battle over unfiltered access to Internet sites will undoubtedly end up in the lap of the Supreme Court, and even if the forces of freedom prevail, as they did with the CDA, Comstock's heirs will continue their campaigns to search out and destroy technological traps for the young. If the cyber-nannies win the battle, queer teenagers like this South Carolina girl may be cut off from the lifeline represented by resources such as *Oasis* and left feeling like the desperate 16-year-old who wrote soap opera actor Ryan Phillippe, "Ryan, the only person in this world I can relate to is your character Billy Douglas on *One Life to Live*. Ryan, I'm so scared. I don't know what to do and I'm afraid of what I might do. You, God, and I are the only ones that know! Ryan, please help!"

[6] Among those urging Congress to mandate filters for public libraries was the Christian Alliance for Sexual Recovery, whose representative, Mark Laaser, asked, "Would you want to provide people with an outlet to express these degrading acts, or would you point them away?" Point them in his direction, perhaps, as clients for his $1,000 cyber-addiction workshops.

[7] The privacy of Internet users is also vulnerable to invasion by government investigators and, in the case of workplace computers, employers. Testifying at Congressional hearings on cyber-privacy in April 2000, GLAAD's Digital Queers coordinator Will Doherty emphasized that "if there is an untimely disclosure of our sexual orientation, that can be very damaging for us with our families or with our jobs."

14

A Niche of Our Own

The growing visibility of lesbian and gay people in the 1990s was not manifested only on the news pages and television and movie screens of America. Lesbian women and gay men were increasingly able to see their reflections in the pages of their own newspapers, magazines, and books and on their own cable television programs. In a further demonstration of the emergence of gay people onto the American landscape, we are receiving the ultimate recognition that this country can bestow: being included in advertising. In Michael Schudson's wonderful phrase, advertising is capitalist realism, the dramatic incarnation of the consumerist ideology that permeates our society. As Schudson put it (making a precise analogy with the official Soviet definition of socialist realism), advertising does not claim to depict life as it is but as it should be—life and lives worth emulating. Thus, to be ignored by advertising is a powerful form of symbolic annihilation, but to be represented in the commercial universe is an important milestone on the road to full citizenship in the republic of consumerism.

Inspired by the optimism of the postwar moment, in 1945 a group of African American newspaper publishers set out to attract mainstream national advertisers to their pages. For this purpose they commissioned a readership survey to collect data on African American consumers in three East Coast cities. Such surveys are not conducted in order to paint a demographically accurate portrait; their rhetorical function is to project an unrepresentative fragment as an image of the whole. The survey performed according to form, concluding, in the words of researcher Dwight Brooks, that, "Black consumers were loyal to national brands, used many of the same products as Whites, had a relatively higher level of education than the national average, and had a fairly high magazine readership." In reporting their data, the researchers compared urban blacks with a national average and, not surprisingly, found a higher level of education (recall that in 1945 the U.S. population was still heavily smalltown and rural). The distortions were not really a problem, however, for the intended audience of the survey: advertisers who needed to be persuaded that African American consumers were worth addressing. Similarly, shortly after the founding of *Ebony* magazine, its publisher initiated a series of market surveys of its readers conducted by the firm of Daniel Starch.

Of particular importance to the advertisers in these studies of African American consumers was the finding that "brand loyalty is greater among Blacks than Whites." This is an insight that would recur decades later as mainstream advertisers began slowly to acknowledge and address gay and lesbian consumers. The gratitude of stigmatized groups to those few companies willing to solicit their patronage is rather sad. Lesbian writer Sarah Schulman cites the explicit appeal by the gay marketing firm Mulryan/Nash: "Many gay men and women are separated from their families. . . . Therefore the mechanisms that normally lead people to choose a product are absent." As Schulman notes, "Since our families do not want us and few national advertisers target us, Mulryan/Nash realize that ad campaigns in gay magazines give gay readers" what they characterize as "an immense obligation to support advertisers who support them."

The road to recognition of gay and lesbian consumers by mainstream advertisers was neither smooth nor short. In 1978, after *Advertising Age* ran an editorial noting but not regretting the relative absence of advertising attention to gays, a gay man wrote asking, "Where's our representation in trade and retail advertising? Where do you see two gay men laughing it up at Burger King? Where's the lesbian couple happily getting into their Chevrolet which came from Avis?" At that time these images were unimaginable, or worse. In the same issue, another correspondent decried any attention given to gays: "I can and do wish to ignore homosexuals in advertising. . . . God, man, what has happened to the sensitivities of your fine publication?"

In 1980 *Advertising Age* noted that most large companies "shy away from being identified with homosexuals" by including them in ad campaigns. At the same time, gay publishers attempted to persuade advertisers that they were overlooking an attractive market. In New York Joseph Di Sabato started a gay marketing company representing seventy-five gay papers around the country, claiming a combined circulation of over a million. In San Francisco the publisher of the *Advocate* began promoting the magazine to advertisers on the basis of claims about its upscale, educated readers. The *Advocate* placed an ad in *Advertising Age* headlined, "It's 1981. Do you know where gay people live?" And the following year San Francisco media consultant Kenneth Maley took an ad to tell the trade magazine's readers that, "Gay men and women may be America's most affluent and least understood market." Not surprisingly, most of the marketing professionals leading the efforts to attract mainstream advertising to gay consumers and gay media were themselves gay. As one observer put it, some argue that because of "gaydar," only gay people should design magazine pages for gay people. In any event, "almost all of the gay-specific agency heads and national magazine art directors are gay men." In 1999 a Philadelphia and L.A.-based ad agency, Gyro, opened a gay/lesbian specialty shop in Los Angeles with the subtle name Gyrohomo ADV. As reported in *Advertising Age* (2/15/99:8), Gyro's Charley McBreaty, himself gay, promised that they will create ads "to the culture, from the culture. . . . I will talk to gays as gays talk to themselves."

As these marketing professionals repeatedly explained to their potential clients, gays (and to a lesser extent, lesbians) were the ultimate yuppie consumers. In the slang of the advertising business, "guppies," as they were sometimes termed, were perfect DINKS—double income, no kids—and therefore, presumably, had lots of disposable income. Once again, no one was needlessly concerned about the large proportion of gay men and lesbians who didn't fit this profile; advertisers weren't interested in reaching them.[1]

The *New York Times* responded to these efforts with a lengthy article in its Sunday magazine in 1982, noting that "for the first time, advertisers are vying for homosexuals' buying power, though they worry about offending mainstream consumers." These worries slowed the process, but only temporarily. In 1987 the Italian liqueur Amaretto Di Saronno was being "positioned" as a hip drink with an ad campaign featuring profiles of suitably hip personalities. One such person was the popular, and openly gay, *Village Voice* columnist Michael Musto. But that ad never ran because a photo of Musto wearing a dress was published in a magazine and the company worried about being associated with someone who might be *too* hip.[2] A few years later the

[1] Contrary to the gilt-edged projections of the marketers and readership surveys, careful analyses conducted by economist Lee Badgett of the University of Massachusetts-Amherst revealed that "if anything, gay men are at a financial disadvantage to heterosexual men, probably because of discrimination." At the same time, the inflated figures used to attract advertisers have been cited as evidence that gay people don't need civil rights protection, as when Justice Scalia argued in his 1996 *Romer v. Evans* dissent that gay people are politically powerful and enjoy "high disposable income."

[2] A Chicago-based gay community directory and Century 21 Real Estate Corporation ran into legal difficulties when they used a cross-dressing image familiar to many Americans who grew up in the 1950s. Their ad, with the caption, EVERY QUEEN DESERVES A CASTLE, showed a

236 A NICHE OF OUR OWN

successful clothing chain the Gap initiated a similar campaign using large celebrity photos, and they happily included several well-known and openly gay figures: playwright Tony Kushner, film director Gus Van Sant, journalist Andrew Sullivan. Despite the rise in anti-lesbian/gay organizing by the religious right in the 1980s, the attractiveness of the lesbian and gay market became increasingly seductive.

Indeed, the seduction of Madison Avenue has been accomplished in part through the efforts of market research firms, such as the Chicago-based Overlooked Opinions and the New York agency Mulryan/Nash, which amassed mailing lists comprising thousands of gay and lesbian individuals and made these available to publishers, ad companies, and direct mail marketers. The first beneficiary of Madison Avenue's growing interest in the lesbian and gay market were newspapers and magazines, which finally were able to attract big money ads from national advertisers.[3]

Perhaps the key factor that moved ad agencies to open the faucet and direct the flow of national advertising dollars to the gay press was the redesign of the *Advocate*, initiated in 1990. After years of depending on sex-oriented ads (especially the lucrative phone-sex businesses that flourished after the onset of the AIDS epidemic), the *Advocate* relegated its sex-related ads to a separate pull-out section in an effort to attract skittish national advertisers. Their initial efforts bore few fruits, but even a sprinkling of advertiser interest provided one of the key ingredients fostering the dramatic spurt in the number of gay and lesbian "lifestyle" magazines in the early 1990s.

In March 1992 a front-page story in the *New York Times* proclaimed "New Gay Press Is Emerging, Claiming Place in Mainstream." Similar articles in *Newsweek* and *USA Today* heralded the move, in *Newsweek*'s words "from closet to mainstream" as "upscale magazines flood the newsstand." These magazines included several that are intended for a lesbian and gay audience—the most successful being *Out* and the *Advocate*—with others more narrowly targeted at gay men (*Genre*), lesbians (*Deneuve*, which changed its name to

---

middle-aged man with rouged cheeks and false eyelashes wearing a tall headdress adorned with pineapple, bananas, and other tropical fruit: the picture was of TV comedian Milton Berle, or Uncle Miltie, as he was known when he was one of television's first superstars, doing his Carmen Miranda shtick. Berle, now in his nineties, was not amused and sued for $6 million. His attorney told *Variety*, "We are deeply concerned that a generation of Americans unfamiliar with Berle's classic shtick are seeing Berle depicted as a homosexual within the pages of this gay magazine. Mr. Television deserves far better."

[3] The success of the gay magazines in attracting national advertising did not, however, guarantee success to the marketing firms that had pushed the envelope. By 1999 both Overlooked Opinions and Mulryan / Nash had gone out of business. Mulryan / Nash's demise was a particularly harsh blow to many small gay publications that were left holding worthless debt.

Curve after Catherine Deneuve threatened legal action, and *Girlfriends*), and even those who are HIV-positive (*POZ*).[4] Among the companies that have advertised in these magazines are American Express, Bank of America, Banana Republic, Benetton, IBM, General Motors, Subaru, Time Warner records, United Airlines, and Sony, in addition to liquor brands such as Absolut Vodka, Miller beer, and Remy Martin cognac.

The *Advocate*, facing serious competition for the attention of national advertisers, eliminated its sex ads altogether in 1992, spinning them off into a new publication, the *Advocate Classifieds*, a venture that eventually spawned a number of new sex-oriented magazines, *Advocate Men* and *Fresh Men*, that rely on classified and porn-video ads. The new *Advocate* was able to attract previously unattainable mainstream ads and to greatly increase its newsstand distribution.

The desexing of the *Advocate* might have inspired magazine entrepreneur Sam Francis, who launched *Arrow*—presumably, as in "straight as an arrow"—but quickly renamed *Hero*, described as a "magazine for the rest of us." The rest of us, it turns out, are well-educated gay men in committed relationships. The magazine gained immediate attention and reached a circulation of 35,000 by the end of 1999. The magazine's focus on "hot monogamy"—the title of a monthly column—was trumpeted by Francis as bringing gay people into mainstream America, and criticized by those, like gay activist Eric Rofes, who see it as "a gay version of *Cosmopolitan*, without the sex."

Gay and lesbian newspapers also benefited from the new interest on the part of advertisers, though they still rely heavily on local businesses and classified ads, including phone-sex operations. In 1994 the *New York Times* reported that at least sixty-five gay and lesbian papers are published nationwide, with a combined circulation nearing three million. Mulryan/Nash reported that ad sales in gay publications in 1998 achieved a 20 percent increase in ad sales compared to less than 10 percent for mainstream newspapers and magazines.

The ambivalence of many lesbian and gay people toward the incorpora-

---

[4] It should surprise no one that lesbian publications fared much less well than those aimed primarily at gay men. In 1999 the advertising director for *Girlfriends* and the lesbian sex-mag *On Our Backs*, Catherine Draper, acknowledged that "when liquor and cigarette and high-end fashion companies talk about tapping into the gay market, they still target the men's magazines rather than the women's." Despite their relative disadvantage, *Girlfriends* and *On Our Backs* reported all-time high ad revenues. Things were not as rosy for smaller, more local lesbian publications: in April 1999, New York's *HX for Her*, the *Women's Central News* of Arizona, and the *L.A. Girl Guide* all ceased publication, largely due to the lack of advertising support.

tion of their images in advertising was captured by critic Danae Clark, who noted that such advertising "appropriates lesbian subcultural style, incorporates its features into commodified representations, and offers it back to lesbian consumers in a packaged form cleansed of identity politics." National advertisers are looking for affluent readers, and they are looking for "comfortable" environments in which to place their ads. Not only do they avoid sex-related advertising, they actively prefer to place ads in "lifestyle" magazines that editorially support a focus on popular entertainment, fashion, and soft news.[5]

The next move in this game may have been made in Australia in 1992, when an automobile dealership ran an ad showing two men, a pair of Dalmatians, a picnic basket, and a Toyota, under the headline "The Family Car." In the United States that same year, the clothing chain Banana Republic ran a series of magazine ads showing couples. Five of the ads showed a man and a woman in romantic poses; the sixth showed two men, arms intertwined. The ad was ambiguous enough to provide deniability, as demonstrated by the publisher of *Vanity Fair*, who said "I just see two guys who are in some way being affectionate. Actually, it looks like something sad. But I don't see gay." On the other hand, the president of Overlooked Opinions was more forthright: "It is a picture that is certainly gay-sensitive, and gay people who see it will interpret it in that way."

"As breakthroughs go, it's not exactly Jackie Robinson joining the Brooklyn Dodgers." Thus *New York Times* columnist Frank Rich greeted "the premiere of the first mainstream television commercial starring uncloseted gay consumers." In April 1994 the Swedish furniture chain Ikea ran the television ad—featuring a middle-aged gay male couple buying a dining table—in the four markets served by its U.S. stores: Houston, New York, Philadelphia, and Washington. While Rich was correct that the ad was not in the category of breaking the racial barrier in professional baseball, it certainly garnered a lot of attention. The ad was reported by newspapers, television news, and magazines, and discussed in articles, columns, and talk shows. On a CNN discussion an antigay speaker objected, "gay relationships are not families," and thus, presumably, shouldn't have dining tables. Ikea was also hedging its bet, allowing the ad to air only in later primetime, even though the commercial

---

[5] An unforeseen consequence of the success of national gay publications in obtaining mainstream advertisers is that they raised their rates accordingly, and seem to have forgotten that small independent presses can't afford to pay the same rate as a big airline. Thus, with the exception of Alyson Books, which is owned by the *Advocate*, the small independent lesbian, gay, and feminist presses are being shut out of advertising in the publications best able to reach their potential readers.

doesn't explicitly refer to the couple as gay. "We recognize the sensitivity of it," said the company's marketing director, "since a consumer cannot choose when a television commercial comes into their home."

The election of Bill Clinton in 1992 and the subsequent furor surrounding the "gays in the military" issue, and the large March on Washington in April 1993, persuaded journalists and publishers as well as advertisers that "gay was in." The title of a book by former National Gay and Lesbian Task Force director Urvashi Vaid represents the trend in book publishing. *Virtual Equality: The Mainstreaming of Gay and Lesbian Liberation* made publishing history in 1993 when Anchor Press paid Vaid an advance of $217,000 for her unwritten book. Other publishers joined in the rush, paying six-figure advances for at least seven different nonfiction lesbian and gay book projects. After years in which mainstream publishers had shunned books written by and for lesbian and gay people, leaving small presses to cultivate writers and audiences, the exploding visibility of gay people and gay issues has raised the tempting prospect of "crossover" best-sellers that would attract nongay as well as gay readers. The success of Randy Shilts's history of the AIDS epidemic, *And the Band Played On*, contributed to this crossover fever, but Michael Denneny, the editor who handled Shilts's work, was skeptical: "Non-gay people are quite willing to praise [gay and lesbian] books, but they feel it's something they don't have to read." Yet even without a substantial crossover readership, these books often do well, largely because there are growing numbers of lesbian and gay readers willing to buy books on gay topics, and because, in the words of a Scribner's editor, "Gay history has come into its own, just as the gay movement has moved into the center of national consciousness."[6]

One measure of the degree to which lesbian and gay people moved into the national spotlight was the appearance of magazine articles and cover stories heralding the unapologetic visibility of gay people. Most dramatic was the amount of attention to lesbians, who had been for so long even more invisible in the mass media than were gay men, and now suddenly seemed to be in journalistic fashion. A 1993 *New York* magazine cover headline set the tone for the year: "Lesbian Chic: The Bold, Brave World of Gay Women."

---

[6] Another factor contributing to the sales of gay books at this juncture was the spread of book-chain superstores, such as Borders and Barnes & Noble, that included well-stocked gay and lesbian sections, and somewhat later, the explosion of Internet-based shopping that brought such books within reach of those unable or unwilling to buy them in person. A significant downside to this development was the immediate and often devastating threat to the viability of the independent gay, lesbian, and feminist bookstores that had served to nurture the community and its literature.

The peak of lesbian media presence was a *Newsweek* cover story in June 1993, showing two women embracing under the banner headline: "LESBIANS: Coming Out Strong. What Are the Limits of Tolerance?" Even more striking were the articles that appeared in women's magazines, not typically known for being sympathetic to lesbians:

- *Mademoiselle* (February 1993): "Women in Love. Young Lesbians: They're fresh, they're proud, they're comfortable with their sexuality. Having staked out their own issues, they're now defining a new style."
- *Vogue* (July 1993): "Sexual Politics: Good-bye to the last taboo. Not too long ago you couldn't say the word *lesbian* on television. Now everyone's gay-girl crazy."
- *Cosmopolitan* (November 1993): "A Matter of Pride: Being a Gay Woman in the Nineties."

- *Glamour* (May 1994): "Do Ask, Do Tell: Lesbians Come Out."

The magazine cover that may have garnered the most attention also focused the public gaze on the growing number of openly lesbian and gay media celebrities. The August 1993 issue of *Vanity Fair* showed popular singer k. d. lang in butch drag, sitting in a barber's chair, being "shaved" by supermodel Cindy Crawford (herself sometimes rumored to be lesbian). The Canadian-born lang, who came out in a 1992 *Advocate* interview, was soon joined by rock stars Melissa Etheridge and Elton John in the small club of openly lesbian and gay singers.

As the 1990s progressed, "lesbian chic" faded and the novelty of gay-oriented advertising subsided. However, interest in marketing to the gay audience remained high and survived efforts to puncture the inflated image of gay affluence. Two trends seemed most likely to continue: steadily growing numbers of mainstream ads in gay and lesbian publications, such as Levi-Strauss's 12-page "advertorial" pushing Dockers khakis, in the November 1999 issue of *Out*; and the use of what marketing experts call "gay vague" images. These images, first used in gay magazine ads, began to appear in mainstream media, and even on television. The two young men shown driving around aimlessly, in a Volkswagen commercial (that happened to debut during the "coming out" episode of *Ellen*) can be—and often are—readily read as gay, but just as easily not thought of this way at all. A Subaru ad with the slogan, "Different Drivers. Different Roads. One Car," shows Subaru vehicles with vanity plates reading XENA LVR (referring to lesbian cult-favorite *Xena, Warrior Princess*) and P-Townie (referring to gay resort

Provincetown, Mass.). Subarbu next plastered billboards in gay neighbor-hoods with an ad whose text—"It's Not a Choice, It's the Way We're Built"—could easily be read as a wink to gay consumers as well as a reference to their trademark 4-wheel drive. One of the ad's developers admitted, "It's apparent to gay people that we're talking about being gay, but straight peo-ple don't know what's going on."[7]

In case anyone thought that advertising to gay consumers was no longer controversial, Anheuser-Busch discovered otherwise when it took out an ad in an April 1999 issue of *EXP* magazine, a free, bimonthly St. Louis publica-tion that is geared toward gays and lesbians. The ad tells people to "Be Your-self and Make It a Bud Light," and depicts two muscled male arms, hands clasping, shown from behind—exactly the sort of anonymous body-part, shot from the rear, image that gay media activists have long criticized news media for using to illustrate gay-related stories.[8] This time, however, gay peo-ple were thrilled—flooding the company's 800-number with congratulatory phone calls, and the cries of outrage came from another quarter. Jerry Fal-well sent his followers an emergency e-mail and followed up in his *Falwell Confidential* weekly newsletter: "Let's keep the heat on Anheuser-Busch so that they understand that pro-family Americans are terribly concerned about homosexual images coming into our homes through reckless advertising campaigns" (it wasn't clear how many pro-family households actually sub-scribed to *EXP* magazine).

As pro and con e-mail ricocheted around the country, and the phones rang off the hook at Anheuser-Busch's pro and con phone lines, a company spokesman expressed surprise "that one print ad placed in select gay-oriented magazines has attracted attention." But perhaps they weren't entirely sur-prised by the reaction they stirred up. The national brewing chains have been sponsoring local gay events for years, despite the potential risk of right-wing backlash. As industry analysts have noted, in the mature U.S. beer market, niches matter more than ever, and brewers are competing fiercely for the gay niche, which is above average in beer consumption. It is also not news that this strategy carries political risks. Anheuser-Busch, Miller, and Coors all have

---

[7] In March 2000, Subaru took another step toward integrating lesbian and gay people into mainstream advertising with a commercial featuring Martina Navratilova along with openly les-bian golfers Juli Inkster and Meg Mallon and skier Diann Rolf-Steinrotter. The TV ads were par-alleled by print ads in *Sports Illustrated for Women* and other sports magazines. The marketing programs director for Subaru America explained that Martina "personifies the attributes of our brand as a go-anywhere, do-anything type of individual."

[8] In 1988, TV journalist Joe Lovett, then a producer at ABC's *20/20*, told me that ABC News had "stock footage" of male couples walking down the street, shot from the rear, that they could draw upon when running gay-content news stories.

made a hit list of the thirteen top "corporate sponsors of homosexuality," compiled by the Family Research Council. The *Wall Street Journal* reported some marketing experts saying that Anheuser-Busch helped fuel the controversy by alerting gay organizations to the ad and the expected backlash.

Nonetheless, Anheuser-Busch seems to have succeeded in its gamble, garnering attention and support from gay people across the country at an apparently small cost in lost business from Falwell's subscribers. However, just a few months later, their arch-rival, the Miller Brewing Company, suffered a failure of nerve while attempting the same maneuver. Miller created a 30-second commercial featuring the Barechest Men—male models from a popular Bay area calendar—frolicking by a pool, playing volleyball, and chugging Miller Genuine Draft, and planned to run the ad on a San Francisco–based gay cable show, *QTV's Xposure Program*. Seems fairly safe, given the San Francisco market. "This is a spot that's regional in nature, only to air on QTV and relevant to the market we're trying to reach," a spokesperson for Miller told the *San Francisco Chronicle*. Almost immediately, however, the company backtracked, insisting that the ad had never been approved. "We are exploring different options regarding placement of this promotional spot, as well as reviewing it and making sure it fits with our marketing programs," said a spokesperson. "It has not been approved. Period. End of story." Whether Miller received any credit from the Family Research Council isn't known, but they were criticized by gay marketers. Howard Buford, head of an ad firm specializing in gay and minority audiences, told the *New York Post*, "That kind of commercial could potentially have meant big business for Miller— and they need it. The Bud ad was a real home run. Now Miller may never catch up. It'll depend on what kind of spin they put on this—and whether people believe them."[9]

At the turn of the new century, advertisers began to pay attention to the powerful new marketing frontier of the Internet, long understood to be heavily populated by gay and lesbian people. *Time* magazine (2/14/00:74) reported estimates that 20 percent of AOL's 21 million subscribers are gay. In the Internet newsletter, *The Industry Standard* (see www.thestandard.com), writer Mark Dolley alerted marketers that, while "the top selling gay magazines, *Out* and *The Advocate*, have monthly circulations of only 100,000 copies or less . . . sites like PlanetOut.com and Gay.com reach millions of gays

---

[9] In August 1997 Reuters reported that Molson, Canada's largest brewery, had produced and planned to air a commercial featuring a passionate kiss between two women. The commercial was approved by the Ontario liquor licensing board, attacked by the American Family Association, and supported by gay journalist Keir MacRae, although with some concern "that Molson's is using lesbian imagery as a male fantasy."

each month, with sites built on the three pillars of successful Web business: content, community, and commerce."

The success of gay-oriented dot-com businesses spurred a reverse crossover, as the Gay Financial Network's Internet Web site became the first gay-oriented company to advertise in many major U.S. business, news, and entertainment publications. In February 2000, gfn.com placed ads in the *Wall Street Journal* (followed by *Entertainment Weekly, Newsweek, Business-Week*, and *People*), promoting gfn.com as a gay-friendly financial news and information site to Internet users, advertisers, and investors.

In February 2000 the *Advocate*'s parent company, Liberation Publications, initiated the purchase of *Out*, which had long been in turmoil with revolving-door editors and plummeting circulation. But before that sale could be completed, the increasingly familiar pattern of new media eating old media made an appearance in the gay realm, as PlanetOut, which enjoys backing from America Online—the recent purchaser of TimeWarner—announced an agreement to acquire Liberation Publications. The merger of the largest gay print publications and the largest gay Web site raised the possibility of achieving an audience approaching respectable size on a national level. PlanetOut, with its 500,000 registered users and its estimated 1.2 million "unique visitors" each month, reaches an audience vastly larger than any yet willing to subscribe to or purchase gay print publications.[10] By early 2001, with the bursting of the late 1990s' dot-com bubble, the acquisition was put on hold.

Toward the end of 2000, critics in the gay press were concerned about the blurring of whatever distinction might have existed between the *Advocate* and *Out*, as the magazines seemed increasingly indistinguishable in their focus on entertainment and celebrities. These concerns were deepened by the entanglements of both the *Advocate* and *PlanetOut* in the politically controversial Millennium March on Washington, which were seen as compromising their editorial independence.

The next step in the seemingly relentless march toward consolidation was taken in November 2000 when PlanetOut and Gay.com announced plans to merge, creating PlanetOut Partners but maintaining their separate sites, thus increasing their appeal to advertisers while eliminating their need to compete

---

[10] The power of the Internet for organizing was demonstrated with the March 2000 launching of StopDrLaura.com, a Web site encouraging and coordinating opposition to homophobic radio host Laura Schlessinger and her proposed TV show. Adding to more conventional efforts by GLAAD, the Web site received 35 million hits by August 2000, by which point major sponsors, including Geico, Kraft, American Express, United Airlines, ToysRUs, Xerox, AT&T, Gateway, and Sears, dropped Dr. Laura. Suffering from low ratings and drowning in bad publicity, Paramount canceled the show in March 2001.

for subscribers. The prospect of this unprecedented degree of consolidation in the gay press was a cause for concern that tempered the enthusiasm urged by the executives of the media organizations. Even more than in the case of mainstream media there are reasons to worry about the concentration of ownership and the loss of competition. The growing consolidation of Internet companies raised another set of concerns among the community of Web pioneers. University of Pennsylvania computer scientist David Farber, one of those credited with creating the Internet, warned that as single companies begin to control both Internet content and systems for gaining access to that content, the Web could resemble a shopping mall with no prime space available for startups with little money. Lesbian author and Internet innovator Patricia Nell Warren, a founder of the youth-oriented Web site the *Oasis*, echoed these warnings with specific reference to GLBT "netizens":

> Already we see the emergence of gay big business—banking, advertising, investment, media conglomerates, mega-malls, mega-sites. Already it's questionable whether everything GLBT on the Net can be found through our own search engines. A publicist tells me that cost of promoting a new GLBT site to the Net is now $5000 minimum. Who can afford this?
>
> If the Net is continue to nurture the "gay community," and keep it inclusive, it's important not to forget the original reasons why the Net attracted us: low cost, grassroots access, ease in finding each other, inclusiveness, the dignity of the individual.

ARE WE BEING SERVED?

The lesbian and gay movement that grew up in the decades before Stonewall was nurtured and disseminated through the newsletters, magazines, "bar rags," and newspapers that helped forge a sense of community both within and beyond the borders of gay urban ghettos. By reporting the stories and reflecting the lives of people who only appeared in the pages of mainstream journalism as perverts, security risks, and child molesters, the lesbian and gay media laid the ground for the struggle that brought about a radical shift in public consciousness and discourse.

Thirty years after Stonewall the *New York Times*, which barely acknowledged the riots that shattered that hot June night, and which refused to use the term *gay* until 1987, is notably attentive to the lives and concerns of lesbian and gay citizens. As the push for broad and equitable coverage in the mainstream press began to succeed, the mission of the lesbian and gay press became less clear. Weekly and biweekly newspapers and magazines found themselves reporting old news that their readers were likely to have read in their daily newspapers, or online at Gay.com or even at a mainstream Web portal such as Yahoo, which offers lesbian and gay news.[11] The national gay and lesbian magazines responded by shifting their coverage more in the direction of pop culture, fashion, and consumerism, a move that is also in keeping with their growing access to national mainstream advertising dollars.[12]

The local gay and lesbian press has fared better in many ways, despite their lack of access to national advertising support. According to William Waybourn, whose Washington-based Window Media owns publications in Atlanta, Houston, and New Orleans, "Anything that deals on a local level is drawing great interest." As gay marketer Todd Evans explained, "By and large, gays and lesbians, like the population at large, need to know what's going on in their local community Friday night, and the best place for the gay community are the local community publications." In addition to covering local events and community activities, the local press serves as a Yellow Pages for lesbian and gay doctors, lawyers, plumbers, insurance sellers, real estate agents, and car dealerships, in addition to the familiar and profitable personal and sex-industry ads. At the close of the 1990s, Chicago and Los Angeles each boasted ten local gay papers, South Florida had seven, and towns and cities across the country supported numerous local publications.[13]

---

[11] The challenges to the gay press presented by growing mainstream coverage is reminiscent of the situation of the African American press described by Bernard Roscho decades earlier: "The truly big racial stories have grown beyond [the Negro media's] scope for a variety of reasons. They are caught in the time-lag of the weekly press . . . they lack the financial resources to chase distant stories on their own . . . they are outgunned by the immediacy of television and the breadth of national magazines. As a result, now the big race stories are everybody's story, the Negro papers are usually out last with the least. . . . The world watched on television or listened to radio as the voice of Martin Luther King rang out from the steps of the Lincoln Memorial. What more could the Negro press possibly contribute in specialized coverage?" Although this was as exaggerated then as an exact analogy to today's gay press would be, there is much that is, and was, precisely on target.

[12] Chasing national advertising by eschewing political coverage is no guarantee of success, however, as *Out* magazine learned. After firing British editor James Collard, hired in order to transform the magazine, publisher Henry Scott told a reporter, "We're not interested in going back to becoming a ghetto magazine. We are not a news magazine. We do not compete with the *Advocate*. . . . Furthermore, we are not a magazine for poor people." Within a few months, as circulation continued to fall, Scott was out, *Out* was up for sale, and, as we've noted, in February 2000 it was bought—by the *Advocate*.

[13] After one South Florida gay magazine folded in early 2000, one publisher asked, "How many publications do you need for 300,000 people?" complaining that "the market is not large enough to sustain the incredible amount of publications" already there.

The strength of the local gay press led to a movement toward regional consolidation. In August 2000 Window Media merged Atlanta's *Southern Voice* and New Orleans's *Impact News* into a weekly *Southern Voice* distributed in more than thirty cities across the South, accumulating a potential readership of 100,000 that would be the largest of any lesbian and gay newspaper. In 2001, Window Media moved north, buying the *Washington Blade* and its offshoot the *New York Blade News*.

In the larger markets local publications follow the trend toward ever-more sharply defined target markets. The ten Los Angeles publications are highly niched. According to Todd Evans, "There's Hispanic, African American, leather, bar-oriented, a circuit party publication, two lesbian. It's unusual for that many even in such a big market. But I think that's the trend."

Market segmentation can readily be seen in the flowering of publications addressed to particular constituencies or interests. Some recent examples:

- *Women in the Life* began in 1994 as a four-page newsletter targeted to African American lesbians, and within five years it had become a monthly magazine.
- *Alternative Family Magazine* was launched in March 1998 as a national magazine for gay and lesbian parents and their families, and by June 1999 it was being distributed through major bookstore chains.
- Jimm Tran, former editor of *Celebrasian*, a Toronto-based newsletter, created *Dragün* as a glossy magazine for the gay Asian community. Beginning in June 1999, the magazine has been a sell-out success—its Web site records over 100,000 hits per week—and has begun expanding into the American market.
- As the new century dawned, new publications were planned for gay people at both ends of the age spectrum. New York's Pride Senior Network announced the start of a quarterly newspaper, the *Networker*, for the aging lesbian and gay community, with an initial circulation of 20,000. At the same time, 22-year-old Jerry Dunn promised that his new quarterly magazine, *Joey*, would be a *Seventeen* or *YM* for gay boys.[14]

14 *Joey* is entering a market already served by *XY*, a San Francisco–based magazine for gay male teens founded in 1996 that reported a 1999 national circulation of 80,000, with 20,000 subscribers. The magazine's 24-year-old editor told the *San Francisco Chronicle*: "I don't think there's a magazine in the country that means more to its readers. I say that because we're dealing specifically with a demographic of gay teenagers who are not living in L.A. or New York, or some place where being gay is accepted. There's really no other forum for them to read about that experience." A reader responded: "The article asserts that *XY* is a voice for gay teens. It

The growing segmentation within lesbian and gay journalism does not diminish the sharpness of the dilemmas facing minority media: the definition of their mission and the nature of their professional role. Just as gay publications seeking mainstream advertising revenue began segregating and then, in many cases, eliminating the sex-related ads that supported them in earlier years, many lesbian and gay newspapers have sought to raise their journalistic stature by adopting mainstream models. Most notably, the lesbian and gay press is torn between acknowledging its historic role as a committed advocate for the interests of a marginalized community and a desire to be seen as fulfilling the professional role of objective journalism.

As most historians and analysts of journalism have noted, objectivity is a fiction adopted by journalists as a way of codifying and justifying their practices. The theory of objectivity, which assumes the possibility of describing events without imposing any bias or interpretation, invariably misrepresents the realities of journalistic work. The selection and framing of stories, the choices of sources and quotes, the placement of stories and of elements within stories—all reflect and reveal presuppositions and prejudices that are far from objective. To a large extent these subjective factors might be invisible to editors, reporters, and audiences precisely because they are shared—the "commonsense" assumptions that embody a dominant ideology. The conventions of professional journalism have developed, in part, in order to provide guideposts for journalists seeking to make sense out of the myriad events that might, but mostly never will, be reported each day, and to justify their choices to those who might have differing views. In this sense, objectivity is, in sociologist Gaye Tuchman's term, a strategic ritual.

Objective journalism arose in the era of industrialization, with the birth of a mass medium that was seeking a heterogeneous mass audience by avoiding the appearance of partisanship, while promoting the cult of facts and balance. Objective journalism gives enormous power to official sources, upon whom reporters become dependent for the "facts" with which to answer the basic who/what/when/where (and sometimes, why) questions that editors and readers expect. Legitimate sources also become essential as the providers of statements, which are the only acceptable form of opinion; two opposing opinions constitute balance, and thus ensure objectivity.

---

seems to me that the $40 annual subscription ($5.95 cover price) of *XY* would deter many youth from reading the magazine regularly, precluding it from being a truly strong resource for youth. In addition, because of its strong disposition toward the fashion and beauty industry, the images in the magazine do not necessarily represent the diversity of gay youth." Those images, however, might well appeal to older readers, who can afford the cover price and are not worried about their parents finding the magazine in their bedrooms.

Michael Schudson defined a reporter operating under this system as "someone who is faithful to sources, attuned to the conventional wisdom, serving the political culture of media institutions, and committed to a narrow range of public, literary expression." Among the many drawbacks of this role is the inability of mainstream journalism to recognize or reflect changing conditions. As James Carey noted, "The canons of objective reporting filter historically new phenomena through an outmoded linguistic machinery that grossly distorts the nature of these events." The emergence of a self-conscious gay community and political movement is a perfect case in point, as demonstrated by the response of the *New York Times*. Beginning in 1963, with the front-page headline, "Growth of Overt Homosexuality in City Provokes Wide Concern," continuing with the minimal attention paid to Stonewall and subsequent events, and the refusal to use the term *gay*, the *Times* filtered out and denied the transformations in both gay and mainstream society that were occurring under its nose.

The *New York Times*, and mainstream journalism in general, has widened its lens and updated its linguistic machinery in the past three decades. Lesbian and gay people are now written about and usually allowed to speak for themselves on the issues that affect their lives. Where does this leave the gay press? All too often, the gay press seems caught in a bind, frequently scooped by the mainstream press on stories that once might have been ignored by straight media, and yet reluctant to adopt a forthright advocacy role and relinquish the label of objectivity. For many years the biggest and generally most respected gay newspaper, the weekly *Washington Blade*, took the cult of objectivity to fetishistic lengths, refusing even to include an editorial page (although the vast majority of U.S. newspapers have editorial sections that are considered strictly separate in personnel and control from the news divisions).

The insistence on objectivity reveals a confusion between honesty and objectivity in journalism. If objectivity, as described in the curricula of journalism programs, is undeniably illusory, it is possible to engage in journalism that is both honest and professional without pretending to objectivity. What this entails is a commitment to telling the truth, not hiding or obfuscating facts that embarrass one's allies, but at the same time it permits journalists to seek out the stories that matter to their community, frame them in a way that reflects that community's reality, and allow people to speak for themselves. By aping the pretensions of mainstream journalism, minority media risk losing their reason for being, while still not fooling anyone. No one picks up a gay paper expecting the magisterial aloofness of the *New York Times*, nor should they.

In 1992, *Philadelphia Gay News* editor John Mandes, eager to portray his paper as objective, proudly told a *Philadelphia Daily News* reporter that he declined to cover an ACT UP demonstration against George Bush because "every time ACT UP burps, it's not news," and editorialized that "ACT UP demonstrations are not news any longer." As a new arrival in town, Mandes may have been ignorant of the furor over the police riot at an ACT UP demonstration on the same spot just eight months earlier, or the continuing tension between demonstrators and police, but he was certainly pursuing the goal he described to another reporter, "to make the weekly conform more to the canons of 'objective' journalism."

Sometimes the pursuit of objectivity can reach absurd proportions. In 1998 Katie Szymanski, a reporter for the *New York Blade News* (an offshoot of the *Washington Blade*), was fired after she appeared in the audience for an episode of the *Ricki Lake Show* and spoke briefly from the floor, condemning the ex-gay "conversion" movement. When the show was aired, Szymanski, who had helped recruit guests for the show, was identified by a graphic as a *Blade* staffer. *Washington Blade* executive editor Lisa Keen instructed the New York editor to fire Syzmanski because her "voluntary appearance as an 'activist' on a show addressing a subject our newspaper covers is a serious violation of our standards. . . . It seriously undermines the confidence readers might have in her ability to report the news in as objective a manner as possible."[15] Former *Philadelphia Gay News* editor John Mandes, now teaching journalism at the University of Denver, applauded, "I would have fired her too."

One of Mandes's first moves after joining the *Philadelphia Gay News* in 1991 was to incorporate the Associated Press wire service as a source of news. The use of "wire feed" by gay newspapers has become a common practice, motivated in part by the appearance of professionalism presumably conferred by the AP label, and in part by simple economics. However, the savings achieved by resorting to AP's feed come at a cost. When a gay paper downloads a story from the AP's Web site, it pays a relatively small fee (pro-rated by its circulation) that is even lower than the absurdly small fees the gay press pays to its writers. Thus, misguided frugality and the search for respectability combine to further erode the economic viability of gay journalism. True, when a gay-related story occurs in some remote part of the country it may only be reported by a local AP stringer. But much of the time the gay press

---

[15] Apparently, Keen didn't feel that her coauthorship with attorney Suzanne Goldberg of a book, *Strangers to the Law: Gay People on Trial*, wouldn't undermine readers' confidence in the *Blade*'s coverage of legal issues concerning gay people.

has come to rely on AP's feed for stories that could easily be covered by free-lance gay journalists. Gay journalists are also more likely to seek out lesbian and gay sources, and reflect less conventional assumptions about the events being reported. If the gay press is unwilling or unable adequately to support writers, whether staffers or freelance, it will undermine its ability to provide perspectives that will never be found in mainstream coverage. In a 1992 *Gay Community News* article on the growing use of AP sources by the gay press, freelance reporter Bruce Mirken commented, "Gay and lesbian publications should never use wire service copy . . . without verifying its accuracy with sources from our community. . . . If we're going to simply take the word of the non-gay media, what is the point of even having a gay and lesbian press?"

One of the few freelancers able to navigate the treacherous waters of the gay press is San Diego–based Rex Wockner, who has succeeded in utilizing the new opportunities offered by the Internet to operate a clipping service, along with a weekly column on PlanetOut's Web site. Wockner collects gay-related news from contacts and publications around the world and feeds them back to over ninety outlets from San Francisco to Kansas, and from Estonia to Thailand. Tom Reilly of PlanetOut describes him as a "one-man gay AP," and *San Francisco Chronicle* reporter Elaine Herscher agreed that his international coverage "gives me a sense of what's going on all over the world that I wouldn't get any other way." The speed and scope of the Internet has broadened the reach of journalists like Wockner and vastly increased the rapidity with which they span the globe, making them truly competitive with mainstream news sources. Wockner notes, "In the old days, Activist A had to call Reporter B at Paper C and hope that the editor was interested. . . . The net has changed all that. Now it takes 10 minutes to reach millions." Completing the circle, it seems, one of Wockner's outlets, the Web news-site GayToday, is edited by veteran activist Jack Nichols, who was a founder of the *Homosexual Citizen* in 1966.

Radio programs produced for and by lesbian and gay people are available on nearly one hundred public and community radio stations in the United States and Canada. Some of these programs have aired for many years, such as the weekly gay programming on WXPN-FM in Philadelphia, broadcast since the 1970s. A few gay and lesbian-oriented programs have been able to break into, and survive on, commercial radio stations. Openly gay talk show hosts Karel and Andrew on Los Angeles's KFI-AM were popular with general audiences from 1999 to 2001, and Alan Amberg has succeeded in hosting *LesBi-Gay* as a drive-time program on Chicago's WSBC-AM and WCJF-AM, attracting ads from Miller Brewing Company and a local Ford dealership.

With the rapid expansion of cable television it was to be expected that lesbian and gay programming would begin to appear, and several fledgling enterprises were born in the early 1990s. Marvin Schwam, a New York businessman, founded Gay Entertainment Television, offering three weekly shows—*Party Talk*, *Inside/Out*, and *Makostyle*—via cable outlets in Los Angeles, Chicago, New York, Miami, and San Francisco. A lesbian-produced program, *Dyke TV*, is carried by cable systems in more than a dozen cities.

In 1992 David Surber, an advertising executive, decided to produce a video magazine for lesbians and gay men, and that September the first two-hour installment of *Network Q* was mailed to subscribers. The video magazine consisted of reports and interviews covering topics of interest to lesbian and gay people, such as National Coming Out Day, lesbian and gay comedians, travel and resorts, political struggles, being out on campus, and the AIDS Memorial Quilt. As one 40-year-old man wrote, "It's like our very own *60 Minutes*." Many subscribers live in rural areas, far from urban centers of lesbian and gay life, and have noted that the video magazine gives them a "feeling of being part of gay America" and "relieves the sense of isolation." By the beginning of 1994 there were two thousand subscribers, representing all fifty states and twelve foreign countries, and it was estimated that each program was seen by 24,000 viewers. But with a yearly subscription cost of $199 for twelve issues, the video magazine was not a solution to the isolation experienced by millions of lesbian and gay people who do not see their realities or their concerns reflected in the mass media. In 1995 *Network Q* abandoned the video-magazine format in favor of syndicating shows to local public television stations, joining *In the Life* in the ranks of lesbian and gay-produced television magazine shows.

As the new century began, the rapidly expanding technology of the Internet-based media offered a vehicle for radio broadcasting to move from local to global audiences. Gay radio professional John McMullen initiated an all-gay radio station in 1997 that, by 1998, was renamed GAYBC. In 2000 the GAYBC Radio Network operated a 24-hour radio Web site, offering a mix of original live programming and repeats. Regular hosts on GAYBC included Margarethe Cammermeyer, the much decorated army officer who unsuccessfully fought against dismissal from the military. In February 2000, GAYBC, partnered with Gay.com, made history of sorts when journalist Michelangelo Signorile hosted Democratic presidential candidate Bill Bradley on a live hookup, reaching listeners through the Internet and permitting call-in as well as e-mailed questions and responses.

15

Facing the Future

Once the post-Stonewall gay movement began attracting attention through its insistence on militant visibility, mainstream journalists fell into the habit of beginning articles on the phenomenon by playing on the words of Oscar Wilde's lover, Lord Alfred Douglas's most famous line. As one reporter after another would write, the love that dare not speak its name has become the love that won't shut up. A few gay characters appearing on TV in the mid-1970s prompted columnist Nicholas Van Hoffman to proclaim 1976 as "the Year of the Fag." Much as this smattering of lesbian and gay images in the media might have frightened such horsemen of the apocalypse as Van Hoffman and the Reverend Jerry Falwell, they were, in fact, few and far between, and invariably dropped for a brief appearance into otherwise wholly heterosexual surroundings.

By the late 1990s, while things had changed to a dramatic degree, they have also stayed the same. Gays, lesbians, bisexuals, and transgendered people have all become reasonably familiar presences on the various stages of America's media-dominated culture. News professionals—editors, reporters, talk show hosts, columnists, and members of the punditocracy—now include gay-related issues and events as a regular category of news, and we make the front pages and the network evening news with regularity. Yet those appearances are almost invariably in the context of some controversy centering on our right to pursue our lives in ways that heterosexuals take for granted. In recent times the most prominent topics for journalistic attention to gay people—leaving aside the AIDS epidemic, increasingly defined by the news media as a "nongay" story—have been the exclusion of gay people from service in the military and from the institution of civil marriage. If invisibility was the defining attribute of gay people in the past, we have in the last fifty years or so moved to a position of relative visibility for a group that encompasses fewer than 10 percent of society. But as we're learning, visibility, like truth, is rarely pure and never simple.

Writing about black popular culture, Stuart Hall remarked that "what replaces invisibility is a kind of carefully regulated, segregated visibility," and in so noting he acknowledged the complexity and ambiguity of progress in media representations.[1] Stereotyping is one step beyond the initial stage of sheer invisibility that minorities have to move through on their way to even token representation. In the 1960s comedian Carl Reiner offered scripts for a television series he hoped to star in; but as one network executive later put it, "the scripts were 'de-Jewishized' and 'Midwesternized,' and the final result was *The Dick Van Dyke Show*." In the present, when Jewish characters (sometimes played by Jewish actors who have not been required to change their names) appear with some frequency, they "rarely get beyond the bounds of familiar and generally comforting stereotypes."

For African Americans, who entered the media stage in the dual roles of villain and victim (of violence and/or ridicule), relative success means playing what Anthony Appiah has called "Saints":

> Does the Saint exist to address the guilt of white audiences, afraid that black people are angry at them, wanting to be forgiven, seeking a black person who is not only admirable and lovable, but who loves white people back? Or is it simply that Hollywood has decided, after decades of lobbying by the NAACP's Hollywood chapter that, outside crime movies, blacks had better project good images, characters who can win the NAACP's "image awards"?

But African Americans, symbolized in this context by Saint Sidney Poitier in the movies of the 1960s and Saint Bill Cosby on television in the 1980s, represent an extreme example of minority images produced in a way that majorities can enjoy and minorities can't (shouldn't?) complain about. As Herman Gray notes, the positive images of blacks on TV's sitcoms "deflect attention from the persistence of racism, inequality, and differential power." In Sut Jhally and Justin Lewis's analysis, the very success of the Cosby show

---

[1] Segregated visibility can almost be taken literally. U.S. TV's Nielsen ratings consistently reveal wide disparities between black and nonblack households, which routinely have completely different lists of top ten prime-time programs. Sociologist Darnell Hunt noted that black characters in 1999 were concentrated on the fringe "weblets" UPN and WB, which accounted for more than 44 percent of all black characters in prime time.

254 FACING THE FUTURE

can be seen by white viewers to imply "the failure of the majority of black people," thus contributing, in the title of their book, to a more "enlightened racism." Other groups still find themselves more frequently relegated to the victim and villain roles blacks may have *partially* abandoned.[2] Media executives, now cautious in casting bad guys, find it easier to write the roles as Arab terrorists or Latino drug dealers.

Lesbians and gay men are still up for grabs as victims and villains. In an analysis of the homophobia at the heart of Oliver Stone's *JFK*, Michael Rogin notes that the films that dominated the Oscars in 1990 and 1991, *Driving Miss Daisy* and *Dances with Wolves*, glorified "unthreatening African and Native Americans," whereas

> Three of the five best picture nominees at the 1992 Academy Awards were homophobic at their core: A homosexual rape at the age of 11 is the buried trauma for the protagonist of *Prince of Tides*. The serial killer in *Silence of the Lambs* is a man trapped in a woman's body, a transvestite aspiring to be a transsexual. . . . *Silence of the Lambs* received the Best Picture and four other awards; *JFK* was nominated for eight awards and the winner of two. Moreover, *Basic Instinct*, the top-grossing film in the weeks surrounding the award ceremony . . . features three bisexual women and one lesbian as its menaces.

March 2000 offered a replay, as *American Beauty* swept the top Oscar categories, but with an updated twist. The film recounts a sort of "coming out" by a straight white-collar worker who discovers freedom through a forbidden sexual obsession. The plot's central mystery is finally resolved through the revelation of the repressed homosexuality of the next door neighbor, a homophobic ex-marine who terrorizes his wife and son and who kills the protagonist after his own tortured sexual advances are rebuffed. The cliché image of the repressed homosexual is clinched by the revelation of his prized possession: a swastika-emblazoned Nazi dinner plate. If militarism and fascism were linked to repressed homosexuality in films of past decades, now this tired trope can be used to add "depth" to a character. The film's carefully calculated transgressiveness gives just the right touch of independence and bogus avant gardism that Hollywood so loves about itself.

Still, how does a film that gives us yet another murderous closet case man-

---

[2] It's important to note that this point applies to fictional media; when it comes to news programs and "reality-based" shows like *Cops* and *America's Most Wanted*, minority criminals predominate.

age to win the best picture Oscar from an officially gay-friendly Motion Picture Academy? Well, for one thing, the film also includes a gay couple who are shown as adjusted and well-integrated into the vacuous suburban world. They are also the only couple that is portrayed as happy, but that might be because we see so little of them beyond several brief moments of comic relief. The film's primary defense against the charge of homophobia, however, resides in the openly gay identity of its screenwriter, Alan Ball. Ball, who had previously written scripts for TV sitcoms, described *American Beauty* as a story about "people looking for love and acceptance, like everybody else," although this hardly seems to describe any of the characters in the movie. The same month that the film opened, a new sitcom written by Ball debuted on ABC. *Oh Grow Up*—a buddy comedy about three thirtysomething male roommates, one of whom has just separated from his wife after realizing that he's gay—was axed before the end of the year, but Ball seems destined for continued media success as an openly gay writer who plays by the rules.[3]

At the end of the century, American television networks found themselves mired in a struggle over the representation of minorities on their flagship prime-time programs. It's almost enough to make you feel sorry for network executives. As recently as 1980, when fewer than 5 percent of U.S. households had VCRs and less than a quarter had cable, they could count on dividing a mass audience amounting to 90 percent of the television audience. By 1997 that number had shrunk to 49 percent, and now the Internet is starting to eat into their dwindling audience share. The familiar strategy of assembling a large, common-denominator audience to sell to advertisers is no longer surefire, as upstart "weblets" like UPN and WB offer programs tailored to attractive market segments like young adults, and cable programmers unrestrained by skittish advertisers can steal audiences with "edgy" programs far sexier and riskier than networks allow. And as if all that weren't enough, along come the representatives of organized racial and ethnic minorities, complaining that they are once again nearly invisible on prime-time network programs.

The latest round of this struggle over media representation began in the summer of 1999 when NAACP president Kweisi Mfume denounced the lineup of new network programs slated for the 1999 fall season as a "virtual whitewash." None of the new series announced for the fall included a lead character who was not white, and the NAACP's protest, soon joined by Latino and Asian

---

[3] Ball's scripts abound in newly gay-permissible jokes: When Ford, the gay character, says, "I like Celine Dion," his ex-wife, a regular character, replies, "That should have tipped me off right there." "Honey," Ford reproaches, "you promised to be nice tonight." And she snaps, "Yeah, and you promised to love, honor, and not go Nancy on me."

American groups, struck a sour public relations note. Meetings ensued, both between the networks and the minority associations as well as behind the scenes at the networks, and in September the *New York Times* reported that "TV Networks Rush to Add Minority Roles" to many of these shows.

By the end of the year the NAACP had made deals with the networks that were intended to "increase opportunities for people of color in the network television industry" both in front of and behind the camera. NBC agreed to hire at least one new minority writer for each of its returning shows, and all the networks pledged to bring on minority interns and engage in diversity training. But in the end, once the PR smoke had cleared and the press conference mirrors put away, the realities of network TV remained as they were.

During the fall of 1999, as the networks were meeting with the NAACP and other minority groups, CBS announced a new drama, *City of Angels*, set in an inner-city hospital and featuring a predominantly black cast as well as a multiracial crew. Series coexecutive producer Paris Barclay, the most successful African American TV director, was quoted in the *Los Angeles Times*: "It's going to change the look and landscape of television very quickly. It's a bold and courageous step. It will accelerate the process of diversity by years." In November 2000 CBS canceled the series, which had only been watched by an average of 7.4 million viewers, making it No. 80 among prime-time network programs.

When it comes down to the bottom line—and in the industry (as it's appropriately termed), it always does come down to the bottom line—what matters is what advertisers are willing to pay for. Advertisers know—or at least believe—that the audience wants to see its own face reflected on the screen, and the audience that matters most is overwhelmingly white and, not coincidentally, middle class and heterosexual, as well.

Just as the NAACP began its campaign to increase the numbers of racial minorities on network programs, the Gay and Lesbian Alliance Against Defamation (GLAAD) was celebrating a record number of openly lesbian and gay characters slated for the 1999–2000 season. As media critics were quick to note, the seventeen gay characters slated for the four major networks was "about equal to the combined representation of significant black, Latino and Asian characters." Leaving aside the familiar tendency to equate gay with white—and certainly, while *Spin City*'s Carter Heywood is a notable exception, television's queers are as white-washed as their straight counterparts—the divide-and-conquer journalistic strategy fails to grasp the more interesting realities these numbers reflect.

As the networks have increasingly factored sophisticated niche-marketing strategies into their calculations, they have stiffened their corporate backbones when faced with conservative outrage at any positive depictions of gay people. Even before *Ellen*'s explosive coming out, network executives were timidly opening their doors to sympathetic if secondary gay characters on such hit shows as *Roseanne, Melrose Place, Northern Exposure,* and *Friends.* By the end of the decade gay writers, directors, and producers began to be more public about their sexuality—coming out of the glass closets so familiar in Hollywood—and using their newly visible gayness as a weapon in the cultural wars.[4]

Gay and lesbian characters have become familiar visitors and even regulars on several sitcoms and dramatic programs but they are still odd men and women out in a straight world. *NYPD Blue*'s "gay John," the empathetic receptionist emoting in the background, is perhaps typical of the sympathetic images now permitted. Confined to a stereotypical characterization—thus avoiding the need for coming out—but treated with a certain respect by the other characters, "gay John" is a tame role model of the safe queer. *Will & Grace*'s infinitely more flamboyant Jack McFarland, atwitter with camp jokes and innuendo, is possible because he's so neatly balanced by the "straight gay" Will Truman, who plays George Burns to Jack's Gracie Allen. Meanwhile, over at the TV high school, Jack McPhee of *Dawson's Creek* spent months agonizing before coming out and then months more before daring to kiss another man; and *Party of Five*'s Julia Salinger reenacted a TV cliché: trying a same-sex kiss while reaffirming her heterosexuality.[5]

Television's new realism regarding lesbian and gay people is apparently translated into a license to be joked about; after all, we're all sophisticated now.[6] Complain and you'll likely be told that the writer, director, or producer is gay, and besides, haven't we gotten to the point where we can take a joke?

In the case of African Americans, television has created an entire stream of essentially segregated programming (e.g., the sitcoms on UPN), watched by

[4] *Frasier* writer David Lee was among the most vocal critics of Paramount Studio's commitment to producing a TV program for homophobic radio counselor Dr. Laura Schlessinger.

[5] The master of this particular trope is TV writer-producer David Kelley, who has used the ploy on *L.A. Law, Picket Fences,* and *Ally McBeal*; at the same time, he has yet to include a regular lesbian or gay character on any of his hit shows.

[6] On the April 26, 1999, episode of *Ally McBeal*, lawyer Richard Fish, invariably treated as a comical character, challenges a hostile witness: "Are you a lesbian? . . . Your honor, I have nothing against lesbians. In fact, put two of them together and . . . The point is, a lot of lesbians in early attempts to deny their homosexuality—or, in part, to account for it—attribute their not liking men to the misguided notion that men are bad—evil, even. These women tend to grow up hating them, it colors their outlook, their opinions, it could be coloring the testimony of the witness. This bears on her credibility, judge. She could be a man-hating, vicious lesbian. The court certainly has a right to know."

African American audiences and nearly invisible to white Americans.[7] Queers are unlikely to be offered this sort of programming, so we need to push for the best available options and images within the mainstream of entertainment fare. As in the past, progress is likely to occur in small increments. Media executives operate much like remote-controlled robots on Mars: testing the environment, making a small step forward, then testing again. Their goal is to remain just at the edge of cultural change, not too far out in front of most people (especially those in their target audience), but not too far behind, either. And by moving along the cultural frontier, the media signal to the rest of society where the lines are currently drawn in its shifting sands.

In the end, all the fuss over network minority representation reflects the bind we're all caught in: this is a media-dominated society and being left off the media's center stage is a form of symbolic annihilation. The networks *could* tell protestors that fighting over the shrinking pie of network prime-time programming is silly, but they're caught in their own trap, as they also want to maintain the fiction that they occupy America's cultural center.

In 1993, as he was retiring from TV journalism, John Chancellor lamented the loss of "a shared experience that we used to have . . . where you knew that most of the country was watching similar programs put out by people of about the same background and age and attitude toward the country. This society is full of people going off on their own and doing crazy things right now, and it's going to get worse." You can just see the suits nodding in sorrowful agreement. "Good night, Chet." "Good night, David."

LOOKING BACKWARD

When Edward Bellamy published his utopian novel, *Looking Backward*, in 1888, he imagined a young man named Julian West falling asleep in 1887 and awaking to the Boston of 2000. Bellamy's hero is astounded by the transformations wrought in those 113 years, as he encounters a world in which crime, war, and poverty have been banished, and equality of the sexes and general social amity achieved. If we imagine a Julia West falling asleep in the more recent year of 1950 and awakening in the first year of the 21st century, she too would encounter transformations that, while not as radical as those proposed

---

[7] In contrast to TV's persistent segregation, Hollywood movies have demonstrated strong crossover potential. In the summer of 2000, four films with African American stars and directors broke records for "black-themed" movies: *Shaft: Still the Man*, *Big Momma's House*, *Scary Movie*, and *Nutty Professor II* (the latter two abounded in the homophobic humor that the Wayans brothers and Eddie Murphy seemingly find irresistible).

by Bellamy, would nevertheless have amazed anyone transported from mid-century America to the present.

Our midcentury Julia West would awake to a world in which the Soviet Union has disappeared and the Cold War that shaped the politics of 1950 lives on mostly in the hearts and minds of Miami's Cuban American community. The globe once divided between the Communists and the "free world" is now dominated by a seemingly unchallenged "free market" global capitalism. The world she now encounters is also one in which previous barriers have crumbled and institutional categories blurred.

America in 1950, just emerging from two decades of depression and war, was experiencing both the boom of a population explosion and an unprecedented migration from the cities to the suburbs that were springing up around them, linked by an ever-expanding web of highways. Long-distance telephone calls were a rare and expensive occurrence, and air travel was an elite luxury. Remote parts of the continent and the globe were truly distant places, from which news arrived via intermediaries of foreign correspondents heard on the radio and read in the newspaper and weekly newsmagazines. Mass entertainment was found at the local movie theater and around the living room radio. In 1950 a new invention called television was beginning to intrude on the consciousness of the country, but it was really only radio with pictures, more of a novelty than a significant social force.

Fifty years later, at the start of the 21st century, television is the voracious behemoth that has eaten or transformed all other media and is now staring into the jaws of the new king of the food chain, the omnivorous Internet. Television began its march through the media of the 1950s by overthrowing the dominance of the movie industry and then uniting with a weakened studio system to create a powerful new concentration of entertainment production and distribution. At the same time, the new medium insinuated itself into the fabric of American journalism, gradually using its ability to show as well as tell in order to supplant print as the primary vehicle for news.

In 1964, sociologist Harold Wilensky analyzed a large body of survey data on "life style and mass culture" and concluded that, "Television, the most 'massified' of the mass media, the one with the largest and most heterogeneous audience, has become central to the leisure routine of majorities at every level. The usual differences in media exposure and response among age, sex, and class categories—easy to exaggerate in any case—have virtually disappeared in the case of television." By the 1980s, as cable increased the breadth of television content, the medium consolidated its hold over other domains of mass entertainment, becoming the dominant vehicle for sports spectatorship and a rival to radio in the creation of pop musical careers and trends.

The hallmark of the late twentieth century in the media industries (and adjacent/overlapping territories, such as the Internet) was the weakening of boundaries that previously distinguished arenas, enterprises, institutions, and professions. In some instances the blurring of boundaries was a direct result of technological innovations (satellite transmission, the Web), and in others, of corporate consolidation that united previously distinct (even competitive) entities. Entertainment media—the rapidly conglomerating TV / film / cable / publishing / music / sports / Internet megasauruses that can be seen grazing in Los Angeles and New York—represent the pattern even more dramatically than in the case of journalism. Here there is no threat to professional norms in pursuing corporate profits across industry boundaries. Quite the opposite, it's called synergy, and it promotes company performance.

Along with the consolidation of industry segments into giant corporations, we are witnessing the ever finer slicing of audiences (aka markets) into ever-smaller demographic segments. Two factors combine to motivate this shift: the steady erosion of the mass common-denominator audiences once delivered by the networks, and the exploding sophistication of marketing data bases and analytic techniques. In the past networks demanded content that would attract everyone (at least, everyone who counted) while offending no one (at least, no one who counted). Those who didn't count included most minorities, queers among them, even when we were barely acknowledged as a legitimate minority. Now, in contrast, producers and sponsors are more than willing to target (somewhat) narrow segments, while certainly being willing to risk offending other (also, in their market-driven view, narrow) segments.

The second half of the twentieth century has witnessed the inexorable triumph of entertainment, as a commercially dominated media system seeks to attract audiences—potential customers for sponsors—by packaging every category of media product, from news to sports to gossip to comedy and drama, as entertainment. Next to "dead air" the worst sin of media is to be boring, to permit or even encourage the dreaded flipping of the remote. The business of producing and distributing entertainment lies at the core of American media and therefore at the heart of American culture.

Our midcentury Julia West would have gone to sleep at a time when homosexuality was still the love that dare not speak it name. Homosexual acts were illegal throughout the United States (and most of the rest of the world), and the government was fueling the growing bonfire of Cold War hysteria by hunting down and persecuting "sexual perverts" in government and elsewhere. Being publicly gay was unthinkable for nearly everyone, even had the media been interested in representing the perspectives of people defined by the police and the courts as criminals, by the churches as sinners, and by psychiatrists as mentally ill.

The gay world, to the degree that the term applied, was divided between a marginalized and stigmatized overt fringe—those who would not or could not hide, and who were steady targets of official oppression and extortion; and a hidden iceberg of outwardly normal men and women—many "confirmed bachelors" and "spinsters" and many married but physically and/or emotionally unfaithful. Miraculously, in the ferment of those postwar years, small groups of homosexual men and women began to organize, in Jim Kepner's words, "obscurely, even apologetically, and with no access to non-gay media." Still, Kepner continued, "we asserted our existence, sought freedom from persecution, sparked courage in a few thousand of our fellows, sought to define and open up *The Unmentionable Subject.*"

Throughout the 1950s and 1960s, small groups of gay people began to cohere, gathering in the bars that were, for the most part, the only available public space, and beginning to knit a community together via the pages of newsletters and small magazines. Taking advantage of occasional cracks in the fabric of mainstream media, even at the risk of ridicule and reprisal, a few brave queers were heard and seen speaking for themselves, alerting others to the possibility of resisting the junta of church, state, and medicine. And they also signaled to the straight world that they would not remain hidden forever. As Seymour Krim put it in the *Village Voice* a decade before Stonewall, "Like it or not, we will force our way into open society and you'll have to acknowledge us."

Homosexuals in the second half of the century came together as a conscious grouping by adopting the peculiarly American identity of a minority akin to (but overlapping with) the racial, ethnic, or religious minorities that are a dominant feature of our cultural and political topography. By asserting minority status—claiming, on the basis of a loose reading of Kinsey, to be 10 percent of the population—gay people were able to fit into a set of familiar rhetorical frames, decrying discrimination and demanding equal rights under the law. As with the political, economic, and cultural claims of racial minorities and women, the struggles of gay people provoked resistance and derision, hostility and reprisal. Still, with perseverance and growing numbers, attitudes began to change, barriers began to fall, and the terms of the debate became more even-handed. Bigotry continues to intrude on our private and our political lives, and violence is all too familiar, but gay people have taken possession of a small but highly visible corner of the public sphere. We are players; but what is the game?

American culture has proved once again to be enormously elastic, absorbing much of gay "style" and sensibility, while remaining on guard against accusations of queerness. The great American bargain offered to successive minorities continues to be: assimilate, but on our terms. By all means, add your flavoring to the national stew, but keep it subtle enough not to threaten the dominance of white, middle-class, Christian, hetero-normativity. We welcome any style that can be repackaged and sold to other markets—whether it's gay disco in the 1970s or African American hip-hop in the 1990s—but we do insist on inspecting all goods at the border and we reserve the right to demonize and marginalize those who refuse to play by our rules.

Our midcentury Julia West would wake up to a world in which politics has become a wholly owned subsidiary of corporate capitalism, played out through the media like other spectator sports, as the two major league parties face each other in ritual combat. But as in sports, it matters little who wins the political Superbowl, as both teams are more alike than they differ in policy or programs, and citizens have adopted the role of couch potato fans, following the race but not expecting to participate.

The homophile movement of the 1950s and 1960s sought to shift the terms of the American cultural consensus, first whispering in the ears of professionals that homosexuals were not necessarily criminal, sinful, or sick, and then trying to break their enforced silence by publicly proclaiming that "Gay Is Good." The gay liberation movement of the 1970s, largely allied with the left-leaning peace and civil rights movements of that era, saw itself as part of a widespread attack on the repressive fabric of Western culture. By the time the AIDS epidemic exploded in 1981, the resurgent right wing then represented by the Moral Majority had set gays firmly in their gun-sights as a major target (and fund-raising opportunity). For the next decade gay people were fighting on two fronts: resisting the virulent homophobia of political enemies while simultaneously organizing in response to an unprecedented medical crisis that was long ignored by both government and media.

In the last decade of the twentieth century gay people were no longer invisible—as a group; but many, if not most, lesbians and gay men remain at least partially closeted. The public stages of media and politics became open to lesbian and gay people to an extent that would have been inconceivable to our Julia West as she fell asleep in 1950. But as always, the price of access to the corridors of power is firmly exacted: play by our rules if you want to stay in the game. What was once called the gay movement is now dressed for success as a constituency of the Democratic Party, offering money and votes in exchange for limited—if hardly trivial—gains. At the same time, we have had to swallow both insult and actual injury: "Don't ask, Don't tell," and the

Defense of Marriage Act were products of the Clinton administration, which called itself the most "gay friendly" ever. And gay Republicans are still congratulating themselves whenever a candidate will even take their money.

Edward Bellamy's 2000 is a utopian world of dazzling social and technological achievements; a garden of roses without thorns. Our Julia West would not wake to such a wondrous world, but if she were gay, she would truly marvel. True, a third of the states still criminalize sodomy, and only thirteen states and approximately 150 municipalities and counties offer protection against discrimination on the basis of sexual orientation. At the same time, there are openly queer individuals and groups in high schools all across the country, and very few teenagers will grow up without knowing anyone who is gay; none will grow up without seeing gay people depicted on the large and small screens that absorb so much of their time and attention.

We may not have reached Bellamy's 21st century, but we have traveled far in the past half century. It is the words of William Blake that might best conclude our tale:

Children of the future Age,
Reading this indignant page:
Know that in a former time,
Love! Sweet Love! Was thought a crime.

SOURCES

In the interest of brevity, source notes are limited to the following concise listings, organized by chapter. All works cited in the text or below are listed in the alphabetical bibliography that follows. A number of the pieces cited are reprinted in *The Columbia Reader on Lesbians and Gay Men in Media, Society, and Politics*, which I edited with James Woods—here referred to as G&W.

There are several key works on the history of lesbian, gay, bisexual, and transgendered people in the United States during the past fifty years, and on their relations with various media. The works (by category) I have relied upon most heavily are Alwood 1996 (for mainstream journalism); D'Emilio 1983 and Loughery 1998 (gay history); Russo 1987 (homosexuality and the movies); and Streitmatter 1995 (the gay press). Two key works that appeared too late to be incorporated here are Capsuto 2000 (on gays and television) and Chasin 2000 (on the lesbian and gay market). David Wyatt maintains a very useful Web site that lists queer characters on television (http://home.cc.umanitoba.ca/~Ewyatt/tv-characters.html).

CHAPTER 1: THE MEDIATED SOCIETY

Mass Media and American Society: Good sources on the state of the mass media are Turow (1997a and 1997b), and Budd et al. (1999). References to Barry Diller are in Ebner (1995), Dullea (1993), and La Ferla (2001). Marshall Herskovitz is quoted by Gail Shister (in her "Television" column) in the *Philadelphia Inquirer*, July 14, 1999. The racial profile of the 1998 and 1999 TV season, and the presence of gays in television, are discussed in Brownfield (1999). **Television as the Mainstream:** Cultivation theory and the Cultural Indicators Project is described in Gerbner and Gross (1976), Gerbner et al. (1994), and Shanahan and Morgan (1999). Cultural studies emphasizing resistance is exemplified by Fiske (1987). For Sarah Kozloff's quotation, see Kozloff (1987:43). Reuven Frank is quoted in Epstein (1974:4). For a study of TV characters in the 1991 season, see Nardi (1992). **Sexual Minorities and the Media:** For Patricia Turner's recollections, see Turner (1994:xiii); B. D. Wong's recollections are quoted in Southgate (1994). Cuban American student quoted in O'Neil (1984:47–48). Dyer's analysis of stereotypes (Dyer 1977a) is reprinted in G&W

(1999:300). See Friedrich (1986:48) on Jewish assimilation in Hollywood. For attitudes toward gay people, see Yang (1997). Patullo's defense of antigay discrimination (1992) is reprinted in G&W (1999:613). **Subversion and Resistance:** See Hodges and Hutter (1974), reprinted in G&W (1999:551). For Ahad Ha-'Am quote, see Ha-'Am (1970:320). Raymond Williams's quotation is from Williams (1977:111). For Babuscio on camp, see Dyer (1977b); Dyer's quotation is from Cohen and Dyer (1980:177).

CHAPTER 2: COMING OUT AND COMING TOGETHER

The Homosexual in Midcentury America: For accounts of gay life in America at midcentury, see D'Emilio (1983) and Loughery (1998). On the Kinsey Report, see Bronski (1984:77). For figures in the Kinsey Report, see Kinsey, Pomeroy, and Martin (1948:656). For the quotation from *The Homosexual in America*, see Cory (1951:13–14); for quotations from *The Homosexual and His Society*, see Cory and LeRoy (1963:240). Cory later abandoned his pseudonym to critique gay activism in Sagarin (1973). **Giving Voice to the Voiceless:** The best overall source on the lesbian and gay press is Streitmatter (1995). Lisa Ben's account of *Vice Versa* appears in Marcus (1992; rpt. in G&W 1999:443–45). Jim Kepner's comments on *Vice Versa* are quoted in Streitmatter (1995:2). For Kepner's account of *ONE*, along with important examples of early gay press writings and comments on the movement, see Kepner (1998). John D'Emilio (1983) covers the gay press (quoted comment, 115). Evelyn Hooker's recollections are in Marcus (1992; rpt. in G&W 1999:169–74). For Hal Call's comments, see Streitmatter (1995:33). **Provoking Concern:** The best source on mainstream journalism and gay people is Alwood (1996). Krim's *Village Voice* article is quoted in Kepner (1998:336). For Randy Wicker's efforts with WBAI and the *New York Times* (*NYT*), as well as the *Times*'s coverage in the mid-1960s, see Alwood (1996: ch. 2). For the quoted recollection of *Life*'s 1964 article, see Loughery (1998:258). *Time*'s January 1966 essay and the response in the *Ladder* is reprinted in G&W (1999:356–61). **The Voice Gets Louder:** For accounts of the 1960s gay rights movement and its press, see D'Emilio (1983; 1992), Loughery (1998), and Streitmatter (1995). On Kameny's linguistic innovations, see Lee (1981). **Coming Out in the Nation's Living Rooms:** For further details, see Alwood (1996: ch. 3).

CHAPTER 3: STONEWALL AND BEYOND

"Homo Nest Raided, Queen Bees Stinging Mad": On media accounts of Stonewall, see Alwood (1996: ch. 4). The *New York Daily News* article is reprinted in G&W (1999:364). Jay and Young's 1972 *Out of the Closets* was reissued in 1992. On the struggle over ads in Canada, see Lee (1981); and on the post-Stonewall movement, Marotta (1981: *NYT* quote, 170). **"Turning Their Condition into Politics":** For accounts of early 1970s media-related activism, including quotations from Arthur Evans and Merle Miller, see Marotta (1981), Alwood (1996), Loughery (1998). Midge Decter (1980) on gay activists is reprinted in G&W (1999):601–611). For Dennis Altman's recollections, see Altman (1981:21). **Expressing Outrage:** On the fight over *Marcus Welby, M.D.*, see Alwood (1996: ch. 7), Loughery (1998:342–43), Levine (1981), and Capsuto (2000). Kathryn Montgomery (1981) covers media activism in the 1970s; see also Montgomery (1989). Russo quote is from 1986 article. **Talking Back to the Media:** For *Newsweek* on gay power in San Francisco, see Fraker (1977). For General Westmoreland's suit against CBS, see Klaidman and Beauchamp (1988:166).

CHAPTER 4: AT THE MOVIES

"A Queer Feeling Every Time I Look at You": On film stereotypes, see Dyer (1977a) and Sheldon (1977), excerpted in G&W (1999:297–301 and 301–306, respectively). For exhaustive accounts of homosexuality in film, see Russo (1987); on lesbians in film, see Weiss (1992). **"Show Me a Happy Homosexual and I'll Show You a Gay Corpse":** For films of the 1960s and 1970s, see Russo (1987). On British legal history, see Weeks (1981:105). Pauline Kael's review of *The Children's Hour* is cited in Byron (1981). Jewelle Gomez's recollections of *Sister George* appear in Brandt (1999:167). For the *NYT* interview with Cliff Gorman, see Klemesrud (1968). **Friedkin Delivers Gay Corpses:** On the struggle over *Cruising*, see Tucker (1979), reprinted in Shore, Case, and Daly (1982:322–29), and Russo (1987). On the Ramrod shootings, see Kaiser (1997:274–75). **Getting the Word Out:** On the Navajo film project, see Worth and Adair (1997). For transcripts of *Word Is Out* interviews, see Adair and Adair (1978). On criticism of *Word Is Out*, see Waugh (1988). For Dyer's comments on the film, see Dyer (1990:243). Kameny is quoted in Marotta (1981:62–63). On the Combahee River Collective statement, see Moraga and Anzaldúa (1981:210–18). For D'Emilio on coming out, see D'Emilio (1983:235–36); for his later thoughts, see D'Emilio (1992:249). On gay Toronto and *The Body Politic*, see Lee (1977). For Waugh's comment, see Waugh (1988:265). **Gay Films for Straight Audiences:** Russo (1987) is a good source on all of these films. Also, see Farber (1981) on *Partners* and *Personal Best*, Byron (1982) on making *Making Love*. For lesbian responses to *Personal Best*, see Ellsworth (1986). **Universal or Particular?:** For Russo's comment on independent gay films, see Russo (1986:34). For viewers' and screenwriter Cooper's comments on *Desert Hearts*, see Husten (1987). See Russo (1987:315) for Donna Deitch's statements in *Ms.* magazine. On critical reaction to *Parting Glances*, see Weiss (1986:7) and Russo (1987:312). Cowan's letter appears in the *NYTBR*, March 9, 1980. Lehmann-Haupt reviews David Leavitt's novel in the *NYT*, September 11, 1986, and Edmund White's in the *NYT*, March 17, 1988. For *Newsweek*'s feature, see Clemons (1988). William Henry reviewed McNally in *Time*, November 13, 1989; and Michiko Kakutani reviewed Dale Peck in the *NYT*, February 9, 1993. For Richard Christiansen's assessment of *Angels in America*, see Christiansen (1994); and see Achebe's characterization of Western critics in Achebe (1976:11). McCarthy (1989) recalls James Baldwin. For Michael Denneny's report, see Denneny (1989), reprinted in G&W (1999:583–88).

CHAPTER 5: TELEVISION TAKES OVER

New Medium, Old Message: The most comprehensive source on gays and television is Capsuto (2000). For Nixon's response to the gay TV character, see Warren (1999). On TV's treatment of gays, see Henry (1987). On *Adam and Yves*, see Capsuto (2000:151–52). See Guthmann (1986) on the making of *Dynasty* and Maupin's criticisms. **No Sex, Please, We're Queer:** See D'Acci (1994) on *Cagney and Lacey*. Moritz (1993) analyzes *Heartbeat*; O'Conner and Tucker, both 1989, review *The Women of Brewster Place*. On the concerns of the Fox executive over the gay kiss on *Melrose Place*, see Seplow (1994). Zerbisias (1995) discusses *Serving in Silence*. On a polled audience response to a gay kiss, see Kim (1995); and on the choice of Asian American Ling Woo to kiss Ally McBeal, see Lee (1999).

CHAPTER 6: AIDS AND THE MEDIA

Rumors of a "Gay Cancer": For accounts of media responses to AIDS, see Albert (1986) (reprinted in G&W 1999:393–402), Kinsella (1989), and Shilts (1987). **Circling the Wagons:** Waxman is quoted in Shilts (1987:143). On early AIDS coverage in the *Philadelphia Inquirer*, see Chastain (1982a, 1982b). Federal official William Grigg is quoted in Tucker (1997:69). On the impact of Rock Hudson's announcement on media coverage, see Milavsky (1988). For actors' concerns about kissing, see Judell (1986). **Natural Squeamishness:** On the media's reluctance to advertise condoms, see Flinn (1996), Wells (1998), Peterkin (1998), Oldham (1999), and Plaster (2000). On the media's reluctance to cover AIDS, see Kinsella (1989), and ibid. (1989:87–105) for the story of *Newsweek*'s April 1983 cover. See Gallagher (1991), on Kimberly Bergalis. Lewis (1992) praised Arthur Ashe. Peter Jennings on the plant fungus story is quoted in Kinsella (1988:120). **Media Activism in a Crisis:** See Alwood (1996, ch. 11) and Kantrowitz (1998) on GLAAD. On Andy Rooney's suspension by CBS, see Bull (1990) and Goodman (1990). For the Museum of Modern Art's avoidance of AIDS graphics, see Crimp and Rolston (1990:16). Peter Jennings's 1989 *AIDS Quarterly* remarks are quoted in Treichler (1999:130).

CHAPTER 7: JOURNALISM'S CLOSET OPENS

Burying and Marrying: For the *NYT*'s obituary on Copland, see Rockwell (1990). *Washington Post* ombudsman E. R. Shipp discusses the Gielgud obituary in Shipp (2000). Nardi (1990) discusses obituary practices. On the *Salina (Kan.) Journal*'s running of a gay wedding announcement, see Pyle (1993). For the *NYT*'s story on the lesbian wedding, see Colton (1999); also see Staples (1999) for editorial the same month. On Vermont civil unions, see Stephenson (2000). For the centenary article on Copland, see Tommasini (1999); also see Schwarz (1994) for the earlier *Times* article on gay composers. **All the News Not Fit to Print:** On practices and changes at the *New York Times*, see Alwood (1996), Anson (1993), DeStefano (1986), Kaiser (1997), and Signorile (1992a, 1992b) (reprinted in G&W 1999:375–86). For Schanberg quotation, see Anson (1993). On the fallout from Stanley Kauffman's 1966 essays, see Alwood (1996:65–69); also see Alwood (1996:84) for Albin Krebs's recollections. For Jane Brody's 1996 defense of her 1971 articles, see Kaiser (1997:229). On Jahr's 1975 travel article, see DeStefano (1986). For Kaiser on Rosenthal, see Signorile (1992a, 1992b). On the news media's handling of the Greenwich Village shootings, see Pierson (1982) (reprinted in G&W 1999:369–76). For the Canadian papers' responses to the word *gay*, see Lee (1981). Jeffrey Schmalz is quoted in Signorile (1992a, 1992b). **The Gray Lady Goes Gay:** On the transformation of the *New York Times*, see Alwood (1996), Anson (1993), DeStefano (1986), Kaiser (1992, 1997), and Signorile (1992a, 1992b). For the continued resistance to the word *gay*, see Stein (1991). On the *Times*'s retraction regarding the lesbian parents story, see Alwood (1996:231). Jeffrey Schmalz's comments on the coverage of gays in the military are from a personal communication (September 1993). The "Culture Briefs" quote from Richard Berke in the *Washington Times* is reported in the April-May issue of the antigay *Lambda Report*. **Coming Out in the Newsroom:** On Jeffrey Schmalz's coming out, subsequent career, and death, see Signorile (1992) (reprinted in G&W 1999:378), and Alwood (1996:264). For speeches to NLGJA by Joseph Lelyveld and Arthur Sulzberger Jr., see

Rosenkrantz (1992). For Barbara Raab's comments on lesbian reporters, see Eddings (1994:48). On Max Robinson's silence about his illness, see Harper (1991).

CHAPTER 8: BREAKING THE CODE OF SILENCE

Naming Names: On the politics of outing, see Signorile (1993) and Gross (1993) (also see G&W 1999:417–36). For the *NYT*'s coverage of the first NLGJA convention, see J. Gross (1992). On the Jewish press's treatment of John Garfield, see Rosenthal (1993). For Maupin's comments, see Mallinger (1990). Henry's January 1990 *Time* article is reprinted in Gross (1993:205–207). **Outing The Pentagon:** On the outing of Pete Williams and its aftermath, see Signorile (1993) and Gross (1993). For articles quoted, see McWilliams (1991), Phillips (1991), and Williams (1991). On communal responsibility as discussed by legal scholars, see Rubenstein (1997) and Wilkins (1993). For Cal Thomas's outing of Dean Hamer, see Thomas (1995). **Kinda Ask, Sorta Tell:** On the outing of Steve Gunderson, see Gross (1993:93–96). See Rotello (1995) (reprinted in G&W 1999:433) on Jann Wenner's outing. For Jim Kolbe on coming out, see Willey (1996). On the outing of Barbara Mikulski, see Keen (1996). Maria Miro Johnson (1999) reported Signorile's speech. On Joel Wachs's coming out, see Link (1999). For the *NYT*'s profile of Pete Williams, see Sciolino (1991). On the media silence over Donna Brazile's lesbianism, see Bedard (1999). David Smith is quoted in the *Atlanta Southern Voice* (editorial, 11/4/99). For Sullivan's views on the Pete Williams outing, see Sullivan (1995:82); for his change of tune on outing, see Sullivan (1999). The *NYT*'s view of Sullivan's article is quoted in the *New York Post*'s "Page Six" feature (12/14/99). For Madonna's response to outing, see *Vanity Fair* (March 2000), 244.

CHAPTER 9: HOLLYWOOD UNDER PRESSURE

AIDS Victims and Villains: For Michael Denneny on promoting *And the Band Played On*, see Harris (1998). Weiss (1986) analyzed *An Early Frost*; King (1985) and Leahy (1986) discuss Aiden Quinn's decision to star; on the making of *An Early Frost*, see Buxton (1992); also see Treichler (1999:178) on NBC's promotional material. On ABC's *Afterschool Special*, "Just a Regular Kid," see O'Connor (1987), and O'Connor (1988) on *Midnight Caller*. **A Kinder, Gentler Hollywood:** For Shilts on Hollywood homophobia, see Lew (1991). On gay activism in Hollywood in the early 1990s, see Sadownick (1992); quote from Joe Ezterhas appears in Sadownick (1991). For GLAAD's response to *Longtime Companion*'s reviews, see Schwartz (1990). On the 1992 Oscars, see Weir (1992) and Signorile (1993:309–320). **Queering the "Straight" Text:** Goldstein is quoted in Russo (1987:316). On African American music as cultural background, see Mercer and Julien (1994:199), Hall (1992:22), Turner (1994:155–56). Also see Bronski (1991) (reprinted in G&W 1999:245–51), Sontag (1967:290), Steiner (1980:180), Van Leer (1995:4), and Cory (1951:4). Spacks is cited in Weiss (1992:30). On cultural "poaching," see de Certeau (1984); also see Doty (1993:3–4) and White (1987:162). On *Cagney & Lacey*, see D'Acci (1994:30) and Hands (1995:50); on *Dynasty* fans, see Feuer (1989).

CHAPTER 10: HOLLYWOOD'S GAY NINETIES

"I feel pretty and witty and . . . Hey!": Millman (1995) foreshadowed Ellen's coming out. For Ellen DeGeneres's reticence, see Soren (1995). On the PR campaign preceding the coming out episode, see Statemen (1997). For Paul Shulman's views on advertisers, see Bruni (1996). On DeGeneres's absence of glamour, see Thompson (1997); on Ivan Reitman's support for Anne Heche, see Weiner (1997). Hadleigh (1986, 1991, 1994, 1996, 1997) comprise interviews with deceased lesbian and gay celebrities. On DeGeneres's reluctant activism, see Handy (1997), Williams (1998). For lesbian reader's reaction to *Ellen*, see Milvy (1997). **Still Villainous After All These Years:** Orth (1997, 1999) represents sensationalist coverage of Cunanan (*Larry King Live* appearance, March 13, 1999). Also see Cindy Adams's *New York Post* column for July 16, 1997. Crowley (1997) and Soar (2000) critique the media's handling of the Cunanan story. Achenbach (1997) disputes HIV rumor. On Walter Jenkins's arrest, see Collins (1998:183–85). For San Diego's "tearoom TV," see Turegano (1998); on the focus of these stories during sweeps, see Rozansky (1998) and Goldstein (1998). On the protests at the Philadelphia TV station, see Wiener (1998). Regarding the double standard for public sex, see Siegel (1998). On Oakland University's surveillance, see Murray (1999); also see Mayhood (1999) and Tyler (1999) on the vice campaigns in Columbus, Ohio, and Elkhart, Ind. **Sad Young Men:** On the sad young man stereotype, see Dyer (1993). See Capsuto (2000) on recent TV. For the *Quantum Leap* episode, see McConnell (1992). Isherwood (1994) interviewed Wilson Cruz. See Cloud (1997) on the openness among teens. For P. K. Simonds on TV and gay teens, see DeCaro (1999). On the lack of furor over *Dawson's Creek*, see Bauder (1999). **Some of My Best Friends Are Celibate:** On TV's Asian celibate bachelors, see Hamamoto (1994:6–10). See Ansen (1996) on drag queens in film. Carpenter (1999) criticized Ellen DeGeneres. Baldwin (1998) interviewed Sean Hayes; also see D'Erasmo (1998) on *Will & Grace* and D'Erasmo (1999) on *Queer as Folk*. See Jacobs (1998) on *Will & Grace* in *Entertainment Weekly*; also see Graham (1999) in *USA Today*; and for the cast's involvement with politics, see Herscher (1999a) and Waxman (2000). On reactions to *Queer as Folk*, see Lyall (1999); Richard Kramer is quoted in Brownfield (1999); on plans for the U.S. version, see Weinraub (2000); for *TV Guide*'s review, see Roush (2000).

CHAPTER 11: BEYOND PRIME TIME

Adam and Steve and Phil and Oprah: The best source on queers and talk shows is Gamson (1998); see also Grindstaff (1997). Dichter is quoted in Ehrenreich (1983:45); also see Ehrenreich (1983:50) on *Playboy*. See Gamson (1998) for the following: Heaton and Wilson quoted (31); *Springer* producers quoted (61); Angela Gardner quoted (155, 178). On Donahue and Paul Cameron, see Newton (2000). **The Tongue-Tied Public Square:** On the establishment of PBS, see Aufderheide (1991:174); for ITVS and *P.O.V.*, see Mookas (1992) and Kauffman (1991:39). For Riggs on *Tongues Untied*, see Kloer (1991). See Buchanan (1989) on culture and Vance (1989, 1990) on the culture wars. On Riggs, *P.O.V.*, and *Stop the Church* under attack, see People for the American Way (1992:17), Goodman (1991), and Ledbetter (1997:188). On Texaco's ending of its PBS sponsorship, see Ehrenstein (1992). For tales of *Tales of the City*, see Rich (1994a, 1994b) and Carman (1994). On *And the Band Played On*, see Maupin (1994). For *More Tales of the City*, see Hoffman (1998) and McCauley (1998). See Ledbetter (1997:14) for cable's challenge to PBS. On reactions to *It's Elementary*, see Ness (1999) and Morantz (1999). **Getting Over the Rainbow:** See Nestle (1987:113) on the 1950s; and Dyer (1986:141–94) on gay men and Judy Garland. See Brownstein (1998) on disco; and Gill (1995:106–113) on the 1970s

David Bowie. On *Rocky Horror*, see Austin (1981); and Koenig (2000) on *Sound of Music* singalongs. On lesbian musicians, see Gill (1995:143–51) and Dickinson (2000). See Braindrop (1991) on queer audiences. On k. d. lang's and Melissa Etheridge's coming out, see Kasindorf (1993) and Bennetts (1993); also see Lemon (1992:44) and Broderick (1992) on lang. See Anderson-Minshall (2000) and Moon (2000) on Sinéad O'Connor; and Griffiths (1999) on Ricky Martin. **Locker-room Closets:** On sports homophobia, see Lipsyte (1991) and Bull (1995). On Billie Jean King, see Amdur (1981), Casey (1981), and Ross (1981). Fleischman (1981) interviewed Navratilova. See Lipsyte (1993) and Bull (1995) on Louganis; for his own story, see Louganis (1995) and Louganis and Marcus (1995). On coverage of the Gay Games, see Woog (1992). On homophobia in football and baseball, see Kettman (1998). See Whitam and Mathy (1986:122) on cross-cultural studies; and Tobin (2000) on gay soccer stars. See Lipsyte (1999) on Billy Bean. On the LPGA and Ben Wright, see Juliano (1995), Mechem (1995), and Potter (1995). See Kort (1998) on Spencer-Devlin. On the WNBA's lesbian fans, see Fisher (1998), Gustkey (2001) and Pucin (2001) on the L.A. Sparks, and Woodell (1998).

CHAPTER 12: MORNING PAPERS, AFTERNOON SOAPS

Coming Out in the Comics: On the comics as reassurance, see Daniels (1971:4). On responses to Lawrence's coming out, see Lawler, Sparkes, and Wood (1994). On homoeroticism in Batman, see Wertham (1954:189). Mark Miller is quoted in McGinty (2000). Matt Groening is quoted in Hartinger (1993:67). *Queer Nation* creator Chris Cooper is interviewed in Glam (1999). **You're the First Person I Have Ever Told:** On the lesbian character on *All My Children*, see Stone (1983). On daytime TV's resistance to gay characters, see LeCuyer (1991). Gross (1996) analyzes the letters to Ryan Phillippe. On "para-social interaction," see Horton and Wohl (1956); also see Jensen (1992:17). For Rodney Wilson's story, see Ruenzel (1994) (reprinted in G&W 1999:278–85). For Eden Riegel on *All My Children*, see Rothaus (2000b).

CHAPTER 13: OLD STORIES AND NEW TECHNOLOGIES

The Good Parts: On porn's value to isolated gays, see Mercer and Julien (1994:195). For Dorothy Allison's first encounter with porn, see Allison (1994:187). For the history of homoerotic images, see Waugh (1996); also see Ellenzweig (1992). On gay male porn video, see John Burger (1995; quotations, 34, 45). See Henderson (1991) on lesbian porn; see Fung (1988) on racism endemic to pornography (both reprinted in G&W 1999:506–526). Strossen (1995) describes *Miller v. California*. On the influence of *Regina v. Hicklin* and the role of Comstock, see Kendrick (1987). See Stevenson (1997) on hard-core theaters. On the porn industry's belated adoption of safer sex, see Umlaut (1989). See Hollibaugh (1983) and Hunter (1995) on early 1980s "sex wars." On the Dworkin/MacKinnon ordinance, see Duggan, Hunter, and Vance (1985); also see Strossen (1995:181). On the victory for pro-sex feminism, see Findlay (1996) and Brownworth (1991). **Somewhere There's a Place For Us:** For Greg Gordon on radio, see Price (1993). On the appeal of the Internet to gay teens, see Silberman (1994) and Walsh (1994) (both reprinted in G&W 1999:537–44); also see Gabriel (1995) and, on Israeli teens, Nir (1998). Lewis (1995) quotes Tom Reilly. For Daniel Montgomery's story, see Byrnes (1995) and Weise (1995a, 1995b). For the

Senate's debate on the CDA, see Andrews (1995a, 1995b). The Supreme Court's CDA ruling is quoted in Jenkins (1998:213). On cyber-filters' blocking of politicians, see Bowman (2000) and Hunter (2000). On cyber-addiction, see Goldstein (2000). GLAAD's report on filters is *Access Denied* (GLAAD 1997). For Will Doherty on cyber-privacy, see Chibbaro (2000).

CHAPTER 14: A NICHE OF OUR OWN

Movement to Market: See Schudson (1984:210–33) on advertising. On African American consumers, see Brooks (1995). See Schulman (1998:129) on gay marketing. See letters to the editor, *Advertising Age*, July 10, 1978, 104. On gay ad agencies, see Kahn (1994:24). For Scalia on gay income, see Alsop (1999a). On Milton Berle's suit, see *Press Pass Q*(1999). On changes at the *Advocate*, see Johnson (1991) and Donaton (1992). On *Hero* magazine, see Egan (2000). For the finances of lesbian magazines, see Davis (1999). On lesbian consumers, see Clark (1991). On Ikea's ad, see Rich (1994a). See Denneny (1989) on crossover best-sellers (reprinted in G&W 1999:583–88). For Scribner's editor on gay history, see Italie (1993). On Subaru's ads, see Alsop (1999b) and Elliott (2000); for quote from ad man, see Palmer (2000). For Anheuser-Busch, see Ford (1999) and Roeper (1999). On the Miller ad, see Herscher (1999b) and Richard Johnson (1999). For gays on the Web, see Dolley (2000); on gfn.com, see Alsop (2000); on the *Advocate*-PlanetOut merger, see Freiberg (2000). For criticism of consolidation, see Crain (2000). On the PlanetOut-Gay.com merger, see Kirby (2000). On concerns over the Net's future, see Warren (2000). **Are We Being Served?** On the African American press, see Roscho (1967). For *Out*'s editorial changes, see Swanson (1999); and for its sale, see Abelson (2000). On the expansion of the gay press, see Rothman (1999). For comment from the South Florida publisher, see Rothaus (2000a). On recent gay publications, see Woodlee (1999), Noh (2000), and Grau (2000). On journalistic rituals and routines, see Tuchman (1972, 1978). For *XY* magazine, see Vaziri (1999). On objective journalism, see Schudson (1995:105) and Carey (1969/1997:140). For John Mandes and the *Philadelphia Gay News*, see Shea (1992) and Fish (1991). On the *New York Blade* and Katie Syzmanski, see Osborne (1998). On the use by the gay press of AP's wire service (including Mirken quote), see Wofford (1992). On Wockner, see Silberman (1998). For gay cable's inroads, see Savage (1999) and Closs (1994) (reprinted G&W 1999:466–73). On GayBC's web-casting, see Wadewitz (2000).

CHAPTER 15: FACING THE FUTURE

Visibility and Its Discontents: See Hall (1992:24) on segregated visibility. For U.S. TV programming and Nielsen data, see Elber (2000). On TV's jews, see O'Connor (1990). See Appiah (1993:83) on "Saints." On TV's blacks, see Gray (1986:239); also see Jhally and Lewis (1992:137) on "enlightened racism." For "reality-based" TV, see Seplow (1995). On the 1992 Oscars, see Rogin (1993:5). For the confrontation between the networks and the NAACP, see Weinraub (1999). For Barclay on *City of Angels*, see Jensen, Braxton, and Calvo (2000). On gay TV characters, see Dretzka (1999). For behind-the-scenes gays in TV, see Ehrenstein (1996) (reprinted in G&W 1999:335–40). On John Chancellor's sign-off, see Clark (1993). **Looking Backward:** See Wilensky (1964:195) on TV. See Kepner (1998:393) on gay journalism, and quotes Krim (336).

BIBLIOGRAPHY

Abelson, Reed. 2000. "Out Magazine Acquired by the Advocate, a Key Rival." *New York Times*, February 21, C12.

Achebe, Chinua. 1976. "Colonialist Criticism." *Morning Yet on Creation Day*. New York: Anchor.

Achenbach, Joel. 1997. "The Killer Virus Motive: Unfounded Rumor Casts HIV as a Villain in Slayings." *Washington Post*, July 19, F1.

Adair, Nancy and Casey Adair. 1978. *Word Is Out: Stories of Some of Our Lives*. New York: Dell.

Advertising Age. Letters to the Editor. July 10, 1978, 104–105.

Albert, Edward. 1986. "Illness and Deviance: The Response of the Press to AIDS." In D. Feldman and T. Johnson, eds., *Social Dimensions of Aids*, 163–78. New York: Praeger.

Allison, Dorothy. 1994. "A Personal History of Lesbian Porn." *Skin: Talking About Sex, Class, and Literature*. Ithaca, N.Y.: Firebrand.

Alsop, Ronald. 1999a. "Are Gay People More Affluent? Advertisers Say Yes, Activists No." *Wall Street Journal*, December 30.

——. 1999b. "Cracking the Gay Market Code: How Marketers Plant Subtle Symbols in Ads." *Wall Street Journal*, June 29.

——. 2000. "Web Site Sets Gay-themed Ads for Big, National Publications." *Wall Street Journal*, February 17.

Altman, Dennis. 1971. *Homosexual: Oppression and Liberation*. New York: Avon.

——. 1981. *Coming Out in the Seventies*. Boston: Alyson.

Alwood, Edward. 1996. *Straight News: Gays, Lesbians, and the News Media*. New York: Columbia University Press.

Amdur, Neil. 1981. "Homosexuality Causes Sports Tremors." *New York Times*, May 12, B11, 12.

Anderson-Minshall, Diane. 2000. "Sinéad O'Connor Is No Man's Woman." *Curve*, June 27.

Andrews, Edmund. 1995a. "On-line Porn May Be Illegal." *New York Times*, June 15.

——. 1995b. "Panel Backs Smut Ban on Internet." *New York Times*, March 24.

Ansen, David. 1996. "Gay Films Are a Drag." *Newsweek*, March 18, 71.

Anson, Sam. 1993. "The Best of Times, the Worst of Times." *Esquire* (March): 103–110, 182–88.

Appiah, K. Anthony. 1993. "'No Bad Nigger': Blacks as the Ethical Principle in the Movies." In Marjorie Garber et al., eds., *Media Spectacles*, 77–90. New York: Routledge.

Associated Press. 1996. "Gay and Lesbian Net Surfers: A Dream Market in an Online World" June 24.

Aufderheide, Pat. 1991. "Public Television and the Public Sphere." *Critical Studies in Mass Communications* 8: 168–83.

Austin, Bruce. 1981. "Portrait of a Cult Film Audience: *The Rocky Horror Picture Show*." *Journal of Communication* 31.2: 43–54.

Babuscio, Jack. "Camp and the Gay Sensibility." In Dyer, ed., *Gays and Film*, 40–57.

Baldwin, Kristen. 1998. "Full-Mettle Jack." *Entertainment Weekly*, October 23, 27.

Bauder, David. 1999. "*Dawson* Gay Story Taken in Stride." Associated Press, March 16.

Bedard, Paul. 1999. "Outlook." *U.S. News and World Report*, October 18.

Bennetts, Leslie. 1993. "k. d. lang Cuts it Close." *Vanity Fair* (August): 94–98, 142–46.

Boswell, John. 1980. *Christianity, Social Tolerance, and Homosexuality: Gay People in Western Europe from the Beginning of the Christian Era to the Fourteenth Century*. Chicago: University of Chicago Press.

Bowman, Lisa. 2000. "Filtering Programs Block Candidate Sites." *ZDNN*, November 8. (See www.zdnet.com/zdnn/stories/news/0,4586,2651471,00.html.)

Braindrop, Lily. 1991. "Pop Goes Queer." *The Advocate*, October 8, 37.

Brandt, Eric, ed. 1999. *Dangerous Liaisons: Blacks, Gays, and the Struggle for Equality*. New York: New Press.

Braunstein, Peter. 1998. "The Last Days of Gay Disco." *Village Voice*, June 24.

Broderick, Frank. 1992. "Tid Bits: k. d. lang Comes Out." *Au Courant*, June 15, 5.

Bronski, Michael. 1984. *Culture Clash: The Making of Gay Sensibility*. Boston: South End Press.

——. 1991. "How Homophobia Hurts the Publishing Industry." *Gay Community News*, July 21, 8–9.

Brooks, Dwight. 1995. "In Their Own Words: Advertisers' Construction of an African-American Consumer Market, the World War II Era." *Howard Journal of Communications* 6.1–2: 32–52.

Brownfield, Paul. 1999. "Americanized vs. Sanitized." *Los Angeles Times*, November 21.

Brownworth, Victoria. 1991. "Butch and Femme: Who's on Top?" *San Francisco Bay Times*, January, 4–5, 9.

Bruni, Frank. 1996. "It May Be a Closet Door, But It's Already Open." *New York Times*, October 13, B1.

Buchanan, Patrick. 1989. "How Can We Clean Up Our Art Act?" *Washington Post*, June 19.

Budd, Mike, Steve Craig, and Clay Steinman. 1999. *Consuming Environments: Television and Commercial Culture*. New Brunswick: Rutgers University Press.

Bull, Chris. 1990. "Andy, We Hardly Knew Ye: And Now, a Few Homophobic Minutes with Andy Rooney." *The Advocate*, February 27, 10–13.

——. 1995. "Disclosure." *The Advocate*, March 21, 28–34.

Burger, John. 1995. *One-Handed Histories: The Eroto-Politics of Gay Male Video Pornography*. New York: Harrington Park.

Buxton, Rodney. 1992. "Broadcast Formats, Fictional Narratives, and Controversy: Network Television's Depiction of AIDS, 1983–1991." Ph.D. diss., University of Texas, Austin.

Byrnes, Susan. 1995. "Parents Suspect Cyberspace 'Kidnap.'" *Seattle Times*, June 2.

Byron, Stuart. 1981. "Rules of the Game." *Village Voice*, November 11, 48

——. 1982. "How 'Making Love' Got made." *Village Voice*, February 3, 38–40.

Capsuto, Steven. 2000. *Alternate Channels: The Uncensored Story of Gay and Lesbian Images on Radio and Television*. New York: Ballantine Books.

Carey, James. 1969. "The Communications Revolution and the Professional Communicator." *Sociological Monographs* (January): 23–38. Reprinted in Munson and Warren, eds., *James Carey: A Critical Reader*, 128–43. Minneapolis: University of Minnesota Press, 1997.

Carman, John. 1994. "PBS Backs Out of Sequel to *Tales of the City*." *San Francisco Chronicle*, April 8.

Carpenter, Dale. 1999. "The Triumph of *Will*." *OutRight*, January 18.

Casey, Helen. 1981. "Sex, Scandal, and Sport." *Gay Information* (Australia), vol. 8 (Summer): 4–6.

Chasin, Alexandra. 2000. *Selling Out: The Gay and Lesbian Movement Goes to Market*. New York: St. Martin's.

Chastain, Sue. 1982a. "A Baffling Disease Turns Deadly to More Than Gays." *Philadelphia Inquirer*, June 20, 1A.

——. 1982b. "'Gay Plague' Has Instilled Fear of the Unknown." *Philadelphia Inquirer*, June 20, 1G.

Chibbaro, Lou. 2000. "House Hearing Mulls 'Cyber-privacy Threats." *Washington Blade*, April 14.

Christiansen, Richard. 1994. "'Angels' Reaches Beyond Gay Issues." *Chicago Daily News*, March 21.

Clark, Danae. 1991. "Commodity Lesbianism." In Gail Dines and Jean Humez, eds., *Gender, Race, and Class in Media*. Thousand Oaks, Calif.: Sage.

Clark, Kenneth. 1993. "John Chancellor, a Founding Father of TV News, Ready to Sign Off." *Philadelphia Inquirer*, June 29, E6.

Clemons, Walter. 1988. "Out of the Closet Onto the Shelves." *Newsweek*, March 21, 72–74.

Closs, Larry. 1994. "I Want My Gay TV." *Out* (September): 60–66, 120–23.

Cloud, John. 1997. "Out, Proud, and Very Young." *Time*, December 8.

Cohen, Derek and Richard Dyer. 1980. "The Politics of Gay Culture." In Gay Left Collective, eds., *Homosexuality: Power and Politics*, 172–86. London: Allison and Busby.

Collins, Gail. 1998. *Scorpion Tongues: The Irresistible History of Gossip in American Politics*. New York: Harcourt Brace.

Colton, Michael. 1999. "Why Is This Wedding Different from All Other Weddings?" *New York Times*, September 26.

Corry, John. 1993. "Off the Straight and Narrow." *The American Spectator* (September): 9, 48.

Cory, Donald Webster (pseudonym of Edward Sagarin: see below). 1951. *The Homosexual in America: A Subjective Approach*. New York: Greenberg.

Cory, Donald Webster and John LeRoy. 1963. *The Homosexual and His Society: A View from Within*. New York: Citadel Press.

Crain, Chris. 2000. "Welcome to Planet Advo-Out." *Southern Voice*, November 16.

Crimp, Douglas and Adam Rolston. 1990. *AIDS Demo Graphics*. Seattle: Bay Press.

Crowley, Harry. 1997. "Homicidal Homosexual." *The Advocate*, September 2, 24–33.

D'Acci, Julie. 1994. *Defining Women: Television and the Case of "Cagney and Lacey."* Chapel Hill: University of North Carolina Press.

D'Emilio, John. 1983. *Sexual Politics, Sexual Communities: The Making of a Homosexual Minority in the United States, 1940–1970*. Chicago: University of Chicago Press.

——. 1992. *Making Trouble: Essays on Gay History, Politics, and the University*. New York: Routledge.

D'Erasmo, Stacey. 1998. "We're Watching . . ." *Out* (December): 100–103, 166.

——. 1999. "You Can't Do That on Television." *Out* (September): 93–95, 172.

Daniels, Lee. 1971. *Comix: A History of Comic Books in America*. New York: Bonanza Books.

Davis, Natalie. 1999. "Targeting Women: Can Lesbian Publications Survive in Today's Market?" *Press Pass Q* (here and below: Internet gay and lesbian newsletter), June 4.

De Certeau, Michel. 1984. *The Practice of Everyday Life*. Berkeley: University of California Press.

DeCaro, Frank. 1999. "In with the Out Crowd: To Be Young and Gay Is No Longer a Prime-time Taboo." *TV Guide*, May 1–7.

Decter, Midge. 1980. "The Boys on the Beach." *Commentary* (September): 35–48.

Denneny, Michael. 1989. "Chasing the Crossover Audience and Other Self-Defeating Strategies." *Out/Look* (Winter): 16–21.

DeStefano, George. 1986. "*The New York Times* vs. Gay America." *The Advocate*, December 9.

Dickinson, Chris. 2000. "Country Undetectable: Gay Artists in Country Music." *Journal of Country Music* 21.1.

Dolley, Mark. 2000. "Gold at the End of the Rainbow: Marketing to Gays." *The Industry Standard*, February 2. (See www.netstandard.com.)

Donaton, Scott. 1992. "Redesigned *Advocate* Trying Its First TV Ads." *Advertising Age*, June 1, 41.

Doty, Alexander. 1993. *Making Things Perfectly Queer: Interpreting Mass Culture*. Minneapolis: University of Minnesota Press.

Doty, Robert. 1963. "Growth of Overt Homosexuality in City Provokes Wide Concern." *New York Times*, December 17, 1.

Dretzka, Gary. 1999. "One Minority Has Managed to Find a Place on Television and in Film." *Chicago Tribune*, August 10.

Duggan, Lisa, Nan Hunter, and Carole Vance. 1985. "False Promises: Feminist Antipornography Legislation." Reprinted in Lisa Duggan and Nan Hunter, *Sex Wars: Sexual Dissent and Political Culture*, 43–67. New York: Routledge, 1995.

Dullea, Georgia. 1993. "Always Room for Old Beaus." *New York Times*, December 23, C1, 6.

Dyer, Richard. 1977a. "Stereotyping." In Dyer, ed. *Gays and Film*. 27–39.

——. 1986. *Heavenly Bodies: Film Stars and Society*. New York: St. Martin's.

——. 1990. *Now You See It: Studies on Lesbian and Gay Film*. New York: Routledge.

——. 1993. "Coming Out as Going In: The Image of the Homosexual as a Sad Young Man." *The Matter of Images: Essays on Representations*, 73–92. London: Routledge.

Dyer, Richard, ed. 1977b. *Gays and Film*. London: British Film Institute.

Ebner, Mark. 1995. "The Gay Mafia." *Spy* (May-June): 42–49.

Eddings, Keith. 1994. "Should Gays Cover Gay issues?" *Columbia Journalism Review* (March-April): 47–49.

Egan, Dan. 2000. "One-Time Utah Whiz Kid Makes Waves with a Unique Magazine." *Salt Lake Tribune*, January 3.

Ehrenreich, Barbara. 1983. *The Hearts of Men: American Dreams and the Flight from Commitment.* New York: Anchor.

Ehrenstein, David. 1992. "Talking Pictures." *The Advocate*, May 5, 72.

——. 1996. "More Than Friends." *Los Angeles Magazine* (May).

——. 1998. *Open Secret: Gay Hollywood, 1928–1998.* New York: Morrow.

Elber, Lynn. 2000. "Study: Blacks on TV are Segregated." *AP News*, February 25.

Ellenzweig, Allen. 1992. *The Homoerotic Photograph.* New York: Columbia University Press.

Elliott, Stuart. 2000. "Advertising: Martina Navratilova Enters the National Mainstream Market in a Campaign for Subaru." *New York Times*, March 13, C14.

Ellsworth, Elizabeth. 1986. "Illicit Pleasures: Feminist Spectators and *Personal Best*." *Wide Angle* 8.2: 46–56.

Epstein, Edward. 1974. *News from Nowhere: Television and the News.* New York: Vintage.

Farber, Stephen. 1981. "Jerry Fallwell Won't Be Too Gay About This." *Los Angeles* (December): 134–48.

Feeney, Mary. 2000. "Lesbian Press Fights Its Own Barriers." *Hartford Courant*, August 16.

Feuer, Jane. 1989. "Reading *Dynasty*: Television and Reception Theory." *South Atlantic Quarterly* 88.2: 443–59.

Findlay, Heather. 1996. "A Winner in the Lesbian Sex Wars?" *Harvard Gay and Lesbian Review* 3.3: 27–30.

Fish, Larry. 1991. "Gay Newspaper's New Objective." *Philadelphia Inquirer*, October 14.

Fisher, Marc. 1998. "Caught in the Mystics' Net: Basketball Team's Diverse Fan Base Is in a League of Its Own." *Washington Post*, August 4, C1.

Fiske, John. 1987. *Television Culture.* New York: Routledge.

Fleischman, Bill. 1981. "Women's Tennis Stays in Shape: Tour Has Withstood Backlash of King-Navratilova Revelations." *Philadelphia Daily News*, December 16.

Flinn, John. 1996. "Fear of Condom Ads." *New York Times*, January 6, 19.

Ford, Dave. 1999. "Intoxicated by Bud Light's Gay-themed Ads." *San Francisco Examiner*, May 13.

Foucault, Michel. 1978. *The History of Sexuality.* Vol, 1, *An Introduction.* Translated by Robert Hurley. New York: Random House.

Fraker, Susan. 1977. "Gay Power in San Francisco." *Newsweek*, June 6, 25.

Freiberg, Peter. 2000. "PlanetOut Buys Advocate." *Washington Blade*, March 24.

Friedrich, Otto. 1986. *City of Nets: A Portrait of Hollywood in the 1940s.* London: Headline.

Fung, Richard. 1988. "Looking for My Penis: The Eroticized Asian in Gay Video Porn." In Bad Object Choices, ed., *How Do I Look?*, 148–60. Seattle: Bay Press.

Gabriel, Trip. 1995. "Some On-Line Discoveries Give Gay Youths a Path to Themselves." *New York Times*, July 2, 1.

Gallagher, John. 1991. "The AIDS Media Circus: Hype and Hysteria Behind the Headlines." *The Advocate* (September 10): 32–37.

Gamson, Joshua. 1998. *Freaks Talk Back: Tabloid Talk Shows and Sexual Nonconformity*. Chicago: University of Chicago Press.

Gerbner, George and Larry Gross. 1976. "Living with Television." *Journal of Communication* 26.2: 172–99.

Gerbner, George, Larry Gross, Michael Morgan, and Nancy Signorielli. 1994. "Growing Up with Television: The Cultivation Perspective." In Jennings Bryant and Dolf Zillmann, eds., *Media Effects: Advances in Theory and Research*, 17–42. Hillsdale, N.J.: Lawrence Erlbaum Associates.

Gill, John. 1995. *Queer Noises: Male and Female Homosexuality in Twentieth-Century Music*. Minneapolis: University of Minnesota Press.

GLAAD (Gay and Lesbian Alliance Against Defamation). 1997. *Access Denied: An Impact of Internet Filtering Software on the Gay and Lesbian Community*. (See www.glaad.org/access_denied).

Glam, Ernie. 1999 "Hero Worship: *Queer Nation* Makes a Splash in Cyberspace, Where Many Gay Comic Strips Find a Home." *New York Blade*, January 29, 19.

Goldstein, Richard. 1998. "Camera [in the Can]." *Village Voice*, May 12.

——. 2000. "Modem Madness: The Panic Over Cybersex Addiction." *Village Voice*, June 7.

Gomez, Jewelle. 1999. "Black Lesbians: Passing, Stereotypes, and Transformation." In Brandt, ed. *Dangerous Liaisons*, 161–77.

Goodman, Walter. 1990 "Why Andy Rooney Had to Go, Guilty or Not." *New York Times*, February 13.

——. 1991. "Prime Time vs. the Art of Ridicule." *New York Times*, September 1, B21.

Graham, Jefferson. 1999. "Man Trouble, More in Store for *Will*." *USA Today*, September 1.

Grau, Rawley. 2000. "Sunrise, Sunset: New Publications Target the Old and the Young." *Press Pass Q*, January 28.

Gray, Herman. 1986. "Television and the New Black Man: Black Male Images in Prime-Time Situation Comedies." *Media, Culture, and Society* 8.

Griffiths, John. 1999. "Ricky Martin: Cross Appeal." *The Advocate*, July 6, 27–37.

Grindstaff, Laura. 1997. "Producing Trash, Class, and the Money Shot: A Behind-the-Scenes Account of Daytime TV Talk Shows." In James Lull and Stephen Hinerman, *Media Scandals*, 164–202. New York: Columbia University Press.

Gross, Jane. 1992. "Gay Journalists Gather to Complain and to Celebrate Progress at Work." *New York Times*, June 29, B6.

——. 1993. *Contested Closets: The Politics and Ethics of Outing*. Minneapolis: University of Minnesota Press.

——. 1996. "You're the First Person I've Ever Told: Letters to a Fictional Gay Teen." In Michael Bronski, ed., *Taking Liberties: Gay Male Essays on Politics, Culture, and Art*, 369–86. New York: Kysak Books.

Gross, Larry and James Woods, eds. 1999. *The Columbia Reader on Lesbians and Gay Men in Media, Society and Politics*. New York: Columbia University Press.

Gross, Larry, Jay Ruby, and John Katz, eds. 1988. *Image Ethics: The Moral Rights of Subjects in Photography, Film, and Television*. New York: Oxford University Press.

Gustkey, Earl. 2001. "Sparks Are Altering Marketing Strategy: In Addition to Targeting Families, WNBA Club Recruiting Lesbian Fans at Rally." *Los Angeles Times*, May 4.

Guthmann, Edward. 1986. "Delicious Dynasty: The Behind-the-Scenes Story of a Television Phenomenon." *The Advocate*, January 7, 43–49.

Ha-'Am, Ahad (Asher Ginzberg). 1970. "Moses." In Leon Simon, ed., *Selected Essays of Ahad Ha-'Am*, 306–330. New York: Atheneum.

Hadleigh, Boze. 1986. *Conversations with My Elders.* New York: St. Martin's.

——. 1991. *The Vinyl Closet: Gays in the Music World.* San Diego: Los Hombres Press.

——. 1994. *Hollywood Lesbians.* New York: Barricade Books.

——. 1996. *Hollywood Gays.* New York: Barricade Books.

——. 1997. *Sing Out: Gays and Lesbians in the Music World.* New York: Barricade Books.

Hall, Stuart. 1992. "What Is This 'Black' in Black Popular Culture?" In Gina Dent, ed., *Black Popular Culture*, 21–33. Seattle: Bay Press.

Hamamoto, Darrell. 1994. *Monitored Peril: Asian Americans and the Politics of TV Representation.* Minneapolis: University of Minnesota Press.

Hands, Tanya. 1995. "'Doin' It Our Way': Queer Reception, Television, and Lesbian Audiences." Master's thesis, Annenberg School, University of Pennsylvania, Philadelphia.

Handy, Bruce. 1997. "Roll Over, Ward Cleaver, and Tell Ozzie Nelson the News: Ellen DeGeneres Is Poised to Become TV's First Openly Gay Star. Is America Ready or Not?" *Time*, April 14, 78–85.

Harper, Phillip Brian. 1991. "Eloquence and Epitaph: Black Nationalism and the Homophobic Impulse in Responses to the Death of Max Robinson." *Social Text* 28: 68–86.

Harris, Paul. 1998. "Pressing Concerns; Editor Michael Denneny Discusses Writing in the Age of AIDS." *A&U* (April): 43–45.

Hartinger, Brett. 1993. "Mainstream Comics Discover Gay Issues." *The Advocate*, May 4, 66–67.

Henderson, Lisa. 1991. "Lesbian Pornography: Cultural Transgression and Sexual Demystification." In Sally Munt, ed., *New Lesbian Criticism*, 173–91. New York: Columbia University Press.

Henry, William. 1987. "That Certain Subject." *Channels* (April): 43–45.

——. 1990. "Forcing Gays Out of the Closet." *Time*, January 29, 67.

Herscher, Elaine. 1999a. "Cast of 'Will & Grace' Comes Out Against Pro22." *San Francisco Chronicle*, December 8.

——. 1999b. "First Major Ad Starring Gays May Air on TV Spot for Miller Beer Set for Cable in S.F." *San Francisco Chronicle*, July 14.

Hodges, Andrew and David Hutter. 1974. *With Downcast Gays: Aspects of Homosexual Self Oppression.* Toronto: Pink Triangle Press (rpt., 1977).

Hoffman, Wayne. 1998. "Back in Time: Armistead Maupin Returns to 28 Barbary Lane with *More Tales of the City.*" *Washington Blade*, June 5.

Hollibaugh, Amber. 1983. "The Erotophobic Voice of Women: Building a Movement for the 19th Century." *New York Native*, September 26, 32–35.

Horton, Donald and Richard Wohl. 1956. "Mass Communication and Para-Social Interaction: Observation on Intimacy at a Distance." *Psychiatry* 19.3: 188–211.

Humphreys, Laud. 1970. *Tearoom Trade: Impersonal Sex in Public Places.* Chicago: Aldine.

Hunter, Christopher. 2000. "Don't Let McCain Censor the Net." *Salon*, October 25. (See www.salon.com/tech/log/2000/10/25/filter_legislation/index.html.)

Hunter, Nan. 1995. "Contextualizing the Sexuality Debates: A Chronology." In Lisa Duggan and Nan Hunter, *Sex Wars: Sexual Dissent and Political Culture*, 16–29. New York: Routledge.

Husten, Jan. 1987. "Fans Make *Desert Hearts* a Cult Classic." *Gay Community News*, January 25, 8–9.

Isherwood, Charles. 1994. "His So-Called Life." *The Advocate*, November 1, 59–60.

Italie, Hillel. 1993. "Market for Lesbian, Gay Books Is Booming." *Philadelphia Inquirer*, August 12, E1.

Jacobs, A. J. 1998. "When Gay Men Happen to Straight Women." *Entertainment Weekly*, October 23, 20–27.

Jay, Karla and Allen Young, eds. 1972. *Out of the Closets: Voices of Gay Liberation.* New York: Douglas.

——. 1992. *Out of the Closets: Voices of Gay Liberation.* 2d ed. New York: New York University Press.

Jenkins, Philip. 1998. *Moral Panic: Changing Concepts of the Child Molester in Modern America*. New Haven: Yale University Press.

Jensen, Elizabeth, Greg Braxton, and Dana Calvo. 2000. "NBC, NAACP in Pact to Boost Minorities in TV." *Los Angeles Times*, January 6.

Jensen, Joli. 1992. "Fandom as Pathology: The Consequences of Characterization." In Lisa Lewis, ed., *The Adoring Audience: Fan Culture and Popular Media*, 9–29. London: Routledge.

Jhally, Sut and Justin Lewis. 1992. *Enlightened Racism: The Cosby Show, Audiences, and the Myth of the American Dream.* Boulder, Colo.: Westview.

Johnson, Bradley. 1991. "Gay Title Gets Serious Redesign." *Advertising Age*, July 8, 31.

Johnson, Maria Miro. 1999. "Gay Officials Convene in Providence: Editor Who 'Outed' National Figures Explains Standards." *Providence Journal-Bulletin*, November 20.

Johnson, Richard. 1999. "Miller Pulls Plug on Gay Beer Ad." *New York Post*, July 13.

Judell, Brandon. 1986. "At the Colbys: The Politics of Kissing." *The Advocate*, January 7, 48.

Juliano, Joe. 1995. "Female Golfers Teed Off at Broadcaster's Quote." *Philadelphia Inquirer*, May 13.

Kahn, Eve M. 1994. "The Glass Closet." *Print* 48.5 (September-October): 21–31, 115.

Kaiser, Charles. 1992. "The Max Factor: Charles Kaiser Gets Max Frankel on the Record." *NYQ*, April 5, 43–46.

——. 1997. *The Gay Metropolis: 1940–1976.* Boston: Houghton Mifflin.

Kantrowitz, Arnie. 1998. "The Issues Change, and So Do the Tactics." *New York Blade*, September 18, 17.

Kasindorf, Jeanie. 1993. "Lesbian Chic: The Bold, Brave New World of Gay Women." *New York*, May 10, 30–37.

Katz, Jonathan Ned. 1976. *Gay American History: Lesbians and Gay Men in the USA.* New York: Thomas Crowell.

Kauffman, Debra. 1991. "A Very Unusual Point of View." *Producers Quarterly* (November): 38–41.

Keen, Lisa. 1996. "Mikulski Swept by Outing Fray." *Washington Blade*, November 1.

Keen, Lisa and Suzanne Goldberg. 1998. *Strangers to the Law: Gay People on Trial.* Ann Arbor: University of Michigan Press.

Kendrick, Walter. 1987. *The Secret Museum: Pornography in Modern Culture.* New York: Viking.

Kepner, Jim. 1998. *Rough News—Daring Views: 1950s' Pioneer Gay Press Journalism*, New York: Harrington Park.

Kettmann, Steve. 1998. "Out of Bounds." *The New Republic*, November 16.

Kim, Albert. 1995. "Poll: Divided We Stand." *Entertainment Weekly*, September 8, 27.

King, Bill. 1985. "'Early Frost' Covers New Ground in Television." *Atlanta Journal-Constitution*, November 11, TV section, 4–5.

Kinsella, James. 1989. *Covering the Plague: AIDS and the American Media*. New Brunswick: Rutgers University Press.

Kinsey, Alfred C., Wardell B. Pomeroy, and Clyde E. Martin. *Sexual Behavior in the Human Male*. Philadelphia: Saunders, 1948.

Kirby, Cathy. 2000. "PlanetOut.com, Gay.com to Unite." *San Francisco Chronicle*, November 16.

Klaidman, Stephen and Tom Beauchamp. 1987. *The Virtuous Journalist*. New York: Oxford University Press.

Klemesrud, Judy. 1968. "You Don't Have to Be One to Play One." *New York Times*, September 29, B1.

Kloer, Phil. 1991. "Voice in *Tongues* Echoes Filmmaker's Experience." *Atlanta Constitution*, July 16, E8.

Koenig, Rhoda. 2000. "The 'Karaoke Sound of Music' Has Audiences Singing Along." *Wall Street Journal*, January 21.

Kopay, David and Perry Young. 1977. *The David Kopay Story: An Extraordinary Self-Revelation*. New York: Donald Fine.

Kort, Michele. 1998. "Muffin Spencer-Devlin." *The Advocate*, August 18, 57.

Kozloff, Sarah Ruth. 1987. "Narrative Theory and Television." In Robert Allen, ed., *Channels of Discourse*, 42–73. Chapel Hill: University of North Carolina Press.

Kuczynski, Alex. 2000. "Following NBC's Lead, ABC Outlines Minority Hiring Plan." *New York Times*, January 8.

La Ferla, Ruth. 2001. "For Diller and Von Furstenberg, a Merger." *New York Times*, February 3, B2.

Lawler, Stan, Alan Sparkes, and Jennifer Wood. 1994. "When Lawrence Came Out: Taking the Funnies Seriously." Paper delivered at the Annual Conference of the International Communication Association, Sydney, July.

Leahy, Michael. 1986. "Why This Young Hunk Risked Playing an AIDS Victim." *TV Guide*, April 26, 34–38.

LeCuyer, A. Grey. 1991. "Why Daytime Isn't Gaytime." *Soap Opera Weekly*, January 15, 20–22.

Ledbetter, James. 1997. *Made Possible By: The Death of Public Broadcasting in the United States*. New York: Verso.

Lee, Chisun. 1999. "The Ling Thing: *Ally McBeal* Uses Ancient Oriental Secret." *Village Voice*, December 1.

Lee, John Alan. 1977. "Going Public: A Study in the Sociology of Gay Liberation." *Journal of Homosexuality* 3.1: 49–78.

——. 1981. "Don't Use That Word! Gay, Meaning Homosexual." In L. Salter, ed., *Communication Studies in Canada*, 3–19. Toronto: Butterworth.

Lemon, Brendan. 1992. "Virgin Territory: Music's Purest Vocalist Opens Up." *The Advocate*, June 16, 34–46.

Levine, Richard. 1981. "How the Gay Lobby Has Changed Television." *TV Guide* (May 30): 2–6.

Lew, Julie. 1991. "Why the Movies Are Ignoring AIDS." *New York Times*, August 18, H18.

Lewis, Claude. 1992. "Ashe's Star Quality Extended Far Beyond the Tennis Courts." *Philadelphia Inquirer*, April 15, A19.

Lewis, Peter. 1995. "Planet Out's Gay Services on Virtual Horizon." *New York Times*, August 21, D3.

Link, David. 1999. "A Councilman's Coming Out: The Yawn Heard 'Round Los Angeles." *Los Angeles Times*, November 17.

Lipsyte, Robert. 1991. "Discriminating Views and the Gay Athlete." *New York Times*, May 24, B12.

———. 1993. "Louganis Approaches the Edge of the Stage, and Leaps." *New York Times*, September 19, S11.

———. 1999. "A Major League Player's Life of Isolation and Subterfuge." *New York Times*, September 6, S11.

Louganis, Greg. 1995. "Breaking the Silence." *People*, March 6, 64–74.

Louganis, Greg and Eric Marcus. 1995. *Breaking the Surface*. New York: Random House.

Loughery, John. 1998. *The Other Side of Silence*. New York: Holt.

Lyall, Sarah. 1999. "Three Gay Guys on British TV: What's the Fuss?" *New York Times*, April 15.

Mallinger, Scott. 1990. "Come Out, Come Out, Whoever You Are: The Politics Of Outing." *Au Courant*, May 14.

Marcus, Eric. 1992. *Making History: The Struggle for Lesbian and Gay Rights*. New York: HarperCollins.

Marotta, Toby. 1981. *The Politics of Homosexuality*. Boston: Houghton Mifflin.

Maupin, Armistead. 1994. "A Line That Commercial TV Won't Cross." *New York Times*, January 9, H29.

Mayhood, Kevin. 1999. "Dozens Charged with Indecency in City Park." *Columbus Dispatch*, November 6.

McCarthy, Mary. 1989. "A Memory of James Baldwin." *New York Review of Books*, April 27, 24.

McCauley, Stephen. 1998. "The Yellow Brick Road to 70's San Francisco." *New York Times*, June 7, "Arts and Leisure," 37.

McConnell, Vicki. 1992. "Changing Channels." *The Advocate*, January 14, 70–72.

McGinty, Stephen. 2000. "Gay Superheroes Come Out of the Comic Closet." *London Times*, February 27.

McWilliams, Michael. 1991. "Will Magazine's 'Outing' of Gulf War Spokesman Change Pentagon Policy Toward Gays?" *Detroit News*, August 3, C1, C12.

Mechem, Charles. 1995. "LGBA Column Is Cruelty Disguised as Commentary." *USA Today*, May 23.

Mercer, Kobena and Isaac Julien. 1994. "True Confessions." In Thelma Golden, ed., *Black: Representations of Masculinity in Contemporary American Art*, 191–200. New York: Abrams.

Milavsky, Ron. 1988. "AIDS and the Media." Paper presented at the Annual Meeting of the American Psychological Association, Atlanta, August 15.

Miller, Merle. 1971. *On Being Different: What It Means to Be a Homosexual*. New York: Random House.

Millman, Joyce. 1995. "The Sitcom That Dare Not Speak Its Name." *San Francisco Examiner*, March 19.

Milvy, Erika. 1997. "It's Not a Secret, But Still Exciting." *New York Times*, April 10, C1.

Mitchell, Elvis. 2000. "Nurtured by TV, Black Comics Are Breaking Boundaries at the Box Office. " *New York Times*, August 14.

Montgomery, Kathryn. 1981. "Gay Activists and the Networks." *Journal of Communication* 31.3: 49–57.

——. 1989. *Target: Prime Time.* New York: Oxford University Press.

Mookas, Ioannis. 1992. "Senate Kills Restrictions on Public TV Funding." *NYQ*, June 21, 12.

Moon, Tom. 2000. "The Transfiguration of Sinéad O'Connor." *Philadelphia Inquirer*, June 11, I1.

Moraga, Cherrie and Gloria Anzaldúa. 1981. *This Bridge Called My Back: Writings by Radical Women of Color.* Watertown, Mass.: Persephone Press.

Morantz, Dave. 1999. "Gay Documentary Spurs Controversy." *Omaha World-Herald*, June 13, E1.

Moritz, Marguerite. 1993. "Old Strategies for New Texts: How American Television Is Creating and Treating Lesbian Characters." In Jeffrey Ringer, ed., *Queer Words, Queer Images: Communication and the Construction of Homosexuality*, 122–142. New York: New York University Press.

Murray, Diana. 1999. "2 Men Accused of Sexual Activity in OU Bathroom." *Oakland (Mich.) Press*, October 6.

Nardi, Peter. 1990. "AIDS and Obituaries: The Perpetuation of Stigma in the Press." In Douglas Feldman, ed., *Culture and AIDS*, 159–68. New York: Praeger.

——. 1992. *Diversity on Prime-Time Television.* A Report of the Media Image Coalition of Minorities and Women. Los Angeles: County Commission on Human Relations, January 30.

Ness, Carol. 1999. "Public TV Finds It's Elementary." *San Francisco Examiner*, June 6.

Nestle, Joan. 1987. *A Restricted Country.* Ithaca, N.Y.: Firebrand.

Newton, Esther. 2000. "My Date with Phil Donahue: A Queer Intellectual in TV Land." Paper presented at the annual meeting of the American Anthropological Association, November.

Nir, Lilach. 1998. "A Site of Their Own: Gay Teenagers' Involvement Patterns in IRC and Newsgroups." Paper presented to the International Communication Association's 48th Annual Meeting, Jerusalem.

Noh, David. 2000. "Year of the Dragün: Magazine for Gay Asians Makes Debut." *Washington Blade*, February 4.

O'Connor, John. 1987. " 'Just a Regular Kid,' About AIDS." *New York Times*, September 9.

——. 1988. "Debated Episode on AIDS." *New York Times*, December 13, C22.

——. 1989. "In 'Brewster Place,' Women Lead the Way." *New York Times*, March 19.

——. 1990. "They're Funny, Lovable, Heroic—and Jewish." *New York Times*, July 15, 25.

O'Neil, Sean. 1984. "The Role of Mass Media and Other Socialization Agents in the Identity Formation of Gay Males." In Sari Thomas, ed., *Studies in Communication* 1:201–206. Norwood, N.J.: Ablex.

Oldham, Jennifer. 1999. "Contraceptives Get Good Reception on Prime Time." *Los Angeles Times*, April 15, C1.

Orth, Maureen. 1997. "The Versace Murder: On the Trail of the Gay Serial Killer." *Vanity Fair* (September): 268–336.

———. 1999. *Vulgar Favors: Andrew Cunanan, Gianni Versace, and the Largest Failed Manhunt in U.S. History.* New York: Delacorte.

Osborne, Duncan. 1998. "'NY Blade' Axes Reporter for Speaking Out Against Anti-Gay Violence." *Lesbian and Gay New York,* December 31, 6, 21.

Palmer, Kimberly. 2000. "Gay Consumers in the Driver's Seat." *Washington Post,* July 4.

Parvin, Paige. 2000. "'Southern Voice' Goes Regional." *Southern Voice,* August 3.

Patullo, E. L. 1992 "Straight Talk About Gays." *Commentary* (December): 21–24.

People for the American Way. 1992. *Attacks on Broadcasting: Who's Who on the Right.* Washington, D.C.: PFAW.

Peterkin, Thomas. 1998. "Furor Over Ad's Gay Scenes." *Scotland on Sunday,* August 9, 6.

Phillips, Marshall Alan. 1991. "Hypocritical Rule of Invisibility Reigns." *Los Angeles Times,* August 7, 7.

Pierson, Randall. 1982. "Uptight on Gay News: Can the Straight Press Get the Gay Story Straight? Is Anyone Even Trying?" *Columbia Journalism Review* (March-April): 25–33.

Plaster, Gip. 2000. "More Ads in Gay Press, But No Condom Ads." (See www.gayscribe.com, February 2.)

Potter, Jerry. 1995. "Controversy Resurrects Old Theme." *USA Today,* May 14.

Press Pass Q. 1999. "Uncle Miltie's a Drag." Vol. 1.10, August 13.

Price, Deb. 1993. "Friendly Voices: Gay Radio Eases Isolation." *Detroit News,* March 4.

Price, Deb and Joyce Murdoch. 1995. *And Say Hi to Joyce.* New York: Doubleday.

Pucin, Diane. 2001. "Sparks Reach Out and Break New Ground." *Los Angeles Times,* May 6.

Pyle, George. 1993. "A Man Marries a Man? Print It!" *New York Times,* August 11, A15 (op-ed piece).

Rich, Frank. 1994a. "Gay Shopping Spree." *New York Times,* April 3, 1994, E11.

———. 1994b. "The Plot Thickens at PBS." *New York Times,* April 4, 17.

Rockwell, John. 1990. "Why Aaron Copland and American Music Are Synonymous." *New York Times,* December 4, B1.

Roeper, Richard. 1999. "Falwell Brews Up Tempest in Beer Stein Over 'Gay Ad.'" *Chicago Sun Times,* May 5.

Rogin, Michael. 1993. "Body and Soul Murder: *JFK.*" In Marjorie Garber et al., eds., *Media Spectacles,* 3–22. New York: Routledge.

Roscho, Bernard. 1967. "What the Black Press Said Last Summer." *Columbia Journalism Review* 6: 6–7.

Rosencrantz, Glenn. 1992. "Welcome to the Gay 90s." *Washington Journalism Review* (December): 31–35.

Rosenthal, Samuel. 1993. "Golden Boychick: Star-Audience Relations Between John Garfield and the Contemporary American Jewish Community." Master's thesis, Annenberg School, University of Pennsylvania, Philadelphia.

Ross, Rosemarie. 1981. "Women Athletes Will Pay for Billie Jean's Scandal." *Philadelphia Journal,* May 7, 41.

Rotello, Gabriel. 1995. "The Inning of Outing." *The Advocate,* April 18, 80.

Rothaus, Steve. 2000a. "OUTLOOKS: Market for Gay Press in South Florida May Be Saturated." *Miami Herald*, March 9.
——. 2000b. "OUTLOOKS: Permanent Lesbian Role Is a Bold Move for Soap." *Miami Herald*, December 28.
Rothman, Cliff. 1999. "Gay Regionals Lead Growth in Publishing." *Los Angeles Times*, November 12.
Roush, Matt. 2000. "Boogie Nights—Showtime's Risky, Frisky Gay Gamble." *TV Guide*, December 2–8.
Rozansky, Michael. 1998. "'Shocking' Exposes That Make the Rounds." *Philadelphia Inquirer*, November 16, C5.
Rubenstein, William. 1997. "In Communities Begin Responsibilities: Obligations at the Gay Bar." *Hastings Law Journal* 48: 1101–1136.
Ruenzel, David. 1994. "A Lesson in Tolerance." *Teacher* (September): 24–29.
Russo, Vito. 1981. *The Celluloid Closet: Homosexuality in the Movies*. New York: Harper and Row.
——. 1986. "When the Gaze Is Gay: A State of Being." *Film Comment* (April): 32–34.
——. 1987. *The Celluloid Closet: Homosexuality in the Movies*. 2d ed. New York: Harper and Row.
Sadownick, Doug. 1991. "Storming the Celluloid Closet: Activists Take Aim at Hollywood." *Village Voice*, July 2, 31–32.
——. 1992. "Gay in Hollywood." *US* (April): 61–67.
Sagarin, Edward. 1973. "The Good Guys, the Bad Guys, and the Gay Guys." *Contemporary Sociology* 2.1: 3–13.
Savage, Todd. 1999. "Radio Active." *The Advocate*, September 14, 80–81.
Schudson, Michael. 1984. *Advertising, the Uneasy Persuasion*. New York: Basic Books.
——. 1995. *The Power of News*. Cambridge: Harvard University Press.
Schulman, Sarah. 1998. *Stagestruck: Theater, AIDS, and the Marketing of Gay America*. Durham, N.C.: Duke University Press.
Schwartz, Karin. 1990. "*Longtime Companion* Reviews." *OutWeek*, June 27, 60, 70.
Schwarz, K. Robert. 1994. "Composers' Closets Open for All to See." *New York Times*, June 19, H1.
Sciolino, Elaine. 1991. "Voice of the Pentagon Delivers Press Curbs with a Deftness Honed on TV." *New York Times*, February 8, A6.
Seplow, Stephen. 1994. "Gays on TV: A New Image Is Coming Out." *Philadelphia Inquirer*, October 17, A1, 5.
——. 1995. "TV's Having a Devil of a Time Choosing Bad Guys." *Philadelphia Inquirer*, July 2, L1.
Shanahan, James and Michael Morgan. 1999. *Television and Its Viewers: Cultivation Theory and Research*. Cambridge: Cambridge University Press.
Shea, Kathleen. 1992. "Mandate for Mandes." *Philadelphia Daily News*, July 6, 33.
Sheldon, Caroline. 1977. "Lesbians and Film: Some Thoughts." In Dyer, ed., *Gays and Film*, 5–26.
Shilts, Randy. 1987. *And the Band Played On: Politics, People, and the AIDS Epidemic*. New York: St. Martin's.
Shipp, E. R. 2000. "An Obit's Silence." *Washington Post*, June 4.
Shore, Elliott, Patricia Case, and Laura Daly, eds. 1982. *Alternative Papers: Selections from the Alternative Press, 1979–1980*. Philadelphia: Temple University Press

Siegel, Marc. 1998. "Sex in Public Not Lewd—Just a Mood." *UCLA Daily Bruin* (November 16) (reprinted at www.gaytoday.badpuppy.com/viewpoint/111698.html).

Signorile, Michelangelo. 1992a. "Out at *The New York Times*, Part 1." *The Advocate*, May 5, 34–42.

——. 1992b. "Out at *The New York Times*, Part 2." *The Advocate*, May 19, 38–42.

——. 1993. *Queer in America: Sex, the Media, and the Closets of Power.* New York: Random House.

Silberman, Steve. 1994. "We're Teen, We're Queer, and We've Got E-Mail." *Wired* (December): 1–3.

——. 1998. "Wiring the Gay World." *Wired* (August).

Soar, Matthew. 2000. "Andrew Cunanan in the Houseboat, with the Bloody Versace Scarf: The Media and the 'Gay Serial Killer.'" *Jump Cut* 43: 48–55.

Sontag, Susan. 1967. "Notes on Camp." *Against Interpretation, and Other Essays*, 275–92. New York: Delta.

Soren, Tabitha. 1995. "Ellen DeGeneres—Unzipped." *USA Weekend*, November 24.

Southgate, Martha. 1994. "A Funny Thing Happened on the Way to Prime Time." *New York Times Magazine*, October 30, 52–55.

Staples, Brent. 1999. "Editorial Observer: Why Same-Sex Marriage Is the Crucial Issue." *New York Times*, September 5, D10.

Stateman, Alison. 1997. "Face the Nation: The Publicity Behind Ellen's 'Coming Out.'" *Public Relations Tactics* (July): 1, 15, 27.

Stein, Edward. 1991. "Scholarly Advice." *Gay Community News*, July 21, 1, 6.

Steiner, George. 1980. "The Cleric of Treason." *The New Yorker*, December 8.

Stephenson, Heather. 2000. "Newspapers Say Weddings, Unions All the Same to Them." *Rutland (Vt.) Herald and Times Argus*, July 23.

Stevenson, Jack. 1997. "From the Bedroom to the Bijou: A Secret History of American Gay Sex Cinema." *Film Quarterly* 51.1 (Fall): 24–28.

Stone, Laurie. 1983. "Just Friends." *Village Voice*, December 6, 69.

Streitmatter, Rodger. 1995. *Unspeakable: The Rise of the Gay and Lesbian Press in America.* Boston: Faber and Faber.

Strossen, Nadine. 1995. *Defending Pornography: Free Speech, Sex, and the Fight for Women's Rights.* New York: Scribner.

Sullivan, Andrew. 1995. *Virtually Normal.* New York: Knopf.

——. 1999. "Not a Straight Story: When It Comes to Public Figures Disclosing Their Sexuality, the New Rule Is Kinda Ask, Sorta Tell." *New York Times Magazine*, December 12, 64.

Swanson, Carl. 1999. "Off the Record." *New York Observer*, May 24.

Thomas, Cal. 1995. Syndicated column, *Los Angeles Times Syndicate*, November 2.

Thompson, Gary. 1997. "Male Movie Audience Doesn't Care What the Heche She Is—She's Sexy." *Philadelphia Daily News*, April 30.

Tobin, Jeffrey. 2000. "Soccer." In George Haggerty, ed., *Gay Histories and Cultures*, 524–25. New York: Garland.

Tommasini, Anthony. 1999. "Composers for the Common Man." *New York Times*, November 21, B1.

Treichler, Paula. 1999. *How to Have Theory in an Epidemic: Cultural Chronicles of AIDS.* Durham, N.C.: Duke University Press.

Tuchman, Gaye. 1972. "Objectivity as Strategic Ritual: An Examination of Newsmen's Notions of Objectivity." *American Journal of Sociology* 77: 660–79.

——. 1978. *Making News.* New York: Free Press.

Tucker, Ken. 1989. "Sharing an Address—and Friendship." *Philadelphia Inquirer,* March 19, L1, 13.

Tucker, Scott. 1979. "Sex, Death, and Free Speech: The Fight to Stop Friedkin's *Cruising.*" *The Body Politic* 58 (November): 23–27.

——. 1997. *The Queer Question: Essays on Desire and Democracy.* Boston: South End Press.

Turegano, Preston. 1998. "Timing and Legality of Sex Report Questionable." *San Diego Union-Tribune,* March 2, E1.

Turner, Patricia. 1994. *Ceramic Uncles and Celluloid Mammies.* New York: Anchor.

Turow, Joseph. 1997a. *Breaking Up America: Advertising and the New Media World.* Chicago: University of Chicago Press.

——. 1997b. *Media Systems in Society: Understanding Industries, Strategies, and Power.* Boston: Addison Wesley.

Tyler, David. 1999. "Park Board Chief Quits After Plea to Indecency." *Chicago Tribune,* November 21.

Tyler, Parker. 1972. *Screening the Sexes: Homosexuality in the Movies.* New York: Anchor.

Umlaut, John. 1989. "Fright, Cameras, Action!" *OutWeek,* August 29, 34–37, 80.

Van Leer, David. 1995. *The Queening of America: Gay Culture in Straight Society.* New York: Routledge.

Vance, Carole. 1989. "The War on Culture." *Art in America* (September): 39–45.

——. 1990. "Misunderstanding Obscenity." *Art in America* (May): 49–55.

Vaziri, Aidin. 1999. "A Voice for Gay Teens." *San Francisco Chronicle,* June 13.

Wadewitz, Mikel. 2000. "Gay Talk via Virtual Airwaves." *The Advocate,* March 14, 18.

Walsh, Jeff. 1994. "Logging On, Coming Out." *The Advocate,* October 18, 6.

Warren, James. 1999. "Nixon on Tape Expounds on Welfare and Homosexuality." *Chicago Tribune,* November 7.

Warren, Patricia Nell. 2000. "Chasing Rainbows: GLBT Identity and the Internet." *Cybersocket* (March). (See www.cybersocket.com.)

Waugh, Thomas. 1988. "Lesbian and Gay Documentary: Minority Self-Imaging, Oppositional Film Practice, and the Question of Image Ethics." In Gross, Ruby, and Katz, eds., *Image Ethics,* 248–72.

——. 1996. *Hard to Imagine: Gay Male Eroticism in Film and Photography from Their Beginnings to Stonewall.* New York: Columbia University Press.

Waxman, Sharon. 2000. "Will & Grace Under Fire." *George* (February).

Weeks, Jeffrey. 1977. *Coming Out: Homosexual Politics in Britain from the Nineteenth Century to the Present.* London: Quartet Books.

——. 1981. *Sex, Politics, and Society: The Regulation of Sexuality Since 1800.* London: Longman.

Weiner, Jennifer. 1997. "*Ellen* Didn't Open Closet." *Philadelphia Inquirer,* May 4.

Weinraub, Bernard. 1999. "Stung by Criticism of Fall Shows, TV Networks Add Minority Roles." *New York Times,* September 20, A1.

——. 2000. "A Controversial British Series Seduces Showtime." *New York Times,* May 14.

Weir, John. 1992. "Gay-Bashing, Villainy and the Oscars." *New York Times*, March 29, H17, 22.

Weise, Elizabeth. 1995a. "Cyberspace Runaway." Associated Press, June 5.

——. 1995b. "Cyberspace Suspect Also a Teen." Associated Press, June 7.

Weiss, Andrea. 1986. "From the Margins: New Images of Gays in the Cinema." *Cineaste* 15.1: 4–8.

——. 1992. *Vampires and Violets: Lesbians in Film*. New York: Penguin.

Wells, Melanie. 1998. "Sex May Sell, But as for Condoms, Networks Aren't Buying." *USA Today*, November 30, 9B.

Wertham, Frederic. 1954. *Seduction of the Innocent*. New York: Rinehart.

Whitam, Frederick and Robin Mathy. 1986. *Male Homosexuality in Four Societies: Brazil, Guatemala, the Philippines, and the United States*. New York: Praeger.

White, Mimi. 1987. "Ideological Analysis and Television." In Robert Allen, ed., *Channels of Discourse*, 134–71. Chapel Hill: University of North Carolina Press.

Wiener, Jennifer. 1998. "Protest at Ch. 10 Ends in 9 Arrests." *Philadelphia Inquirer*, November 13, B8.

Wilensky, Harold. 1964. "Mass Society and Mass Culture: Interdependence or Independence?" *American Sociological Review* 29.2: 173–97.

Wilkins, David. 1993. "Two Paths to the Mountaintop? The Role of Legal Education in Shaping the Values of Black Corporate Lawyers." *Stanford Law Review* 45 (July): 1981–2026.

Willey, Keven. 1996. "Kolbe Steps Forward: Gay Lawmaker Gets Priorities Straight." *Arizona Republic*, August 4.

Williams, Francis. 1998. "Over Here and Out." *The Guardian*, April 21, 4.

Williams, Marjorie. 1991. "Is It Any of Your Business?" *Washington Monthly* (September): 39–44.

Williams, Raymond. 1977. *Marxism and Literature*. Oxford: Oxford University Press.

Wofford, Carrie. 1992. "Arrival or Assimilation?" *Gay Community News*, March 22, 3, 5, 6.

Wolfenden Report: Report of the Committee on Homosexual Offences and Prostitution. 1964. New York: Lancer.

Woodell, Debbie. 1998. "League Woos Lesbian Fans." *Baltimore Sun*, January 11, 6L.

Woodlee, Yolanda. 1999. "Toilings of a Trailblazer." *Washington Post*, April 29.

Woog, Dan. 1992. "Tackling the Issue: Gay and Lesbian Journalists Wrestle for Mainstream Sports Coverage." *The Advocate*, September 8, 54–55.

Worth Sol and John Adair. 1997 (rev. ed., edited by Richard Chalfen). *Through Navajo Eyes: An Exploration in Film Communication and Anthropology*. Albuquerque: University of New Mexico Press.

Yang, Alan. 1997. "The Polls—Trends: Attitudes Towards Homosexuality." *Public Opinion Quarterly* 61: 447–507.

Zerbisias, Antonia. 1995. "Networks Stifle Slightest Hint of Gays' Sex Lives." *Toronto Star*, February 4, L10.

INDEX